JOURNEY OF THE SOUL

A Handbook for Esoteric Psychology and Astrology

Edition 7
March 2018

Leoni Hodgson

All rights reserved

Copyright © Leoni Hodgson 2018

No part of this publication may be reproduced, stored in a retrieval system, or transmitted in any form or by any means, electronic, mechanical, photocopying, recording or otherwise, without the prior written permission of the author.

ISBN: 978-0-6483012-0-2

Email: leoni@bigpond.net.au

www.brisbanegoodwill.com

Esoteric Psychology is the Science of the Soul. It is the study of the energies of the soul, how it affects human psychology and determines what a man should be. This science studies the evolution of consciousness, those stages of crises and growth that occur as the energies of the soul seek to fuse with and express through, the forces of the personality. This study provides the basis for this book, the Journey of the Soul.

About this Book

This book was conceived around 1990-1991 when I began teaching exoteric and esoteric astrology, seven ray seminars and personal development courses. I wrote small booklets for each of those courses. In that period, I studied Esoteric Psychology with the University of the Seven Rays. The Director was renowned teacher of esoteric studies, Michael Robbins. For my thesis, to gain a *Masters in Esoteric Psychology*, I combined these booklets, added the knowledge I was gaining and the *Journey of the Soul* was born.

During the middle and late 1990's I joined the faculty of the University of the Seven Rays and studied for a further five years with Robbins, gaining a *Doctor of Philosophy in Esotericism* in 2000. During this period and into the new millennium I taught seven Esoteric Psychology Courses; each course was 2 years long and a new one would start as the old course finished.

Journey of the Soul (JOS) was the course workbook along with Alice A. Bailey's *Esoteric Psychology, volume II*. Other reference material came from Helena Blavatsky's *Secret Doctrine* and *Patanjali's Raja Yoga Sutras*. Over that period, the contents of *Journey of the Soul* were tested in the class format and continually refined so that the concepts would be clear for students. This has continued through several editions. Now the book is being made available for worldwide distribution via Amazon as edition 7. It has been re-formatted to letter-size, a new ISBN number has been added and a few inner changes have been made.

The *Journey of the Soul* continues to evolve, just as consciousness does, which is what the book is all about.

About the Author

Hodgson has studied various branches of esotericism through the Theosophical Society, Co-Freemasonry, the University of the Seven Rays (degrees in Esoteric Psychology and Esoteric Philosophy), in astrology (PMAFA 1983), Esoteric Healing and Raja Yoga. She is an accomplished teacher and counsellor in these modalities.

Acknowledgments

This book is dedicated to the world service work of the Tibetan Master Djwhal Khul.

Loving thanks to my husband Jim who supports me in every way in all my endeavours. Grateful thanks to all my friends and co-workers who have assisted me through the years.

Ideas, concepts and most quotes come primarily from the series of books written by Alice A. Bailey, published by Lucis Trust.

Foreword

Leoni Hodgson the author of "Journey of the Soul" has produced a very valuable resource in this edition, as a product of her teaching experience and in-class students over many years. Leoni, through her valuable experience and knowledge of the Esoteric Wisdom teachings has been instrumental in leading many students to find their soul path journey. It is a joy to see such a valuable teaching tool being made available to the wider public.

The book gives the knowledge of the constitution of man and the importance of his evolving consciousness by introducing Esoteric Psychology as a means to finding one's individual destiny or soul potential for the current life and lives to come.

"Journey of the Soul" focuses on how Esoteric Psychology as given in the Ageless Wisdom teachings, aids the unfoldment of the soul's potential, with expanded awareness, leading to expanded consciousness, through knowledge of not only the universal macrocosmic view of the bigger picture, but also from the microcosmic view of individual man and how he fits into the grand scheme of the 'whole'. Through this book one can easily imagine the picture of "as above, so below", that the patterns are repeated throughout the Universes, Solar Systems to the individual and that we are all part of the whole grand scheme, that we are not separate, but all part of the "one soul" of humanity.

This book explores in great analytical detail that aids the individual to understand the crisis and stages of growth that occur as the soul seeks to express Itself through the personality. Esoteric Psychology is essentially the Science of the Soul – the highest spiritual aspect of the human being. The task of the personality is to seek integration with the soul by developing the highest aspect of it various natures. This book is not only a "go to" book for invaluable information which covers cosmology, hierarchies of kingdoms, the evolution of consciousness, it is also a "how to" book as one studies one's individual characteristics through the application of the Seven Rays, the Planets, the Signs and specific areas of life indicated by the houses in one's astrology chart. Essentially this about the science of energy and how we can be participants in the directing of those energies that enhance our ability to stand in Spiritual Being.

Given the critical nature of world conditions many are questioning the meaning and purpose of their life to help make sense of relationships and events we see, global, nationally and individually and this book provides a wonderful guideline to achieving a sense of purpose and opportunities through life's challenges to achieve new insight that enables each person to contribute to the global goodwill for peace.

For those who are just enquirers of the path this book serves a wonderful insight into the purpose and meaning of life, which can whet the appetite and enthusiasm to venture into deeper study. This book is valuable to the student of astrology as the quick guide to learning how to interpret one's own astrology chart and those of others. This goes towards not only understanding oneself but also creates more tolerance of others as we all struggle towards greater light and understanding.

Many blessings Leoni for your valuable contribution to enhancing awareness and insight.

Kay Hannan,

BA majoring in Welfare. Sociology and Psychology.
Administration Co-ordination for Faculty and Students Morya School of Meditation

Introduction

What is the Soul?

With his famous equation E= mc2, Albert Einstein proved that everything in the universe is energy. Esotericism is the science of the world of energies, while occultism is the science of energy manipulation. Both esotericists and occultists say the same thing: There is naught in the world but energy.

The Atom of atoms is only energy and God Himself is naught but energy. [1]

All living creatures are composed of a variety of different energies. In man, the physical body is the densest. At the highest is the energy we call spirit. Between the physical body and spirit is an energy field called the soul. The soul is the connecting bridge between the physical and spiritual. It is that aspect called the evolving consciousness, intelligence or wisdom. The soul is that cohering, driving force behind every human being. We are born into physical incarnation under soul impulse. The cause of all diseases is a block to soul energy somewhere in the personality nature. The soul (driven forwards by spiritual force) has a definite program or plan it wants to achieve in the incarnation. The physical incarnation begins to die when the soul turns its interest away from it. Our whole life begins, blooms, reaches maximum potential, unravels and ends according to the Plan of the Soul. Therefore, it is practical to understand the soul and its purpose.

What is the Journey of the Soul?

When you study humanity, it is obvious that people are unequal in development. Consciousness or soul ranges from gross ignorance of higher spiritual realities to that of an enlightened master such as Jesus Christ and Gautama Buddha. Between these two poles, the mass of humanity is found.

The journey of the soul is the series of lives that men and women go through in order to transform their consciousness from a state of ignorance to that of enlightenment. This is the purpose of incarnation - through life experience and to become loving and compassionate souls. It is the reason we are born on earth. The journey is the evolution of the soul or consciousness aspect.

What is Esoteric Psychology?

Over the ages, Sages and Yogis have given us various systems and techniques to bring about this transformation in consciousness. Just as scientists in the world study energy intelligently and attempt to manipulate it and unleash its power for human consumption, so have these wise ones. Excepting that, their goal is to unleash the power of spirit latent in human beings. Vedanta has given us Raja Yoga, Buddhists the Noble Eightfold Way and Christianity the Ten Commandments. These systems are designed to bring about the evolution of consciousness so that an evolved spiritual being emerges from the chrysalis that is ordinary man.

To this end, the Tibetan Master Djwhal Khul has given us Esoteric Psychology. It draws upon all the previous teachings, adds to the science of Astrology and modern psychology and introduces the Science of the Seven Rays. This latter science is but a study of the various energies that make up a human being and their intelligent mixing and harmonising.

Esoteric Psychology is the Science of the Soul. It is the study of soul energy, how it affects human psychology and determines what a man should be. This science studies the evolution of consciousness.

The Master Djwhal Khul and Alice Bailey

Most of the books attributed to Alice A. Bailey were actually dictated telepathically to her by a very advanced soul called the Master Djwhal Khul - also known at DK or the Tibetan Master. [2] A brief biography of Khul is in the "Hierarchy V" section and a drawing of him is towards the back of the book. When making reference to these books I have used the names Bailey, the Tibetan and DK inter-changeably. But always, when using "Bailey" I am referring to the thoughts of Djwhal Khul.

---

1 Bailey, Alice A. Discipleship in the New Age II, 303
2 Bailey, Alice A. The Unfinished Autobiography, 162-3

Table of Contents

CHAPTER 1: THE LARGER PICTURE 1
    1. The Cosmos and the Solar System 3
    2. The Hierarchies and the Kingdoms 13

CHAPTER 2: THE EVOLUTION OF CONSCIOUSNESS 23
    1. The Constitution of Man 25
    2. Levels of Consciousness 35
    3. The Initiations 39

CHAPTER 3: ESOTERIC PSYCHOLOGY 45
    1. Introduction to Esoteric Psychology 47
    2. Psychology Disorders 51
    3. Problems of Mystics and Disciples 71

CHAPTER 4: THE SEVEN RAYS 83
    1. The Seven Rays And Psychology 84
    2. The Ray Chart 101

CHAPTER 5: ESOTERIC ASTROLOGY 107
    1. The Signs 111
    2. The Planets 125
    3. The Houses 133
    4. Planets in Signs and Houses 137
    5. Astrology Readings 167

CHAPTER 6: SPIRITUAL PRACTISES 175
    1. Meditation 177
    2. The Practise of Right Detachment 187
    3. The Masters and Service 189

APPENDIX 193
    1. Glossary 193
    2. Seven RayS Questionnaire and Charts 197
    3. Bibliography 205

CHAPTER 1: THE LARGER PICTURE

Given the fact of the finiteness of man and of his life, given the tremendous periphery of the cosmos and the minute nature of our planet, given the vastness of the universe and the realisation that it is but one of countless greater and smaller universes, yet there is present in men and upon our planet a factor and a quality which can enable all these facts to be seen and realised as parts in a whole and which permits man to expand his sense of awareness and identity so that the form aspects of life offer no barrier to his all-embracing spirit. [1]

---

[1] Bailey, Alice A. Esoteric Psychology II, 219

1. THE COSMOS AND THE SOLAR SYSTEM

This chapter lays the framework for the journey of the soul. It gives a brief overview of the universe and solar system, the larger setting for the evolution of all souls in all Kingdoms.

1. The Appearance and Disappearance of Universes

The Wisdom Teachings, most particularly 'The Secret Doctrine' written by renowned esotericist Helena Blavatsky, say that the appearance, disappearance and rest periods between universes, is cyclical.

> The appearance and disappearance of the Universe are pictured as an outbreathing and inbreathing of "the Great Breath," which is eternal and which, being Motion, is one of the three aspects of the Absolute—Abstract Space and Duration being the other two. When the "Great Breath" is projected, it is called the Divine Breath and is regarded as the breathing of the Unknowable Deity—the One Existence—which breathes out a thought, as it were, which becomes the Kosmos. (See "Isis Unveiled.") So also is it when the Divine Breath is inspired again the Universe disappears into the bosom of "the Great Mother," who then sleeps "wrapped in her invisible robes." [1]

2. "God"

The Divine Breath has many names. The most common is "God", or to esotericists the Logos. The latter is Greek for "word", a relative term, generally used to signify Creator. Here is an esoteric description of this force.

> That sumtotal of manifestation which can be called Nature, or God and which is the aggregate of all the states of consciousness. This is the God [of] Christians; this is the force, or energy, which the scientist recognises; and this is the Universal Mind, or the Oversoul of the philosopher. This, again, is the intelligent Will which controls, formulates, binds, constructs, develops and brings all to an ultimate perfection. This is that Perfection which is inherent in matter itself and the tendency which is latent in the atom, in man and in all that is. This interpretation does not look upon it as the result of an outside Deity pouring His energy and wisdom upon a waiting world, but rather as something which is latent within that world itself, that lies hidden at the heart of the atom, within the heart of man himself, within the planet and within the solar system. It is that something which drives all on toward the goal and is the force which is gradually bringing order out of chaos; ultimate perfection out of temporary imperfection; good out of seeming evil. [2]

3. The Triune Nature of the Universe - Spirit, Soul, Body

At the birth of a universe and while it runs its course the Universal Life demonstrates three aspects. In Christian terms God is a Trinity - Spirit, Soul and Body. Esotericists call these three aspects Life, Quality and Appearance. All lives are built upon this model; all are in the process of developing the potential of these three principles. This is the ultimate purpose of the journey of the soul - to become in fact, the triple Deity.

Blavatsky gives a deeply esoteric description of the birth of a new universe and the involvement of the Trinity or the three aspects. The following quote comes from archaic writings called the Stanzas of Dzyan.

> [Stanza 3] And Light drops one solitary Ray into the waters, into the Mother Deep. The ray shoots through the Virgin-Egg .. [causing] .. the Eternal Egg to thrill and drop the non-eternal (periodical) Germ, which condenses into the World Egg [3]

---

1 Blavatsky, Helena; The Secret Doctrine 1, 43
2 Bailey, Alice A. The Consciousness of the Atom, 21-22
3 Blavatsky, Helena; The Secret Doctrine I, 64

The 1st Logos or Aspect: this is the initiating power of Deity and of nature. In the stanza, it is "Light". When the time is right, under Cosmic Law, it triggers the process that brings a universe into being. On lower levels, this 1st aspect is related to the 1st ray, to birth and death, beginnings and endings, the monad, father and spiritual awareness.

The 2nd Logos or Aspect: this is the building and unifying force of Deity. In the stanza, it is the "Ray". It fertilises the egg, the universe to be. In manifestation, its force is the 2nd ray, it is the son or soul aspect in the Father-Son-Mother trilogy. Related to quality, it is the impetus behind the development of love-wisdom consciousness.

The 3rd Logos or Aspect: this is the universe itself in incarnation. In the stanza, it is the "World Egg". Terms synonymous with the philosophical aspect of the Third-Logos are "Mahat or Intelligence". [1] This force - in manifestation the 3rd ray, brings about the appearance of form and the instinctual intelligence of the body nature.

1. Spirit	*2. Soul*	*3. Body*
1st Aspect	2nd Aspect	3rd Aspect
Electric Fire	Solar Fire	Fire by Friction
Father	Son	Mother (Holy Ghost)
Life	Quality	Appearance
Awareness	Consciousness	Instinct
1st Ray	2nd Ray	3rd Ray
Will-Power	Love Wisdom	Intelligence

This chart gives a list of associated terms related to the three aspects.

The Three Major Fires of the Universe

The Bible tells us that "God is a consuming fire". [2] Occultism gives three fires or energies in the universe and each is related to one or other of the three aspects of Deity. The blending and activity of these fires produce all that exists.

1. *Electric Fire (1st Logos):* (the 1st ray, monadic power, the power of spirit). This first fire is the power of God, seen by the human eye as lightning and electricity. It is the force that drives all lives along the evolutionary path. In advanced human beings, it demonstrates as dynamic spiritual power.

2. *Solar Fire (2nd Logos):* (the 2nd ray, soul radiation, power of the soul). The second fire is the soul or consciousness aspect of God. It causes a spiral-cyclic motion in atoms that creates relationships and awareness. At the level of an advanced soul it demonstrates as love, wisdom, kindness, compassion and understanding.

3. *Fire by Friction (3rd Logos):* (personality force). This 3rd ray fire animates the atoms of matter, causing activity. It brings the universe into physical existence and gives instinctual intelligence to substance. This is the vitalising fire of the physical body and the sum-total of individual kundalini (the power of Life).

4. The Primordial Seven

In the Bible, these are the seven Archangels that stand before the throne of God. Esotericism calls them the highest Beings in existence, the Builders, Dhyan Chohans and the primal Seven Rays. The Seven Rays Lords in our solar system are distant reflections of these seven. These Highest Seven channel the three fires and adding their own force, build the universe. They achieve this by directing their agents, the Deva Kingdom (Army of the Voice).

> Ultimately the creators of all the manifested Universe .. they inform and guide it; they are the intelligent Beings who adjust and control evolution, embodying in themselves those manifestations of the ONE LAW, which we know as "The Laws of Nature." [3]

Fohat, Lord of Fire

The collective fire of the universe wielded by the Seven Archangels, is called Fohat. This force is the messenger of their will - the fiery whirlwind, the electric vital power. The gradual application of Fohat on the evolutionary path to all atoms in the universe, transforms the lowest of forms eventually into the highest.

> It is divine Purpose, actively functioning. [4]

---
1 Barborka, Geoffrey; The Divine Plan, 503
2 Bible, Deuteronomy, 4:24
3 Blavatsky, Helena; The Secret Doctrine I, 22
4 Bailey, Alice A. The Soul and its Mechanism, 99

5. The Universe has Seven Cosmic Planes

As building work begins in the universe, numberless universes, stars and solar systems ranging over seven great planes appear. Each of the Seven Cosmic Planes has a kingdom or class of life living upon it.

1. Keep in mind that the universe is not like a box with levels stacked one on top of each other. We understand the structure of the universe to be similar to that of an atom, with a (spiritual) nucleus at the centre and with the planes surrounding it. The planes interpenetrate.

2. On the first, highest or innermost plane the bodies of expression are created from the finest of substance. The most evolved beings in the universe, those who direct the affairs of the universal system, are here. Substance grows gradually denser down the planes, with the seventh plane being the densest. This means the bodies of expression grow coarser on each subsequent lower plane. As consciousness ascends the planes, finer bodies are utilised.

3. Each cosmic level has seven subplanes. This means that there are 49 subplanes in the universe. (*See this in the long thin diagram*).

4. Each subplane divides seven times again. This makes 7 x 7 x 7 or 343 mini-planes in the universe. If we think of each mini-plane as a step or rung on a ladder of ascending consciousness, then there are 343 steps to climb in the universe. This is our task, to ascend (in consciousness), from the bottom or outermost levels of the universe, to the top or innermost.

The Seven Cosmic Planes

1	Cosmic Logoic Plane	
2	Cosmic Monadic Plane	
3	Cosmic Atmic Plane	
4	Cosmic Buddhic Plane	
5	Cosmic Mental Plane	
6	Cosmic Emotional Plane	
7	Cosmic Physical Plane The 7 subplanes of our solar system	Logoic Monadic Atmic Buddhic Mental Emotional Physical

Diagrams:

They show the seven vast planes of the Cosmos. These planes are subdivided into many smaller subplanes. The two higher diagrams show the cosmos as if planes are stacked one on another, while the lower diagram shows the planes in their truer spheroidal form. Our solar system is the bottom or outermost seventh plane.

The arrows represent the monads (see later sections on the Hierarchies and Constitution of Man) streaming out into the universe from the central spiritual Sun on the Path of Outgoing or Involution; then returning on the Path of Return or Evolution.

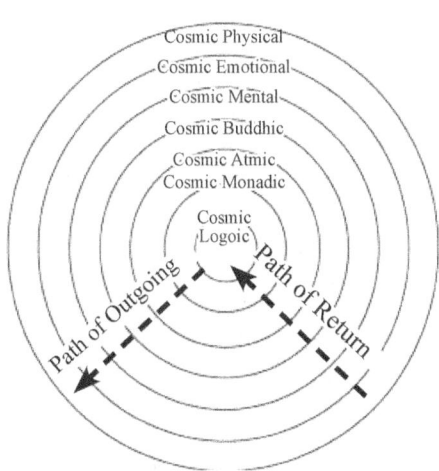

The Seven Planes of the Solar System

The bottom seventh plane of the Cosmic System - the Cosmic Physical, is where solar systems are found. This is where our solar system is located. The seven planes of our solar system are the seven subplanes of the Cosmic Physical Plane. Esoteric writings tell us that:

> A solar Logos.. His ring-pass-not comprises the entire circumference of the solar system..
> The Sun is the physical body of the solar Logos. [1]

We have bodies on all seven planes, but most are still embryonic. Meaning, most people have not yet awakened in consciousness in the higher bodies. The seven planes of our system are the levels through which consciousness ascends as we evolve.

- *7th Physical Plane*: the tangible physical bodies of all forms in all kingdoms are located on this plane. Man has a dense component and an etheric aspect to his physical body. Primeval man was conscious at this level.

- *6th Astral Plane*: man's body of expression at this level is the emotional body. Most of humanity are at this level, are awake emotionally, having climbed one step of the ladder in consciousness.

- *5th Mental Plane:* the body of expression on the lower mental, is the mental unit. This is where man learns to think analytically. On the higher three subplanes the body of expression is the egoic lotus or body of the soul. This is where soul consciousness and love-wisdom unfolds.

- *4th Buddhic Plane*: the body of expression here is the buddhic vehicle. This is where we develop spiritual intuition or instant knowing. Buddhi and intuition are synonyms.

- *3rd Atmic Plane:* the body of expression is the spiritual. On this plane man develops spiritual awareness. Those who have reached this level are Masters, meaning, they have mastered the forces of the lower five planes of the system.

- *2nd Monadic Plane:* this is the plane of the monads, the divine seeds or sparks. At this level we find avatars such as Christ and Gautama Buddha.

- *1st Logoic Plane:* work in the solar system is completed when this God-conscious level is reached. Then, consciousness ascends to the Cosmic Astral Plane and so on.

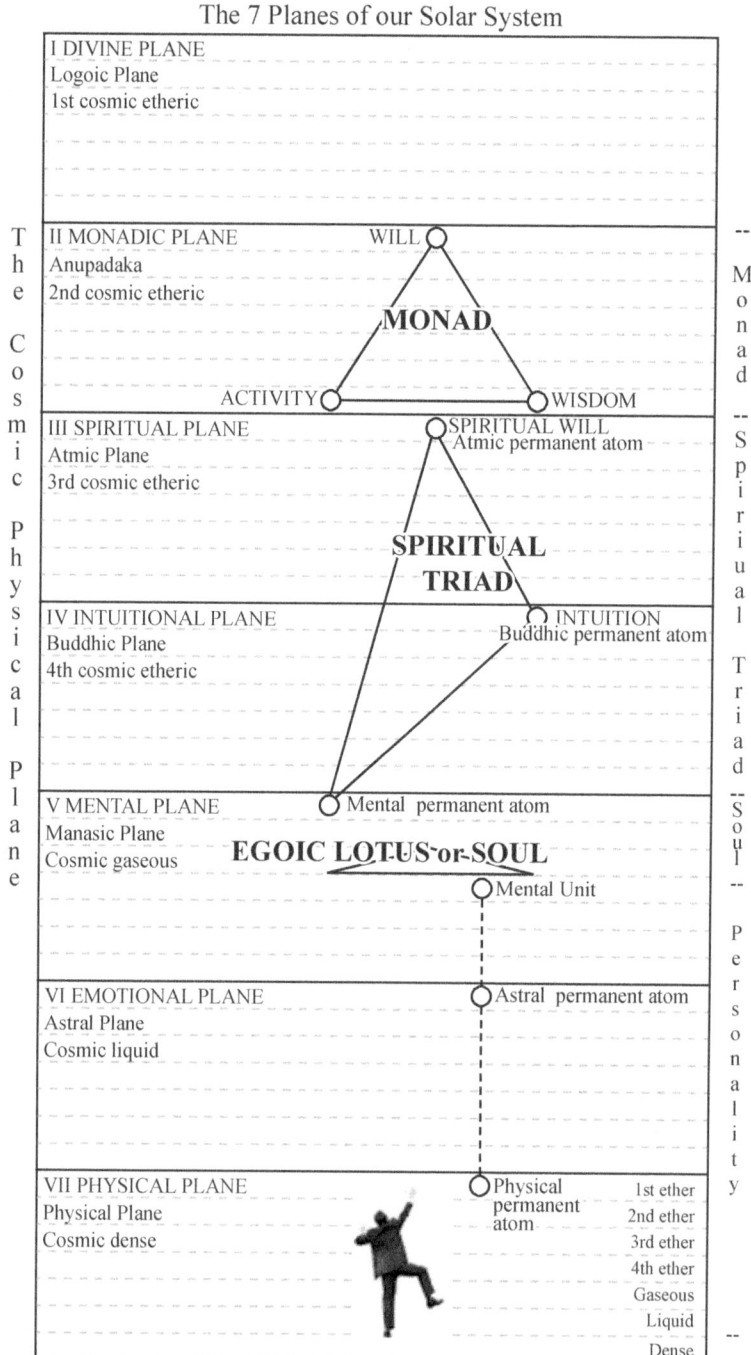

Based on Chart III, A Treatise on Cosmic Fire, p117

The 7 Planes of our Solar System

The Constitution of Man

---
1 Bailey, Alice A. A Treatise on Cosmic Fire, 255

6. The Solar Logos and a Solar Scheme

The Oversoul of the solar system or solar scheme is a cosmic being called the Solar Logos. The principle or quality in process of development by the Solar Logos is intelligent love.

> The aim of evolution for us is love dominated by intelligence—or intelligence dominated by love. [1]

It may help to think of a Solar Scheme as a university for the development of consciousness and enlightenment. The Solar Logos is the head of the school. The planets (petals) are like different classes.

There are ten Planet Schemes or classes in our system, each known by its densest planet. Hence, ours is the Earth Scheme class. Other schemes in our solar system are Vulcan, Mercury, Venus, Mars, Jupiter, Saturn, Neptune, Uranus and Pluto.

Each Planet Scheme is the manifestation of a Life called a planet Logos or Heavenly Man. The planet Logos is the ensouling life of his planet scheme, just as the Solar Logos is the ensouling life of the whole solar system. Each Planet Scheme is a force centre in the body of the Solar Logos. Earth's planet Logos is known as Sanat Kumara.

The ten Planet schemes are all in manifestation together, each proceeding on its own lines at different stages of growth. Hence, the schemes differ in age or stages of development.

The Solar Logos sends wave after wave of fiery force (Fohat) around the ten schemes. This is the force of evolution at work.

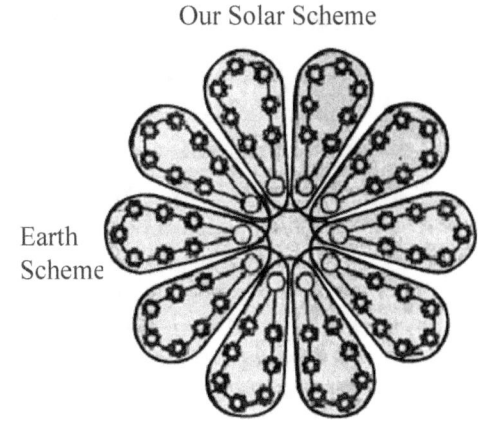

Drawing by E. Gardner in Chains and Rounds, depicting the ten schemes, with their globes and rounds.

7. Three Outpourings of Involution and Evolution

The Solar Logos provides the fuel or energy that starts, evolves and then brings the evolutionary process to fulfilment. This occurs in three outpourings.

1. The 1st outpouring from the 3rd Creative Logos drives down through all the seven planes. It vivifies universal substance and causes every atom of matter to vibrate.
2. The 2nd outpouring from the 2nd Spirit-Matter Logos forms the six planes below the first, producing form.
3. The 3rd outpouring from the Unmanifested Logos, manifested in the universe as the force of the 1st ray. It formed humanity and gave him the spark of spirit.

> The first ray of Will or Power is the first aspect of the All-self and in the third outpouring came down to the fifth plane [2]

> The fourth kingdom, the human, was formed [3]

In the diagram, the unlinked dots are connected by man's egoic lotus.

Man begins his journey on the lowest Physical Plane. Next, he climbs (in consciousness) to the sixth Astral Plane. He arrives at the fifth Mental Plane as he develops his mind. Later, he becomes spiritual in consciousness when he builds the link (the antahkarana), from his mind to the upper Mental Plane (connects the dots).

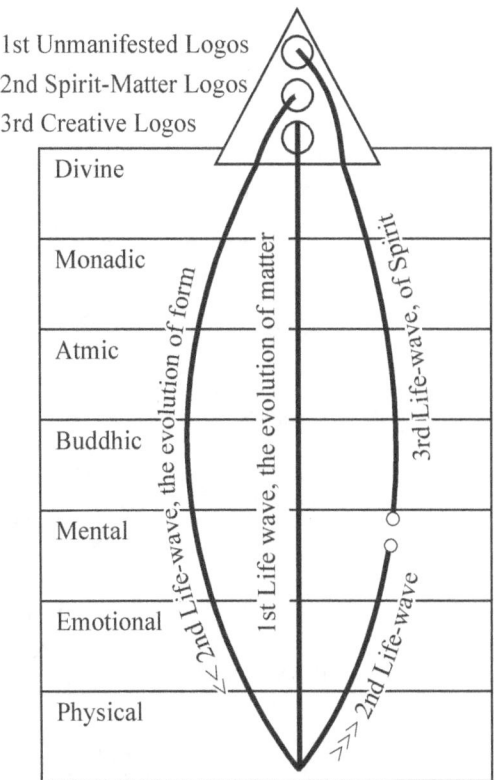

Simple drawing printed in an early Theosophist magazine, showing the three outpourings. The gap between the two dots is where the antahkarana is built.

---

1 Bailey, Alice A. A Treatise on Cosmic Fire, 576
2 Ibid, 586
3 Ibid, 584

8. God at Work in the Earth Scheme - Globes and Rounds

This section gives a brief overview of the evolutionary work in the Earth Scheme, as it is driven forwards by the Earth Logos wielding spirit-fire or Fohat.

The life force of a planetary Logos circulating through the seven chains in a scheme. [1]

The Logos uses fiery force to stimulate the spiritual fire in all kingdoms, creating the urge to progress forward. The overall plan is to drive all souls through the Mineral, Vegetable, Animal and Human Kingdoms in an orderly sequence, then through higher superhuman kingdoms until they reach Deity.

Globes A globe is just another name for a planet, the physical field upon which evolution takes place. Each major cycle of evolution happens on forty-nine globes. The Logos takes incarnation through this series of forty-nine globes as part of a plan to evolve all lives in all kingdoms.

Only one globe is fully in incarnation at one time. Referring to the Earth Scheme diagram, the globe in focus today is at the bottom (D), the earth we live on today. Note that the scheme covers the planes from Atmic to Physical. Each globe experience offers bodies of a different grade of substance.

Rounds These are cycles of spirit-fire projected by the Logos around a globe. This fiery force drives all lives onwards and upwards on the Path of Evolution. Each round repeats on a higher scale, the evolutionary work of the preceding round.

A Round:	One cycle of spirit-fire, on a globe.
A Globe Round:	Seven cycles of spirit-fire, on a globe.
A Planet Round:	One complete cycle round the seven globes of a chain (with its seven cycles on each globe).
Seven Planet Rounds:	Seven times the previous stage. This is one complete evolutionary work in one Chain. (One kalpa, or manvantara or Day of Brahma).
A Scheme Round:	Seven planet rounds over the seven Chains of a Scheme.

Chains A Chain is seven planets.

In each Chain, globes (A and B) develop the forms that incoming souls will use.

In the Human Kingdom, on globes C, D, E, the mind (the 5th Principle) is developed.

On F, Buddhi or intuition (the 6th Principle) is developed.

On G, Atma, the spiritual (7th Principle) is developed.

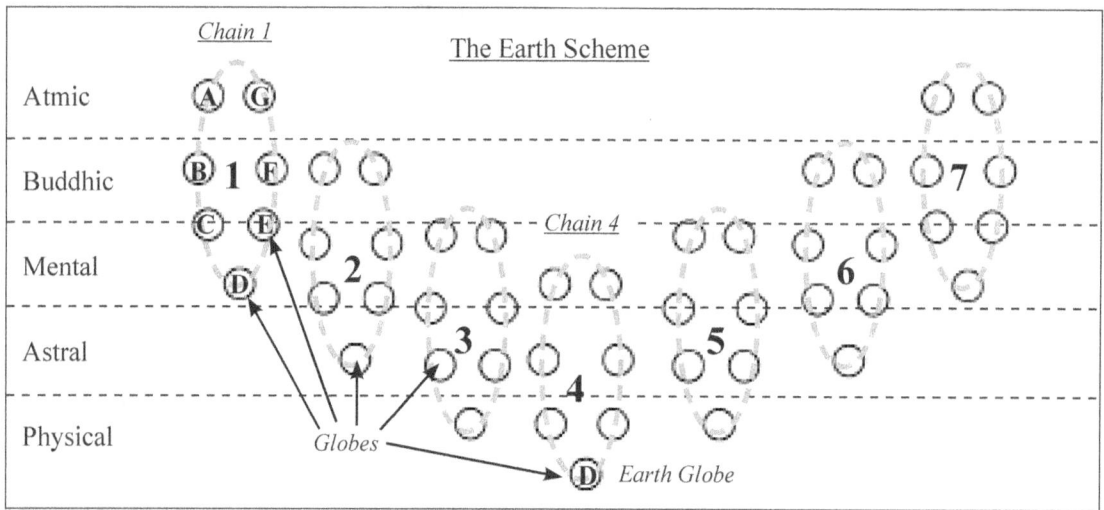

Diagram: The horizontal lines in the diagram show that globes lie on different planes or sub-planes. On the downward arc, the forms used by the monads grow successively denser until in the 4th chain, deepest concretion is reached. This is where we are now. Then on the upward arc forms are lighter.

---

1 Bailey, Alice A. *A Treatise on Cosmic Fire*, 459

1. Progress of the Life Wave from globe to globe

a. Globe A manifests first.

b. The first monads to appear on Globe A are those of the Dhyani Chohan Kingdoms (the deva/ angel or nature-builder kingdoms); which did not graduate from the last chain before it ended. Then gradually, all other kingdoms appear. The Dhyan Chohans are guardians for man. Co-mingling with animal man when he appears on the planet, they develop little by little the full type of humanity. This is a great sacrifice on their part.

> They lose their high intelligence and spirituality of Devaship [1]

c. Over vast periods, seven rounds of fiery logoic force cycle through each of the seven kingdoms. (A globe round). Each round conditions the Seven Root Races of each kingdom. These root-races are simply seven sequential, evolutionary developments that demonstrate as improved bodies and expansions in consciousness. Here is the general plan:

  - Cycle 1 energises the 3rd Elemental Kingdom (nature's building spirits), cycle 2 the 2nd Elemental Kingdom and cycle 3 the 1st Elemental Kingdom.
  - Cycle 4 energises the Mineral Kingdom, cycle 5 energises the Vegetable Kingdom and cycle 6 energises the Animal Kingdom, developing its seven Root Races.
  - The 7th Cycle energises the Human Kingdom, developing its seven Root Races.
    While this seems to suggest work is going on in one kingdom at a time, when we examine nature it is clear that all kingdoms are evolving simultaneously.

d. Then the Life-Wave moves all kingdoms to Globe 'B' and the same process occurs. Then onto 'C' through to 'G'. In his book 'The Divine Plan', Geoffrey Barborka suggests that cycles are occurring on several Globes at once. For example, when the third Cycle on Globe A is in process, so is the second Cycle on Globe 'B' and the first on Globe 'C', etc.

e. When the Life Wave makes a final move from one globe to the next, the previous globe goes into a period of relative dormancy. But it maintains a seed group called "sishtas", which are seeds for future bodies when the Life-Wave returns in the next Planet Round.

f. On the seventh and last Planet Round, when life moves finally to Globe 'B', Globe A dies. The moon is an example of a dead globe. This occurs sequentially on all globes. When the Life-Wave moves to the next Chain, taking all lives with it, the whole of the previous Chain disintegrates. Eventually, so will the scheme. At this ultimate stage, all monads will have merged back into the over-presiding Deity or be held over for a future opportunity.

2. Progress from Kingdom to Kingdom

On the Ladder of Life diagram (Hierarchies Section), the Kingdoms of Nature are shown occupying specific evolutionary rungs. The plan is that in a predetermined period, all monads should move up into the next higher kingdom or rung. The most crucial stage of the whole process involves the Human Kingdom. The kingdoms below are either unconscious or semi-intelligent, while the kingdoms above are super-conscious. The Human Kingdom links the higher and lower kingdoms and is the bridge through which self-consciousness and then the superconscious state is attained.

a. It takes one complete work in a Chain or Manvantara period (seven Planet Rounds), for the souls in a kingdom to mount one rung of the Ladder of Life. [2]

b. If we apply this rule to our current Human Kingdom (in the 4th Chain in the 4th Round) then our monads started working with us:

  - In the Mineral Kingdom in the 1st Chain.
  - We graduated into the Vegetable Kingdom in the 2nd Chain
  - Graduated into the animal in the 3rd Chain.
  - Then into the Human Kingdom in the 4th or current Chain.

---
1 The Mahatma Letters to A. P. Sinnett, 94
2 Barborka, Geoffrey; The Divine Plan, 263

3. The Rounds and the development of "Principles"

> A principle .. is the germ or.. seed.. which embodies some aspect of the divine unfolding consciousness. [1]

Man is developing seven principles or aspects of consciousness. The principles being individually developed varies and this depends upon the spiritual status of the person. For instance, the dense physical body (sthula-sarira), which was counted as a principle in Blavatsky's work, no longer applies. Humanity has progressed past that point. The principles being developed by "little evolved man" [2] today are as follows:

1st Principle:	**Etheric Body**	The vital body. The expression and vehicle of the soul.
2nd Principle:	**Prana**	The life principle of energy, the breath of Life.
3rd Principle:	**Kama**	Desire.
4th Principle:	**Lower mind**	Concrete mind.
5th Principle:	**Manas**	Higher or abstract mind.
6th Principle:	**Buddhi**	Universal Soul or Mind, man's spiritual soul; Christ force, intuition.
7th Principle:	**Atma**	Spiritual Will.

a. In advanced man, the principles being developed are (1) Prana, (2) Kama, (3) Lower Manas, (4) Higher Manas, (5) Buddhi, (6) Atma, (7) the Monad. [3]

b. One principle develops per round, on each of the seven planes. All seven principles are developed by the end of the seven rounds. Each round works through seven root races and one principle develops in each race.

c. We are currently in the 4th Round of the 5th Root Race, where lower-mind is being developed. The higher focus for advanced people is the 5th principle of higher Manas, which will be fully developed in humanity in the future fifth round. In the meantime, aspirants and disciples can develop higher Manas, Buddhi and even Atma in this fourth round if they seize the opportunity.

- The Principles and the 49 Fires

In our system, the seven planes subdivide into 7 subplanes, making 49 subplanes. The fire of God drives souls up the subplanes, developing each of the seven principles. Each subplane represents an aspect of this fire and mastery over each subplane is mastery over its fire. The goal of evolution, of the rounds, is to develop the Seven Principles and light these 49 fires. God is "a Consuming Fire" and as we "light our fires" we can channel more spiritual fire.

> The object of the cyclical journey of the seven Rounds is to complete the full development of the seven principles .. thus "lighting" all the Forty-Nine Fires. [4]

Development of the Seven Human Principles during Rounds and Races

Principles	Planes	Etheric	Prana	Kama	Lower mind	Manas higher	Buddhi	Atma	Rounds
1. Atma	Atmic	○	○	○	○	○	○	●	7th Round
2. Buddhi	Buddhic	○	○	○	○	○	●	○	6th Round
3. Manas	Mental higher	○	○	○	○	●	○	○	5th Round
4. Lower mind	Mental lower	○	○	○	●	○	○	○	4th Round
5. Kama-manas	Astral	○	○	●	○	○	○	○	3rd Round
6. Prana	Physical	○	●	○	○	○	○	○	2nd Round
7. Etheric Body	Physical	●	○	○	○	○	○	○	1st Round
		Race 1	Race 2	Race 3	Race 4	Race 5	Race 6	Race 7	

Each dark circle indicates the principle being developed in the round. We are currently in the 4th round.

---

1 Bailey, Alice A. Esoteric Healing, 611
2 Bailey, Alice A. The Treatise on Cosmic Fire, 265
3 Bailey, Alice A. The Light of the Soul, 74
4 Barborka, Geoffrey; The Divine Plan, 185

4. The Seven Root-Races of Man

All kingdoms in nature go through seven evolutionary developments in each round. In the Human Kingdom these seven developments are called *Seven Root Races*. Within each root-race are seven sub-races. The following information comes from Helena Blavatsky's 'The Secret Doctrine'.

- The 1st Root Race - the "First Born" or "Self-born".

When the Logoic Life Wave moved from the 3rd globe to our 4th Earth globe, the most basic human forms were created to house the incoming Human Monads. Lunar Pitris - beings who graduated from the Human Kingdom in the Moon Chain, created these forms by projecting "astral shadows" (chhayas) of themselves. The first human forms were pale copies of their creators, non-physical, mindless and speechless. Evolution was slow. This race reproduced by fission, like amoebas and developed the "hearing" sense and its organ.

> [They] .. could only project out of themselves shadowy men [1]

Halfway through each race, the seeds of the next race are sown and the human form begins to develop modifications that will be required in the future. Eventually there are so many with these new modifications, the new race gains ascendancy.

- The 2nd Root Race - the "Sweat-born" and the "Boneless".

This race emanated from the 1st Race. Sexless, they reproduced by: (1) "Budding": a small portion of the parent breaks off and grows to the size of the original. (2) "Sporing": a single cell thrown off that reproduces the features of the parent. This race developed the touch sense and made chant-like sounds.

- The 3rd Root Race - Lemurian.

This first physical race came into existence approximately 18 million years ago. The body developed a bony structure. There was a division of the sexes, male and female and true sexual union began. The mental faculties awakened when animal man received the seed of intelligence (individualisation) at the midpoint of this race. [2] The final subraces of Lemuria developed monosyllabic speech and were "golden coloured, yellow-complexioned men" [3]. They "built large cities, cultivated arts and sciences and knew astronomy, architecture and mathematics to perfection". "The first war that earth knew was the result of man's eyes and senses being opened, which made him see that the daughters of his Brethren were fairer than his own". There was a serious incident in this race called "The Fall of the Angels" when monads refused to incarnate. The prepared forms remained mindless and "monsters they bred".

Lemuria was centred in the Pacific Ocean region. Destroyed by volcanic action, later it sank. Australia is the largest relic and "the only pure and direct descendants are Australians" - aborigines.

- The 4th Root Race - the Atlantean.

This race developed the taste and sight senses, physical eyes and speech. The giant physiques of the previous race diminished as symmetry and beauty of form developed. The civilization of the Atlanteans was greater even than that of the Egyptians, but unfortunately, under the influence of wicked rulers the Atlanteans became a nation of greedy, materialistic magicians. A Great War between the forces of good and evil eventually led to the untimely submersion of Atlantis. Amongst the remnants are the principle isles of Polynesia. The last group of animals to enter the Human Kingdom did so in the middle period of this race. The Subraces of this Root Race are called: 1 Rmoahal. 2: Tlavatli. 3 Toltec. 4 Turanian. 5 Semite. 6 Akkadian 7 Mongolian.

- The 5th Root Race - the Aryan.

Subraces are: 1 Hindu. 2 Arabian. 3 Persian. 4 Keltic. 5 Teutonic. We are currently in the 5th sub-race and the 6th sub-race is forming. The future 6th Root Race will be coloured to a great extent by the 6th ray and will be intuitive. The final 7th Root Race will merge the male-female genders.

> ***The journey of the soul continues as consciousness expands from race to race, from round to round and from hierarchy to hierarchy.***

---

[1] Blavatsky, Helena; The Secret Doctrine II, 95
[2] Gathered from Bailey, Alice A. Initiation Human and Solar, 28-34
[3] Blavatsky, Helena; The Secret Doctrine II, 198. All subsequent information on this page comes from this book.

9. The Laws of Nature

There are eighteen laws that govern the universe. The highest law is God's purpose; then there are three major universal laws, seven minor laws of the solar system and seven basic laws of the soul.

1. The Three Major Laws of the Universe [1]

Law of the 1st Aspect - the Law of Synthesis. This law governs spiritual activity. It drives the monads into manifestation, then abstracts them, blending and synthesising them again with their spiritual source. On an individual level this law begins to govern man when he arrives at the Path of Initiation.

Law of the 2nd Aspect - the Law of Attraction. This law governs soul activity. It refines form and evolves consciousness. It governs relationships of all types on all levels - sexual relationships, personal relationships, those between groups, races, nations, etc. Related to this law is the "Law of Love.. the law of the astral plane" [2]. Its work in man is evolving desire and personality love into soul love. The Spiritual Hierarchy of Masters wields this law.

Law of the 3rd Aspect - the Law of Economy. This is the law governing matter. All bodies are manipulated under this law to make them fit the needs of the soul.

2. Seven Systemic Laws [3] of the Solar System concern the form side of life.

1. The Law of Vibration - Logoic Plane
2. The Law of Cohesion - Monadic Plane
3. The Law of Disintegration - Atmic Plane
4. The Law of Magnetic Control - Buddhic Plane
5. The Law of Fixation - Mental Plane
6. The Law of Love - Astral Plane
7. The Law of Sacrifice and Death - Physical Plane

3. Seven Laws of the Soul [4] concern the evolution of consciousness

1. The Law of Sacrifice
2. The Law of Magnetic Impulse
3. The Law of Service
4. The Law of Repulse
5. The Law of Group Progress
6. The Law of Expansive Response
7. The Law of the Lower Four

The Law of Karma, of Cause and Effect

This important law has a most profound effect on every living creature in the universe. Karma is a Sanskrit term, the popular name given to the universal process of cause and effect. For every action, there is an equal reaction. The underlying premise is that, harmony and rhythm are fundamental aspects of nature. Whenever this harmony is disturbed, nature seeks to restore balance. In a sense it is related to the 1st Law of the Solar System, the Law of Vibration. Karma is produced according to the vibration we emit. We are freed from karma when we are in harmony with Deity and there is no response within us to the vibrations of the three worlds of man.

Every action that occurs is impressed upon *Akasa*, the "infinite omnipresent material of this universe", [5] producing a karmic seed that is recorded in the Akashic Record. In one life or another, the seed ripens and man is forced to respond to a karmic event. If response is negative, evil karma follows. If response is positive, good karma follows. If response is balanced, no karma follows. Spiritually, this latter is the desired result - to walk through life in perfect equilibrium. This frees us from the Wheel of Rebirth. There is nothing personal in this law, it subjects every living entity in the universe to its equal and fair effect. We are all required to harmonise ourselves with the universal flow.

In man, the primary producer of his karma is his mind and the thoughts he thinks. Evil thoughts bring evil karmic reactions, kind and loving thoughts bring kind and loving reactions. Everything that happens to us is attributable either to our own karma or to family, group, racial or national karma. We and those we associate with create all that happens to us because of how we use our minds. Accepting this as a fact is empowering, releasing us from the belief that we are victims of life.

> *This completes this section on the cosmos and solar system. It covered God at work creating the universe round by round and driving all lives up through the various levels and planes according to Divine Law.*

---

[1] Bailey, Alice A. A Treatise on Cosmic Fire, 6
[2] Ibid, 569
[3] Ibid, 6
[4] Gathered from Bailey, Alice A. Esoteric Psychology II, 85-200
[5] Bailey, Alice A. The Soul and its Mechanism, 97

2. THE HIERARCHIES AND THE KINGDOMS

Hierarchies are groups of intelligent, semi-intelligent and ignorant forces that are responsible for the appearance of the universe and all its workings. From the very highest to the very lowest, the hierarchies are groups on all levels through which the Divine Monads work, carrying out the will of God as He manifests his purpose in time and space.

The monads are Sparks of God, the seeds of immortal spiritual life anchored in the hearts of all living beings. They constitute the incarnated presence of God the Father. They stream forth in groups (monadic essence) at the birth of a universe. Circling through all its levels, they trace a path repeated in countless universes - a journey from ignorance to spiritual enlightenment. Then, when the universe closes, they remain. Here are some important quotes.

> Monads are eternal, unitary, individual life-centers, consciousness-centers, deathless during any solar manvantara .. the ultimate elements of the universe. [1]
>
> The monads are not discrete principles, limited or conditioned, but rays from that one universal absolute Principle. [2]
>
> These hierarchies .. in their totality .. are the informing lives of .. all interplanetary space. [3]
>
> They are the mediators between Spirit and matter. [4]
>
> Each hierarchy, whether it be sun, planet, or man himself, is an aggregate of monads, all connected by unbreakable bonds—not of matter or of thought, but of the essence of the universe. [5]
>
> The Rays carry in their Hearts all the Seeds of Form; the Hierarchies use the forms. The Rays are vehicles; the Hierarchies are the users of the vehicles. [6]
>
> [The Hierarchies] stretch endlessly in either direction. [7]

If the 4th Human Hierarchy is the middle point, series of hierarchies extend above, inhabited by beings that grow less material and more spiritual. Similarly, a series of subhuman hierarchies descend downwards. The hierarchies form a series of steps through which consciousness ascends. The plan is that, at an allotted time, the lives in a hierarchy will step up (in consciousness), to the next hierarchy. The bodies that have been used do not ascend. Their material is reused by the lower hierarchy that is about to graduate to that level.

> The lives which compose a hierarchy pass in ordered cycles into the next above .. It is consciousness and realisation which (is) being transferred and the consciousness of one hierarchy expands into that of the next higher. [8]

The hierarchies are divided into the intelligent and those that are not. The higher hierarchies, those groups of spiritual beings on the inner planes of the cosmos, are the intelligent forces who control the evolutionary processes. They institute the laws of the cosmos, directing an infinite number of semi-intelligent builders to carry out their plans.

> The whole universe is ruled by intelligent and semi-intelligent Forces and Powers. [9]

The supreme authority or ruler of a hierarchy is called a Hierarch or Manu (also Silent Watcher, Planetary Spirit, Logos). The name of the Manu of the 5th Root Race is "Vaivasvata Manu". [10]

---

1 Purucker, Geoffrey de; Occult Glossary, 2nd ed., 111
2 Blavatsky, Helena; The Secret Doctrine II, 167
3 Bailey, Alice A. A Treatise on Cosmic Fire, 1195-6
4 Ibid, 1195-6
5 Blavatsky, Helena; Collected Writings, XII, 645
6 Ibid, 645
7 Purucker, Geoffrey de; Occult Glossary, 2nd ed., 86
8 Bailey, Alice A. A Treatise on Cosmic Fire, 1208
9 Blavatsky, Helena; The Secret Doctrine I, 287
10 Bailey, Alice A. Initiation Human and Solar, 41

1. The Hierarchy of Compassion, the Intelligent Architects of the Cosmos

The Hierarchy of Compassion [1] is a cosmic model applicable to any system and scheme. "Men" on the ninth rung are not exclusive to our earth humanity. It simply indicates that the human stage must be experienced. These are the superhuman beings and levels in a universe according to the Eastern Wisdom model. The name of the hierarchy suggests that the ultimate task is to develop compassion.

1.	Adi-Buddhi	Primordial Wisdom, Primeval Universal Mind, the goal of this hierarchy.
2.	Universal Buddhi	Maha-Buddhi, Mahat, Universal Mind, the soul or vehicle of Spirit, the first primeval reflection of the formless Cause.
3.	Universal Light or Life	Daiviprakriti, Fohat: divine light or fire emanating from the Logos.
4.	Seven Sons of Light	The Seven Silent Watchers, the Primordial Seven, the universal Lords of the Seven Rays.
5.	Dhyani-Buddhas	Seven Buddhas of Meditation. They are the prototypes of the Buddhas we see on earth.
6.	Dhyani-Bodhisattvas	Meditative Ones, or Celestial Bodhisattvas. They emanate from the Dhyani Buddhas. There are seven. Each is a silent Watcher of one globe in a planet chain.
7.	Super-Terrestrial Bodhisattvas	These seven emanate from the Dhyani-Bodhisattvas and watch over one of the Seven Root-Races of one Globe Round.
8.	Terrestrial Buddhas	Also called Manus, there is one for each of the Seven Root-Races.
9.	Men	The first rung of the hierarchy.

2. The Hierarchy Scheme of Earth - The Ladder of Life

This hierarchy is specific to earth. The circle, representing the One Life, the source of all monads, is outside the Earth Scheme. It is Paramatman, the Supreme Soul or Spirit; the source of Atman, a synonym for the spiritual soul.

1. The Hierarch or head of the Earth Scheme, the planet Logos, is represented by the apex of the triangle.
2. The falling rays picture the descent of the monads to earth. They come down in waves or classes to one or other of the rungs.
3. The Ladder of Life has ten rungs, ten ascending levels of consciousness. On each rung a class of monads, works though a specific Kingdom in Nature.
4. Having descended, the monads commence their cycling following the great evolutionary journey known as the 'Circle of Necessity'. Their immediate goal is to attain a self-conscious independent existence. [2] Their ultimate goal is to return to Paramatman.
5. Each rung stands for one evolutionary degree of attainment. The goal of each class or kingdom is to graduate to the next higher rung.
6. The monads work their way upwards from the lowest Elemental Kingdom, to the first, using the vehicles on each rung.
7. So for instance our 4th Human Hierarchy monads used elemental vehicles to mount the first three steps, then mineral, vegetable and animal bodies to mount the next three steps. In the Human Kingdom they are using human bodies. When their lower extensions (us) reach the first Dhyani-Chohanic Kingdom - or become soul conscious; our monads also graduate, becoming monads of the 5th Hierarchy of Souls.

Ladder of Life

1. Class I. Dhyan-Chohanic Kingdom
2. Class II. Dhyan-Chohanic Kingdom
3. Class III. Dhyan-Chohanic Kingdom
4. Human Kingdom
5. Animal Kingdom
6. Plant Kingdom
7. Mineral Kingdom
8. Class I Elemental Kingdom
9. Class II Elemental Kingdom
10. Class III Elemental Kingdom

---
1 Gathered from Barborka; The Divine Plan, 67-73
2 Ibid, 58

3. The Seven Creative Hierarchies connected with the Human Kingdom

These seven creative hierarchies are primarily concerned with the Human Kingdom. Do not confuse the number of each of these seven hierarchies with those given on the Ladder of Life, which covers all the kingdoms in nature. The Seven Creative Hierarchies are helping us to develop the seven principles referred to previously in "The Rounds and the development of Principles" section.

The creative hierarchies are in the etheric body of the Logos, so their function is to provide a structure upon which the various lives on each plane can model themselves. They link earth kingdoms to the cosmic galactic powers of the constellations. There are twelve creative hierarchies but five of them (the hierarchies associated with Pisces, Aries, Taurus, Gemini, Cancer) no longer work directly to produce man. However, their forces are still very potent in the astrology zodiac and in man's psychology and life.

The 7 Creative Hierarchies in Active Expression

Cosmic Physical Plane

Plane	*No.*	*Hierarchy Name*	*Sign - Ruler*	*Colour*
Logoic Plane	I	The Burning Sons of Desire	Leo - Sun	Orange
Monadic Plane	II	Prototypes of the Monads	Virgo - Jupiter	Blue
Atmic Plane	III	The Triads	Libra - Saturn	Green
Buddhic plane	IV	Human Hierarchy Lords of Sacrifice	Scorpio - Mercury	Yellow
Mental Plane	V	Solar Angels	Capricorn - Venus	Indigo
Astral Plane	VI	Lunar Lords	Sagittarius - Mars	Red
Physical Plane	VII	Elemental lives	Aquarius - Moon	Violet

Our task is to develop the principles, powers and knowledge that each of these hierarchies represent. As each principle is developed, controlled and expressed we ascend one evolutionary level in the system. Advanced man is trying to become conscious in each of the four hierarchies higher than the personality, the lower mental level.

Hierarchy I: The Divine Flames. The highest hierarchy is holy and originates from the Heart of the Central Spiritual Sun. They are called the Burning Sons of Desire and represent the "longing of the Father for the Mother" that underlies the drive towards spiritual union. The monads in this Hierarchy represent the "God" aspect to man

Hierarchy II: The Divine Builders. This hierarchy contains the prototypes of our monads, but they are not the monads, they are far higher.

Hierarchy III: The Triads. This hierarchy holds the potencies of Spirit, Soul and Intellect. It works on the Atmic Plane, holding the archetype or blueprint of man's spiritual nature.

Hierarchy IV: The Human Hierarchy (see the following pages).

Hierarchy V: The Hierarchy of Souls (see the following pages).

Hierarchies: VI and VII: these semi-intelligent hierarchies provide the substance for the forms of the lower mind, emotions and physical etheric bodies. These two hierarchies, along with the 4th and 5th, produce man as he is in incarnation.

Where man is concerned, the fourth, fifth, sixth and seventh Hierarchies are, during the cycle of incarnation, his very self.[1]

These hierarchies build man's bodies of expression and the Solar Angels help him develop and use them. Advanced man's immediate spiritual task is to perfectly merge within his nature the 4th and 5th hierarchies. Most people however are still working to fully develop and manage hierarchies 5, 6 and 7.

---
1 Bailey, Alice A. Esoteric Astrology, 42

1. Hierarchy IV - the Hierarchy of Human Monads [1]

The 4th Hierarchy or Class of Human Monads (there are sixty thousand million) [2] is not man as we know him in the three worlds. These monads set the ideal pattern or model for us.

> The fourth kingdom in nature (is) the lowest manifestation of the fourth creative Hierarchy. [3]

Through the evolutionary process, man in the three worlds aspires to become perfect as his Father in Heaven (the monad) is perfect. Energised by ceaseless persevering devotion, sacrificing their high position to raise the lives of lower hierarchies to the status of themselves, these monadic "Lords of Will and Sacrifice" are our essential prototypes.

> The Lords of Will and Sacrifice come down into manifestation, sacrificing their high position and opportunities upon the higher planes of manifestation in order to redeem matter and raise .. (the lower Creative Hierarchies) to the status of Themselves [4]

Strategically placed between the subhuman kingdoms and superhuman, the Human Hierarchy links the higher and lower. In man, spirit and matter are united through the intellect. Lower kingdoms can attain the self-consciousness and then superconscious states through the Human Hierarchy. This is its great service to the system. It is how all lives working in the subhuman kingdoms can find spiritual liberation, by moving up through the Human Kingdom into superhuman realms.

Because it is the 4th Kingdom in nature, it follows that the ray which governs it and which is its soul ray, is the 4th Ray of Harmony through Conflict.

> The egoic ray of the Life which informs the human family is this fourth ray [5]

When human history is studied, we see that the conflict aspect has ruled. This will change in the future when a dominant number of individuals transform their natures and are distinguished by harmlessness and harmony instead of war and anger.

> This fourth ray of conflict is the ray whose energies .. bring about harmony and at-one-ment. The result of this harmonising activity is beauty, but it is a beauty that is achieved through struggle. [6]

The personality ray of humanity is the 5th of Concrete Mind and Knowledge. Hence man's natural curiosity "to know, to find and discover".

> The personality ray is the fifth ray of knowledge through discrimination [7]

Man is a combination of both the human and deva evolutions. Using deva essence, lesser devas build his lower bodies while higher devas (Solar Angels) build his wisdom body the egoic lotus. All the centres in our human bodies are composed of deva essence.

> From the most esoteric standpoint "Man is a deva;" he is Spirit and deva substance, united through the work of conscious deva energy. [8]

Man is an embryonic God. All the ingredients are within him. His task in time and space is to bring his God potential into full flowering.

The ultimate plan for the Human Kingdom on earth is profound. Once the consciousness of God has manifested through humanity as a whole (the 5th Kingdom manifesting through the 4th), the 4th Kingdom will be a great station of light in the solar system. It will be a powerhouse of such potency and a focal point of such energy that our kingdom will be a factor in not only the solar system but also affecting seven systems of which ours is one. [9]

---

1 Bailey, Alice A. A Treatise on Cosmic Fire, 1203
2 Bailey, Alice A. A Treatise on Cosmic Fire, 579. There are 35 thousand million 2nd ray monads; 20 thousand million 3rd ray Monads; 5 thousand million 1st ray Monads.
3 Bailey, Alice A. Esoteric Psychology I, 344
4 Bailey, Alice A. Esoteric Astrology, 116
5 Bailey, Alice A. Esoteric Psychology I, 343
6 Bailey, Alice A. Esoteric Psychology II, 92
7 Bailey, Alice A. Esoteric Psychology I, 343
8 Bailey, Alice A. A Treatise on Cosmic Fire, 729
9 Gathered from Bailey, Alice A. Esoteric Psychology II, 217

2. Hierarchy V - the Hierarchy of Souls, the Spiritual Hierarchy, the Kingdom of God on Earth

The 5th Hierarchy is a deva or angelic hierarchy. [1] When our current humanity was about to step from the Animal to the Human Kingdom, this was promoted and managed by Deva Lords of Flame or Solar Angels (Agnishvattas). They came to earth and the Spiritual Hierarchy came into being.

> They created the nucleus of the Hierarchy [2]

The Angels help man to expand his consciousness and step from the 4th into the 5th Kingdom. As souls step up the two kingdoms slowly merge. This has been happening over the past two thousand years and will come to completion during the incoming Aquarian Age in the 22nd and 23rd centuries. The 5th Kingdom will manifest on earth when most men and women become soul conscious.

> The fifth kingdom in nature, the spiritual, will emerge out of the fifth root race. (This work is) under the guidance of the Christ [3]

This will change world civilisation dramatically. Instead of the "conflict" aspect of the 4th ray dominating consciousness, the "harmony" aspect will. Humanity will be a centre of goodwill.

> The Kingdom of God is .. a vast and integrated group of soul-infused persons, radiating love and spiritual intention, motivated by goodwill [4]

The distinction between the 5th and 4th kingdoms is one of consciousness. Members of the 5th kingdom are here on earth already. Readers of the book could be full or partial members. The first step into this higher kingdom is taken when goodwill begins to drive our actions, which means we are on the Path.

> A spiritual intention, motivated by goodwill .. has taken the first step into the spiritual kingdom [5]

Personnel of the 5th Spiritual Hierarchy

Sanat Kumara, the Lord of the World

The Three Buddhas of Activity

Reflections of the 3 major and 4 minor Rays

The 3 Departmental Heads

Ray 1 The Manu	Ray 2 The Christ	Ray 3 Mahachohan
Develop racial bodies, politics, government.	[Bodhisattva/ Lord Maitreya] Guides man's spiritual destiny.	Responsible for world civilisation.
Master Morya	Master Koot Humi	The Venetian Master
Master Jupiter	Master Djwhal Khul	Minor rays:
	A European Master	Ray 4 Master Serapis
		Ray 5 Master Hilarion
		Ray 6 Master Jesus
		Ray 7 Master Rakoczi

Master Koot Humi

Master Morya

Sanat Kumara: he is the Logos of Earth, the representative of the Manu, the Hierarch of Earth. Other names by which he is known are the One Initiator, the Ancient of Days and the Eternal Youth. He came to earth from Venus (this is the Venus chain in the Earth Scheme), as custodian for the evolution of life on earth. Shamballa is his seat of government, the 'Centre where the Will of God is known'. The Spiritual Hierarchy is his ashram.

The Christ: he is known in the East as Lord Maitreya, the Bodhisattva, the Imam Mahdi and in the West as the World Teacher. He is the Lord of Love and of Compassion, while his brother the Buddha is the Lord of Wisdom. Christ's task is to oversee and guide the spiritual destinies of men.

---

1 Gathered from Bailey, Alice A. A Treatise on Cosmic Fire, 605
2 Bailey, Alice A. Telepathy and the Etheric Vehicle, 132
3 Bailey, Alice A. Discipleship in the New Age I, 32
4 Bailey, Alice A. Discipleship in the New Age II, 407-8
5 Bailey, Alice A. Initiation Human and Solar, 10

Master Morya: amongst his pupils are many Europeans and Americans. A Rajput Prince, he is the head of all esoteric organisations in the world and of the 1st Ray Ashram of souls.

Master Koot Humi: this Master has many pupils everywhere. Of Kashmiri origin, the family originally came from India. He is on the 2nd Love-Wisdom ray and head of the 2nd Ray Ashram of souls.

Master Djwhal Khul: in 1934, Blavatsky wrote in the first person of *Djwhal Khul*:

> [I am] a Tibetan disciple of a certain degree and this tells you but little, for all are disciples from the humblest aspirant up to and beyond The Christ Himself. I live in a physical body like other men on the borders of Tibet and at times (from the exoteric standpoint) preside over a large group of Tibetan Lamas, when my other duties permit. [1]

In 1919, Alice Bailey began writing the 'blue books', which she described as being telepathically dictated to her by Djwhal Khul. The purpose of the books is given below.

> If the information given raises the aspiration and the will-to-serve from the plane of the emotions to that of the mind (the plane where the Masters can be found) they will have served their purpose. [2]

4. The Animal, Vegetable and Mineral Kingdoms

On the Ladder of Life, these are kingdoms 5, 6 and 7. Do not confuse this number scheme with the Creative Hierarchies specifically related to the Human Kingdom, which are different.

Each kingdom is a reservoir of power and of vitality to the next kingdom. The Vegetable Kingdom draws its sustenance from the sun, water and earth. The Animal Kingdom draws sustenance primarily from the sun, water and the Vegetable Kingdom. Humanity draws from the sun, water, vegetable and animal world. Man's responsibility is to stimulate the instinct of animals until individualisation for them is possible. He must foster the perfume-producing faculty of the Vegetable Kingdom and adapt plant life to the myriad uses of man and of animals. With the Mineral Kingdom he must work alchemically and chemically.

1. The Animal Kingdom

Up until 200 years ago, animals preyed on humans and continually wiped out small groups trying to establish themselves. The devastation was terrible and the karmic result is the current cruelty visited on animals.

> Devastation wrought by animals .. lies at the root of man's cruelty to animals [3]

The incoming 7th ray will cause a great destruction of the present animal forms and they will be dramatically refined as a result. Under its effect man will learn to use the power of thought to control and direct animals and this will eventually bridge the gap between the Animal Kingdom and man. One by one, these animal lives are prepared and brought to the door of individualisation. There they wait, until it opens for them to receive the spark of intelligence and enter the Human Kingdom. Domestic animals that live in close and intimate proximity with human beings, such as cats and dogs, are the most advanced members of the Animal Kingdom.

2. The Vegetable Kingdom

This is the only kingdom on earth in which three rays have fully blended - the indigo ray 2, yellow ray 4 and light blue ray 6; into a green that has spread over the planet. Supremely beautiful, the Vegetable Kingdom is closely related to the deva kingdom and the more aromatic the perfume the more evolved the plant life.

> Its highest form of activity, is demonstrated by the perfume of its highest forms of life. [4]

3. The Mineral Kingdom

This kingdom has seven main groups that each correspond to the Seven Rays. It is undergoing initiation by sound and fire, a process began in the 20th Century World Wars.

---

[1] Bailey, Alice A. Ponder on this, Extract from a Statement by the Tibetan.
[2] Ibid
[3] Bailey, Alice A. Esoteric Psychology I, 256
[4] Ibid, 197

5. The Deva or Angelic Kingdom

The Deva or Angelic Kingdom in its many grades and levels build the universe and the forms through which spirit incarnates for experience in the different kingdoms. This kingdom is also called the 'Army of the Voice' because its members sweep into power when duly commanded. These angel messengers are the agents of karmic and cosmic laws and their ranks stretch from the lesser nature spirits to the highest of Heavenly Spirits.

> The Order of the angels is hierarchical. On the lower rungs of the angelic ladder of life are the lesser nature spirits, brownies and gnomes, associated with the element of earth; fairies and sylphs with that of air; undines or nereids with water; and salamanders with fire. Above them, as previously stated, are angels and Archangels in an ascending scale of evolutionary stature, reaching up to the Seven Mighty Spirits before the Throne. [1]

A book on this subject that is highly recommended is 'The Kingdom of the Gods', by Geoffrey Hodson. He was a true higher clairvoyant who saw and communicated with devas. The paintings and sketches below are images of devas he saw and had drawn. Note the general similarity of the centre picture with the Christian version of angels.

FAIRY JOY

Mountain Deva, Cape Town, South Africa

GRASS ELF

EARTH GNOME

Humans and devas are partners. The Deva Kingdom is feminine, the Human Kingdom is masculine. Inextricably linked, two sides of a whole; together they form the body of the Logos. They are parallel evolutions and at different stages of the path, units within either can cross into the other kingdom for experience. According to Theosophist E. L. Gardner, these two kingdoms are one stream in the Elemental Kingdom but separate into two streams in the middle of the Mineral Kingdom. The deva stream passes through jewels, grasses, insects and birds and the human through metals, mosses, shrubs, trees and animals. The two streams merge again beyond the human stage. [2] While not discounting what Gardner wrote, Bailey said the two evolutions touch in the Vegetable Kingdom, separate in the Animal and Human Kingdoms, make contact again on the Buddhic Plane and finally merge on the Monadic Plane. [3] In the seventh round the human and deva kingdoms become fully merged. [4]

1. There are two main groups of Devas

a. The Greater Gods or Builders: they are the intelligent devas on the Evolutionary Path that work in grades up to the rank of the planetary Logos. They have many different names: Dhyan-Chohans or Dhyanis, Devas, Angels, Solar Pitris, Solar Angels, Arch Angels, the shining ones, celestial beings, resplendent ones and Elohim. These devas have passed through the human stage.

b. The Lesser Gods or Builders, Lunar Lords or Angels. These subhuman nature spirits are on the Involutionary Path and have yet to pass through the human stage. They form the essence of substance in its many and varied forms of earth, fire, air and water. Ranging from blind and ignorant to semi-intelligent, they produce all the lower-nature bodies in all kingdoms.

---
1 Hodson, Geoffrey; Kingdom of the Gods, 56
2 Gathered from Gardner, E. L; The Web of the Universe, 98
3 Gathered from Bailey, Alice A. A Treatise on Cosmic Fire, 589
4 Ibid, 599

2. Deva work with Humanity

Devas do not understand speech but respond to vibration or sound. Ultra-sensitive to the world of man, every word and sound causes a reaction in deva substance. They make forms according to the nature and persistence of a sound and the intent of its originator. Ugly sounds produce ugly forms, sweeter or sacred sounds produce glorious and magnificent forms. The Solar Logos created the universe by enunciating the AUM.

> In the beginning was the Word and the Word was with God and the Word was God. [1]

Mental Plane: three great groups of angels - the gold, the flame coloured and the white and gold, work on mental levels with lesser angels or devas who vitalise thoughtforms. [2] Amongst this group are the Solar Angels (Agnishvattas) who build and fan into action, man's soul body and consciousness. The great Angel/ Deva Lord, Agni, rules over these devas.

Astral Plane: these devas are called Agnisuryans Builders and are ruled by the deva Lord Varuna. They produce the phenomena called human love, the sex impulse and instinct. They oversee the little elementals that form the emotional body, whose fluctuations control the masses. The immediate evolutionary goal for average man is liberation from their control.

> The mental elemental, the astral elemental and the physical elemental have a definite life of their own .. until the man has reached a relatively high point in evolution. [3]

Physical Plane: these devas are called Agnichaitan builders and are ruled by the deva Lord Kshiti. They are the metals and minerals and build the earth globe and all physical bodies. Connected to the central fires in the bowels of the earth, they purify by fire and are very dangerous to man.

- Some populous deva groups

Violet devas of the physical-etheric subplanes. Their colours range from lavender to deep purple. They control the elementals that build the etheric bodies of all forms on the Physical Plane.

Green devas of the Vegetable Kingdom. The greater devas of this order guard the solitude of the forests and sacred spaces. They direct the elemental fairies and elves of plant life that build and paint flowers, work with fruits, vegetables and all greenery.

White devas of the air and water. They work with electrical phenomena, control the seas, rivers, streams, the water and air elementals. Man's guardian angels come from their ranks. Under the white devas work the elemental sylphs and water fairies, then at a lower level, brownies, gnomes and pixies.

3. Contacting Devas

Rose Fairy

> The deva and human evolution will, during the next five hundred years, become somewhat more conscious of each other and be able therefore more freely to co-operate. [4]

There are people who try to summon devas in magical work, but higher devas cannot be commanded. While this is appropriate in the case of evolved or pure souls who work under due rule and law, it is very inappropriate for the ignorant to attempt this. At that lower level, the only devas that might respond are the blind and unintelligent lesser devas who are very dangerous to man. Anyone who ignorantly attempts to invoke them runs the risk of becoming, "a lost soul". Their rightful masters are the higher devas who choose whether to communicate with man.

Devas are contacted through ritual work. When the vibrations of participants are pure enough and the motive of ritual work is altruistic, ceremonies serve as a common meeting ground. In these circumstances, ask for their assistance and they will oblige. Play beautiful classical music, knowing that they will come and fill the room with beautiful images. The colours violet and white provide a medium through which the two kingdoms can draw closer together.

---

1 Bible, John, 1:1
2 Bailey, Alice A. Externalisation of the Hierarchy, 505
3 Bailey, Alice A. Esoteric Psychology II, 290
4 Bailey, Alice A. Letters on Occult Meditation, 182

4. The Celestial Hierarchy or Hierarchy of Angels

> The seven planetary Spirits or Angels .. are identical with the Dhyan Chohans of the esoteric doctrine and have been transformed into the archangels and the Spirits of the Presence by the Christian Church. [1]

This hierarchy stems from the writings of a convert of St. Paul's - Dionysius. There are nine Orders of Angels that distribute the power of God. It is simply a Christian version of ancient Eastern Lore. The different grades relate somewhat to Dhyani-chohan levels.

Seraphim	They radiate and inspire man with divine love.
Cherubim	Enlighten man with wisdom.
Thrones	Teach men to rule with justice.
Dominions	Rule the activities of the angels.
Virtues	Work miracles.
Powers	Ward off evil spirits.
Principalities	Rule over people and nations.
Archangels	Some texts refer to seven Archangels - Michael, Gabriel, Raphael, Uriel, Chamuel, Jophiel and Zadkiel. They are messengers in matters of great importance.
Angels	Messengers.

Archangel Michael

Perhaps the most famous Archangel is Michael. In esoteric text including the Bible, he leads God's armies against evil forces and defeats them. This happens on many levels, on earth and in the heavens. To complete this section, here is a quote.

> Just as the planet called the earth is regarded as the turning point or the battle-ground between Spirit and matter and is therefore, from that very consideration, of great importance, so our solar system holds an analogous place in the cosmic scheme. The cosmic man, the solar Arjuna, is wrestling for His individualised perfected self-consciousness and for freedom and liberation from the form and from the not-self. So man on this planet battles for similar ideals on his tiny scale; so battle in heaven Michael and His Angels, or the divine Heavenly Men, Whose problem is the same on the higher scale. [2]

Archangel Michael, TattoMagz

This completes this chapter on the larger picture, an overview of the stage setting through which the monads evolve. As they do so, their lower attributes the souls, also evolve - in consciousness. Simultaneously, the forms used by souls evolve. All three streams are ascending on a journey that takes them ever closer to the Source of Life.

---

1 Bailey, Alice A. Esoteric Astrology, 646. Quote from the Secret Doctrine.
2 Bailey, Alice A. A Treatise on Cosmic Fire, 242

CHAPTER 2: THE EVOLUTION OF CONSCIOUSNESS

This is evolution, the process which unfolds the life within all units, the developing urge which eventually merges all units and all groups, until you have that sumtotal of manifestation which can be called Nature, or God and which is the aggregate of all the states of consciousness. [1]

---

[1] Bailey, Alice A. The Consciousness of the Atom, 21

1. THE CONSTITUTION OF MAN

In this section, the various aspects of man and different levels of consciousness are studied. Man "is made in the image of God", is essentially a triune being - Spirit, Soul and Body.

1. Man's Higher Nature or Self

1. The Monad - Source of Consciousness

The monad was initially explored in the Hierarchies section. The Monad is the ultimate source of consciousness, the highest aspect in all living entities in the universe. Wave after wave, Monadic groups (or Sparks of God) stream out from the central Life to circle through the universe from high to low and then from low to high again; a cycle called "the evolution of the monads"[1]. In the process they transform the universe, symbolically, from darkness to light.

The method employed at each level is the same. The monads work through the kingdoms on each level. They expand consciousness/ the soul aspect at each level until that group of souls is ready to ascend to the next higher kingdom. This is a great sacrifice made by the monads, because by falling into incarnation - and during the aeons they are submerged under the veils of matter; they lose their high intelligence and spirituality "to regain them in the end of the.. seventh round"[2]

When this is achieved, the circling of the monad (Circle of Necessity) is complete. The enlightened one is absorbed back into its Source. Here is a wonderful description:

> After the separation between the life-principle .. and the body takes place, the liberated soul — monad, exultingly rejoins the mother and father spirit .. the Adam who has completed the circle of necessity and is freed from the last vestige of his physical encasement. Henceforth, growing more and more radiant at each step of his upward progress, he mounts the shining path that ends at the point from which he started around the GRAND CYCLE.[3]

2. The Spiritual Triad

The Spiritual Triad is the body of expression of the monad. When we refer to our spiritual aspect, this is the Spiritual Triad. The Triad and spirit are synonymous terms. The Triad is triple in nature and its body spans the Spiritual, Intuitional and Mental Planes. These three aspects - the higher potential aspects within us all, are also known as atma-buddhi-manas, "spirit - spiritual soul - spiritual mind". The full force of the Triad is only consciously experienced after the 3rd initiation - when we become fully soul conscious.

The Triad (or simply spirit) works through the soul in the causal body, to develop and expand consciousness.

> Man, in essential essence, is the higher Triad demonstrating through a gradually evolving form, the egoic or causal body and utilising the lower threefold personality as a means to contact the lower three planes. All this has for purpose the development of perfect self-consciousness.[4]

The Planes & Spirit, Soul, Personality

1. Logoic		**GOD**
2. Monadic	△	**THE MONAD**
3. Atmic		**The Spiritual Triad** Spans the 3rd and 4th planes to the top of the 5th.
4. Buddhic		
5. Mental	○	Soul: 3rd subplane
6. Emotional		**The Personality** spans the 7th and 6th planes, up to the 4th subplanes of the 5th Mental.
7. Physical		

---

1 Bailey, Alice A. A Treatise on Cosmic Fire, 176
2 Barborka, Geoffrey; The Divine Plan, 347
3 Blavatsky, Helena; Isis Unveiled 1, 303.
4 Bailey, Alice A. A Treatise on Cosmic Fire, 260-261

3. The Human Soul

Soul arises when Father-Spirit merges with Mother-Matter. It is the Son of the Father and of the Mother, the embodied life of God coming into incarnation to reveal the nature of God, which is essential love. [1]

Everything has a soul, be it an atom, animal, man, planet, galaxy etc, but not all souls are equal in consciousness. The individual soul is a cell in the sumtotal of manifestation, commonly called God. This Oversoul is the aggregate of all the states of consciousness. The soul is the attractive force in nature that holds all forms together so that the life of God can manifest through them. It is the quality which every form manifests, which distinguishes a rose from a cabbage, an elm from a maple etc. All colours, vibrations, qualities, characteristics are the outer manifestations of soul. Subhuman Kingdoms have a group soul and share group karma. Humans have individual souls. This enables individual man to accelerate his spiritual progress if he does the inner work.

- The Solar Angels

The human soul is that part of the mind that has the potential to be illumined. Solar Angels, members of the 5th Hierarchy, bring this about. There are many names by which they are known, such as: Sons of Manas or Mind, Lords of Wisdom, Lords of the Flame and Agnishvattas.

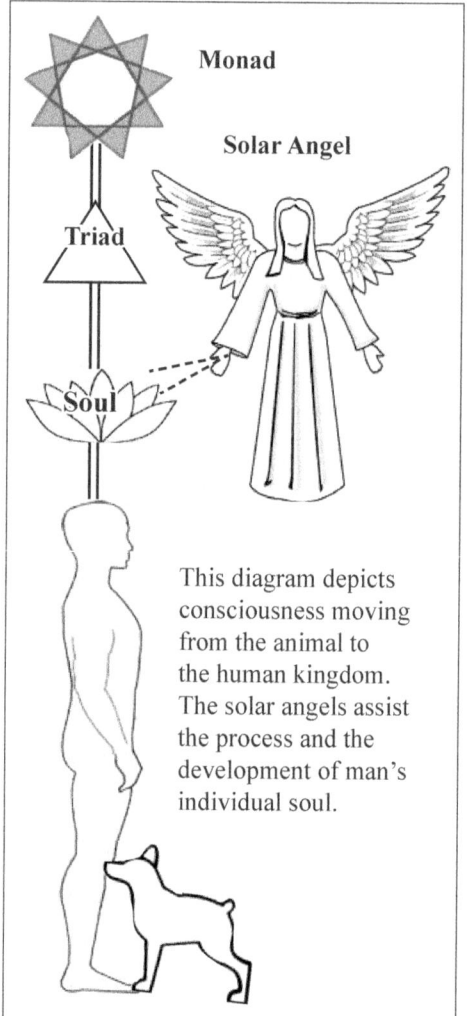

Led by a very advanced angel called Sanat Kumara, the Solar Angels came to earth during the 3rd Root-Race, to help primitive animal-man become truly human and step into the Human Kingdom. (See diagram). They did this by planting a seed of Divine Mind (fiery angelic essence) in animal man. This action is called "individualisation" and from that point onwards, man had an individual soul. From this seed, man builds his soul body. Other names for the soul body are causal body and egoic lotus.

> This fifth hierarchy of Agnishvattas .. embody the "I principle".. They enable (man) to build his own body of causes, to unfold his own egoic lotus and gradually to free himself from the limitations of the form. [2]

- Human Soul

Man's soul is a blend of manas (Universal Mind) and buddhi (Universal Soul). It is that thinking, intelligent, self-conscious and discriminating part of our nature.

In primitive man, the soul is undeveloped, consciousness is ignorant. Ignorance or lack of awareness separates us from our spiritual potential. Ignorant mind identifies with the lower material self, the personality, and is unable to discriminate the true from the false.

> As long as a man is identified with the appearance, these aspects of the mental principle produce in him the "great heresy of separateness." [3]

This diagram depicts consciousness moving from the animal to the human kingdom. The solar angels assist the process and the development of man's individual soul.

On the Path, man discovers his spiritual soul (the 2nd aspect of the Spiritual Triad) and gradually identifies with it. Through the experience of many incarnations gradually his little soul is enlightened, becomes wise and loving. The next step then is to become monadically or spiritually aware.

> The soul is now the dominant factor; consciousness is now identified with itself.. and not with its phenomenal appearance. Later, the soul itself is superseded by the monad. [4]

4. Unfoldment of the Petals of the Egoic Lotus

Soul wisdom is housed in the egoic lotus. Each petal of the lotus represents certain qualities and values. As wisdom unfolds so do the petals of the lotus. It is constructed from mental essence and is anchored on the 3rd subplane of the Mental Plane. Look at the previous diagram "The 7 Planes of our Solar System" to find its location.

---

1 Gathered from Bailey, Alice A. Esoteric Psychology I, 36
2 Bailey, Alice A. A Treatise on Cosmic Fire, 703
3 Bailey, Alice A. Esoteric Psychology I, 38
4 Ibid, 39

The nine-petalled egoic lotus, the heart centre in the monadic consciousness [1]

The lotus has 3 layers, each with 3 petals; all shielding the inner bud that hides the "Jewel in the Lotus" or our spiritual connection. The Angel's task is to ensure the petals (our qualities), are vitalised, nurtured and eventually unfold.

Within the lotus are three (permanent) atoms that connect man with the Mental, Astral and Physical Planes. These atoms assimilate and record experience and preserve memory across lives. Around these atoms the mind, astral and physical bodies are constructed.

As consciousness unfolds, so do the petals. At the same time, consciousness rises from lower to higher chakras, from lower to higher planes.

The three circles of three petals each are called:

1. Knowledge: the outer (orange) petals.
2. Love: the middle (pink) petals.
3. Sacrifice: the inner (yellow) petals.

The general process of petal unfoldment and development of qualities is as follows.

Knowledge Petals 1 to 3 unfold through experience on the Physical Plane.

1. Knowledge-Knowledge petal: unfolds through suffering, a result of breaking karmic law.
2. Knowledge-Love petal: unfolds through physical relationships and the evolution of self-love to love of others.
3. Knowledge-Sacrifice petal: unfolds through suffering, the repercussion of indulging desire.

Love Petals 4 to 6 unfold through Astral Plane or emotional experience.

4. Love-Knowledge petal: unfolds when one understands the causes behind events and the pairs of opposite are consciously balanced.
5. Love-Love petal: unfolds as glamour falls away and focus turns to love of the Real.
6. Love-Sacrifice petal: unfolds by sacrificing personal desire for the group good.

Sacrifice Petals 7 to 9 unfold through experience on the Mental Plane.

7. Sacrifice-Knowledge petal: unfolds when all is given for the good of humanity. The 1st Initiation.
8. Sacrifice-Love petal: unfolds at the 2nd Initiation, as all soul powers are used to serve humanity.
9. Sacrifice-Sacrifice petal: unfolds at the 3rd and 4th Initiations. One is simply a soul at this level.

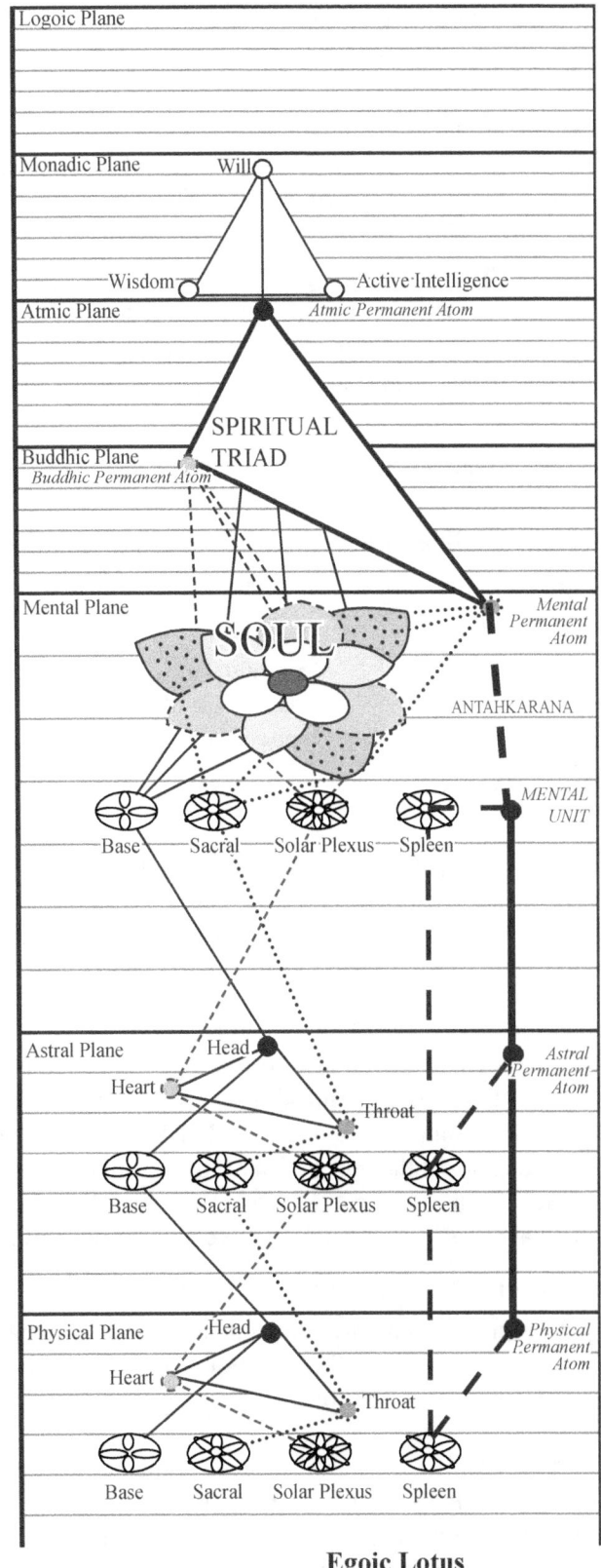

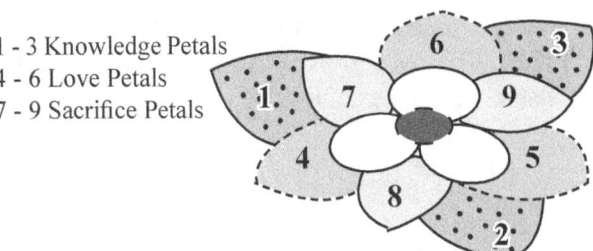

Egoic Lotus

1 - 3 Knowledge Petals
4 - 6 Love Petals
7 - 9 Sacrifice Petals

---

1 Bailey, Alice A. *A Treatise on Cosmic Fire*, 539

- Destruction of the Egoic Lotus

Through aeons the Solar Angel hovers over the developing egoic lotus, fanning its fire (the element of the Mental Plane is fire); until all faculties are developed. Then at the 4th initiation level when all human experience has been met and mastered, spiritual fire makes a direct connection via the antahkarana, to the mental unit. The inner spiritual fire contained in the "Jewel in the Lotus" bursts free, bringing about the lotus' blazing destruction. It is no longer required. Man has reached the Buddhic Plane in his evolution and functions consciously in his intuitional body. The lives, from which the lotus was built disperse.

> The four lower groups of solar Pitris .. [Angels] .. return to the heart of the subjective sun.. the three higher groups are carried.. straight to the central spiritual sun [1]

> The lesser units .. return to the eternal reservoir. They form substance of a very high order and will produce the forms of those existences who, in another cycle, will seek vehicles. [2]

> The Thinker or spiritual entity stands free of the three worlds and functions consciously on the buddhic plane. [3]

5. Man's Triple Connection with his Source - Sutratma, Antahkarana and Creative Threads.

To become consciously aware at the spiritual level, man must build his bridge in consciousness. This bridge has three threads.

Life Thread	[Sutratma and Silver Cord]. It comes directly from the monad and is anchored in the heart. It is the seat of life. When the antahkarana (from monad to brain) is completed it blends all types of spirit-matter consciousness into one living whole.
Consciousness Thread	[Antahkarana]. It comes directly from the soul and anchors in the head in the pineal gland. This is the seat of consciousness.
Creative Thread	It is initiated and constructed by man himself because of mental and spiritual creative work over centuries. A synthesis of the Life and Consciousness Threads, in advanced man it anchors in the throat chakra. [4]

The consciousness thread links the soul to the personality, but in average man is not vitalised so there is very little conscious awareness of the soul. As the personality aligns with the soul a magnetic field between them is established, the thread vitalises and forms the first part of the antahkarana.

Over time the three threads steadily fuse and blend. Then, there comes a point when the aspirant is ready to start building the antahkarana proper, to link his mind via the Spiritual Triad to the monad. Technically, this second stage of the link spans the upper Mental Plane, from the mental unit on the 4th subplane to the manasic permanent atom on 1st Mental Subplane. It bypasses the soul. But the entire bridge extends even past this point, to the monad. The antahkarana is built through creative meditation work.

- Ida, Pingala, Sushumna

In the spinal column are three etheric channels or paths, which houses these three threads - the antahkarana proper, the sutratma and the creative thread. These three paths are also known as the *Ida, Pingala* and *Sushumna*.

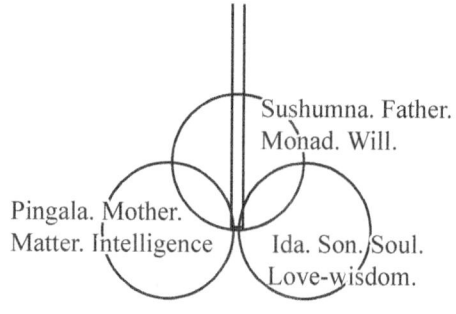

The negative and positive forces of the body, express themselves via the Ida and Pingala nerve routes. When these have been equilibrised, when the antahkarana is built and the monad and personality are related, the sushumna path is safe to use. Then, spiritual man arouses kundalini fire via sushumna and it passes through the centres up the spine, without hindrance. Consequently, the truly spiritual man appears on earth. True saints and yogis are examples.

---

1 Bailey, Alice A. *A Treatise on Cosmic Fire*, 878
2 Ibid, 830-1
3 Ibid, 764
4 Gathered from Bailey, Alice A. *Esoteric Healing*, 153

Alice A. Bailey, *Esoteric Healing*, 184

2. Mans Lower Nature - Mind, Emotions and Physical

1. The Mind - the 6th Sense

The average human mind is like a computer, which tells its programmer what to think and do. The spiritual goal is to control the mind and put the soul in charge.

a. Man's mind distinguishes him from the animals. It is the individualising principle that enables him to know that he exists, feels and knows.

b. The mind creates thoughtforms, concentrates, analyses, associates, sorts, compares, contrasts, deduces, correlates and memorises. It is not well organised in most people who are controlled by the emotions. For younger souls, it is anchored in the sacral centre; in the more advanced the throat.

> The sacral centre   the mental elemental life   Transferred later to the throat centre. [1]

c. Lower mind's job is to build thoughtforms. When a person has an idea, it is the mind's job to form the image of this idea from mental essence. Everyone makes thoughtforms, but the weak-minded, unthinking person makes them unconsciously and they are vague and ill formed. They dissipate quickly. The initiate produces well thought-out thoughtforms, sharply defined and longer lasting. These have a powerful effect on others.

d. Lower mind holds a record of the past; its contents are a combination of the unconscious and conscious aspects of our mind. Every action leaves its impression. Nothing is lost. The records of all our experiences are stored in the subconscious mind. This colours our whole life experience. We are the result of all that we have ever thought, felt and done. When we look at life through the lower concrete mind, we look through a window coloured by all past experiences. When a new image comes into the mind, the existing vibrations modify it. The new thought in turn, modifies the existing mind contents. This is why the mind is called the "slayer of the real". It is impossible to see life clearly, to see reality as it is, through an unpurified mind. Perception at this level is inaccurate. As a result, so-called free-will is not free at all. Tied to lower mind, it behaves in accordance with all existing desires, which are the result of the past. We may aspire to change, to live by higher ideals, but good intentions will be defeated if the mind is not purified.

e. Kama-manas mind: in the average person, the mind seems to be fused with the astral, desire (kama) body. As a result, its natural inclination is to be downward looking into the lower three worlds. This is why there is an instantaneous emotional reaction in such people when they see or hear something they do not like, or when they come across thoughts that are contrary to their own. This mind is not free to act on its own. It is bound to the astral nature. It is its slave.

f. Lower mind is pivotal because it unites either with the soul or with the ego. Lord Gautama Buddha said that the mind could make a man a Buddha or a beast.

g. The mind's ultimate function is to be the instrument of the soul. The immediate spiritual goal is to bring about an alignment between the lower mind and the soul, to detach the mind from its downward gazing tendency and fuse it with the soul. When this occurs, mind's natural inclination is to "look upwards" towards the divine. This is what we want.

- The Brain, the Switchboard of the Mind

The brain is a wonderful and most delicate instrument that receives and transmits information from the thinker that is controlling it, from the five senses of hearing, touch, sight, taste and smell; and from the world.

> [The] brain, that great receiving plate upon the physical plane. [2]

The way the brain relays information from the mind is coloured by the ray that conditions the physical body. A 7th ray brain is more orderly in transmission than the 3rd ray brain. The 3rd ray brain transmits information faster than the 7th ray brain.

For a long time, the personality controls the mind and brain. Instructions emanating from lower mind, coloured by astral desire, play through the brain and drive the physical body out into the world to satisfy the demands of its master - the lower ego.

---

1 Bailey, Alice A. Esoteric Psychology II, 304
2 Bailey, Alice A. Light of the Soul, 412-413

As time passes, gradually an alignment forms from the brain, to the astral body, to the mind and higher to the soul. When this happens, the soul can finally be effective in our daily life. Now it can help the struggling man or woman who is immersed in illusion and glamour. It throws the clear light of reason down into the brain to help us see more clearly. For a long time, the distorting effects of restless mind and lower desire deflect this light. But gradually the mind stills and the brain becomes the eye of the soul in the physical world.

The goal for disciples is to exclude the astral field from this alignment. As the mind becomes synchronised with the meditative attitude of the soul, so does the brain with the mind; and gradually astral disturbance fades. Now impulses from the seventh sense, "the intuition" [1] are received and transmitted by the brain.

The next step is to extend this alignment (antahkarana) from the soul to the Spiritual Triad, to the monad. When complete, this links the monad directly to the brain on the Physical Plane. This final link is the sutratma, the Silver Cord, which absorbs all levels of consciousness into one whole.

> In the centre of the brain, seated in the pineal gland .. is the home of the soul, an outpost of the life of God, a spark of pure spiritual fire. This is the lowest point which pure spiritual life, direct from the monad, our Father in Heaven, contacts or reaches. It is the termination of the sutratma, or thread which links and connects the various sheaths and passes from the monad on its own high plane, via the soul body on the higher levels of the mental plane down into the physical vehicle. [2]

2. The Emotional Body

The emotional body (also called the astral body and desire body) is the feeling body that gives expression to emotions ranging from love and compassion to fear and hate. In advanced man it anchors in the heart centre, giving expression to higher feelings of spiritual love that emanate from the buddhic nature (spiritual soul) on the Buddhic Plane.

In the average person, the emotional field anchors in the solar plexus centre and works through this centre and the desirous sacral centre. At this level, it controls the physical body, driving it to satisfy its desire. It forms attachments, aspires, attracts, repulses and fears. The soul uses this field to make connections with others emotionally. But when the astral nature controls consciousness (as it does in most people), life is filled with turmoil and fear.

The emotional body is simply a great reflector. Unpurified, it takes colour and movement from its surroundings and is affected by every passing desire, sound and motion. The astral nature is the most difficult vehicle to control and for many lives it keeps us trapped in the material world through fear, pain and desire. In most people the emotional body:

a. Forms the basis of how we view life, other people and ourselves.
b. It influences the important decisions, which are based on how we feel.
c. It has the greatest impact upon the physical body and results in either good health if emotional release is primarily positive or impaired health if it is primarily negative.

- Feelings, Emotion and Desire

The mind and astral bodies work together to produce feelings, emotion and desire. As we move through our daily life our astral sense is constantly "feeling" and testing contacts that we make. Feelings are generated all the time, but these may not necessarily evolve into an emotion. It is only when the mind engages, that an emotion is generated.

> The relation between thought and feeling is called by us emotion. [3]

An emotion arises if the mind investigates to discover whether an experience that generated a feeling is "good" or "bad". If the mind determines the experience is good, a positive emotion arises from the astral field. If the mind judges the experience to be bad, a negative emotion rises. Then, emotion evokes desire.

Desire is "a generic term covering the outgoing tendency of spirit towards form life". Desire is the sensuous grasping after that which gives pleasure in the outer life. In the Raja Yoga sutras, Patanjali links desire with attachment.

> 2:7 Desire is attachment to objects of pleasure. [4]

These objects range from the coarsest, to intellectual pursuits and to the mystic seeking union with a god or Master outside of himself. In the normal course of evolution, objects of desire change until ultimately the only desire is to unite with the holiness, sacredness and bliss of God.

---

1 Bailey, Alice A. Esoteric Psychology I, 132
2 Bailey, Alice A. Light of the Soul, 318
3 Bailey, Alice A. Discipleship in the New Age II, 623
4 Bailey, Alice A. Light of the Soul, 135

[Obstacle VI. Lack of dispassion] "addiction to objects." This is the desire for material and sensuous things. It is love of sense perceptions and attraction for all that brings a man back again and again into the condition of physical plane existence. [1]

A vital and important spiritual goal is to purify and control the astral body and train it so it will not respond or react automatically to external events. It should be serene, quiet, clear and mirror-like. This will enable it to reflect soul love and wisdom. A person with a serene astral nature works from the heart chakra and not from the solar plexus. But achieving this state is very difficult. Suppression of emotion causes cancer. A balanced emotional nature is the result of character development and meditation upon God, the soul, the good and beautiful.

3. The Dense Physical Body, the Physical-Etheric Body and the Seven Major Chakras

The Physical Plane has two levels, etheric and dense. The etheric body is built from four subplanes of etheric substance; the dense body from matter of the three lower gaseous, liquid and dense subplanes. The dense physical body is robot-like. On whatever plane consciousness is focused - physical, emotional, mental or spiritual; the forces of that level galvanise the dense body into action.

The physical body gives the soul access to the physical world and this is vital because evolution and the ascension of consciousness can only occur on the physical plane. Therefore, it is wise to look after the physical body and take steps to keep it healthy and strong. This is especially so as we advance spiritually. Then, the body must keep up with the normal demands of outer life as well as cope with the higher forces pouring through it as service obligations are fulfilled. The Bible says

> Know ye not that ye are the temple of God and that the Spirit of God dwelleth in you? [2]

It is a fact that disciples push their bodies to the limit to help, serve and save. A strong and healthy body maximises service potential and helps us move faster to that far, distant shore of spiritual liberation than might otherwise be the case. The state of the physical body will either hinder or help our progress.

> One of the problems which all sincere disciples must solve is to learn to live as if the physical body did not exist. By that I mean that its limitations and the hindrances which it imposes upon the expression of the free, spiritual consciousness are negated by an inner attitude of mind. [3]

- The Etheric Web

Pervading the manifested universe is an all-encompassing or universal etheric web composed of pranic energy - the living essence of the universe. All individual etheric webs are part of this "mother" web.

> The field of space is etheric in nature and its vital body is composed of the totality of etheric bodies of all constellations, solar systems and planets which are found therein. Throughout this cosmic golden web there is a constant circulation of energies and forces. [4]

Underlying the human body is man's individual etheric web. Built from substance from the physical etheric plane, it is composed of threads of force (nadis or nerves) [5] which form the channels along which prana flows. The sumtotal of prana in the body constitutes the etheric web.

The etheric web underlies and interpenetrates the entire dense physical body. Its physical plane equivalent and medium of distribution in the body is the nervous system.

The forces flowing through this web come from various sources, drawn in by the owner's thought and emotional life. They vitalise the physical body, providing brain function, movement, action, vitalisation and anchorage.

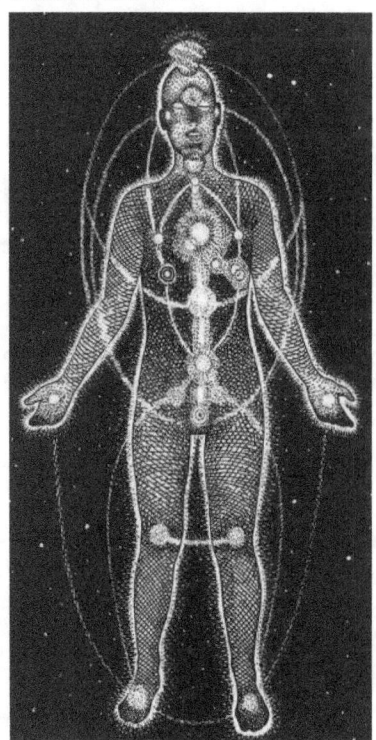

Sketch from Malvin Artley's book *Bodies of Fire*.

---
1 Bailey, Alice A. Light of the Soul, 67
2 Bible, Corinthians, 3:16
3 Bailey, Alice A. Discipleship in the New Age I, 433
4 Bailey, Alice A. Esoteric Astrology, 11
5 Bailey, Alice A. Light of the Soul, 330

- The Chakras or Force Centres

Within the etheric web are many force centres (chakras), formed where the energy lines cross. Seven of these centres are major because they are concerned with the evolution of consciousness - the soul connects with man through these seven centres. They are vitalised and controlled by thoughts and feelings and are safely developed through right thought. Forced development of the centres through intense meditation or other practises is dangerous because etheric-energy is a form of fire. Excessive etheric-fire will disrupt and inflame the unprepared nervous system.

> The centres in the human being deal fundamentally with the FIRE aspect in man, or with his divine spirit. They are definitely connected with the monad, with the will aspect, with immortality, with existence, with the will to live and with the inherent powers of Spirit. [1]

Another point to note is that, many believe the centres to emerge at the front of the body. But the esotericist considers them to lie at the back, outside the physical spine. Here is a quote from Bailey on this subject.

> Let him "learn to work and think with the spine and head and not with the forefront of the body".. This carries the energy downwards by the involutionary route and not upwards by the evolutionary route of the spinal column. [2]

The chakras in the physical-etheric body are mirrored in the astral and mental fields. This is shown on the "Unfoldment of the Petals of the Egoic Lotus" diagram in the previous section.

> These centres are .. [not] .. physical things. They are whirlpools of force that swirl etheric, astral and mental matter into activity of some kind. Because the action is rotary, the result produced in matter is a circular effect that can be seen by the clairvoyant as fiery wheels. [3]

Ignorant, average or unevolved man focuses in the lower chakras, in the region of the sex organs and stomach. Incoming force stimulates these body parts and appetites. As consciousness evolves, focus moves up to the centres above the diaphragm, galvanising man into activity in his mind and soul.

- The Three Lower Major Centres

Base Chakra, animal man consciousness. This centre is related to the physical plane and vitalises the physical body. Individuals with very powerful and selfish lower wills may work through this centre. It awakens fully at the 3rd initiation.

Sacral Chakra, animal man ruled by sex. Those who are still controlled by the sexual nature, work primarily through this centre. At the 1st Initiation, sacral energy begins to be raised to the throat centre.

Solar Plexus Chakra, Atlantean consciousness. Those focused in this centre are "Atlantean" in consciousness. This is because this centre and the emotional life ruled that past race. Related to the Astral Plane, it is the channel for feelings and desires from the crude to subtlest. In average man it works closely with the sacral and base centres so that desire and the lower appetites dominate the life.

- The Four Higher Major Centres

Throat Chakra, Aryan consciousness. Advanced intelligent "Aryan" people who are not yet creative in a spiritual sense focus in this centre, in the mind. It provides the entry point for energy from the Mental Plane. When this centre comes into activity, the first faint orientation of man towards his spiritual nature occurs.

Heart Chakra, aspirants and disciples: it becomes more dominant after the 1st Initiation, which demonstrates as control over the physical nature. When awake it relates man to the Buddhic Plane and the second divine aspect Love-Wisdom. The heart centre is the centre of spiritual love, just as the solar plexus is the seat of personal human love. As we evolve and the heart centre begins to awaken under soul impulse, it draws up the energies of the solar plexus so that desire transmutes into spiritual aspiration. It opens fully at the 4th initiation.

Brow or Ajna Chakra, advanced intelligent men and women, aspirants and disciples focus here. It comes alive prior to the Path and is awakening rapidly in many. The ajna is the seat of personality power and when governed by the materialistic and selfish dominant personality its energies flow down into the solar plexus and sacral centres to feed the lower desires. When it is being influenced by the soul from the crown chakra, aspirants and disciples are being inspired by the soul. It opens fully by the time the third initiation is taken. [4]

---

1 Bailey, Alice A. A Treatise on Cosmic Fire, 165
2 Bailey, Alice A. Esoteric Psychology II, 589
3 Bailey, Alice A. A Treatise on Cosmic Fire, 167
4 Bailey, Alice A. Esoteric Healing, 147

Crown Chakra, Initiates and Masters. This centre is dominant after the 3rd Initiation. It relates man to the Atmic Plane and the 1st aspect of will-power. It provides the soul with its point of entry and exit in the body.

At the 3rd initiation the soul takes full control of the lower nature. It achieves this by raising kundalini fire, the fire of matter residing in the base chakra. As kundalini weaves its way up the spine, etheric substance separating the various centres burns away and the physical body is infused with spiritual power. This process culminates at the 3rd initiation. [1]

At the 4th initiation and via the crown centre, the monad synthesises the centres and transfers all the body and psychic forces up to the head centre, taking full control of the lower nature.

> At the fourth initiation, where atma or pure spirit is in control, where the Spiritual Triad is expressing the nature of the monad. [2]

- The Glands of the Endocrine System

Systematically, the unfoldment of the nervous system parallels that of the etheric web and the endocrine glandular system faithfully mirrors the centres of force, with their interconnecting lines of energy.

The endocrine system is the physical externalisation of the seven major chakras. Conditioned by them, they in turn condition man by secreting directing chemicals or hormones into the blood stream. The relation of chakra to gland is given in the chart below. Two of the most important are the pituitary and the pineal glands. The pituitary is related to the life of the personality, while the pineal is related to the soul.

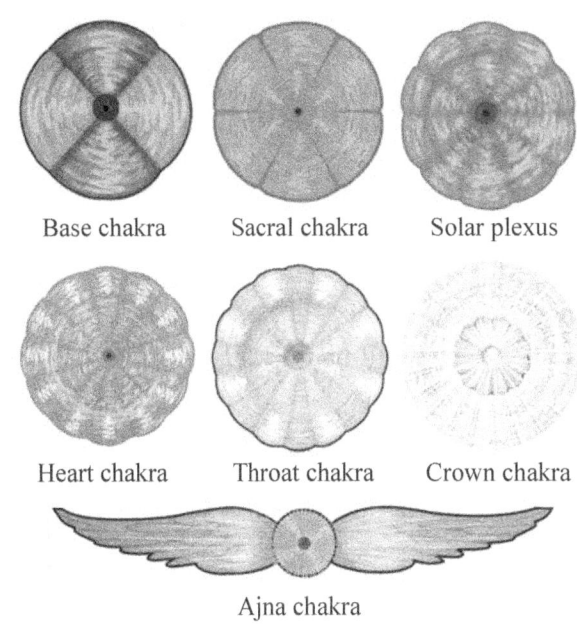

Base chakra Sacral chakra Solar plexus

Heart chakra Throat chakra Crown chakra

Ajna chakra

> The Thread of Life, the Sutratma that links all the sheaths of man with his Heavenly Source, terminates in the Pineal Gland. This is the lowest point to which pure spiritual life and fire descends. The Pineal Gland is the seat of the soul. [3]

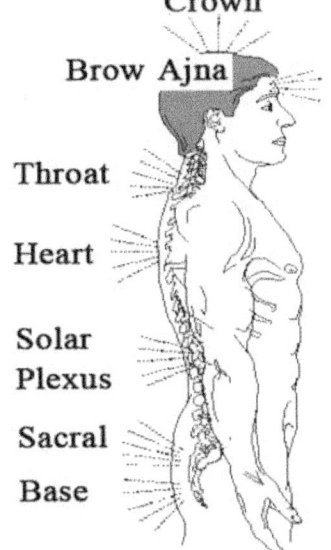

Chakras		Glands	Petals	Planets		Rays
				Initiates Disciples	Ordinary Man	
1	Head	Pineal	960	Vulcan	Pluto	1
2	Ajna	Pituitary	96	Venus	Venus	5
3	Throat	Thyroid	16	Saturn	Earth	3
4	Heart	Thymus	12	Jupiter	Sun	2
5	Solar Plexus	Pancreas	10	Neptune	Mars	6
6	Sacral	Gonads	6	Uranus	Uranus	7
7	Base	Adrenals	4	Pluto	Pluto	1

This chart shows the relationship between chakras, planets and rays. Note that different planets rule and therefore convey different ray energies, at the levels of average man and that of discipleship and initiates.

This completes this section on the Constitution of Man. In each new incarnation the monad - through the soul, appropriates a form, develops the lower bodies and the mechanism of the etheric system. Once this is in place, the soul is ready to continue its journey towards enlightenment.

---

1 Gathered from Bailey, Alice A. Esoteric Psychology II, 62-67
2 Bailey, Alice A. Rays and the Initiations, 225
3 Gathered from Bailey, Alice A. Light of the Soul, 318-319

2. LEVELS OF CONSCIOUSNESS

The evolution of consciousness from ignorance to wisdom or enlightenment is the spiritual goal for man. This section covers the seven expansions of consciousness that we pass through as we journey from the Physical to the Atmic and then to the Monadic Planes. The Solar Angels guide us through this process. They intervene three times, make an impact on man's mind on three different occasions. The results are profound.

1. Solar Angel Impact 1: the "Touch of Appropriation"

The Solar Angels came to earth during the 3rd Root-Race to give animal-man individual souls, thus permitting them to step fully into the Human Kingdom. The first impact of the soul, at that stage of human evolution, is called "individualisation". At that time, the form became aware of for the first time, the touch of the soul. This act is called the "Touch of Appropriation" - the soul appropriates its vehicle.

> At the time of the individualisation of animal-man when the mind principle was implanted. This was the birth hour of the human soul. [1]

This impact awakened animal man (conscious on the physical and astral planes), to consciousness on the Mental [2]. Individualisation, or opening the door to animal souls so that they could step into the Human Kingdom has occurred several times - on the Moon Chain, in the Lemurian 3rd Root Race and in the 4th Atlantean Race. [3] The door between the Human and Animal Kingdoms closed at that point. [4] Blavatsky refers to the door opening again in the 5th Round for a special group of animal-men [5], but that point is obscure.

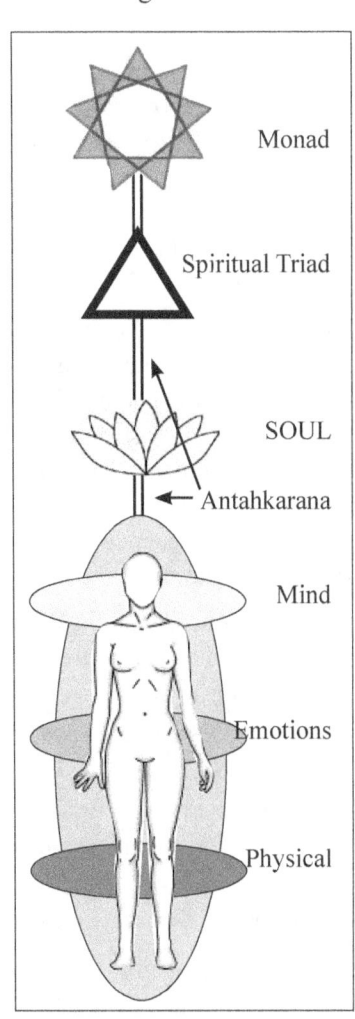

The accompanying drawing links the various levels that consciousness evolves through. It is suggestive only.

1. Lemurian Consciousness - unintelligent man

The lowest level of consciousness is rapidly diminishing and exists in tribal and rural peasants who have not received a modern education and who identify only with the physical appetites of the sacral chakra. As aeons pass, slowly desire for a larger range of satisfactions arises and identification shifts from the physical to the astral, into the world of desire. Atlantean consciousness dawns.

2. Atlantean Consciousness - emotional man

At first desire focuses on basic appetites, the urge to self-preservation and economic satisfaction. Then focus shifts to the solar-plexus centre and the subtler pleasures begin to appeal such as the desire for beauty. Consciousness becomes more astral-mental, or kama-manasic and the trend of life and character improves. The urge for satisfaction is less animal and more emotional. Moods and feelings are recognised and desire for peace and happiness. This is the level on which the masses of humanity are located. They are Atlantean in consciousness.

---

1 Bailey, Alice A. Externalisation of the Hierarchy, 438
2 Gathered from Bailey, Alice A. A Treatise on Cosmic Fire, 348
3 Gathered from Bailey, Alice A. Esoteric Psychology II, 211
4 Gathered from Bailey, Alice A. A Treatise on Cosmic Fire, 459
5 Blavatsky, Helena; The Secret Doctrine I, 184

3. Aryan Consciousness: Intelligent Man - "Personalities"

Advanced people of the world, particularly in the West, are developing the Aryan consciousness. This has nothing to do with a physical race or Nazis but concerns the development of the mind. When the mental body asserts itself and integrates with the emotions and physical body the integrated personality emerges.

> Aryan consciousness .. demonstrates in a two-fold manner as mental power and personality force. [1]

"Personalities" are coordinated and integrated human beings who are emotionally controlled and mentally developed. They are wilful men and women of destiny who try to remake other people to fit into their world. They fall into two groups:

a. Those with no soul contact are urged forward to their destiny by a sense of power, self-love, exalted ambition and a superiority complex. They are determined to reach the top of their domain.

> A personality is a separated .. [and] .. separative human being. [2]

b. Those with a small measure of soul contact, whose methods and motives are a mixture of selfishness and of spiritual vision.

The Leo Lion, arrogant and proud is a symbol of the unregenerated personality. When the ego breaks or capitulates under the weight of the Wheel of Karma, the soul prepares to make another intervention.

2. Solar Angel Impact 2: The "Touch of Acquiescence"

4. Aspirants

Aspirants are becoming aware of the soul and their higher spiritual destiny. Their task is to stabilise their emotions, adapt to fit into their chosen group and learn to love humanity. They are still essentially self-centred.

> Aspirants are preoccupied with their own little affairs and with their own small efforts .. for their own interpretations of truth and for their pet ideals of peace .. All their lives they have fought for an ideal and a dream and they love that more than they love humanity. [3]

The emergencies of life evoke the second soul impact - the "Touch of Acquiescence". This takes place on the battlefield of the Astral Plane - the plane of illusion, amidst emotional turmoil. As emotional purification proceeds, this group come under the growing influence of their souls.

3. Solar Angel impact 3. On the Path of Initiation:

5. Disciples

Disciples are occupied with the integration of personality and soul and are becoming decentralised at a personality level. They are remodelling themselves to fit into the world of souls; mental focus is in the soul and in the world of souls. When the personality is the mask of the soul, only then does it measure up to its true significance - to be the outer face of inner spiritual forces. All through this process, the Solar Angel stimulates the soul into greater activity until finally a "bridge" (the antahkarana) is built between man's lower mind and his spiritual nature. The Laws of the Soul apply during this stage, forcing man to turn towards his spiritual destiny.

The sign influence that is influential at this stage is Scorpio. The battle with the Hydra that lives in the swampy emotions symbolises the struggle that those at this level go through.

> In Scorpio .. the disciple undergoes those tests which will enable him to take the second initiation and demonstrate that the desire nature is subdued and conquered .. This is beautifully expressed for us in the legend of Hercules, the Sun-God who overcomes the nine-headed Hydra or serpent of desire by being forced to his knees and from that position of humility lifts up the serpent into the air. [4]

When this level is successfully passed, the disciple faces all life experiences intelligently and regards the environment as a place of purification and field of service. Here is a wonderful description of the making of a disciple:

---

1 Bailey, Alice A. Esoteric Psychology II, 379
2 Ibid, 264
3 Bailey, Alice A. The Externalisation of the Hierarchy, 310
4 Bailey, Alice A. Esoteric Astrology II, 143-144

For what is a disciple? He is one who seeks to learn a new rhythm, to enter a new field of experience and to follow the steps of that advanced humanity who have trodden ahead of him the path, leading from darkness to light, from the unreal to the real. He has tasted the joys of life in the world of illusion and has learnt their powerlessness to satisfy and hold him. Now he is in a state of transition between the new and the old states of being .. His spiritual perception grows slowly and surely as the brain becomes capable of illumination from the soul, via the mind. As the intuition develops, the radius of awareness grows and new fields of knowledge unfold .. Frequently then he reaches the position in which Arjuna found himself, confronted by enemies who are those of his own household, confused as to his duty and discouraged as he seeks to balance himself between the pairs of opposites .. As he perseveres and struggles, surmounts his problems and brings his desires and thoughts under control .. the Master is found; his group of disciples is contacted; the plan for the immediate share of work he must assume is realized and gradually worked out on the physical plane. [1]

Soul Laws

These laws become operative, they guide life direction and action in disciples and initiates who gradually come under the full influence of the soul.

Law 1. Law of Sacrifice: this law teaches us to give up the lesser for the greater. Under this law, the disciple recognises his area of responsibility, identifies with the whole of which he is a part and learns the true meaning of the words "Having nothing and yet possessing all things". Because nothing is asked for the separated self, all things are given.

Law 2. The Law of Magnetic Impulse: it draws souls to souls. Brother, sister souls find each other and work together, under the influence of this law.

Law 3. The Law of Service: this law brings about identification with group interest and the negation of personal material interests. It instils a heartfelt need to help others.

Law 4. Law of Repulse: under this law, the soul gradually repulses all the layers of matter that bind it. This includes for instance, old friends, acquaintances and life interests with which one no longer has resonance. Ultimately, all that is not spirit is repudiated.

Law 5. Law of Group Progress: under this law, the group is a collective and operates in unison. All individuals in the group progress forward at the same pace.

Final. The two final laws - 6 and 7, are only for the very advanced and concern group work done on the Astral Plane (Law 6, The Law of Expansive Response) and Mental Plane (Law 7, The Law of the Lower Four.) [2]

A helpful chart

Development of Consciousness in the Solar System

	Planes	*Level of Consciousness*	*Status*
1	Logoic	Logoic or God awareness	God
2	Monadic	Monadic awareness	Christ
3	Atmic	Spiritual awareness	Masters
4	Buddhic	Intuitive awareness	Arhats
5	Higher Mental	Soul consciousness - loving, wise	Aspirants, Disciples, Initiates
	Lower Mental	Aryan consciousness - mentally alive	Advanced intelligent man
6	Astral	Atlantean consciousness - emotional	Average emotional man
7	Physical	Lemurian consciousness - animal instincts	Unevolved primitive man

---

1 Bailey, Alice A. Treatise on White Magic, 58-60
2 Bailey, Alice A. Esoteric Psychology II, 85-200

6. Initiates and 7. Masters

The final impact from the soul is the "Touch of Enlightenment", which occurs at the enlightenment initiation (3rd). Those at this level - initiates, work with the Divine Plan for the upliftment of humanity. Destruction of the egoic lotus occurs at the 4th initiation when human experience has been mastered. Then spiritual fire has a direct connection via the antahkarana, to the mind. Man stands free from the hold of the three lower worlds and functions consciously on the Buddhic Plane [1] in the intuitional nature.

After the 3rd initiation, higher initiates begin to align with spirit and consciousness shifts gradually out of the soul into that of the monad. 5th degree Masters or perfected Elder Brethren are adapting the forces of nature, the energies of the rays and the potencies of the zodiacal signs, to world need.

This ends this section on Levels of Consciousness. The journey of the soul is literally a series of ascending expansions of consciousness or initiations.

---

[1] Gathered from Bailey, Alice A. A Treatise on Cosmic Fire, 713, 830, 878

3. THE INITIATIONS

This section covers initiation - milestones that mark specific expansions of consciousness in the life and journey of the soul. Each initiation enables us to function consciously on a higher level than before and to express a greater proportion of wisdom.

Definitions of initiation.

> Initiation is but another name for synthesis and fusion. [1]

> What, therefore, is Initiation?.. It is first of all the entering into a new and wider dimensional world by the expansion of a man's consciousness so that he can include and encompass that which he now excludes and from which he normally separates himself in his thinking and acts. It is, secondly, the entering into man of those energies which are distinctive of the soul and of the soul alone—the forces of intelligent love and of spiritual will. [2]

> The objective of all training given on the Path of Discipleship and up to the third initiation is to induce that clear thinking which will render the disciple free from illusion and give to him that emotional stability and poise which gives no room for the entrance of any of the world glamour. [3]

Each initiation is related to a plane in nature, as outlined in the following chart.

Nine Initiations in our solar system - Rays and Initiations, 340

	Initiation Name	Plane	Chakra affected	Candidates taking the initiation	Ray
1	Birth	Physical	Sacral	Aspirants	7
2	Baptism	Astral	Solar plexus	Disciples	6
3	Transfiguration	Mental	Ajna	Initiates	5
4	Renunciation	Buddhic	Heart	Arhats	4
5	Revelation	Atmic	Base		1
6	Decision	Monadic	Throat		3
7	Resurrection	Logoic	Head		2
8	Transition	Planetary	Hierarchy		4 minor
9	Refusal	Systemic	Shamballa		3 major

The first initiation - control of the physical appetites, is taken on the dense Physical Plane. The second initiation - control of the emotional nature, is taken on the second Astral Plane, etc. Initiations 1 to 5 are the human initiations and "make a man perfect". Initiations 6 to 7 give freedom from the solar system.

The first three initiations lead to enlightenment. [4] The training for these initiations occurs in three schools or halls of learning. These halls are equivalent to kindergarten, high school and university.

Unenlightened man labours in the Hall of Ignorance, then passes into the Hall of Learning to prepare for the 1st Initiation, then into the Hall of Wisdom to prepare for the 2nd and 3rd. After the 3rd, man moves onto the Path of Solar (Sirian) Initiation.

---
1 Bailey, Alice A. Esoteric Astrology, 241
2 Bailey, Alice A. Esoteric Psychology II, 12
3 Bailey, Alice A. Glamour a World Problem, 33
4 This is not the ultimate Buddhist nirvanic enlightenment, but a stage towards it.

1. The Hall of Ignorance

Ignorant and unenlightened man labours here. "Ignorant" in this context is simply ignorance of the inner spiritual realities. There is no central control and focus is on survival and material comfort.

> In the Hall of Ignorance .. man is polarised in the personality or lower self. [1]

Astrology

Pluto and Mars rule in this hall. Mars co-rules the sacral chakra and both planets rule the solar plexus centre. They intensify desire and drive man out to satisfy his lower craving in the "World of the Flesh and the Devil". These influences do their work until the time comes when the cup of pleasure has been fully drained. Then, dissatisfaction brings the aspirant to the Hall of Learning and the Probationary Path.

2. The Hall of Learning or Knowledge - the 1st Initiation

When the mystical experience with its emphasis upon dualism evolves into a yearning for union with the Divine, the portals of initiation have been reached. As this yearning grows and the aspirant struggles to realise the desire for union as a truth and fact, he or she steps onto the Path.

> Students should therefore have in mind the following definite occult concept: The mystical Way leads to the first initiation. Having achieved its purpose, it is then renounced and the "lighted Way" of occultism is then followed, leading to the lighted areas of the higher states of consciousness. [2]

Goal. Prepare for the 1st Initiation (Little Chelaship) [3]

The goal in the Hall of Learning is to prepare for the 1st Initiation, to become a self-conscious individual free "from the control of the physical body and its appetites" [4]. This initiation is taken on the Fixed Cross with the "Sun or ascendant in Leo". [5] "At the first initiation this babe starts on the pilgrimage of the Path". [6] "He passes, at this initiation, out of the Hall of Learning into the Hall of Wisdom". [7]

Candidates for the 1st Initiation - Aspirants

This group includes advanced intelligentsia and mystics. Mystics walk the Path of Love and seek union with God through love and devotion. But there are different types of mystics. The term "mystic" as it is used in this book refers to spiritually inclined people whose state of mind is distinguished by a profound sense of duality. For them God is somewhere "out there" and they yearn to be one with that being "out there". The mystic senses the presence of Deity and from the heights of aspiration, adores him so completely that higher contact sometimes is made. Briefly. But the blissful experience cannot be repeated at will. The antahkarana that enables us to reach the higher levels of Self, has not been built.

> [The mystic] longs ceaselessly for the constant repetition of the ecstatic state to which his prayer, adoration and worship have raised him. He is usually quite unable to repeat this initiation at will. [8]

As mystics pass this stage and start to search with their minds for truth, they find their way to the Path. There are very advanced and intelligent people who walk the Path of Love and therefore technically are mystics. An example was Bede Griffiths, a Benedictine monk who lived in India. He was an intelligent investigator of God and life, an esotericist.

a. A strong personality will be evident and materialistic goals will still be strong. There will be a new sense of reaching for something higher, finer and better.
b. Aspirants will be going through crises in the personal life. There will be attempts to discipline the physical appetites through means such as vegetarianism and exercise.

---
1 Bailey, Alice A. Initiation Human and Solar, 12
2 Bailey, Alice A. The Rays and the Initiations, 666
3 Chelaship is a synonym for "discipleship".
4 Bailey, Alice A. The Rays and the Initiations, 685
5 Gathered from Bailey, Alice A. Esoteric Astrology, 143. The ascendant (ASC) in astrology forms the cusp of the first house or life area.
6 Bailey, Alice A. Initiation Human and Solar, 63
7 Ibid, 84
8 Bailey, Alice A. From Intellect to Intuition, 68

Advice that may help candidates

Encourage a desire to develop healthy physical appetites: play sport, physical fitness, pay attention to diet, fast, consider vegetarianism, pastimes and hobbies which develop and expand the mind and join personal development groups. Control of the physical appetites is a strict requirement for the 1st Initiation.

> No one is accepted (for training by the Masters) whose physical appetites are in any danger of controlling him. This applies particularly to those preparing for the first initiation. [1]

Astrology

Pluto and Vulcan rule the 1st Initiation. [2] Pluto destroys impediments and Vulcan purifies to the very depths.

Chakra Activity

Sacral energies are rising to the throat and focus is moving gradually from sex to higher creative endeavours.

Qualities demonstrated when the 1st is taken

a. There may still be little soul control. [3]
b. There is freedom from the control of the physical appetites. [4]
c. Control of the dense physical has been demonstrated. [5]
d. Sex has become a natural and correct appetite.
e. It marks the beginning of a new life, mode of living, new thought, conscious perception and a new attitude towards relationships. Although negative attitudes persist, such people truly love their fellowmen.
f. The 1st Initiation is the key to entry into the Hall of Wisdom.

3. The Hall of Wisdom - the 2nd and 3rd Initiations

> Having groped his way through the Hall of Ignorance during many ages and having gone to school in the Hall of Learning, he is now entering into the university, or the Hall of Wisdom. When he has passed through that school he will graduate with his degree as a Master of Compassion. [6]

Goal. Take the 2nd Initiation (Chela in the Light)

The 2nd Initiation brings personal crises that make it clear that the emotional life needs to be brought under control. The task is to demonstrate emotional self-control.

Candidates for the 2nd Initiation - Disciples

a. Demonstrate the ability to think in wider terms and to work in groups.
b. Demonstrate mental flexibility and a lack of fanaticism to any truth or spiritual leader. [7]
c. Emotional crises motivate the aspirant to seek relief and seek inner peace.
d. When oriented to the soul, with the entire emotional nature responsive to energies coming from "the Heart of the Sun," the disciple is ready for the second initiation. [8]

Advice to help candidates

Explain the goal of the initiation. Encourage intellectual development and use of the mental will to control the emotions. Encourage emotional disciplines, development of harmlessness in thought and speech, study of the Wisdom Teachings, the practise of meditation, joining a group espousing high ideals, etc.

Astrology

Neptune, Venus and Jupiter rule the 2nd Initiation. Jupiter develops the heart chakra and inclusive attitudes. Venus governs the brow centre and develops the ability to love intelligently. Neptune governs the solar plexus centre and transmutes desire into aspiration. Scorpio is related to these tests and trials.

---

1 Bailey, Alice A. The Rays and the Initiations, 126
2 Gathered from AAB. Esoteric Astrology, 70
3 Gathered from AAB. Esoteric Psychology II, 14
4 Gathered from AAB. The Rays and the Initiations, 685
5 Bailey, Alice A. Initiation Human and Solar, 85
6 Ibid, 10
7 Gathered from AAB. The Rays and the Initiations, 127
8 Gathered from AAB. Esoteric Astrology, 297-8

> In Scorpio .. the disciple undergoes those tests which will enable him to take the second initiation and demonstrate that the desire nature is subdued and conquered and that the lower nature is (being) lifted up in the air (so that the personality is fit) for the world service demanded in Aquarius. [1]

Chakra Activity

Energies are transferring from the solar plexus to the heart. Sacral energy continues to move to the throat centre, via the heart, giving an aspiration to serve. Energies are also starting to flow via the brow centre and the battle is on between the ego and the soul to see who "sits in the driver's seat". This "seat" is the brow or ajna centre.

Qualities Demonstrated when the 2nd Initiation is Taken

a. Desire is under soul control and is being transmuted into love. [2]
b. Emotions are still powerful but there is a new and intelligent response to emotional situations.
c. There is a determination to think in wider and more inclusive terms.
d. Humility is demonstrated and a voiced realisation of the divinity in all men. [3]
e. Aspiration and longing to serve is so strong, rapid development occurs.
f. Those people seeking mental polarisation, who aspire to think and to know and who are demonstrating control of the physical appetites "have taken the second, or are on the verge of so doing." [4]
g. A growing sense of relationships, of a basic unity with all that breathes, and a recognition of the One Life which will lead eventually to that state of expressed brotherhood which it is the goal of the Aquarian Age. [5]
h. The constant reorientation of the soul towards the monad. [6]

Goal: Take the 3rd Initiation (Chela on the Thread, Accepted Discipleship.)

For the 3rd initiation, focus shifts to the control of the mind and the entire personality. This period between the second and the third is called the "greater burning ground", the hardest phase for the sensitive, feeling aspirant who experiences intense suffering as all obstacles to pure spirituality are burnt out of his system. [7] Once the desire nature is under control the pilgrim travels the Path with increased speed and sometimes the 3rd and 4th are taken.

> Once the second initiation is taken the progress will be rapid, the third and fourth following probably in the same life, or the succeeding. [8]

Candidates for the 3rd Initiation - Initiates

a. They approach life from a level tableland of experience and not from the heights of aspiration or fanatical sacrifice. They have an adjusted sense of proportion and are forward-looking towards the soul and not backward looking towards the form nature.

> Temperance in all things, the wise use of all sustaining forms and self-forgetfulness are the hallmark of the disciple [9]

b. The person is seeking to control the mind and manipulate thought matter to overcome illusion. [10]
c. He or she is trying to conform to a higher spiritual Law.
d. They are fully self-conscious .. a *developed* mystic, capable of pure vision, motivated by spiritual intent.. a trained occultist, mentally polarised and profoundly aware of the realities, forces and energies of existence and therefore free from the ordinary glamours and illusions which colour the reactions and life of the average man. [11]

---

1 Bailey, Alice A. Esoteric Astrology, 143
2 Gathered from Bailey, Alice A. Esoteric Healing, 156
3 Bailey, Alice A. The Rays and the Initiations, 679
4 Ibid, 667
5 Gathered from Bailey, Alice A. The Destiny of the Nations, 138
6 Ibid, 120
7 Bailey, Alice A. The Rays and the Initiations, 683-4
8 Bailey, Alice A. Initiation Human and Solar, 84-5
9 Bailey, Alice A. The Rays and the Initiations, 127
10 Gathered from Ibid, 600
11 Gathered from Bailey, Alice A. Esoteric Astrology, 307

Qualities when the 3rd is taken
   a. Personality-soul fusion is complete and the Monadic Ray controls the personality. [1]
   b. There is complete freedom from the claims and demands of the personality. [2]
   c. Consciousness is planetary [3] (or global).
   d. The whole life is an example of selflessness and concern for the rights and well-being of all.
   e. They demonstrate detachment - that outstanding characteristic of the man who has been born again, purified and transfigured. [4]
   f. They are consciously one with the "Father in Heaven" and therefore with all monads. [5]

The Influence of Sirius

Sirius and our solar system are related [6] and forces from that planet govern the Spiritual Hierarchy [7]. Sirius is a major centre of higher consciousness for man and controls the spiritual work taking place on earth. The force emanating from Sirius makes man sensitive to his higher spiritual destiny and draws him towards it.

The ashrams of the Hierarchy receive energy from Sirius. Initiates are being influenced by Sirius after the 2nd Initiation but are not consciously aware of this until after the 3rd. The development of Buddhi, of pure love (love-wisdom) is a major goal. In Masonic terms the Sirian Lodge is:

> The true "Blue Lodge," and to become a candidate in that Lodge, the initiate of the third degree has to become a lowly aspirant. [8]

> The third degree (the first degree of the Lodge on Sirius) [9]

Astrology

Mars and the Moon (veiling a sacred planet) rule the 3rd Initiation. The Moon unveils Uranus when the form nature has been purified; awakening spiritual will. Saturn and Mercury are still influential. From this point on, the influence of Sirius is a key factor in the initiation process and raises consciousness to that of initiate awareness.

Defeat of the personality at the 3rd - the Angel versus the Dweller

Mars brings out the Dweller on the Threshold, the powerful integrated personality for its final battle with the soul and creates conflict to bring this about. The Dweller is a vitalised thoughtform, the sumtotal of lifetimes of illusion, glamour and maya. Always present, it takes cogent form when a re-orientation of the life has taken place consciously and under soul impression and the person is ruled from the Mental Plane.

Here is the scene. On one side stands the Angel of the Presence, revealed by the intuition, on the other side stands the Dweller. The disciple stands in the centre. In the centre of the "burning ground" these two foes meet. The burning ground is that process that disciples go through as they burn up or purify all negativity in the nature. It is a battle to the death that continues until the Dweller is absorbed by the Angel. When that occurs, the personality nature is an obedient servant used by the soul, with whom the initiate now fully identifies. Focus is on world service work.

> Then the lesser light (a true light in its own right) of the personality is absorbed into the greater light of the Angel or soul. The Angel, therefore, "occultly obliterates" the Dweller who becomes lost to sight in the radiant aura of the Angel. [10]

The student's vital role in this battle is to be steadfast, to hold the mind high and steady in the light of wisdom. This allows the Angel to do its work and neutralises the most powerful weapon of the Dweller - restless mind fluctuations and obscuration's.

Chakra Activity

Energy transfers from the base to the crown centre and the two head centres become increasingly active.

---

1 Gathered from Bailey, Alice A. A Treatise on Cosmic Fire, 176
2 Bailey, Alice A. The Rays and the Initiations, 44
3 Gathered from Bailey, Alice A. Esoteric Astrology, 359
4 Bailey, Alice A. From Bethlehem to Calvary, 166
5 Gathered from Bailey, Alice A. Initiation Human and Solar, 19
6 Gathered from Bailey, Alice A. Esoteric Astrology, 641
7 Ibid, 198
8 Bailey, Alice A. The Rays and Initiations, 416
9 Bailey, Alice A. Discipleship in the New Age II, 159
10 Bailey, Alice A. Glamour a World Problem, 269

4. The Path of Solar Initiation - the Higher Initiations

Goal: the 4th Initiation

Initiates at this level are called arhats. They have mastered the Physical, Emotional, Mental and Buddhic Planes, detached from all self-interest and have renounced the personal life. In consciousness they are "one .. with the Logos". [1]

This is a momentous initiation and the point at which the long association with the Solar Angel ends. The egoic lotus shatters because it is no longer required. Man's consciousness links directly with his monad. He is no longer strictly human but is more spiritual. The Solar Angel, released from its long association with its human being returns to the Sun. The Monadic Ray absorbs the soul ray and spirit works directly through the brain without the intermediary of the soul.

Mercury, Saturn and Vulcan rule this initiation.

> Vulcan is the .. planet of isolation for .. it governs the fourth initiation wherein the depths of aloneness are plumbed and the man stands completely isolated .. All desire is renounced; the will of God or the Plan is seen. [2] The initiate knows what he has to do.

Goal: 5th Initiation

Those at this level are called Masters because they have gained mastery over the forces of the five planes that man works through - the Atma, Buddhi, Mental, Astral and the Physical. In consciousness they are one "with the monad" [3]. The 5th Initiation opens the doorway to the cosmos. It "is the first cosmic initiation". [4] At this level, the Masters see for the first time the full intention of the Purpose and Plan of God (the Earth Logos).

> He sees with a new clarity some of the karmic liabilities which have led the planetary Logos to create this planet of suffering, sorrow, pain and struggle .. that on it .. a great redemptive experiment is going forward; its prime implementing factors .. [are] .. the "Sons of God".. chosen, in that far distant time when the fourth kingdom in nature came into being, to carry forward the science of redemption .. of substance, of matter and form and thus proved the possibility of that redemption through their own transfigured personalities—their reward should be their eventual manifestation as expressions of divinity. [5]

Goal: 6th - 9th Initiations

Beings at these levels are truly becoming cosmic. A Chohan of the Sixth Initiation discards all the sheaths beneath the monadic vehicle, from the atmic to the physical. Now one of seven cosmic paths is chosen.

Path I. The Path of Earth Service	Path V. The Ray Path
Path II. The Path of Magnetic Work	Path VI. The Path of the Solar Logos
Path III. The Path of the Planetary Logos	Path VII. The Path of Absolute Sonship [6]
Path IV. Path to Sirius	

The 7th brings freedom from the solar system. [7] These initiates are now able to function on the cosmic Astral Plane. The 8th brings freedom into a higher state of awareness again and the 9th brings freedom from "all enticement". [8] It is only at the ninth that full God consciousness in our system is realised.

> Only, therefore, at the ninth initiation is the human being a full and true expression of divinity .. en rapport with the consciousness of the One in Whom we live and move and have our being. [9]

This ends this section on Initiation. Step by measured step, the soul extends its consciousness up and through these various levels until he or she steps forward as a Master of the energies of Life.

---

1 Bailey, Alice A. Initiation Human and Solar, 19
2 Bailey, Alice A. Esoteric Astrology, 392
3 Bailey, Alice A. Initiation Human and Solar, 19
4 Bailey, Alice A. Esoteric Astrology, 90
5 Bailey, Alice A. Discipleship in the New Age II, 385-6
6 Bailey, Alice A. A Treatise on Cosmic Fire, 1242
7 Gathered from Bailey, Alice A. The Rays and the Initiations, 686
8 Ibid, 686
9 Ibid, 535

CHAPTER 3: ESOTERIC PSYCHOLOGY

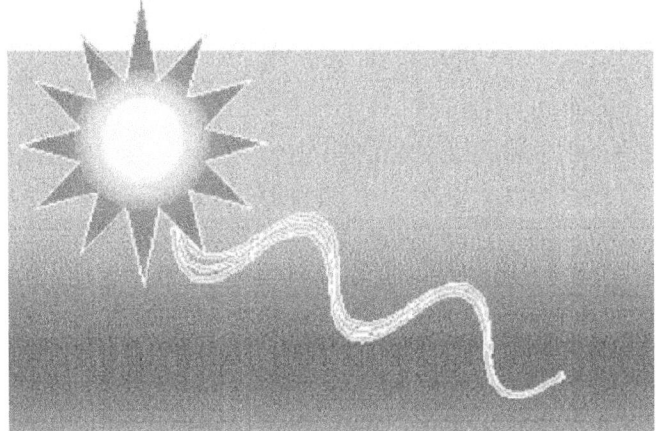

The Psychologists will .. be concerned with the revelation of the fact of the soul and with the new psychology which will be based upon the seven ray types and the new esoteric astrology. Their major task will be to relate, through approved techniques, the soul and the personality, leading to the revelation of divinity through the medium of humanity. [1]

---

[1] Bailey, Alice A. Discipleship in the New Age I, 39

1. INTRODUCTION TO ESOTERIC PSYCHOLOGY

This section examines Esoteric Psychology, the Science of the Soul. The soul is the higher spiritual aspect of a human being. Crises and stages of growth that occur as the soul seeks to fuse with and express itself through its personality nature are studied.

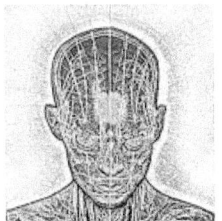

1. Overview of Mental Health

Psychology is what scientists and philosophers of various persuasions have created to try to fill the need to understand the minds and behaviour of man. The need for this arose as humans matured under the influence of the 5th Ray of Mind and became more mental. A positive result is the mass training of the mind in public schools. But as people became more mentally aware they realised they were unhappy and began to look for answers for their feelings of dissatisfaction. This gave rise to the science of psychology and its result, counselling, which has evolved rapidly since these early beginnings. In the 20th Century there were impressive breakthroughs in this new science and Freud and Jung were amongst the forerunners.

Psychological problems as commonly understood are those difficulties encountered when relating to people, the environment and world, because of rigid attitudes and negative beliefs and perceptions. Good mental health is the basis for a creative and joyful life. The essential requirement for good mental health is a flexible mind - the ability to change the mind.

A person who is mentally and spiritually healthy:
  a. Takes responsibility for his or her life and actions.
  b. Is flexible, able to change the mind, is spontaneous, laughs easily and feels free.
  c. Has integrity and honesty, speaks from the depths and not from the surface.
  d. Is content to be his or her own self.
  e. Has courage to face insecurity and go forward into the unknown.
  f. Is socially cooperative and feels integrated with the community.
  g. Has a purpose for living, a holistic outlook and affirms truth and goodness.

1. Neurosis

From late 20th Century psychology, the term *neurosis* was generally used to refer to any mental imbalance that caused distress but did not interfere with rational thought or the ability to function in daily life. Neurotic tendencies are common and manifest in various ways. Examples are depression, acute or chronic anxiety, obsessive-compulsive tendencies and phobias. Neurotic tendencies arise when there is poor ability to adapt to the environment and an inability to change life patterns that could lead to disease.

The steps involved in getting to this stage are:
  a. Desires are repressed.
  b. The ego rationalises these repressions are all right.
  c. For each repression, a negative belief forms such as "It's not OK to cry" or "I'm unlovable".

d. The person's view of self, others and of life becomes rigid, distorted and unrealistic.
e. This builds up inner conflict, tension and stress. The emotion is still trying to get out.
f. Eventually the person feels alienated.
g. This influences behaviour, which becomes rigid or odd.
h. The flow of life energy through the system begins to shut down and alienation from society occurs. The symptoms of the disorder become apparent.

Counsellors guide clients to a better understanding of the past and hold a vision before the person's eyes of how things could improve with a little work. When response is positive, rigid ideas release and mental flexibility restores. This leads to a more expanded and balanced view of the present and future and improved mental health.

2. Psychosis

These are a group of mental disorders more severe than neurosis, commonly lumped under the term insanity. A definition of "psychotic disorder" from the Dictionary of Psychology 1995 and still relevant today is:

> A general cover term for a number of severe mental disorders of organic or emotional origin .. the defining feature is gross impairment in reality testing. That is, the person makes incorrect inferences concerning external reality, makes improper evaluations of the accuracy of his or her thoughts and perceptions and continues to make these errors in the face of contrary evidence. Classic symptoms include delusions, hallucinations, severe regressive behaviours, dramatically inappropriate moods and markedly incoherent speech. The standard clinical literature lists as psychoses: bipolar disorder, brief reactive psychosis, schizophrenia, various organic mental disorders and some of the mood disorders.

It is possible for a person to appear normal, proceed to a neurotic state, then psychotic, then back again. Refer such cases to professionals trained in this area. This includes esoteric psychologists trained to recognise and work with people who are suffering delusion or other psychic disturbances caused by unwise spiritual practises.

3. Bailey said that there are three forms of incurable insanity

a. Organic, due to disease of the brain matter; tumours, abscesses or growths and head structural defects.

b. Idiocy, or a very low-grade human animal because the "true owner" of the body is absent and the soul is unaware of the form. There is also a rare form of possession where the life thread is attached to the original owner of the body, but the consciousness thread is that of another discarnate entity seeking physical plane expression. This is different to the average case of possession, where the distressed true owner seeks to regain its body. These conditions may be learning experiences for carers rather than for the insane.

> These conditions are related far more to the karma of the parents or of those who have charge of the case than to the patient himself. In many of these cases, there is no person present within the form at all, but only an animated living body, informed by the animal soul but not by a human soul.[1]

c. "Astral Maniacs" is a condition caused by an uncontrollable astral body. Mentally little that is wrong, but the mind is unable to stop the man expressing some uncontrollable desire. Here is a description.

> These "astral maniacs" are the most difficult and quite the saddest types to handle because mentally there is little that is wrong with them. The mind, however, cannot control and is definitely relegated to the background; it remains useless and inert whilst the man expresses (with violence or subtlety as the case may be) some basic desire. It may be the desire to kill, or desire to have abnormal sexual experience, or even the desire to be ever on the move and thus constantly active... there is no remedy but the protection of the man from himself and his own actions.[2]

These should be referred to professionals who deal with these sad cases.

> Later in the psychology chapter, there is a section *"Sexual Overstimulation 1: Sexual-Psychopath, Sadist, Serial Killer, Rapist, Murderer"*. It is possible that some people placed there would be better placed in this category - as astral maniacs.

---
1 Bailey, Alice, A: Esoteric Psychology II, 459
2 Ibid, 459

2. Points that distinguish Esoteric Psychology

1. Esoteric psychologists study the esoteric sciences

From an esoteric perspective the major shortcoming in modern exoteric psychology is an incomplete understanding of man's equipment, which results in blame being placed on the personality aspect. The soul is not seriously considered. But it is the integrating principle in man and the cause of the trouble because it pushes man to evolve. This is a major shortcoming. The pioneering psychologists were disciples who gave the great gift of modern psychology to man. However, unless there are important changes:

> It will fall of its own weight and produce (as it is already producing) problems, complexes and diseases of the mind which are direct results of its own methods. [1]

The modern psychologist needs to become proficient in several esoteric branches.
  a. Firstly, gain an esoteric understanding of the constitution of man and of the initiation process. Imbalances in the etheric body and force centres occur at various stages on the evolutionary path, resulting in imbalances in the psychology and physical body. This needs to be understood if correct diagnosis is to be made.
  b. Acquire knowledge of the Seven Rays so that the true nature of a man's temperament and the real subjective cause of his varied reactions and complexes are seen.
  c. Acquire an understanding of Esoteric Astrology, which gives a blueprint of the psychology of a person, the underlying energy disturbances in the nature and the purpose of the soul.

With the gains of modern exoteric psychology added to esoteric knowledge, diagnosis of mental disorders and physical disease with be more factually scientific and accurate.

2. Emphasis is laid upon the soul and relating the personality to the soul

The soul is the initiating factor of a human being's appearance on earth and is the coordinating and integrating centre. The primary goal of the esotericist is to relate the soul and personality. Djwhal Khul (the true author of the two Esoteric Psychology volumes) said:

> The contribution I seek to make to the subject, have to do with the emphasis we shall lay upon the nature of the integrating principle found within all coherent forms [2]

3. Esoteric psychologists study eastern wisdom and knowledge on the mind

The true cause of unhappiness is the basis of Gautama Buddha's teachings. When the mind is ignorant of its true nature, the false "I" arises. This "I" craves happiness and looks for it in the external world. It reaches out and grasps after things, attaches itself to people or objects it thinks will bring it happiness.

If we examine our life, we see it is a continual process of grasping after desired objects. If we get what we want, we have temporary happiness. But after a while, the value that we place on any object diminishes and we grasp after something else. If we do not get what we want, "I" is unhappy. It believes life is unfair or cruel. Then anger and bitterness rises. This is the true cause of our unhappiness and these lead to psychological problems and disease.

There comes a point in time when the long drawn out and painful detachment of man's outer gazing focus and attention from the outer world into the world of spiritual reality must begin. This means that the mind as the primary instrument of the personality needs training so that it will identify with its inner wisdom, the soul. A course in Raja Yoga or Buddhism mind training is needed.

4. Psychology problems are viewed as those of energy

Essentially, we are all energy beings working through fields of energy (mind. emotions, etheric), living in a world of swirling repulsive and attractive forces, interacting with other people's energy fields. The task is to balance and harmonise our energies, which then naturally harmonises all outer relationships.

> As long as we regard our problem as consisting of the inter-relation of many energies, their fusion and their balancing .. we shall arrive at some measure of understanding and subsequent solution. [3]

---
[1] Bailey, Alice A. Esoteric Psychology I, 5
[2] Ibid, 5
[3] Bailey, Alice A. Esoteric Psychology II, 424-5

3. The Goals of the Esoteric Psychologist

Goal 1. Relate the client's soul and personality

The counsellor should give suggestions that will lift the eyes of the client to the soul. For instance, introduce the Wisdom Teachings if it is appropriate. Hearing about the Plan for Humanity, the journey of the soul, reincarnation, karma, etc., can have a powerful impact and bring far-reaching changes. The Law of Rebirth when accepted is a major releasing agent and the recognition of further opportunity and a lengthened sense can bring a sense of peace. The teachings are practical and if adopted lead to sane, joyful and healthy living. The client can accept or reject this information.

Some people have an aversion to "New Age nonsense". In this case, modify terms. Introduce the Law of Karma under the name of "what goes around comes around". Meditation is widely accepted as a way of improving health and life quality and people who may choose not to meditate for spiritual reasons, may do so for health reasons. Many who have had difficulties with fundamentalist or rigid religions may find the words soul, spirit, God, etc, repellent. Find alternative words that describe the same truth. Most Buddhists do not accept that there is a reincarnating soul but do embrace the notion that the mind is capable of being illumined and becoming wise. Substitute the word "soul" with "mind wisdom'. Talk about the purity, beauty and power of one's inner nature.

Age matters. As a person gains life experience and goes through life challenges, especially those that coincide with Saturn transits at ages 28-30, 35, 42-45, 57-59, then there is a natural turning away from peripheral things and a search for deeper meaning. The counsellor can explore a person's values, quality of life and life fulfilment.

Goal 2: Enhance the ability to stand in spiritual being

An important goal to help restore clients to psychological health is to eliminate guilt and any sense of sin. Explain that we are here to learn and so-called "mistakes" or "failures" are a normal and natural part of the process of growing in spirit.

a. Help clients see crises as opportunities for growth and progress. They do not indicate failure.

b. Give an esoteric explanation for the cause of inner conflict and pain. Explain how identification with the lower nature, the personality, has resulted in feelings of unworthiness, powerlessness and low self-esteem. When identification is detached from the personality and re-aligned with the wisdom aspect, suffering goes. Add that the person's soul has initiated the process, that it is seeking integration. Similar crises in past lives have been met successfully because he or she is here now and this period will be survived.

c. Help the person anchor in the present and orient to the future. Recommend meditations to anchor attention in the present such as "observing the breath". Encourage troubled individuals to cultivate a wider life view, to find and join a group that shares the same ideals.

d. Emphasise the fact that the power to heal is found within. One is a soul with all the spiritual power and creativity that this implies. Invoking the "power of the soul", God or Jesus etc., really works.

e. If the mind is deeply troubled, recommend physical activities, filling the present moment with constructive creative effort and finishing one task before starting another. This helps to restore balance.

Goal 3: Help people find and serve in their chosen field

Another important aspect of this work is to help clients discover what it is they would really like to do in terms of a useful and constructive occupation or pastime and support that. Work out a plan, a series of steps that will help him or her reach that goal. For clients who are more spiritually advanced, identify vocations that are in line with their soul's purpose, which are deeply fulfilling and will satisfy a yearning in the heart to help people.

> ***This ends this Introduction to Esoteric Psychology. It is important for students of the wisdom to realise they do not have to be an expert or have a counselling degree to offer esoteric advice and assistance. Simply respond as a good friend would to someone who is troubled and who seeks help and guidance.***

2. PSYCHOLOGY DISORDERS

Evolution has brought humans to a point that innate sensitivity is universal and is growing. While this is a positive step, it has seen the spread of new nervous and mental diseases, the result of man trying to respond to changing conditions. From the esoteric perspective there are psychological problems that affect the wider community, which are dealt with in this chapter. Then there are those that are specific to mystics and disciples and that are addressed in the following chapter.

However, before we go into specifics, it is important to realise that underlying all these disorders is a common root cause - an imbalance in energy. There is an imbalance and disruption of force within a man's own fields on any level and often with the environment. The esoteric approach is to harmonise this imbalance.

> When considering the human being and his expression and existence .. we are really considering energy and the relation or non-relation of forces .. As long as we regard our problem as consisting of the inter-relation of many energies, their fusion and their balancing, plus the final synthesis of two major energies, their fusion and their balancing we shall arrive at some measure of understanding and subsequent solution. [1]

Here is a chart that covers the major disorders affecting the general population.

Three Major Groups of Psychology Problems affecting all Humanity				
1. Cleavage	2. Integration	3. Stimulation		
		Mental disorders	*Delusion*	*Unwise Guidance*
Divisions in the nature that are at war with each other.	When a cleavage heals, the over-inflated ego feels powerful, able to achieve anything.	Mind / thought, becomes rigid, due to a too intense and narrow focus on one line of thought.	Meditation illumines the mind but it causes delusion due to a lack of discrimination.	People believe voices they hear or dreams they have are real and true.

1. Cleavage
This problem arises when there is a division or split within the nature, when two aspects are antagonistic to each other. For example: the mind and emotions are antagonistic to each other, or the environment is very challenging for the person. This gives rise to a sense of duality and problems that range all the way from bipolar disorders to those of the mystic with his adoration of God set up high on a pedestal.

2. Integration
This problem, which is largely that of an over-inflated ego, arises when an inflow of potent illumined mind energy causes a person to lose all sense of balance and proportion. It is caused by the integration or healing of a cleavage within the nature. It is usually only temporary.

3. Stimulation (or more correctly, overstimulation)
This set of disorders arises as the result of an inflow of potent mental or soul energy. Then, because a person's system is unaccustomed to the higher and faster vibration and there is a lack of balance in the thought or emotional life, overstimulation occurs and problems appear.

---
1 Bailey, Alice, A; Esoteric Psychology II, 424. There are references to astrology and the Science of the Seven Rays. These chapters come later in the book.

1. PROBLEMS OF CLEAVAGE [1]

The separative spirit that is so entrenched in human nature is a consequence of the dual nature of universe, of the seeming divide between spirit and matter. But this state is temporary and the opposites over time resolve into the one essential Life or Soul of the Universe. In the meantime, these warring energies play havoc in our psychology.

The cleavage problem is essentially one of energy, of two different energy fields that repulse each other. One is antagonistic with the other and trouble arises. There are many different energy types and groups found in the world. Those that have a similar resonance like each other and those whose energies are different dislike each other. Consequently, cleavages are found everywhere - between individuals, races, religions etc. On an individual level, cleavages occur between the bodies – soul and personality, between the mind and emotions, within the emotional field itself, or between a person and the environment.

In most cases, cleavages do no real harm and cause our various likes and dislikes. But in those who are Atlantean (emotional) in consciousness, they can cause deep distress. The emotions are too powerful and the mind cannot control the emotional swings and resultant fear and anxiety. Dominated by the emotions, the mind imagines terrible things and becomes captive to these fear-images.

If fear and anxiety are not dealt with, if they persist over time, it will gradually undermine health. Energetically, a divide or cleavage forms between the person and something highly disliked about himself or a person or thing in the environment. In extreme cases, this divide may become so severe it interferes with normal life. Raja Yoga creator, Patanjali, described this condition hundreds of years ago. This interpretation is Djwhal Khul's.

> The effect of this [cleavage] may mean that he is an anti-social human being, or unpopular, full of fear of life, or expressing, in many other forms, his inability to tune in on his surroundings. Lack of understanding, of right relationship.. will be evidenced. The cause of the cleavage in this case is usually found somewhere within the astral body itself. [2]

There are three major cleavage groups

1. Cleavage within the astral body

This brings about a cleavage between a person and his environment, with a fear of life so that there is great difficulty relating with or understanding others. This results in miscommunication, isolation and alienation. The following list of modern disorders fits into this group.

- Anxiety Disorders - OCD, Panic Attacks, Phobias, Self-Harm

  Anxiety and fear dominates the following three disorders.

  a. Obsessive-compulsive disorder (OCD): an anxiety disorder characterized by unreasonable thoughts and fears that leads sufferers to do repetitive behaviours (compulsions). They may realize the obsession is not reasonable and try to ignore or stop them, but that only increases the distress and anxiety. Ultimately, they feel driven to perform compulsive acts to ease stressful feelings.

  b. Panic attacks: a sudden episode of intense fear that triggers severe physical reactions when there is no real danger or apparent cause.

  c. Phobias: an overwhelming and unreasonable fear of an object or situation that poses little real danger. Several types of phobias exist such as fear of large and open spaces or in certain social situations; or there are specific phobias such as a fear of snakes, spiders or heights.

Anxiety and self-hatred dominates the following disorders.

  a. Self-harm/ self-injury: sufferers deliberately cut or burn themselves. It is an unhealthy way to cope with emotional pain, anger, frustration and may be followed by guilt, shame and the return of painful emotions.

---
1 Bailey, Alice A. Esoteric Psychology II, 415 - 437
2 Bailey, Alice A. Esoteric Psychology II, 436-437

b. Eating disorders: these commonly co-occur with anxiety disorders. People become obsessed with food and weight. Anorexia nervosa sufferers starve themselves or exercise excessively to avoid putting on weight. Bulimia nervosa is characterized by episodes of binge-eating and feelings of guilt, humiliation and self-loathing, followed by extreme fasting and/or purging. But it is not about food. These are unhealthy ways of trying to cope with emotional problems, of trying to regain control. In both disorders, the sense of self is determined by their weight and their perceptions of it, by body image. They are often depressed for failing to achieve what they consider is the perfect body, which in their mind is the cause of not being universally loved and accepted.

- Bipolar / Manic Depression, Borderline Personality Disorder (BPD)

In these mood-swing disorders the cleavage is within the emotional field, hence the alternating states of euphoria and depression. Patanjali, the originator of Raja Yoga described this disorder.

> 2:15. The quality of activity (rajas) is the characteristic of the emotional or astral nature and, when this is dominant the life is chaotic, violent, emotional and subjected to every mood and feeling. It is primarily the quality of the desire life.

Bipolar / manic-depressive disorder is characterized by alternating moods of mania depression. Borderline Personality Disorder generates significant emotional instability that can lead to other mental and behavioural problems. There may be a severely distorted self-image, feelings of worthlessness and being fundamentally flawed in some way, anger, impulsiveness and frequent mood swings.

2. Cleavage between the mind and emotions

This creates a war between a man's mind and the goals he sets with his emotional nature and desires that would take him in another direction. The thinking man is aware of the strength of the desires, the inability to satisfy them and that there is a part of him that does not want to do so. This creates the cleavage. They occur also when the intellect is not used wisely to discern essentials from nonessentials, between right direction and wrong goals, between satisfactions of the lower nature and higher. This group should cultivate peace.

3. Cleavage between the personality and soul

This produces sequentially a dominant selfish personality and then a practical mystic conscious of the need for fusion and unity. This group should cultivate goodwill.

Therapy: the key to bridging cleavages is to train the mind to be a discerning and integrating tool rather than a critical and separative factor. However, unless the mind is active and the soul is influential, esoteric techniques such as Raja Yoga should be avoided. Although cases are treated on an individual basis, for cleavages within the astral nature itself, Cognitive Therapy is recommended. It is a mind-training therapy designed to deal with specific issues. For the mystically inclined, give appropriate advice from the "Enhance the Ability to Stand in Spiritual Being" section. The ultimate remedy is the development of harmlessness. It bridges all cleavages.

Example of anorexia: Singer Karen Carpenter

Karen was very emotional (Cancer rising and the Sun in Pisces) and was full of fear (Sun opposite Saturn). Her emotional nature dominated her consciousness. (Mars {ruler of the solar plexus chakra} square the Cancer ascendant. Moon conjunct powerful Pluto, opposite Mercury. Sun in Pisces).

Fussy, critical and judgmental (Venus in Aquarius), Karen had obsessive and morbid thoughts about her body (Venus 8th house {8H}, inconjunct the ascendant {ASC} and Uranus). She hated her appearance (Mars square Uranus and ASC) and controlling her food intake (Scorpio/ Mars rules the 6H of diet), was a way of coping with the anxieties she experienced.

Karen brought her negatives through from a previous life. They were triggered again because of harsh criticism she received from an authoritarian in the home - putting her up then pulling her down (Saturn in Virgo 4H, opposite Sun conjunct the MC, the top of the chart).

Like Narcissus, she was obsessed with her body image. It led to her death but in her case the cause was self-loathing and not self-love.

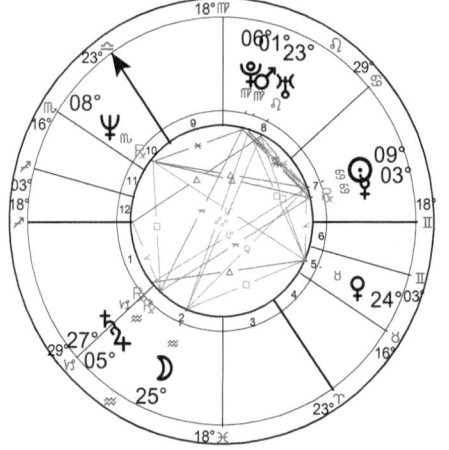

Example of bulimia: Princess Diana

Diana was very emotional and defensive (Sun and Mercury in Cancer); at times emotionally unstable and angry (Moon opposite Uranus-Mars). In self-protection, to try to control life and relationship disappointments, she would detach from her emotions (Moon in Aquarius, square Venus).

Diana disliked her body, her image. We know this because she developed the disorder (Jupiter, ascendant ruler, is retrograde, in judgmental Aquarius {it carries the judgmental 5th ray}, conjunct "the judge", Saturn). She was highly critical of her lack of (to her) lovability, even hated herself, blaming the breakdown of her relationships on this (Venus square Mars in Virgo). By the time this stage was reached, the cleavage in her emotional body was advanced.

With her perception distorted (Jupiter retrograde square Neptune), she thought she was fat (Jupiter).

Bulimia was her chosen method of weight control. First, she would comfort-eat by gorging on food (Sagittarius ascendant). Then feeling disgusted she would purge, vomit it all up (Moon opposite Mars-Pluto). Then she would repeat the habit (Moon dominating her psychology).

Diana brought this pattern through from a previous life. It was triggered again because of devastating and cruel criticism she received when she was a child, about her appearance and how she liked to eat (Mars, ruler of 4th house of family, in Virgo square Venus in Taurus).

Example of bipolar: Amy Winehouse

Amy was born with no planets in water (emotional) signs. This often means great difficulty in connecting with one's emotions excepting in a most superficial way. But the chart gives us more information - the Moon is in harsh Capricorn. This means that Winehouse had a habit of deliberately suppressing her emotions to cope with life and her disappointments in relationships.

This places her in the Atlantean consciousness group. She was unable to handle her emotions through reason (Moon conjunct Neptune {co-ruler of the solar plexus chakra} square Mercury); so she suppressed them.

She was mentally introspective (Mercury retrograde), mentally-emotionally unstable and inclined to depression (Moon in Capricorn, square Mercury).

Her will and confidence were weakened by drug and alcohol addiction. (Neptune square Sun).

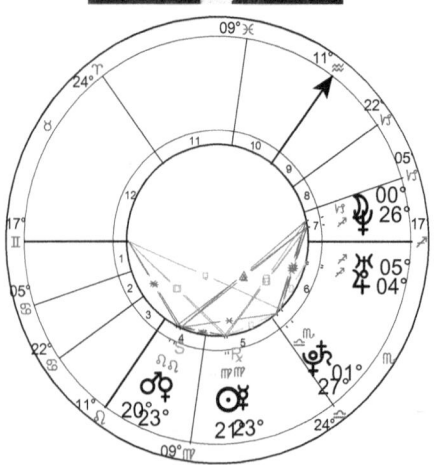

This enabled the old lunar patterns and mood swings / bipolar, to rise again. She was preoccupied with finding fault with herself, about the way she looked, about her "ugliness" and she self-medicated to cope (Sun-Mercury in Virgo square Moon-Neptune). Unable to heal her emotions because they were too deeply buried, as the divide within her deepened, the emotional swings became more accentuated.

Amy brought the pattern, the self-attack thoughts through from a previous life. Abuse and criticism triggered them from childhood traumas she suffered in childhood (Mars in the 4th house. Sun, ruler of 4th, in Virgo in the bipolar pattern), as is so often the case in emotional disturbances.

Emotional pain and her addictions were the death of her (Capricorn rules the 8th house of death. The Moon is in Capricorn, conjunct the "drug" planet Neptune).

2. PROBLEMS OF INTEGRATION [1]

The healing of a cleavage brings its own problems.

> When a man has succeeded.. in healing or bridging certain cleavages is the recognition of an immediate sense of well-being and of demand for expression. [2]

Synthesis and integration brings in an influx of unaccustomed energy which may express itself as high voltage ambition, as a sense of power and as desire for personality influence. If the 1st Power Ray is in a person's makeup via the dominating signs Aries, Leo, Capricorn and Scorpio, it can make a selfish personality even more selfish and egotistical and fuel a burning desire to rule and control others. A potential dictator is created and this can lead to serious troubles and difficulties.

> A sense of power, which makes the man, temporarily at least, selfish, dominant, sure of himself and full of arrogance. He is aware of himself as facing a larger world, a wider horizon and greater opportunities. This larger sense can bring, therefore, serious troubles and difficulties. [3]

What sets this group apart from megalomaniacs, is that they are idealists who are well meaning.

> This type of person, under the influence of this extension of consciousness, is often beautifully motivated and actuated by the highest intentions [4]

There are three major integration problem groups

1. Egomania (narcissism - extreme love of self)

The Narcissistic Personality Disorder (NPD) arises from Greek mythology. Narcissus was renowned for his beauty. He was exceptionally proud, disdained those who loved him and thought he was more beautiful than the gods. Unfortunately, he attracted the attention of Nemesis. In the ancient Greek religion, Nemesis was the goddess who brought retribution to those who were arrogant before the gods. She drew Narcissus to a pool where he saw his own reflection in the water and fell in love with it, not realizing it was merely an image. He died from self-adoration.

Narcissists are vain and selfish people who have an excessive interest in themselves, an extraordinary admiration of their physical appearance and crave admiration. They are preoccupied with issues of personal adequacy, power and prestige and have an excessively grandiose view of their talents. The person under the influence of this problem is often highly motivated. But a lack of sensitivity to the feelings of others breeds trouble and resentment. Unchecked, this can lead eventually to a serious state of egomania.

Therapy: offset these difficulties by helping sufferers realise that they are an integral part of a much greater whole. When successful, personal values will adjust and the exaggerated sense of power will balance out.

- The "Entitlement Generation" of narcissists

This generation born to the "baby boomers" (1965 onwards) was showered with love, told constantly how wonderful they were and deserving of the very best. This gave rise to a generation of self-entitled narcissists. They adore themselves, indulge themselves with their parent's money demanding the very best, pouting when forced to leave their luxurious nest to make their own way in life.

Example of egomania (narcissism) 1: Muammar Gaddafi (time unknown)

Egomania is a 1st ray problem - a too powerful belief in one's own self-importance; and of the 6th ray - a lack of the sense of proportion and fanaticism.

Some think that Muammar Gaddafi was an egomaniac. We do not have his birth time, but he must have had a powerful ascendant sign and ruling planet to match his powerful personality. The Sun, the personality ruler was not particularly strong, being in mutable sign Gemini. But he carried the leadership 1st ray with Pluto in 1st ray Leo, conjunct Mars and semi-square the Sun.

---
1 Bailey, Alice A. Esoteric Psychology II, 437 - 448
2 Ibid, 437
3 Ibid 437
4 Bailey, Alice A. Esoteric Psychology II, 438

He had an Aries ("it's all about me") Moon opposite idealistic and deluding Neptune. Loving and believing in himself and his vision of how the world should be, he thought the Arab World would rally behind him and accept his goals as their goals. They did not. Pluto square Venus shows obsessive love. He demonstrated narcissistic behaviour and Pluto is midpoint the Sun and Neptune. He only saw his own light (Sun no major aspects). He was blinded by his own self-delusion, by his own self-aggrandising thoughts (Mercury square Neptune).

Most dictators have violent deaths. Karmically, the grief, pain, harm and deprivation that has been forced onto others, rebounds upon the perpetrator like a boomerang. Gaddafi was killed by a mob who inflicted terrible injuries upon him before he was shot.

Example of egomania (narcissism) 2: artist Salvador Dali

Many have speculated that self-proclaimed genius Salvador Dali was a narcissist. He said "Each morning when I awake, I experience again a supreme pleasure - that of being Salvador Dali".

There are similarities between the charts of Gaddafi and Dali. Both have very prominent Moon's in "I am" Aries. They were both instinctively very self-aware and believed they were special. Dali cultivated an eccentric and bizarre persona (Moon square Uranus; ASC sextile Sun, Mercury, Mars). However, under this facade, he was fearful and insecure (Moon square Neptune-Uranus, semi-square Saturn).

Dali was wonderfully talented with an art style uniquely his own (Uranus trine Venus) which brought him fame.

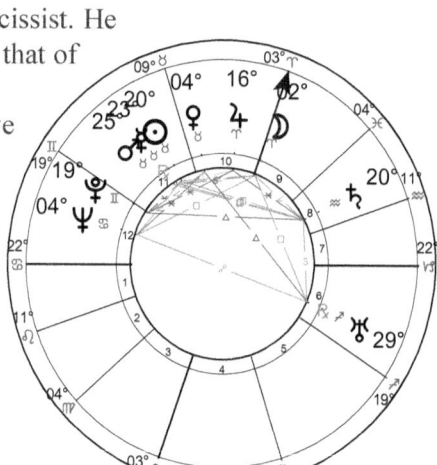

2. Fanaticism (temporary)

While in the "integration" flux period, self-absorption with a tendency to over-emphasise can turn people into fanatics for a time. It is a shorter-lived stage than a later group of fanatics found in the next "Stimulation" problem group of mental-extrovert fanatics. This latter group have a crusading orientation and are deadly serious and dangerous in their causes. The fanatics here are a gentler group and the tendencies weaken as the energy-integration imbalance settles down.

With high motives, these people try to drive everyone along the path that they have travelled, believing that because they have had good outcomes, others can as well. They may spend generously on books, courses, lectures, education etc., to motivate family and friends. For a while they can become great nuisances for those who interact with them.

Therapy: help sufferers recognise the fact that they are demonstrating a lack of respect for the point of view and beliefs of others because they are not recognising differences in background, education, psychology, in the point in evolution and in tradition and heredity. You could also point out (if this is has happened), that they are wasting their money in their attempts to convert others to their way of seeing and interacting in the world.

3. Over-development of the sense of direction or of vocation

When the gap between the emotional body and the mind is bridged, people can be so greatly affected by the vast field of mental activity that has opened they become selfishly preoccupied with their own plans and goals.

Therapy: If the problem is not excessive, then it is best to leave people alone to the directing purpose and guidance of their souls. In time, the energy swings will even out.

More severe sufferers need to be helped to realise and see that they are an integral part of a much greater whole, that they do not exist in a vacuum and their well-being and position in life has been assisted by family, friends and the community. It this is successful, then personal values will adjust and the sense of power will balance out.

Perhaps the group needing most attention are the egomaniacs because they are more extreme and their actions can bring a dangerous backlash. Help such people broaden their perspective by pointing out that there is a lack of wisdom being shown because the point of view and beliefs of others and their backgrounds and circumstances are not being taken into account.

3. PROBLEMS OF STIMULATION [1]

Widespread education and the practise of meditation stimulates the brain cells and increases the vibration of the atoms of the body. Consequently, there is an intensification of the rate of vibration of the whole body system, which if not properly handled, leads to overstimulation in these areas.

Stimulation Problem 1: Mental Problems

This problem affects mentally intense intellectuals. Psychologically unsound, people with this trouble of blind adherence to ideas and personality devotions are everywhere. They are a menace and the condition is contagious. It is a problem of integration - the mind is potent and wants to control. Here is how it arises.

> The thought form of an idea has been potently constructed.. [and is] .. capable of holding a man both mentally and emotionally. If he has no sense of balance, proportion and humour .. he .. can see nothing and believe nothing and work for nothing except that embodied idea which is holding him a captive. Such people are the violent partisans in any group, in any church, order or government. They are frequently sadistic .. willing to sacrifice or to damage anyone who seems to them inimical to their fixed idea of what is right and true. The men who engineered the Spanish Inquisition .. are samples of the worst forms of this line of thought and development. [2]

1. Mental introverts

This group consists of people who may be geniuses or very creative in a positive way. But a third type can have problems - an introverted person with low self-esteem, who becomes captive to dark brooding thoughts. Images of rejections and humiliations pile up to the point that there is:

> The violent and often dangerous expressions of frustration in which the man attempts to release the result of his inner brooding along the chosen line. [3]

Today this problem is a phenomenon amongst youths who commit suicide or shoot their teachers, school associates and others. Authorities report that a common theme is the desire to exact revenge upon those they are angry with. Ray type determines how those affected will vent their frustration. Rays (R) 2, 4 and 6 leads to inner brooding. [4]

When this disorder arises, there is emotional sensitivity and vulnerability (R2), overlaid with a 4th ray tendency to agonise and brood over perceived injustices. Imaginative movies created in the mind replay painful incidents. Anger rises (R4 is the ray of war) and thoughts of revenge. Feeling victimised (R2 and R6 trait), 6th ray fanaticism urges violent action. This highly combustible mix festers away in the mind of the introvert with this problem, quietly and unseen behind closed doors until something triggers an explosion.

Example of mental introvert: Charles Joseph Whitman

Engineering student and former marine, Whitman killed seventeen people and wounded thirty-two in a mass shooting in and around the Tower of the University of Texas. Whitman was never diagnosed, but he was polite, courteous and well-mannered. As far as we know, he never revealed to the world the dark thoughts and menacing urges that he eventually revealed through his rampage. He was deeply introverted and fits into this group.

Three of Whitman's personal planets (Sun, Mercury, Venus) are in Cancer, a sign of introversion. The rulers of Cancer - the Moon (R4) and Neptune (R6) are in cadent houses, which adds to introversion. Mars in the emotional sign Pisces in the 12H of hidden things, is the primary danger signal. A t-square containing the Sun, Moon, Mars (violence, guns) in the 12H and Neptune (delusion), pointed to brooding paranoia. He took his revenge on people through murder.

---

1 Bailey, Alice A. Esoteric Psychology II, 448 - 520
2 Ibid, 455-456
3 Ibid, 461
4 Bailey, Alice A. Esoteric Psychology II, 461

2. Megalomaniacs

This group of people are very different to the first group, because they have an inflated sense of self-esteem and admiration. They harbour delusional thoughts and fantasies about power, relevance and omnipotence. If not checked, these thoughts become so intense they wall their owner off, leading to complete isolation or separateness. Some believe that Jim Jones of the People's Temple cult, dictator Saddam Hussein and psychopath Charles Manson were in this group.

Rays 1 of Will and Power and 5 of Concrete Mind are strong. This gives them a powerful and inflexible will and mental attitudes. Many megalomaniacs have a Taurus or Scorpio Sun sign. These signs carry the 4th Ray of War and the 1st ray of Power and Destruction via rulers Vulcan and Pluto. Often Venus is implicated. It represents a 5th ray intelligence, which is used ruthlessly by the ego - shown in the chart by Venus afflictions. Add a powerful and ruthless ambition and you have all the ingredients in place that could lead to megalomania.

Example of megalomania 1: Jim Jones

Jones was stubborn, persevering and ambitious. His Taurus Sun was trine Saturn in its own sign Capricorn, in the 1st house. These qualities made it easy for him to realise his personal goals and it fostered his megalomania.

Jones' Sun was in the 4H. He acted like a father to "his family" and demanded unquestioning loyalty. He loved absolute power and was obsessed about getting it (Venus, ruler of the Sun, afflicted in Aries, square Pluto). Eventually he destroyed those who opposed his authority (Pluto 7H opposite Saturn 1H).

His was a poisoned chalice. With Lord of Karma Saturn opposite Pluto, any violation of the Law of Love would force upon him a very bitter and harsh price. When he realised he was up against a power greater than his own (the US government), he spitefully killed himself and as many others he could take with him.

Example of megalomania 2: Saddam Hussein (unknown birth time)

Hussein had a Taurus personality which was conjunct revolutionary and brilliant Uranus. He loved absolute power and was obsessed with getting it (ruler of Taurus, Venus, afflicted in Aries, square Pluto). This fed his megalomania.

Dictators usually have hard and violent deaths. Cancer and the Moon naturally rule the 4th house of life endings. The Moon is conjunct violent Mars, which opposes Uranus. Hussein had a sudden and violent death. It is all due to karma. Saturn, Lord of Karma is in the 1st degree of Aries, the sign that naturally rules the ascendant and 1st house. Hussein's ambitions were bloody and he paid for it. If he had been wiser with his dealings with the USA he may have had a happier ending (Saturn trine Pluto, ruler of the US, because of the eagle symbol of Scorpio).

Example of megalomania 3: Charles Manson

Manson was a Scorpio of the lower type - dangerous and lethal (Sun, Mercury, Venus in Scorpio). His megalomaniac pattern is represented by the Sun-Venus conjunction square Saturn; Venus is afflicted in Scorpio. He had a driving ambition, loved being in control and to control all those around him.

Manson brought through his problem from a previous life. Moon (past lives) is exalted in the 10th house in Aquarius in a Grand Cross planet pattern. He needed a group that he could control and manipulate; with the Sun's location in the 7H of "others", he needed to gather people around him and use them to further his plans (Moon square Mercury in Scorpio, square Uranus in Aries, opposite Pluto). His murderous group was called the Manson Family (Pluto in the 4H of family).

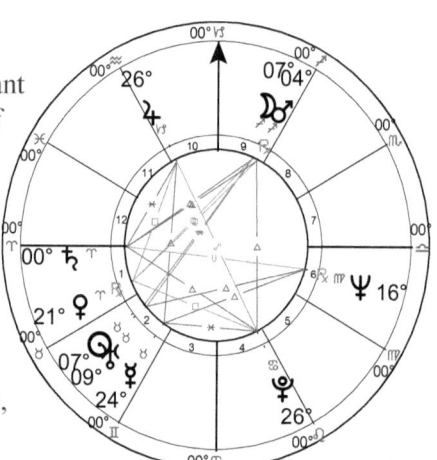

3. Mental extroverts

Two rays dominate this group. Firstly, the 3rd ray of Intelligence that also gives shrewdness and cunning. It is a force that can lead to extroversion and the acting-out of one's inner desire - it is related to the sexual sacral chakra via the throat chakra, which it rules. Ray 3 speeds up the brain so that thought-forms are processed faster and words are skilled and manipulative. White collar criminals usually have this energy in abundance. Secondly, the 6th Ray of Desire and Fanaticism via Mars can produce fanatical, crusading types. When these two forces drive a selfish, unspiritual person then very unpleasant and often dangerous people emerge.

- Mental Extrovert Subgroup 1: Sectarian and Obsessive Fanatics

Sectarians have a narrow-minded adherence to a sect, party or denomination. When coupled with humourless fanaticism, serious trouble can arise. They like to gather believers to support their crusades - crusading is a 6th ray phenomenon. Through pen, word or violent action, they attack those who oppose their point of view. Relentless, they never let up.

Example of Mental Extrovert - Fanatic: Irish cleric Ian Paisley

Birth time is unknown. A fiery crusader for his sectarian cause, mentally brilliant and with powerful oratory, Paisley is a perfect example of this type of fanatic. Hypothetically, he had a 6th ray personality (his Aries Sun is ruled by 6th ray Mars); working through a 3rd ray physical body / brain (Moon - the form in Capricorn ruled by 3rd ray Saturn).

With revolutionary Uranus in religious Pisces, trine calculating Saturn in the death sign Scorpio, he incited the Protestant Northern Ireland Army to war.

Paisley mellowed with age, became more conciliatory with his old political foes, the mark of someone approaching the Path.

- Mental Extrovert Subgroup 2: Stalkers, Cyber-bullies

"Stalking" is defined as an unwanted or obsessive attention by an individual or group toward another person. Stalking behaviours are related to harassment and intimidation and may include following the victim in person or monitoring them. Obsessive devotion is a 6th ray trait. The obsession could be the idolising of a person and wanting to possess his or her love; or if rejection is the motivating impulse, hating that "fallen idol" and wanting to harm or kill. Victims are bombarded with unwanted attention. Bullying is a 1st ray trait, but these people are not courageous. Rather, they manipulate (ray 3) from behind the scenes, behind their computers and from the shadows.

Example of Mental Extrovert - Stalker, Bully: Maria Marchese

The worst case of stalking in the UK up until 2007, occurred when Maria Marchese (45) harassed psychiatrist Dr Jan Falkowski for four years until she was stopped.

She tried to ruin his reputation and threatened to kill his fiancee, bombarding the couple, their families and colleagues with chilling text messages, phone calls and emails for four years. One warned Deborah Pembertont (Falkowski's fiancee), that she would be burnt in her wedding dress, while a second suggested "dig your own grave". A third read: "Your life will end, gunman paid".

Southwark Crown Court was told that Marchese burgled and wrecked the psychiatrist's riverboat home. Having destroyed his marriage plans and relationship, she then accused the doctor of drugging and raping her in his hospital office. To back her claims, she retrieved a condom from his dustbin, smearing herself with its contents to frame him.

Marchese's birthdate is not available. However, her 6th ray obsessive fanaticism is evident; so is her ingenious 3rd ray trickery and deceit. When her photo is examined, she appears to have a 3rd ray physical body and brain. This would then give her a 6th ray (Mars) personality or/ and astral nature. The real problem is the 6th ray, which feeds the desire nature and our yearnings and cravings. Obsessive types will stop at nothing to try to satisfy their 6th ray thirst.

In 2007, the Southwark Crown Court jailed Marchese for nine years.

- Mental Extrovert Subgroup 3: Psychopaths and Sociopaths

Today, a psychopathic disorder is most commonly assessed with the Psychopathy Checklist created by psychologist Robert Hare. It combines "aggressive narcissism" with an "antisocial personality disorder" that may or may not be associated with criminal activity. The psychopath has no concern or empathy for others, it is all about him, what he feels, what he wants, what he believes he has a right to take. Constantly bored and seeking a thrill, he uses his intelligence and glib charm, cunning and manipulative skills, to satisfy his need of the moment. There is poor impulse control. While sociopaths may appear normal most of the time, psychopaths do not. They are openly blatant.

The 3rd ray dominates this group. Restless with a short attention span, they are always looking for distractions, ways, means and opportunities to get what they want. Scheming manipulators, they find it easy to con people. Consequently, these types are naturally drawn to white-collar crimes such as embezzlement, fraud and identity theft. They enjoy the thrill of the game and of the chase.

Example of Mental Extrovert - Sociopath: Nazi surgeon Josef Mengele

Polite and well-mannered Mengele had no hesitation in conducting inhumane surgical experiments on Jewish prisoners in Nazi death camps. There was no regard for the rules of a society or the sanctity of human life, nor compassion for those he abused.

Mengele's personality was in sensitive Pisces, but this did not extend to the masses to whom he was uncaring (Neptune 1H in Cancer, square Moon 4H, the family of man). Stolidly unemotional, Mengele was unfeeling about any pain he inflicted on others (Saturn [3rd ray] in Taurus square Mars). His mind - this time represented by Venus, is debased in Aries and is excited by the infliction of pain and suffering (Venus square Uranus conjunct Mars).

Mengele had a powerful and morbid curiosity about death and other unhealthy and unpleasant things (Sun square Pluto 12H). He wanted to shine in life (Sun in the 10H) and surgical experiments for his Nazi masters was a means to achieve this (Sun sextile Uranus conjunct Mars).

He sacrificed people to achieve his warped ideals (Neptune in Cancer square the Moon in Libra). The 3rd ray flows through both Cancer and Libra.

- Mental Extrovert Subgroup 4: Sexual-Psychopaths 1 - Sadists, Serial Killers, Rapists

This is the most extreme sub-group in the Mental-Extroversion problem. Remember that Bailey said (Esoteric Psychology II, 455-456) that an idea that has been potently constructed can hold a man mentally and emotionally if there is no sense of balance, proportion or humour. Such people brood over their predilection which keeps them captive to the unhealthy thoughtforms they have constructed.

Today, many of these thoughtforms centre around sex and sexually aggressive crimes are increasing.

This is being fed by a new generation of young men who have grown up watching online pornography. Consequently, in many instances, their approach to women and relationships has been corrupted and if this does not balance out trouble lies ahead for them in broken and damaged relationships and marriage.

Today in the west, more victims of sexual crimes are willing to come forward and report what happened to them. This is a most positive development because it is evidence of a legal system that is a little more supportive to the plight of victims. It was not always like that.

The 3rd ray (intelligent manipulation and deceit) and the 6th ray and Mars (cruelty, sadism and sexual sadism) are fundamental to this problem. But when sex is involved, we add Uranus, the 7th ray and Mars, because they rule and control the sexual-sacral chakra. Wherever there is an imbalance in sexual appetite, the sacral chakra is at the root of the problem.

a. The 7th Ray and its Effect

The 7th ray is increasing its influence in humanity. During normal evolution, the rays cycle in and out of incarnation. The last time this force was very active on earth was in early man, in ancient Lemuria. Now that it is coming in again [1] it is bringing in with it many 7th ray types who were living at that time.

---

[1] Bailey, Alice A. Esoteric Psychology I, 190

> A large number of seventh ray [people] are coming into incarnation now and to them is committed the task of organising the activities of the new era and of ending the old methods of life and the old crystallised attitudes to life, to death, to leisure and to the population. [1]

While many are responding to the higher call, many others are bringing through the seeds of sexual perversions which were rampant in Lemuria. These karmic seeds are a result of their own actions and behaviours in that far off time. Then, under the stimulation of the 7th ray, mankind was learning to control his physical body and use his sexual nature. Consequently, the sacral centre was dominant. [2] But unfortunately, in the process of this development, animal appetites became insatiable, resulting in widespread sexual licentiousness and perversion.

> In the infancy of the race, a great mismating, promiscuity and .. perversions took place. [3]

Now the 7th ray is returning, it is pouring its fire through humanity and is stimulating all individual sacral centres. This is the cause of the increased interest in sex today.

> One of the great results of the influence of the incoming seventh ray has been the increase in the mental interest in sex. [4]

The spiritual goal is to use this force in higher creative ways. But under this stimulation, many are finding it difficult to resist the old urges and are bringing them into the light of day. This is why we are seeing an upsurge in sexual perversions.

b. Sexual Psychopaths

Many criminal psychopaths fall into the Sexual Sadism group. Some clinicians argue that psychopaths prefer violent, sexual behaviour. According to Diagnostic and Statistical Manual of Mental Disorders, there are two forms of sadism.

- The first is "Sadistic Personality Disorder," a condition in which someone "is amused by or takes pleasure in the psychological or physical suffering of others."
- The second type of sadism is "Sexual Sadism," a perversion of the erotic instinct in which the suffering of a victim is not just generally enjoyable but intensely arousing, often to the point of orgasm. [5]

Example of Mental Extrovert - Sexual Sadist: Marquis de Sade

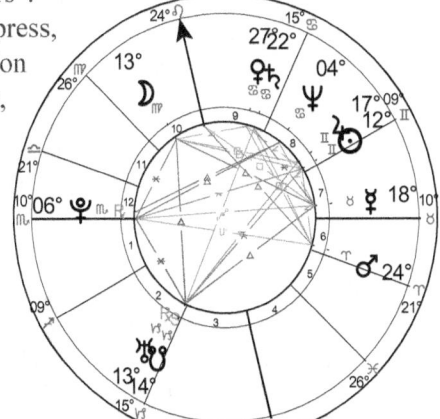

Perhaps the most famous of all sexual sadists is the French writer of depraved and pornographic literature, the Marquis de Sade. He was a proponent of extreme freedom, unrestrained by morality, religion or law. The words sadism and sadist are derived from his name.

Sade was incarcerated in various prisons and in an insane asylum for about 32 years. He spent most of his life in prison for staging sexual orgies that embraced crimes of sadomasochistic violence.

He had sexual Scorpio rising, the lowest types of which can be "monsters". [6] A law unto himself and with evil and sadistic tendencies he yearned to express, he would not be stopped by any sense of decency or fear of karmic retaliation (ASC ruler Pluto conjunct the ascendant and co-ruler Mars - 6th ray in Aries, square Venus and Saturn).

The most problematic aspect is Saturn (3rd ray) in Cancer square Mars, indicating the inhibiting of feelings and calculated sadism that was cold and vicious.

Uranus was in calculating Capricorn, conjunct the south node. Sade had done this in a previous life, where sadism was his "profession". (Uranus trine the Moon in the 10th house, Mars 6H trine MC).

---

1 Bailey, Alice A. The Destiny of the Nations, 30
2 Bailey, Alice A. Esoteric Psychology II, 339
3 Bailey, Alice A. Esoteric Healing, 228
4 Bailey, Alice A. Esoteric Psychology I, 262
5 Http://twistedminds.creativescapism.com/psychologeal-disorders/psychopaths/sadism/
6 Bailey, Alice A. Esoteric Astrology 332

Example of Mental Extrovert - Sexual Sadist and killer: Dennis Rader

Rader was a cold-blooded killer known as the BTK killer (Bind, Torture, Kill). He sent details describing his killings to police and local news outlets, recounting details as if reciting the items on a shopping list.

His sadism and detachment from the suffering of his victims is shown by 6th ray Mars in Aquarius - a 5th ray sign indicating mental detachment. Mars has no aspects to planets, which means this violent side was outside and beyond any central control. A murderous persona controlled him.

His evil tendencies are further shown by the Moon in Capricorn - seeds of the past. The ancient pattern was so powerful it blocked soul influence (Moon conjunct the South Node, opposite ascendant. Venus the soul, debased in Mars' sign Aries). Rader displayed no remorse or sensitivity to his victims and to the terrible things he did. He was not human, but a shell used by evil entities. This was possible because he had the seed within him. Read what Bailey says about this type of obsessed person, which is relevant for sadists like Rader:

> [They] are "shells," obsessed by evil entities.. hence their extreme skill and cunning, based on very ancient evil experience .. devoid of all true feeling .. lacking the light of love and understanding.. [1]

Irredeemable, Rader fits the profile of an "astral maniac" whose focus is sadistic and sexual. Once again, here is the description:

> Mentally there is little that is wrong with them. The mind .. remains useless and inert whilst the man expresses (with violence or subtlety as the case may be) some basic desire. It may be the desire to kill, or desire to have abnormal sexual experience .. something which cannot be controlled.. [2]

Overshadowed by evil, a long period of salvaging must occur, else Rader could end up a lost soul.

- Mental Extrovert Subgroup 4: Sexual-Psychopaths 2 - Paedophiles

Clinically, paedophilia is considered a psychiatric disorder. Although there are paedophiles who are sadists, not all are. Several different types have been identified. Here is a definition.

> Paedophilia, is a psychiatric disorder in persons 16 years of age or older typically characterized by a primary or exclusive sexual interest toward prepubescent children (generally age 11 (or 13) years or younger [3]

The Catholic Church (ruled by Neptune and Mars that carry the 6th ray) is particularly affected but it seems that most if not all religions and government departments that managed children in the 20 Century were involved. Paedophilia is a universal problem. Most people today simply consider the practice to be a gross evil and sexual perversion. The damage, psychologically and physically can wreck soul progress in a life or series of lives. Interestingly, paedophilia is not mentioned in the Bible or other central esoteric writings. But sexual perversion and abuse is. Serious karma waits for those who use their force and power to harm the innocent. This is what the Bible says:

> Matthew 18:6 But whoso shall offend one of these little ones .. it were better for him that a millstone were hanged about his neck and that he were drowned in the depth of the sea. 18:7 .. woe to that man by whom the offence cometh! (King James Version)

Paedophilia and Astrology

The scale of paedophilia was dragged into the public gaze when Pluto, the Arrow of Death moved through (from the 70's) Libra, Scorpio and Sagittarius. As it passes through Capricorn, governments are examining the problem in greater depth and are passing laws to better protect children. Uranus rules new technology and computers, which has enabled the rapid spread of paedophilia and for its ability to reach into the home. The positive side of this is that it is bringing this perversion into the light of day. Latent appetites are emerging and those who cannot rise above them will suffer karmic consequence at some time or other.

---

1 Bailey, Alice A. Esoteric Astrology, 544
2 Bailey, Alice A. Esoteric Psychology II, 459
3 Diagnostic and Statistical Manual of Mental Disorders DSM-IV TR (Text Revision). Arlington, VA, USA: American Psychiatric Publishing, Inc.. 2000-06. p. 943

Therapy: Esoterically, the problem arises in people whose sacral-sexual chakra is powerful and who stimulate inappropriate desire by lusting over sadistic or sexually violent images. The esoteric cure is to divert desire into a positive creative direction, which lifts the excess force into the higher creative throat chakra. The adage "energy follows thought" applies. Obviously, evil and sadistic people must be restrained. But long term the goal is for a more rounded out unfoldment. An important goal for future schools is to train young people to be more balanced in their views, to hold a broader perspective and to value the contribution that can be made to the whole. A technique that will constitute a part of the science of psychology in the future is to evoke the person's soul, so that it can take on the task of breaking down the walls of thought. If the controlling beliefs and perceptions are too strong, then sufferers may take the psychological condition to their grave and into future lives. Then only the hard impact of karma will soften the rigidity of the mental unit and broaden out perception.

Example of Mental Extrovert - Paedophile: Dennis Ferguson

Notorious Australian paedophile Ferguson, kidnapped and raped children.

Ferguson brought the habit through from a previous life. His Moon (the past) is in Sagittarius, which rules animal appetites at the lower level and is a predatory sign. Its lower impulse is "let food be sought". This appetite was huge (Jupiter conjunct the Moon).

The power of this ancient evil controlled Ferguson's mind and consciousness. (Jupiter as co-ruler of Pisces, rules the mind planets Mercury and Venus {the intelligence}, Moon squares Venus).

Ferguson had a warped sense of love and sex (Venus square Uranus), he had unhealthy sexual fantasies (Venus in Pisces. Neptune is the ruler of fantasises and of strange evil).

His impulse was to subjugate children and force his will on them (Moon trine Saturn-Pluto in Leo; the latter sign ruling children). He acted on those impulses, abducting, attacking and raping young people (Mars opposite Mercury, the latter ruling youths).

Note that Ferguson's Mars (6th ray of cruelty), was retrograde when he was born. This is another indication that he brought through his violent sexual tendencies from a previous life. In the current life he was given an opportunity to rehabilitate his tendencies but did not. When by progression Mars passed over Saturn (karma), he was incarcerated and then killed himself on December 31, 2012

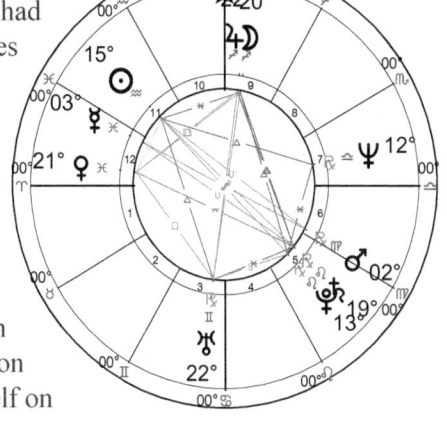

Example of Example of Paedophile 4221 Astrodatabank

This paedophile attacked his children's pre-teen playmates.

Like Ferguson, 4221 had a Sagittarius Moon - he had powerful physical appetites and paedophile tendencies which he brought over from a previous life (Moon-Sun-Saturn T-square. The Sun rules his 5th house of children).

Mars (sex) is the most powerful planet in the chart. It is in its own sign, disposits all other planets, but is retrograde. This again points to a past life sexual issue that needed to be straightened out.

His idea of "love" and sex was skewed and unhealthy (Venus, ruler of the Sun, is debased in Aries, trine Uranus. Mars rules Venus and is retrograde in Scorpio.)

There was unhealthy sexual fantasising (Mars trine Neptune) about children in his local environment (3H).

Details about the end of his life were not available. However, with Scorpio ruling his 8th house of death and Pluto conjunct retributive Saturn opposite his Sun, it would not have been easy.

Stimulation problem 2, arising from Meditation and Illumination

As we become more mystical, we become responsive to powerful new energies and a new world of phenomena. This is when young souls fall prey to delusion. We all go through this experience and the goal is to develop discrimination.

1. Illusion - The Misinterpretation of Ideas

This problem affects intellectuals who misinterpret the truth. Vast illusory thoughtforms form around the varying schools of thought (philosophy, science, religion, sociology, politics, etc.) The truth is misinterpreted because of preconceived personality or narrow conclusions.

Therapy: the intuition or soul apprehension destroys illusion. It develops as we become more inclusive and wise, through occult meditation and the study of symbols - such as astrology.

2. Glamour - Distortion of Reality because of Emotional Bias

Glamour is illusion intensified by desire. It is illusion on the emotional plane and victims are emotional types. Deceived by the appearance of things, they do not look for deeper causes and motives because mental discrimination has not developed. Consequently, they wander through life as if in a mist. Glamour is potent, because the masses function at an astral level. Glamour rises when the ego, unable to accept that others may not see it as being superior, imagines itself to be so anyway and feels self-satisfied and smug as a result. It puts other people down to maintain this pretence. Another version is denial of the truth accompanied by the building of "wish-list" images that depict how things could be and should be.

Therapy: advise sufferers to discontinue any practises to develop lower psychic powers. Explain the difference between the Lemurian, Atlantean and Aryan consciousness, evoking pride of status. Develop the intellect. Avoid the breeders of glamour - *criticism, pride, separativeness*. Align with the soul and evoke light, seeing it flood the mind and astral nature, bringing peace. Practise the Formula for the Dissipation of Glamour.

3. Maya - Glamorous Activity on the Physical Plane

This is the activity produced when glamour and illusion play out on the physical level, in daily life. It is that vital, unthinking, emotional mess in which most people seem to live.

Therapy: the only remedy is to bring all the centres under soul control, achieved at an advanced level. In the meantime, continue with right-living and develop discrimination.

Aspects of Glamour

Name	Plane	Stages of the Path	Therapy
Illusion	Mental	Path of Initiation	Contemplate as a soul, study symbols
Glamour	Astral	Path of Discipleship	Meditate, hold the mind steady in the light
Maya	Physical	Path of Probation	Manipulate force wisely.

Examples of Illusion, Glamour and Maya

colspan
An aspirant reads about the Masters and pupils and aspires to become a student. He realises that he has to begin a process of inner and outer purification to progress spiritually.

1. Illusion	*2. Glamour*
Ideas are misinterpreted. Personal conclusions warp the pure message. *Example: I aspire to be a student of the Masters, so I need to be 100 per cent pure and become an ascetic and retire into a monastery where I will not be contaminated by others.*	Perception of truth is distorted because of emotional bias caused by the breeders of glamour: pride, separativeness and criticism. *Example: I aspire to be a student of the Masters, and I qualify because I am a vegetarian. This makes me a superior person and I feel really good about my exalted status.*
*3. Maya: that intense activity produced when both illusion and glamour act out on the Physical Plane.*	
Withdraws from the world and people.	Swaggers pridefully, talking disdainfully to people.

RAY GLAMOURS [1]

Ray 1
Smugly sees itself as having the divine right of kings to do as it wills because it knows best and others are too weak to stop it. The glamour of ...
- physical strength.
- personal magnetism, personal potency.
- self-centredness, of "the one at the centre."
- selfish personal ambition.
- rulership, of dictatorship, of wide control.
- superimposed will—upon others and upon groups.
- the Messiah complex in the field of politics.
- selfish destiny, of the divine right of kings personally exacted.
- destruction.
- isolation, of aloneness, of aloofness.

Ray 2
Smugly sees itself as being self-sacrificing, selflessly serving, unconditionally loving, worthy of being loved and appreciated. The glamour of ...
- the love of being loved, of popularity.
- personal wisdom.
- selfish responsibility.
- too complete an understanding, which negates right action.
- self-pity, a basic glamour of this ray.
- the Messiah complex, in the world of religion and world need.
- fear, based on undue sensitivity.
- self-sacrifice; selfish service.
- selfish unselfishness, self-satisfaction.

Ray 3
Smugly sees itself as being mentally superior and creative and justified in manipulating others for the greater good. The glamour of ...
- being busy.
- cooperation with the Plan in an individual and not a group way.
- active scheming.
- creative work—without true motive.
- good intentions, which are basically selfish.
- "the spider at the centre."
- "God in the machine."
- devious and continuous manipulation.
- self-importance, from the standpoint of knowing, of efficiency.

Ray 4
Smugly sees itself as being the peacemaker, the creator of harmony or beauty, the alive or self-expressive one. The glamour of ...
- harmony, aiming at personal comfort and satisfaction.
- war.
- conflict, with the objective of imposing righteousness and peace.
- vague artistic perception.
- psychic perception instead of intuition.
- musical perception.
- the pairs of opposites, in the higher sense.

Ray 5
Smugly sees itself as the expert who is always right, the one not swayed by mystical nonsense, who sticks to the facts. The glamour of ...
- materiality, or over-emphasis of form.
- the intellect.
- knowledge and of definition.
- assurance, based on a narrow point of view.
- the form which hides reality.
- organisation.
- the outer, which hides the inner.

Ray 6
Smugly sees itself as the righteous, virtuous, adoring, selflessly serving devotee; the special and chosen one. The glamour of ...
- devotion and idealism.
- adherence to forms and persons.
- loyalties, of creeds.
- emotional response.
- sentimentality.
- interference.
- the lower pairs of opposites.
- World Saviours and Teachers.
- the narrow vision.
- fanaticism.

Ray 7
Smugly sees itself as being a powerful worker of magic, superior in its efficiency and organising skills, being perfect and perfectly presented, following the rules. The glamour of ...
- magical work.
- the relation of the opposites.
- the subterranean powers.
- that which brings together.
- the physical body.
- the mysterious and the secret.
- sex magic.
- the emerging manifested forces.

---

[1] Gathered from Bailey, Alice A. Glamour: a World Problem, 120-125

GLAMOUR DISSIPATION FORMULA
(From 'Glamour a World Problem', 215-221)

PART 1. PREPARATION

1. The preparatory stages
   a. Recognise the glamour to be dissipated, the ways in which it affects your daily life and all relationships.
   b. Using mental focus, align your brain light with the light of your mind, lifting the lower light up into the mind-light, forming a pin point of light like a small torch light. (This light is used to reveal the glamour you want to be rid of).
   c. Briefly meditate on the soul, recognising the power of this greater light.
   d. Build the searchlight. Visualise this blended torch-light connecting with the light of the soul that is on the higher mental plane. Blend these 3 lights, fuse them together, forming a searchlight, ready to be turned in the needed direction.
2. Align the personality with the soul. See the soul accept the personality, forming one unit. Say "I dedicate my personality to the soul."
3. Brace yourself for the work to be done. Turn your mind <u>to the astral plane</u> and focus on the glamour to be eradicated. (Do not focus on yourself or your astral body).

PART 2. THE FORMULA

1. Endeavour to see and hear the soul - the source of light and power, breathing out the **OM** into the mind. Retain and hold this soul light. Feel strong, positive.
2. Build an intense brilliant powerful searchlight generated by this soul light and the 2 lesser lights; a vivid brilliant disc light not yet radiating.
3. Focus all your will behind light.
4. Relate the searchlight being held, and the glamour out there on the astral plane. Briefly affirm that the searchlight will destroy the glamour.
5. Turn on the light. See a broad brilliant beam pour forth from your mind and impact the glamour on the astral plane.
6. Silently say

   The power of the light prevents the appearance of the glamour (Name it).
   The power of the light negates the quality of the glamour from affecting me.
   The power of the light destroys the life behind the glamour.

   Enunciate these words with focused tension, with the mind held steady and with a positive attitude.

7. Sound the OM: see the light impact the glamour, penetrate the glamour and being absorbed by it. See the light slowly dissipate the glamour.
8. Withdraw to the Mental Plane, turn off light, identify with the soul, with God, with the Real.

Glamour is never immediately dissipated because it is of too ancient an origin. But persistent use of this formula will weaken the glamour and slowly it will vanish. Observe the results and continue if the glamour is being weakened. Otherwise discontinue the formulas use.

Stimulation problem 3. Guidance and Dreams

1. Guidance

Because man is increasingly becoming mystical, the guidance problem is widespread. It occurs when a person believes he hears voices or urges (God, the Christ, Baba, etc.), commanding him to actions of one sort or another. But usually only a person's own internal dialogue is heard.

This type of guidance may sweep people into quite harmless activities, but not always. Susceptible people who open themselves to blind, unreasoning guidance may become negative, impressionable automatons, helpless victims of circumstance, self-hypnotised tools used by others.

Wise teachers such as Gautama Buddha tell us that blind acquiescence and acceptance is not asked of students. The goal of all true teaching is to develop the mind and intellect, so that students can reason their way to enlightenment.

The desire to contact revered Saints and Masters is natural, but mystics are inclined to want this so powerfully, they imagine communications that in fact are only the product of their wish-life. It is naive to think that these advanced beings would make direct contact with people who are still ignorant of the truth, or who have not built the inner mechanism through purification and right living that makes such contact possible. It does not happen according to the Master Djwhal Khul. To think otherwise is to be deluded. The Master Djwhal Khul said for instance, that there was an astral effigy of him "living" on the Astral Plane, which had been constructed by devotees. Here is a quote on the subject to prove the point.

> In the early stages and whilst under illusion and glamour, that which is contacted is a vision of the astral, illusory form upon the planes of glamour and illusion. This is not, therefore, a glimpse of the Master Himself, but of His astral symbol, or of the form built by His devoted disciples and followers. [1]

- Sources from which guidance can come:
  a. Supposedly from God. Those susceptible to this problem are introverts who are mystically inclined and naive about religion. Sometimes there is the recovery of old spiritual tendencies from a previous life that appear new and as divine injunctions coming from God. People wanting to escape from life's difficulties may join a church and blindly follow the "will of God", believing they hear God speak to them.
  b. Words previously heard and remembered, ranging from the very good to very bad. They replay through the mind and susceptible people believe the person or entity is talking to them.
  c. From contacts made by the person on the Astral or Mental Planes. These planes are full of thoughtforms that may be used by undesirable entities demanding blind and unquestioning acceptance.
  d. From trained minds giving instruction to disciples. But true initiates do not try to control their students in such a manner.
  e. From a man's own soul when through meditation, discipline and service, he has established contact and there is a direct channel of communication from soul to mind to brain. But misinterpretations can occur in the undeveloped mind if the character is not pure and the personality nature still controls.

Therapy: for "Illusion", encourage the development of the intuition. For "Glamour", snap people out of their delusion by explaining the difference between the Lemurian, Atlantean and Aryan levels of consciousness; evoking pride of status. Encourage the development of discrimination and cessation of criticism, pridefulness and separativeness.

For "Guidance" problems, all spiritual practises should stop and those affected should be directed to find creative mental and physical interests. Any voice that demands control of the life or that has personality or separative implications should be rejected. Sometimes, being a cynic is a healthy thing.

A therapy technique which can be used for all types of psychological problems is for the sufferer to consciously invoke the power of the soul using affirmations. However, it is only effective when mental focus can be held. A simple version of this technique is to affirm "I invoke soul light and love" while visualising white light pouring through the personality vehicles and life, cleansing and purifying all aspects of the lower nature. "I wash myself through with love and light" is another. Including a thought that the source of the light is from God, Jesus, spirit, the soul, etc., or the healing force of nature (for sceptics); will make the practice more powerful and beneficial.

---
1 Bailey, Alice A. Esoteric Psychology II, 357-358

2. Dreams

A distressing dream life is simply the expression of frustrated desire. There are three main causes and when these three types of frustration exist, you will frequently have a vivid, unwholesome dream life, physical liabilities of many kinds and a steadily deepening unhappiness.

a. Sex frustration: it leads to an overemphasis on sex, an uncontrolled sex thought life and sexual jealousies.
b. Frustrated ambition: it dams up the life force, producing constant inner fret, envy, hatred, bitterness and intense dislike of the successful. It causes abnormalities of many kinds.
c. Frustrated love. Disappointment spills over into the dream life.

Therapy: some therapists believe dream interpretation will help current problems. But there is danger with such work. For instance, it could bring to the surface things that are undesirable in the unrecognised wish-life or penetrate the past and tap into ancient racial evil. On a more mundane level, it could cause sleep disorders. Although dreams can come from the soul and sometimes from higher sources, students should leave the Science of Dreams alone. Recommended therapy is to deal with the underlying frustration by filling the life with constructive and creative projects and to invoke the power of the soul through meditation and positive affirmations.

4. MISCELLANEOUS

1. Depression

Wholesale depression is seriously affecting all of humanity and the primary cause is the lowered physical vitality of the race. [1] The ray governing humanity is the 4th Ray of Harmony through Conflict and the path of least resistance for many when they feel unhappy is to initiate conflict with the perceived perpetrator or cause of the pain. When carried on for an extended period it is very debilitating to the system wish-life or penetrate into the. Under the influence of the 4th ray, uncontrolled emotional bodies can swing rapidly back and forth from exhilaration to depression.

The main psychological cause of depression occurs when people feel inadequate and unable to measure up to presented opportunities. This affects everyone including people who are deeply self-absorbed and introspective aspirants and disciples who are troubled by a sense of failure.

> Depression is as frequently a result, based upon a sensed incapacity to measure up to the realised opportunity. The man sees and knows too much. He can no longer be satisfied with the old measure of living, with the old satisfactions, and with the old idealisms. He has touched and now longs for the larger measures, for the new and vibrant ideas, and for the broader vision. The way of life of the soul has gripped and attracts him. But his nature, his environment, his equipment and his opportunities appear somehow to frustrate him consistently, and he feels he cannot march forward into this new and wonderful world. He feels the need to temporise and to live in the same state of mind as heretofore, or so he thinks, and so he decides. [2]

Bailey said that there was a "glamour of depression" and he said as much to one of his disciples.

> The glamour of depression, based on a sense of spiritual inferiority which is not warranted, being not based on facts. As an instance of this—read the list of failings which you give. My brother, even if there is some basis of truth in your enumeration, still your replies remain untruthful, for you omit all recollection or reference to the other side of the picture. You are centred in your mind in the involutionary reactions of the personality vehicles. Yet, you are, as you well know, in preparation for certain steps forward upon the Path. A clear vision of yourself is needed.. [3]

Therapy: depression is widespread and affects all people. Advise sufferers to cultivate and express goodwill. A meditation or visualisation exercise which is helpful is to imagine creating a beautiful garden. Spend a few minutes every day, tending and creating this garden, filling it with fragrant and beautiful flowers, bushes and trees. Tending to a physical garden will also help. It is very therapeutic to be outside in the sun and working with the magical Plant Kingdom. Disciples are told to ignore depression and continue service work.

---

1 Bailey, Alice A. Esoteric Psychology II, 512
2 Bailey, Alice A. Esoteric Psychology II, 466
3 Bailey, Alice A. Discipleship in the New Age I, 425

2. Dyslexia - a development of the future 6th Subrace?

Dyslexia is a specific learning disability that is neurological in origin. It is characterized by difficulties with accurate and / or fluent word recognition and by poor spelling and decoding abilities. Secondary consequences may include problems in reading comprehension and reduced reading experience that can impede growth of vocabulary and background knowledge. [1]

Simply, dyslexia is a specific learning disability and while there are different types, what they have in common is the difficulty in reading comprehension. Intelligence and sight are normal, but when the dyslexic tries to read, words look scrambled. If reading did not exist, no one would know there was a problem.

- The Problem - the left-brain is not operating like it "should"

Brain scans of dyslexics reveal that the left-brain under performs during reading. It is responsible for words, logic, numbers, analysis, lists, linearity and sequential thinking. The left-brain assembles letters and words like carriages of a train, that all flow smoothly when the engine moves forward. The right brain is the creative brain and deals in areas, space and patterns.

In the average person, the right and left hemispheres of the brain work synchronously. The right brain forms a picture and the left-brain supplies detail. This does not happen with dyslexics and this is at the root of the difficulty. The right brain sees a word as a drawing, a sketch, not a line-up of sounds. A dyslexic person said that when he reads "the words move on the page, just like the ripples on a swimming pool". [2] Consequently, dyslexics make a mess of reading and writing. Most dyslexics have low academic results in comparison with higher IQ results. This happens because they cannot learn a new lesson the traditional way.

Forcing dyslexics to learn left-brain ways of reading and writing is like making an iPhone use methodology that is fifty years old. The only real problem for dyslexics is that they are born into a world that does not yet have appropriate educational materials that meet their needs. This will have to be created by dyslexics themselves.

- Changes in the dyslexic brain

Scientists have recorded differences in the dyslexic brain. Firstly, the left hemisphere that is usually larger, is smaller in dyslexics, is equal in size to the right hemisphere. Secondly, the thalamus, a vital communication centre that receives information from the senses and relays these to the cerebral cortex; has smaller neurons in those areas that are related to sight and hearing (the area most affecting dyslexics). Thirdly, the cerebral cortex, the master part of the brain, has extra cells. [3] No one seems to know what this means and some scientists hypothesise that the dyslexic brain is an inferior model that is fundamentally flawed, a throwback to a time when man did not need to read. But not Dr. Gordon Sherman PhD [4], a leader in the field of dyslexia research and education for over thirty years. This is what he thinks:

> Nature loves diversity .. Diversity propels evolution by enhancing a species' ability to adapt to changing environments.. While a dyslexic brain may not be ideally suited for processing certain sequential and linguistic information, perhaps its symmetry and connection differences constitute an ideal design for other kinds of processing. Teachers of children and adults with dyslexia often remark that many have unusual strengths [and] a disproportionate number may have exceptional strengths.. [5]

Dr. Sherman hypothesises that this brain is possibly a new evolutionary model. Many millions are affected - rough estimates are about 7% of people of the world's population. It seems that nature is experimenting and people like Dr. Sherman think that possibly the adaptations seen in dyslexics are stepping stones to more sophisticated and right-brain thinking in the future. This fits with esoteric thought.

- An opinion

Humanity evolves, developing different faculties one after another. The concrete mind and its power of analysis is currently being developed. But now and over-lapping this work, the next faculty of the abstract mind is being developed. This is an important statement for our topic because it gives credence to Sherman's hypothesis that the dyslexic brain is an evolutionary advancement.

---

1 IDA Board of Directors, Nov. 12, 2002.
2 http://www.beingdyslexic.co.uk/forums/index.php?showtopic=7745
3 Gathered from Dr. Gordon Sherman, Brain Research and Reading
4 http://www.thenewgrange.org/gordon-sherman/
5 http://www.greatschools.org/special-education/LD-ADHD/775-structural-brain-differences-in-kids-with-dyslexia.gs

> [The abstract mind is] the pattern building faculty, or the mind which works with the blue prints upon which the forms are modelled. [1]

Note the use of the words "the pattern building faculty", linking the abstract mind to the right brain. The abstract mind works with the concrete mind to help it grasp and interpret the unseen. This abstract mind comprehends or senses inner realities or truths that are not concrete or tangible. The mind of man is gradually evolving from thinking logically to reasoning more abstractly. This fits Sherman's hypothesis that the dyslexic brain favouring as it does right-brain activity, is possibly a new evolutionary model.

- Famous dyslexics

Nature compensates and what dyslexics seem to lack on one hand, they make up in a special area of talent or expertise. Alexander Faludy was born severe dyslexia. In 1998 he became the youngest undergraduate at the University of Cambridge. He overcame this impediment by having all his study books put onto tape. Famous scientists such as Albert Einstein, Thomas Edison and Michael Faraday are suspected by some of having the condition, but this is not proven. Diagnosed dyslexics are actor Anthony Hopkins, movie director Steven Spielberg, activist Erin Brockovich, singer writer John Lennon, chef Jamie Oliver, artist Pablo Picasso, neuroscientist John Skoyles and entrepreneur Richard Branson

- Astrology

The main planet to examine is Mercury, which is the primary significator of the mind and communication on all levels. It also rules the abstract mind - with Uranus and the intuition which is instant knowing. In dyslexics, Mercury will show how a person performs and copes.

Uranus, is also important. Dyslexics often seem to be very gifted and can excel in both the arts and science. Uranus rules science and evolution by giving the gift of spontaneous and independent activity.

Example of Dyslexia: Richard Branson

Branson's mind: when he was born, his mind was very introspective and he struggled to communicate with the outer world. It was a past-life and karmic thing. Dyslexia compounded this, making his situation more extreme. (Mercury is unaspected to all planets excepting to Saturn, semi-square Mercury, in the 12th house of self-undoing).

Branson suffered pain and isolation as a child. (Sun-Mercury in the 12H of isolation, with no major planet aspects). These are major psychological afflictions, which would incapacitate most people for life. Branson said he had hell at school. Dyslexia was the cause of his suffering. (Mercury rules the 3rd house of school and the bullying planet Mars, is in this house).

Branson's soul-purpose is represented by his Sun because it rules his Leo ascendant. This is most interesting, because it means that his sense of isolation and communication difficulty was part of his spiritual destiny and service. Perhaps the task of this most successful businessman was to show the world that dyslexia was no impediment to material world success.

It is obvious that Branson is an advanced soul. Apart from his ability to rise above adversity and entrepreneurial brilliance (which means his inner integration is in place), he is an ethical business magnate (a highly unusual type in the greedy business world of today) and a philanthropist who uses his money, power and influence to "do good in the world". [2] Uranus' influence flows through advanced souls (via the Sun in advanced Leo types) and this accounts for Branson's entrepreneurial brilliance and forward thinking vision.

This ends this section on Psychology Disorders. All humanity suffers from these problems. The next section covers those disorders peculiar to Mystics and Disciples.

---

1 Bailey, Alice A. Treatise on White Magic, 365
2 http://www.startupceo.co.za/2012/10/29/richard-branson-age-is-an-advantage/

3. PROBLEMS OF MYSTICS AND DISCIPLES [1]

There are three main divisions in this group:

1. Chakra development	2. Psychic Powers	3 Group problems
Chakra development causes energy imbalances that affect the nature.	Emotionally inclined mystics develop lower psychic powers and become deluded.	Some egos find it hard to integrate harmoniously into a group

1. PROBLEMS DUE TO CHAKRA DEVELOPMENT

Ordinary man is ruled by his lower cravings and consequently pours his force through the three lower centres associated with these cravings - the base, sacral and solar plexus. On the Path, there is an ordered transference of energy from lower to higher centres that causes problems.

1. Evolution of consciousness and transference of energy in the chakras

- First Transference – Sacral to Throat - 1st Initiation

The first transference lasts several lives. The centres below the diaphragm are fully awakened and active, with the solar plexus dominating the life. It receives energy streams from the base and sacral centres and when it begins to deflect them to the higher centres, it means the personality is now the highly intelligent citizen and aspirant. He is conscious of the dualism of his nature and is ready to tread the Probationary Path. [2]

    The heart and throat centres become active. Sacral force rises to the throat and solar plexus force to the heart. The latter transference is yet of so small a measure that the effect of the transference is almost negligible. This period is a long and very difficult one lasting several lives. But gradually group consciousness develops and man moves towards the 2nd Initiation.

- Second Transference – Solar Plexus to Heart - 2nd Initiation

In this period, the ajna centre becomes active and dominant so that personality life is selfish, powerful, but also very creative. This is the zenith of the personality life. All centres below the head are active and functioning. The centres below the diaphragm are subordinated to the throat and ajna centres and are conditioned by the ambitious man.

> The ajna centre is vivid and potent; the throat centre is intensely active and the heart centre is rapidly awakening. [3]

Powerful ambition replaces the life of feeling and mystical effort. This is an appropriate development designed to round out the nature. It is only temporary. In the current or in a future life the mystic will emerge again when the mind is fully awakened and desire for mental satisfaction is satiated. Then a life based on spiritual values will attract him again. For a period, he will be drawn to both the world of man and the world of souls.

> As yet, however, his reactions are still selfishly motivated though—at the same time—he is subject to cycles of vision and periods of spiritual effort. The mystical life is definitely attracting him. He is becoming the mystic. [4]

Gradually, as selfless service is expressed, the heart centre opens and draws up purified astral energy from the refined solar plexus chakra. This is the second transference.

---

1 Bailey, Alice A. Esoteric Psychology II, 520 - 622
2 Ibid, 525
3 Gathered from AAB. Esoteric Psychology II, 526
4 Bailey, Alice A. Esoteric Psychology II, 525

- Third Transference – Base to Crown - 3rd Initiation

In the spiritually advanced man the head centre is radiantly active. The soul pours its energy into all centres via the head. This awakens the base centre and draws all the psychic energies up to the head centre, up to the soul.

> (With) the awakening of the centre at the base of the spine. Then the great Polar opposites, as symbolised and expressed by the head centre (the organ of spiritual energy) and the centre at the base of the spine (the organ of the material forces) are fused and blended and from this time on the man is controlled only from above, by the soul.[1]

2. Problems caused through chakra transference

The reason why there is so much illness and nervous trouble in those who strive spiritually is because of the stress put on the physical body by the rapid shift of forces. Bailey said that:

> The widespread disease and ill-health found everywhere at this time is caused by a mass transference which is steadily going forward in the race.[2]

a. The solar plexus centre is highly active, releasing astral forces into humanity, causing fear, desire of a wrong kind and many other emotional upsets.

b. Over-activity of a lower centre overstimulates the organs in that area, with congestion and inflammation.

c. There is intense activity in the higher centre, reduced activity in the lower and the forces swing back and forth. This accounts for the uneven life of the aspirant. This results in congestion, inflammation and disease in the higher centre and devitalisation in the lower region.

d. A serious problem is the premature awakening of kundalini fire, the fire that animates Physical Plane life. It resides in the base chakra. As kundalini rises up the body, it steadily increases the vibration of all atoms and burns dross from the etheric body. This process occurs naturally with steady spiritual growth. But unwise breathing or spiritual exercises can prematurely awaken kundalini, resulting in body damage, insanity and even death. The golden rule is - leave kundalini alone!

Therapy: do not brood on the physical condition or on the region of transference. The practise of spiritual disciplines such as right-detachment and meditation will help stabilise the fluctuating energies, as will endeavouring to live a stable and practical life of service. Esoteric healing and chakra balancing will also help.

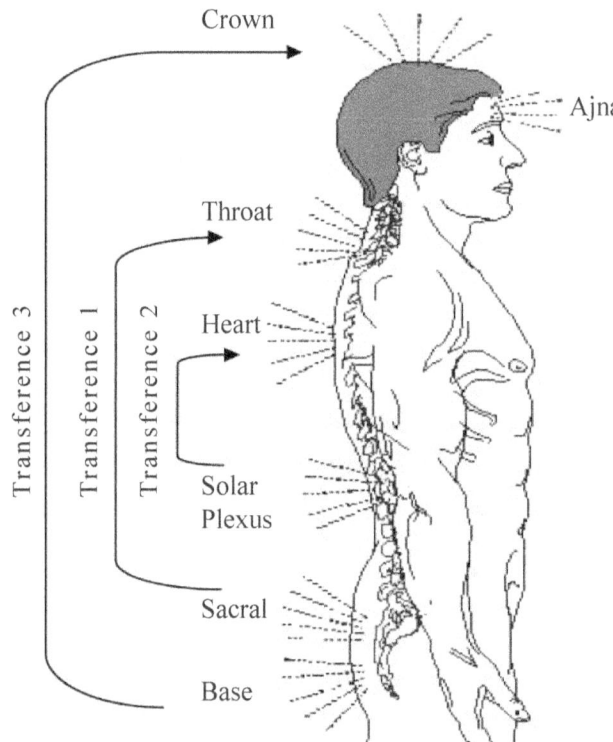

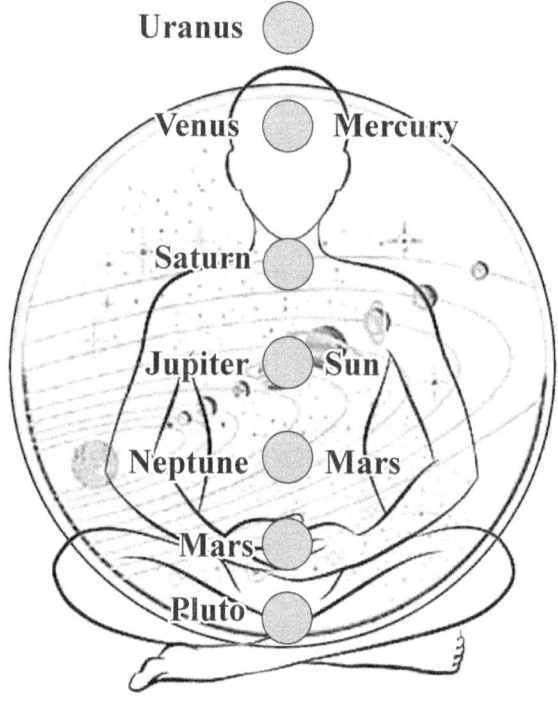

The planets in our solar system are the major chakras in the etheric body of the Solar Logos.

---
1 Bailey, Alice A. Esoteric Psychology II, 527
2 Ibid, 545

Chakras and Levels of Consciousness	Glands and disorders
1. CROWN. 1000 Petals. Occultist. Initiate. Master. Dominant after 3rd Initiation.[1] Relates man to spirit. Provides the soul its point of entry and exit in the body. From the crown, all centres are synthesised and when kundalini in the base chakra rises their force is transferred to the head centre. When this occurs, man is controlled only from above, by the soul. "At the 4th Initiation, the monad takes control and individual experience in the lower worlds is complete." [2]	Pineal gland. Problems: inflammation of the brain, tumours. In extreme cases premature awakening can lead to insanity.
2. Ajna. 96 Petals. Aspirant. Disciple. Mystic. Dominant after 2nd Initiation. The seat of personality power. Represents the highest form of creative intelligence in man. The organ of imagination. Comes alive prior to passing onto the Probationary Path.[3] 1st degree initiate: the ajna ruled personality is intelligent and effective on the Physical Plane, but focus is (still partially) materialistic and selfish. The ajna energies sweep down into the lower centres. 2nd degree initiate: when the disciple holds the mind "steady in the light", soul energy flows into the heart centre. It is fully functional by the time the third initiation is taken. [4]	Pituitary gland. Eyes, lower brain, nervous system, sinuses. Problems: headache, nerve difficulties, neuritis, serious eye trouble.
3. THROAT. 16 Petals. Creative Artists. All advanced humanity. The intelligentsia. The transference upwards of energy from the sacral centre to the throat - the 1st Transference, occurs as the physical appetites are being purified. All individuals focused in the higher centre are becoming mentally creative. This centre is related to the Mental Plane.	Thyroid gland. Alimentary canal, arms, bronchial tree, larynx, lymphatic system, shoulders, speech, trachea, upper lungs. Problems: breathing, speech.
4. HEART. 12 Petals. All types of spiritual people. Starts to becomes more dominant after the 1st Initiation, because this initiation relates man to the Buddhic Plane of intuition and the second divine aspect Love-Wisdom. As the heart centre begins to awaken under soul impulse it draws up the energies of the solar plexus, controlling the desire nature. It fully opens at the 4th Initiation.	Thymus gland. Arteries, breasts, capillaries, heart, lungs, vagus nerve, veins. Problems: AIDS, cardiovascular, autoimmune diseases.
5. SOLAR PLEXUS. 10 Petals. Average humanity. It is related to the Astral Plane and expresses feelings and desires from the crudest to the subtle. It works closely with the sacral and base centres, with desires focused in the lower appetites. In more advanced man it gives desire for recognition and for improved life quality. In the person approaching the 2nd Initiation it acts as a clearing ground for the energies of the lower centres, which begin to be gathered up by the solar plexus and transferred to the heart centre - the 2nd Transference.	Pancreas gland. Digestive organs, bowel, gallbladder, liver, spleen, stomach. Problems: cancers caused by repression of emotions digestive, emotional and nervous problems, skin disorders. .
6. SACRAL. 6 Petals. Low grade animal type of men. Below the 1st Initiation. Individuals focused in this centre focus on food and sex. At the 1st Initiation sacral energies begin to be raised to the throat centre - the 1st Transference. Eventually the creative output of the aspirant will work primarily though this higher point. The sacral centre is related to the four etheric subplanes of the Physical Plane.	The gonads. Etheric body, reproduction, sex. Problems: difficulty with conception, reproduction and sex, venereal diseases.
7. BASE. 4 Petals. People with powerful, selfish wills focus in this centre as well as in the ajna. This centre is related to the Physical Plane and vitalises the dense physical body structure. It is awakened in its true and final sense at the 3rd Initiation.	Adrenals. The back, bladder, bones, flesh, kidneys, skeleton, skin, teeth. Problems: with the adrenals, urinary tract and dense physical structure.

1 This chart is based on information from AAB Esoteric Healing, 45.
2 Gathered from Bailey, Alice A. Externalisation of the Hierarchy, 567
3 Bailey, Alice A. Esoteric Psychology II, 304
4 Bailey, Alice A. Esoteric Healing, 147

2. PSYCHIC POWERS

1. Problems concerning the Psychic Powers

There are two sets of powers latent in our equipment: lower animal powers and the higher Divine powers. Higher psychics are advanced disciples and initiates. Lower psychics are Atlantean in consciousness. They use solar plexus centre power, which opens the door to the Astral Plane.

Psychic Powers in the Animal, Human and Divine Kingdoms: *Esoteric Psychology II*, 559

Animal	Human	Divine
1. The four major instincts	*The five major instincts*	*The five transmuted instincts.*
a. Self preservation	Creative self-preservation	Immortality.
b. Sex	Sex. Human love	Attraction.
c. Herd instinct	Gregariousness	Group consciousness.
d. Curiosity	Enquiry, analysis, self-assertion	Evolutionary urge, Self-control
2. The Five senses	*The five senses*	*The five senses.*
a. Touch	Touch. Contact	Understanding.
b. Hearing	Hearing. Sound	Response to the Word.
c. Sight	Seeing, Perspective	The mystical vision.
d. Taste (embryonic)	Taste. Discrimination	Intuition
e. Smell (acute)	Smell, Emotional idealism	Spiritual discernment.
3. Lower psychic powers	*The human correspondences*	*Higher psychic powers.*
a. Clairvoyance	Extension through vision	The mystical vision.
b. Clairaudience	Extension through hearing	Telepathy. Inspiration.
c. Mediumship	Intercourse. Speech	Mediatorship.
d. Materialisation	Invention	Creativity.
e. Divination	Foresight. Planning	Prevision.
f. Healing through animal magnetism	Healing through science	Healing through spiritual magic.

1. Three groups of people consciously or unconsciously use the lower psychic powers.

a. Those whose evolutionary stage is low.
b. Those who brought them over from Atlantean times. In that ancient period humans fully expressed the lower psychic powers, along with animals. These should be left behind.
c. The mystic. Meditation and aspiration overstimulate the solar plexus centre, opening a door to the Astral Plane. Images may be of a very high order (angels, saints etc.). But if phenomena are seen, it is evidence that consciousness is working on the Astral Plane. This is where we learn to distinguish truth from error. Those who mistake the unreal for the real have not yet developed discrimination.

> In all cases .. where there is colour, form and phenomena analogous to .. that .. upon the physical plane then there is to be seen the "duplicating phenomena" of the astral plane. [1]

2. Psychism, so-called, can be divided into the following two groups:

Higher Psychism	*Lower Psychism*
Divine	Animal
Controlled	Uncontrolled
Positive	Negative
Intelligently applied	Automatic
Mediatorship	Mediumship [2]

---
1 Gathered from Bailey, Alice A. *Esoteric Psychology II*, 568
2 Bailey, Alice A. *Externalisation of the Hierarchy*, 8

3. Arresting the lower psychic powers

Atlantean (emotional in consciousness) Psychism

Cultivate a spirit of true humility; train the intellect to think, refuse to use these powers and reject all contacts or messages that feed the ego and the sense of being superior or special. This will eventually close the solar plexus centre and the open door to the Astral Plane. It will also atrophy that part of the inner mechanism that has made these powers available and cause them to die out. The true disciple and mystic is mentally polarised and vision is free from the deluding reactions of the solar plexus centre and Astral Plane.

Aryan (mental in consciousness) Psychism

a. If the astral door has been opened due to certain practises (such as "sitting for development"), these should be stopped and contact with those teaching them terminated. Focus on work and social obligations, physical plane interests and responsibilities. Leave devotional practices alone until the psyche has stabilised.

b. If the door is open because of inherited activities from previous lives and an over-active solar plexus centre, focus should be on building a strong and healthy physical body, emphasising higher goals and a life of service. Wearing and surrounding oneself with the colour yellow that stimulates mental activity will help.

c. In serious cases where there is a violent fight against the psychic activity, a nervous breakdown and loss of mental control, the person needs protective seclusion, rest and a light diet. Their trouble is not mental but is related to the solar plexus and should be treated as such.

Arresting Psychism in an advanced Mystic, Disciple and Occultist

In this case, the work must be more scientific and focused on balancing the centres.

2. Problems concerning the Development of Mystical Vision [1]

Mystical vision is the process of sensing the goal, of contacting the ideal and of visioning the many symbols that veil the soul. Mystical literature of all world religions is full of these visions. The mystical approach is the right way for many, provided it does not extend to hallucination and fanaticism.

1. Devitalisation

When mystics live entirely in the world of aspiration, drawn constantly upwards to that which is idealised, they become impractical and ungrounded. Energies that should be vitalising the physical body feed the forces of the astral body, or are diverted from the heart outwards, devitalising the physical body.

2. Delusion

This occurs when spiritual imaginings, wishes and longings completely absorb a mystic's attention to the detriment of common sense. Becoming obsessed by this powerful dream, they mistake it for reality. They suffer serious psychological difficulties that are induced by the ecstasy of their vision and some have even died. Such people are victims of a hallucination that has disrupted sane and healthy living.

Therapy: the psychologist should gently develop in the mystic a cycle of doubt, leading even to a temporary agnosticism. The result would be a rapid establishing of the desired equilibrium. Encourage a normal physical life with its ordinary interests, fulfilling obligations and responsibilities.

3. Delirium (modern term is "schizophrenia")

When delusion and devitalisation are chronic without inner control or right proportion, outer expression becomes abnormal ranging from fanaticism to sadism and insanity. The mystic is obsessed by his own peculiar thoughtform of truth and reality. He has only one idea in his head. His mind is not active for his brain has become the instrument of his astral nature and registers only his fanatical devotion and emotional obsession.

The following description of schizophrenia fits the esoteric description of delirium. It is a group of severe brain disorders in which people interpret reality abnormally. Schizophrenia may result in combinations of hallucinations, delusions and disordered thinking and behaviour. It is not a split or multiple personality disorder but refers to a disruption of the usual balance of emotions and thinking. Sufferers believe that something is real and true even when contrary evidence is shown. Logic and reason does not help. Experts say about 1% of the population are affected.

---

1 Bailey, Alice A. Esoteric Psychology II, 598-606

- Modern Delirium Subgroup: Paranoia

Paranoia is a mental condition characterized by delusions of persecution, unwarranted jealousy, or exaggerated self-importance. It may be an aspect of chronic personality disorder, of drug abuse, or of schizophrenia.

Therapy: In all problems where there is excess emotion, physical and mental activity is recommended. However, grounding the physical body is of the utmost importance. Recuperative periods should be spent amongst the beauty of nature and in sunbathing. Wearing all shades of violet and lavender will help to soothe the nervous system.

Where there is devitalisation, the sufferer should stop all spiritual practices and focus on physical pursuits. The psychologist should gently develop in the mystic a cycle of doubt, leading even to a temporary agnosticism. The result would be a rapid establishing of the desired equilibrium. Encourage a normal physical life.

If the damage is so extensive that it is irreparable, then only a new incarnation will retrieve the situation. The task then is to become aware of the mind's tendency to think delusory thought and to be practical in life approach. This includes making an effort to ground the spiritual vision in outer constructive service.

4. Abnormal detachment or dissociation - mystical-emotional types

This problem starts when mystics or emotional spiritually-inclined people see nothing but their vision and spend all their time registering that vision through dreaming, wishing, sexual longings and agonising aspiration. Such people can sever all normal relations with their surroundings and outer responsibilities, so that they live entirely in their manufactured world, detached and unmoved by people or life. The mental fortress becomes impenetrable to the soul and it may require a new incarnation to establish inner balance.

The modern term Dissociative Disorder covers many conditions. Here is a definition: "Someone with a dissociative disorder escapes reality in ways that are involuntary and unhealthy. The symptoms of dissociative disorders — ranging from amnesia to alternate identities — usually develop as a reaction to trauma and help keep difficult memories at bay". [1]

- Dissociation Subgroup 1: Split or Multiple Personalities, Possession

The parent term today for split and multiple personalities is "dissociation" and sometimes "alternate personalities". The medical cause is given as "identity fragmentation". With the Alternate Personality Disorder, different personas or fragments of the same persona, appear to rotate through consciousness.

a. Esoteric Cause 1: Aversion to life

The basic cause is the soul's dislike or avoidance of life. It is a problem of "duality". The universe is dual; it is both Spirit and Matter. So is man, he is both spirit and body and is currently in the process of dissociating from the personality and identifying with the soul. This natural technique of evolution is being used unnaturally at times to help people deal unnaturally with life difficulties and trauma. A precedent for this was set in the dawn of man's history, an incident called the "Fall of the Angels" These angels refused to incarnate because of their aversion for the bodies they had to inhabit, considering them too gross.

Aversion is a reaction that arises when we cannot get what we want. It is the opposite of "attachment". We become attached to objects or people we like and avoid those we dislike or hate. But if this avoidance tendency becomes so extreme that it interferes with normal day to day function, a serious problem has arisen.

b. Esoteric Cause 2: Weak Etheric Connection

It is possible for souls who have a great aversion to incarnation but who are already here, to withdraw. One obvious way is to kill the physical body. But the condition being analysed is when consciousness withdraws, leaving the body alive. This latter is possible where there is a weak connection between the etheric energy field and the physical body, which means that the owner of the body only has a weak grip upon it. Mystics are particularly affected and the problem is widespread.

The problem of a weak etheric link will be compounded if the person is also doing mystical meditations which intensely yearn for union with God or the Divine. This throws open the Astral Plane door.

> The impact of the higher spiritual forces upon the .. mystically motivated people is producing serious and widespread trouble, breaking down protective etheric barriers and throwing the doors wide open on to the astral plane. [2]

---
1 www.mayoclinic.org/diseases
2 Bailey, Alice A. Esoteric Psychology II, 487

If this happens, consciousness may slip out, by design or accidentally; leaving the body open for invasion. Bodies can be taken over (possessed) by foreign entities, which then communicate through the vehicle.

> Sometimes this possession alternates between the two individuals concerned. Sometimes more than two are concerned and several persons upon the inner side of life use the same physical body. [1]

If the owner struggles to reclaim the body, then he or she comes through for as long as the connection is held. Otherwise, if the soul does not want to stay, the body is left vacant for any passing entity to occupy.

c. Astrology

There are several planets and signs that are associated with dissociation problems.

- Gemini: it is related to the etheric body [2] and is the intermediary as far as essentials are concerned, between the soul and body. As previously said, possession happens sometimes when a body is left empty because the connection to the etheric vehicle is weak, enabling its owner to separate off from the etheric.
- Mercury: it rules the concrete mind and message relaying. In dissociation problems the concrete mind's normal function which relays information from the outer world via the senses to the mind and vice versa, is impaired. Consciousness has split off from mind and has retreated into its own safe imaginary world or place on the Astral Plane of delusion. Mercury's situation in the chart is central to understanding why a soul should choose to dissociate. Mercury also rules the etheric vehicle, through Gemini. [3]
- The Moon: it rules the form nature and energy circulation round and through the etheric vehicle. [4] It also rules the past and it will show if the escapist impulse came through from another life.
- Neptune: it gives hyper-sensitivity and a yearning for something higher and finer. Misused, an aversion to life could arise.
- Mars: it "is the planet which rules and controls the physical vehicle". [5] Mars also rules the solar plexus chakra (with Neptune). It is through this centre that escape is made away from the physical world into the emotional. Possession cannot happen when the mind is stronger than the emotions.

In emotional types, afflictions to Mercury, the Moon and the ascendant which is related to the new incarnation, may symbolise a weak etheric connection.

Example of Multiple Personalities: Chris Costner Sizemore (Three Faced of Eve fame)

There is evidence from Sizemore's bio's and astrology that she was Atlantean (emotionally ruled) in consciousness and that she brought this problem in from another life. (Moon square Neptune. These two planets represent Atlantean consciousness.) This escapist pattern dominated her consciousness (Moon-Neptune are on the 10H - 1H angles).

Neptune on the ascendant weakened the soul's grip on the physical body and indicates a wide-open Astral Plane door which permitted entry to discarnate entities.

Her consciousness and mind were not strong enough to withstand psychic invasion. (Sun square Pluto in Cancer, a sign related to astralism. Mercury weakened in watery Pisces that is related to the Astral Plane. Moon trine Mercury indicates the ease with which astralism dominated the mind).

The pattern for a weak etheric-body connection is present. (Moon square Neptune; Mercury square Mars the physical body in Gemini, a sign related to the etheric). Consequently, Sizemore by choice or by coercion, found it easy to vacate the body.

Therapy: the remedy for Atlantean people with these problems is always the same. Avoid all spiritual practises and live a full physical life attending carefully to the details of family and life responsibilities. Developing the mind through study helps to build up mental strength.

---
1 Bailey, Alice A. Esoteric Psychology II, 420
2 Bailey, Alice A. Esoteric Astrology II, 352
3 Gathered from Bailey, Alice A. Esoteric Astrology, 352
4 Bailey, Alice A. Esoteric Healing, 143 The etheric vehicle from the circulatory angle, is governed by the Moon, as it veils Vulcan.
5 Bailey, Alice A. Esoteric Astrology, 210

- Dissociation Subgroup 2: Sudden Infant Death Syndrome (SIDS)

> Death.. is a great and universal heritage; all forms die, for such is the law of life [1]

SIDS is the unexplained death, usually during sleep, of a seemingly healthy baby. It is sometimes called crib death. The exact cause is unknown yet to science.

During normal sleep, we "die" to the physical plane. The consciousness thread is withdrawn and the owner of the body travels elsewhere. The life-thread remains intact so that the dweller can return to the body. In SIDS the consciousness thread withdraws at sleep and at the same time or sometime later, so does the life thread.

Early withdrawal from incarnation can be an intelligent decision made by the soul for a specific karmic or growth experience purpose. SIDS seems to fit this category exactly. In this case, souls deliberately leave the doorway into and out of life open, to facilitate an early death. The motivating cause is to expunge individual, family or group karmic debts. This karmic debt may not belong specifically to the soul who has made an early departure but belong to the bereft parents.

> [In] cases of sudden death. There the activity is the result of the destroyer, or the first divine aspect .. individual karmic necessity may not be involved .. [there may be] .. karmic group involvement, or .. relationships and obligations established in past lives... on occasion the "soul may leave the door of protection open so that the forces of death itself may enter anew .. in order more rapidly to obliterate past penalties" [2]

The following quote will be shocking to those who hold to the sanctity of life. The master Djwhal Khul said that sometimes an advanced soul will extinguish the life of its form if it is "not normal". This includes infants as well as the elderly. Esoterically then, the fight by modern science to keep alive very early born and undeveloped babies, or people in comas or in a vegetative state no matter what, is a violation of the natural Laws of Nature. Note that he is not advocating suicide.

> Frequently, today, lives are preserved.. that could be well permitted liberation. They serve no useful purpose and cause much pain and suffering to forms which nature (left to herself) would not long use and would extinguish. Through our overemphasis on the value of form life and through the universal fear of death and through our uncertainty as to the fact of immortality and also through our deep attachment to form, we arrest the natural processes and hold the life, which is struggling to be free, confined to bodies quite unfitted to the purposes of the soul.. This preservation is, in the majority of cases, enforced by the subject's group and not by the subject himself—frequently an unconscious invalid, an old person whose response apparatus of contact and response is imperfect, *or a baby who is not normal.* [3]

The means to make this early exit seems to be linked to the pineal gland. Normally, this gland, which is the physical plane anchorage of the soul, remains active until the infant is firmly anchored in the incarnation.

> the pineal gland in the head. This remains active during infancy and until the will-to-be is sufficiently established so that the incarnating person is firmly anchored in physical incarnation. [4]

But if it is the soul's design that the physical incarnation should be terminated after only a few weeks or months, then at the appropriate time, a signal is sent from the soul to terminate the connection to the pineal gland causing physical body death. But remember, the soul lives on to have another incarnation when the time or conditions are right.

Astrology Planets and Signs involved:
- The Sun: because the sutratma, the life thread, is anchored in the heart and the Sun rules the heart.
- Gemini, Mercury and the Moon: because they govern the etheric body which withdraws at death.
- Uranus: because its 7th ray governs the physical etheric plane and its action is sudden. It is also a ruler of the crown chakra, of which the pineal gland is its physical plane anchorage.
- Saturn: it is the Lord of Karma.
- Pluto: it is the Lord of Death.
- Venus: which represents the soul and perhaps the ascendant which represents soul purpose.

---

1 Bailey, Alice A. Esoteric Healing, 233
2 Ibid, 471-472
3 Ibid, 350-351
4 Ibid, 145

Example of SIDS child died at 4 months of age. Chart from Astrodatabank #14675

This was a karmic life for this soul, which planned for an early death. The astrological evidence is as follows. (The soul-purpose ascendant is in Capricorn, ruled by Saturn the Lord of Karma. It is the ruler of the chart, that is, of the physical incarnation. Saturn is in the 8th house of death, inconjunct the ascendant the soul-purpose point, which is also the physical body birth point).

There seems to have been a problem with the heart. (Saturn is in Leo, which rules the heart. Often this indicates a heart impairment. To support this hypothesis, the Sun is in the 12th house, indicating hospitalisation and is afflicted by Mars, Uranus and Neptune).

The life thread is anchored in the heart, which in the case of SIDS has an early withdrawal. The early death and sudden withdrawal was part of the soul's plan. (Venus the soul, is t-square Uranus {sudden release}, because of a karmic cause {Saturn in 8H of death, inconjunct the ascendant}. Uranus also rules the pineal gland through which death can come).

There is a deliberately weakened connection between the physical body (ascendant) and the etheric body, allowing early death to occur. (Mercury conjunct the ascendant, square Pluto, Lord of Death).

What is behind this? Why a SIDS incarnation? It appears to be a lesson for the parents. A hypothesis is that the parents in a previous life (Moon and nodes fall in the 10th/ 4th houses), because of social lifestyle choices, perhaps drugs (Moon in Libra semi-square Neptune), ignored a child which suffered as a result (Moon opposite Chiron, conjunct south node). The karmic experience was for the parents, to learn to have greater appreciation and care for any child which should come into their care.

- Dissociation Subgroup 3: Autism (autism spectrum disorder, ASD)

ASD is defined as a serious developmental problem characterized by great difficulty in communicating and forming relationships because of avoidance and dissociation tendencies. These are 5th ray "cleavage" traits - one part of the nature is out of touch with another, bringing ASD under its auspices. Here is a quote.

> In the activity of [the 5th ray] will be found eventually the source of many psychological disorders and mental trouble. Cleavage [causes] **gaps in the relation of the physical body to the subtle bodies which show as imbecilities and psychological troubles.** [1]

In ASD, brain and nervous system function is impaired. Scientists who have studied autism say there are fewer alpha and beta waves, which points to under-connectivity especially in important strategic areas that have to do with the emotions and relating. They now believe autism is a genetic disorder. This also fits with the esoteric understanding that individual disease is mostly karmic and therefore comes through an inherited gene.

a. It is also possible we are dealing with souls who greatly dislike physical incarnation and who try to avoid it and this creates the cleavage.

> The withdrawal of the self-conscious aspect of the dweller in the body .. due to that dweller's great dislike for physical incarnation. [2]

Some may be finding a doorway into other worlds and escaping through that door. The physical body remains healthy and strong, but only minimal response is present.

> when the "doorway out into the other worlds" is discovered and becomes .. a way of escape from the difficulties of life and a short cut out of conscious physical experience. The connection then between the mystic and his physical vehicle .. gets looser and looser until the man spends most of his time out of his body in a condition of semi-trance or a deep sleep condition. [3]

b. Another option is that while normal at first, a child withdraws inwardly and refuses to engage with the world in the first few vital years of life. If so, its ability to do so could be permanently impaired because of damage to the central nervous system activities. An explanation comes from Patanjali's Eastern classic on Raja Yoga (Bailey version "Light of the Soul", page 21).

---

1 Bailey, Alice A; Esoteric Healing, 302.
2 Bailey, Alice A. Esoteric Psychology II, 419
3 Bailey, Alice A. Esoteric Psychology II, 610

In this section, Patanjali is warning that an incorrect meditation technique could damage brain-nerve-sense activity. However, the matter discussed is also relevant for our discussion on autism.

> Book I:10 The vrittis are those activities of the mind [that relate] the sense employed and that which is sensed. Passivity (sleep) is based upon the quiescent state of the vrittis (or upon the non-perception of the senses.) By withdrawing himself from active sense perception, by no longer utilising the "outward-going" consciousness and by abstracting that consciousness from the periphery to the centre, he can bring on a condition of passivity,—a lack of awareness.. a form of trance. [1]

Simply, the vrittis are nerve activities that convey messages to and from the brain so that we are aware of what is going on around us. Psychological dissociation - whether through an incorrect meditation technique or just by refusing to engage with the outer world, is dangerous because it will impair the vrittis - nerve functionality. Nerves (nadis) linking the posterior parts of the brain with the frontal socialising lobe, begin to atrophy, isolating the person from the outer world. This is why early intervention is vital to turn autism around in a child. It can make dramatic improvements. Greater success seems to come with programs using love, play and encouragement that invite the child to engage. Love seems to be the key. Emotionally sensitive children have an absolute need for a home structure that is loving and orderly. This will help them feel comfortable and encourage them to stay.

Look for communication problems that translate into brainwave and nervous system under-connectivity - afflictions to Mercury and Venus, or to planets in Gemini and Aquarius.

Example of Autism: Jett Travolta

Travolta had a classic aversion to life pattern in his chart - the Sun was square Neptune. He brought through a heavy pattern from past-life incarnations via his Moon - a sense that form-life means death (Moon square Pluto, Moon in the 8th house of death). The power of the soul to influence the life was weak (Venus in detriment in Aries. Ruler of Aries Mars in the watery sign Pisces). A weak etheric connection, enabled consciousness to slip away. (Mercury representing the etheric in Pisces, square ascendant). He had seizures - a result of a weak etheric connection. (Mars wide opposition to Moon, the other ruler of the etheric, in Mercury's sign, Virgo). The door to the Astral Plane was open at birth. (Mercury in Pisces square ascendant. Pisces-Neptune are related to the Astral Plane. Neptune square the Sun). There was a malfunction between mind and brain (Mercury semi-square "Saturn - brain").[2] It was not as severe as it could have been. Jett was high-functioning. As a soul, he reversed withdrawal and decided to stay. He was surrounded by love, which was what he needed to heal childhood wounds (Venus trine Chiron), incurred in another life.

Soul purpose: this was to find mental and life balance, to be fully grounded in the incarnation and in the physical body. (Esoteric ruler of the Sagittarius ascendant, Earth, is in Libra, opposite the Sun.)

3. Problems with the Revelation of Light and Power [3]

The problem of the light in the head occurs in the advanced man, aspirant or disciple who has learnt to focus mentally and who is meditating. The inflow of the light of the soul brings the brain cells into functioning activity. The pituitary body is involved; the ajna centre is active and is merging its field with the head centre. The unified magnetic field can become so brilliant it is seen with the eyes closed or sensed as a diffused misty light inside or outside the head. Sometimes physical blindness and poor sight is due to the presence of this light, unrecognised and unused, producing an effect upon the eyes and optic nerve.

This is a physiological and not a psychic power and is quite different to clairvoyance. Not all occult students see this light. It depends upon temperament, the quality of the physical cells of the brain, the nature of the work and the extent of the magnetic field. Second Ray types are more easily affected. Problems will not occur if people are active in service work.

Therapy: make no effort to see the light in the head. Use the mind and energies in selfless service.

---

1 Bailey, Alice A. Light of the Soul, 21-22
2 Bailey, Alice A. Esoteric Astrology, 299
3 Bailey, Alice A. Esoteric Psychology II, 606-615

3. DISEASES CONNECTED WITH GROUP THOUGHT [1]

When people go into group work and still have aggressive and prideful egos, when they have not done the inner work or developed the inclusive qualities; then they usually cause trouble. They want the influence and power of the teacher or leader of the group and make trouble to get it. If they do not curb these tendencies, they influence others to think and feel like they do, expanding their discontent and jealousy. Shut off from real group interactions they may be ejected from the group. Or what is more damaging, they destroy the group and psychically harm the teacher. As decentralisation occurs there is an easier response to the higher influences of group work and people make the necessary adaptations to fit in.

1. The group problem of criticism

The life of a group hinges upon the central figures in the group and they pay the price for any group weakness. From every side and in every group there streams in on the group leader directed criticism, poisonous thoughts, untruths, destructive gossip, unspoken jealousies, frustrated ambitions, desire to see the leader superseded by themselves or by someone else and many other forms of selfishness and mental pride. The "sitting in judgment" and idle critical gossip can not only kill the leader through accumulated poison and distress but also kill the group life. Criticism is a virulent poison and group criticism, voiced or strongly felt will eventually damage the criticiser, but will hurt the one who is criticised more. One ambitious, disloyal person can wreck a group. One selfless, noncritical, consecrated person can swing the group into successful work.

In such a case, group leaders must continue the work, retreat within, speak the truth with love and refuse to become bitter. They have the challenging task of waiting until members learn the lessons of cooperation, silence and loving appreciation of the problems with which all group leaders are faced. It also provides an opportunity for the leader to work off karma.

Therapy: practise the art of silence. One cannot enter the higher spiritual realms until there has been restraint of speech and control of thought, with consequent harmlessness on the Physical Plane. We imprison ourselves on the planet by what we think, say and do when motivated by selfishness or spite. Each time we stop thinking a negative thought, each time we stop speaking wrong words, little by little, those ties that hold us are severed. Appropriate silence is the hallmark of the disciple. Replace a judgmental thought with a loving one. Learn to preserve that inner silence that promotes holiness.

2. The group problem of "smothering" and of the "umbilical cord"

The reverse of the previous problem occurs when the devotion and personality love of group members smothers the leader. Piscean age people (in consciousness), can remained attached to the group and drain the life of the leaders if the umbilical cord is not cut. Or, when aroused to hate or dislike, can violently disrupt the tie, causing much distress and unnecessary suffering to the group as well as to the leader.

Therapy: group members must be independent and leave the teacher space in which to move. When training instruction is complete, the cord must be cut. Then the group can progress and live its life as a self-directing agent even when the leader passes away.

This ends this section on the Problems of Mystics and Disciples. These disorders primarily concern the etheric centres, delusion and group work. Living a balanced life helps the first condition, the development of discrimination the second, and harmlessness is the outstanding quality that harmonises all our interactions with others.

---
[1] Ibid, 617-621

CHAPTER 4: THE SEVEN RAYS

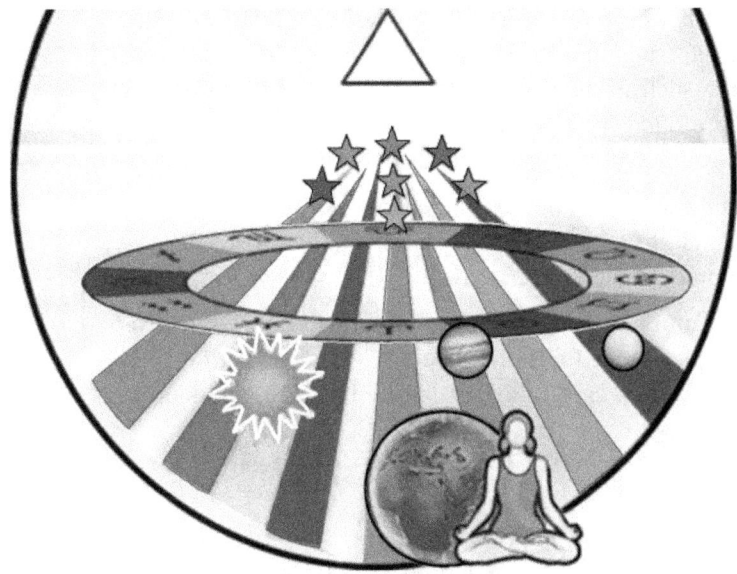

We are taught in the esoteric philosophy that seven great divine Emanations, Aeons or Spirits (in Whom we live and move and have our being) came forth from God at the time of the Creation. The same teaching can also be traced in the Holy Bible. Upon one or other of these seven Rays, the souls of all forms of life are to be found as well as the forms themselves. These seven rays produce the seven major psychological types. [1]

---

1 Bailey, Alice A. Discipleship in the New Age I, xiii

1. THE SEVEN RAYS AND PSYCHOLOGY

The Primordial Seven - also known as Seven Archangels, are the source of power and light for the Seven Rays in our solar system. Streaming through "seven stars of the Great Bear" [1] **via the twelve zodiacal constellations and planets, the Seven Rays build and animate all life in our solar system. Each ray has its own unique vibration and colour and they build and condition all forms - all physical bodies, soul and spiritual vehicles. All find their rhythm and pattern from one or other of these rays.**

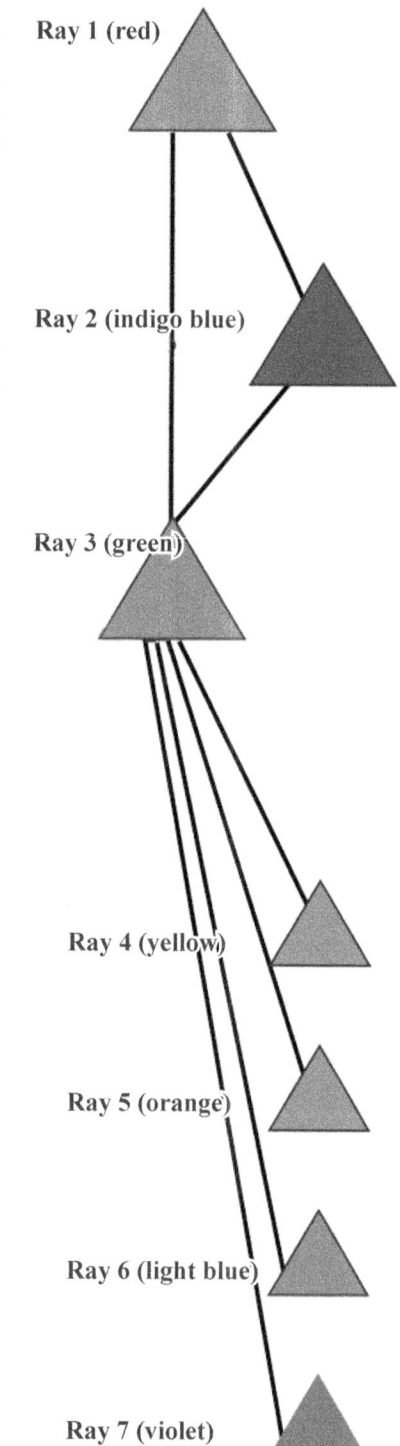

These seven forces are sometimes referred to as seven intelligent beings or Ray Lords. They are obedient to instruction coming from the Highest Source - God, transmitted by intermediaries such as the Seven Archangels, to manifest the Plan of God on earth. In a very profound sense, they represent Divine Consciousness and the heavenly "brain" through which the commands of God are expressed.

> The seven rays are the sum total of the divine Consciousness, of the Universal Mind.. Symbolically, They may be regarded as constituting the brain of the divine Heavenly Man. [2]

The rays come into activity and pass out again, under the rhythmic impulse of nature. In other words, just as we (as souls) use our physical bodies and leave when the physical body dies, so do the rays come in and provide and condition forms and then depart.

1. Three Major Rays of Aspect [3]

The major rays are the forces of Deity, the minor rays are off-shoots of these. The major rays create a desire to synthesise the life and unite with the whole, whether this is in an inclusive and higher sense, or selfishly for egotistical reasons.

> The three great rays, which constitute the sum total of the divine manifestation, are.. in their totality, the manifested Deity, the Word in incarnation. They are the expression of the creative purpose and the synthesis of life, quality and appearance. [4]

- **Ray 1 of Power or Will.**

This is the force of the 1st spiritual aspect, the power of God. It governs life and death. In human psychology, it gives an impressive will, power to endure and rulership ability.

- **Ray 2 of Love-Wisdom.**

This is the primary ray of our Solar Logos, which means love and wisdom are the primary qualities being developed in the system. The other six rays are subrays of this Second Ray. This makes them no less powerful in their effect. The Lord of this ray is in close touch with the heart of Deity.

This force cultivates and colours consciousness in all forms in all kingdoms of nature, developing the mind so that wisdom can come to the fore. To man, it gives the gift of love and wisdom.

---

1 Bailey, Alice A. Esoteric Astrology, 85
2 Bailey, Alice A. Esoteric Psychology I, 59
3 Ibid, 22-28
4 Ibid, 158

- **Ray 3 of Active Intelligence.**

It is the force of the 3rd aspect, fertile, adaptable and vigorous. Its gift to man is physical endurance and an active intelligence that is comfortable navigating the material and financial worlds.

2. The Four Minor Rays of Attribute.

All the rays resonate with one of the 7 planes: Ray (R) 1 with the Logoic Plane, R2 with the Monadic and R3 with the Atmic Plane. The lowers rays are synthesised by ray 3 and the bodies they energise are coordinated from the Atmic level. The lower rays (related to the Mental Plane (R5), Astral Plane (R6) and Physical Plane (R7); are more concerned with the details of man's personality life; ray 4 (Buddhic Plane), brings man into harmony with God.

> The major Rays of Aspect embody the entire story; the minor Rays of Attribute contribute the detail in process and enterprise. [1]

- **Ray 4 of Harmony, Beauty and Art.**

It gives the potential for harmony, produced through conflict. In man it fosters a love of beauty and gives the gift of being able to combine sounds, colour and music, so that the creative power and beauty of God can manifest on earth. This ray is now coming into power.

- **Ray 5 of Concrete Knowledge and Science.**

It gives the attribute of concrete knowledge through which man can concretise his concepts and build thoughtforms and thus bring his visions, dreams and ideas into being. Its influence is active currently.

- **Ray 6 of Devotion and Idealism.**

Here is a detailed description: "Devotion grows out of and is the fruit of dissatisfaction, plus the use of the faculty of choice. According to the depths of a man's discontent and of his power to see clearly, he passes from one point of temporary satisfaction to another, each time demonstrating his devotion to a desire, to a personality, to an ideal and to a vision, until he finally unifies himself with the .. Oversoul or God". [2]

- **Ray 7 of Ceremonial Order or Magic.**

This ray is now coming into power. Forced regimentation is its early and lower manifestation, a precursor to the appearance of divine order.

3. Three Objectives in Studying the Rays

a. It throws light upon history.
b. It clarifies our knowledge of man.
c. It gives a practical method of analysis to apply on ourselves and others. The Master Djwhal Khul made a profound statement when he gave an esoteric interpretation of the meaning of "psychology".

> The true meaning of "psychology" is the "word of the soul." It is the sound, producing an effect in matter, which a particular ray may make. [3]

In this statement, we get the sense of God being creative in the universe. Its seven tones or rays radiate out, creating and colouring the consciousness of all that exists.

The goal of Esoteric Psychology is to bring the personality ray into harmony with the soul ray, then with the Monadic Ray, prior to integration with the expansiveness of Deity. It is a matter of synchronising man's vibration with the harmony of the whole. Disciples are asked to introduce this new science of consciousness into mainstream psychology.

> You belong to the new school which is entrusted with the task of producing the new, esoteric psychology, based upon the five rays which are manifesting through every human being—the soul ray, the personality ray and the rays of the three bodies of the personality. [4]

---

1 Bailey, Alice A. Esoteric Astrology, 631
2 Bailey, Alice A. Education in the New Age, 22
3 Bailey, Alice A. Esoteric Psychology I, 8
4 Bailey, Alice A. Discipleship in the New Age I, 644

RAY I: WILL-POWER

Major ray: 1st Aspect, 1st Logos, electric fire, the colour red.

Energy: it builds and destroys, a boundless power that is destructive and hard. It is also the dynamic germinating force seeding new life. In man, it confers natural power, great inner fortitude and a rocklike ability to endure in face of all obstacles. It is the ray of the occultist and of born leaders.

Some of the Names of the Lord of Ray One: Lord of Death; Liberator from Form; The Fiery Element producing shattering; The Will that breaks into the Garden; The Ravisher of Souls; The Finger of God; The Breath that Blasts; The Lightning which Annihilates; The Most High; Lord of the Burning Ground.

Ray 1 Soul in control: disciples express ray 1 force with dynamic power, purpose, strength, courage and truthfulness arising from absolute fearlessness. Prepared to stand alone they are steadfast and can endure against all obstacles. Their will is to achieve spiritual liberation, freedom and right human relations for all.

- Vocations: leaders, managers, supervisors, politics, the forces. Any career requiring great will power, strength, stamina and the ability to stand firm in the face of all obstruction. To destroy if necessary.
- Spiritual conscience: to preserve spiritual principles and values.
- Greatest contribution: strengthening and liberating others.
- Goals: to be powerful and benevolent leaders who serve the highest good and free people from bondage and oppression.
- Most Joyous Activity: to discard all nonessentials and be in perfect freedom.
- Sense of sacredness: the exhilaration at being in the presence of the power of Deity and identification with the One Self,
- Heart's desire: to be *The One and only*.

Ray 1 unregenerated personality: it is a law unto itself, proud, ambitious for power, wilful, hard, arrogant, obstinate, angry and dominating. Full of self-importance, it wants to control others. Liking isolation, determined to do things entirely on its own and its way, it tolerates no interference. It calls attention to itself as being the first and best in everything. It asserts its authority by intimidating opponents with its power and annihilates all opposition. It takes charge noticeably, strutting arrogantly, trampling over anyone foolish enough to get in its way. Gathering followers easily, it will use them as weapons to get its way if necessary.

Ray 1 Mind: an intense, fast and powerful mind that synthesises facts, focuses on principles and that sees the broad picture. Laser-like with diamond clear thought processes, it easily separates out the essential from nonessential and concentrates, organises and prioritises. It is independent, outspoken, decisive and firm in thought and speech. Its weaknesses are jumping to conclusions, making assumptions and aggression.

Ray 1 Astral Body: (uncommon, disciples only. Seven disciples in Djwhal Khul's [DK] group had this field).[1] With a fiery and intense emotional field, these disciples are not "touchy-feely" people. Standoffish, they have difficulty relating emotionally with others. The intense power of this field could erupt periodically with volcanic outbursts.

Strengths

Courage, detachment, fearlessness, independence, large mindedness, strength of will. Dynamic power to lead, govern, direct and initiate processes; power to destroy and liberate old forms, to establish and enforce the law; power to synthesise and centralise, to preserve values. It gives independence and detachment.

Weaknesses

Angry, arrogant, control issues, cruel, hard, impatient, inhibited, isolationist, power-hungry, separative, stubborn, unrelenting ambition and pride, violent, wilful.

Famous figures

Adolf Hitler, Anwar Sadat, Bismarck, Thomas Carlyle, Charlemagne, Franklin Roosevelt, Hercules, Nikita Khrushchev, General Kitchener, Mikhail Gorbachev, Margaret Thatcher, Mohandas Gandhi, Mussolini, Napoleon, General Patton, Paul Keating, Walt Whitman, Winston Churchill.

Signs

Aries

Leo

Capricorn

Planets

Vulcan

Pluto

---

1 Based on the chart later in the section "Rays of the Tibetan's Disciples". Data is from Bailey, Alice A. Discipleship in the New Age I and Michael Robbins' "Tapestry of the Gods".

Ray 1 Physical-Etheric Body: (uncommon, disciples). It is lanky but steely strong; a stiff, awkward body that avoids human contact. Lean and mean is a good description. The ray 1 brain expresses ideas sharply and assertively.

Ray 1 Soul-Personality Integration Technique - ACLRI Method

Alignment. The ray 1 personality is powerful and is ruthless in its fight to get to the top. It cries:

> The love of power must dominate. There must also be repudiation of those forms which wield no power.

A driving force impels it forward.

> Stand up. Press outward into life. Achieve a goal. For you, there must be not a circle, but a line. Prepare the form. Let the eyes look forward, not to either side. Let the ears be closed to all the outer voices and the hands clenched, the body braced and mind alert.

But eventually, the pinnacle of the personality life begins to exhaust itself. Then, unable to find life satisfaction, the searcher turns within and hears with the inner voice, the soul ...

> Emotion is not used in furthering the Plan. Love takes its place.

Crisis. Karmic retribution brings a major crisis - those who destroy are eventually destroyed. Alone, depressed, discouraged and in mental pain, an inner plea for assistance is made. Only then will the soul respond.

Light. In the ensuing quiet, soul light streams in and reveals the destruction and devastation the person has been responsible for, the arid isolation of the life; but also, the next step forward and the required developmental steps.

- Vices to eliminate: pride, isolationism, self-pity, use of power to destroy and control, arrogance and insensitivity to people's feelings.
- Virtues to cultivate: tenderness, humility, sympathy, tolerance, patience and inclusiveness.
- Use of the ray 1 integration word *"inclusiveness"* to soften the hardness.

Revelation. The disciple finds his or her part to play in the Spiritual Plan, a heart centred vocation. Ray 1 souls lead the fight for the higher and greater good.

> The symbol of a moving point of light appears above the brow. The keynote of the life though uttered not, yet still is clearly heard: 'I move to power. I am the One. We are a Unity in power. And all is for the power and the glory of the One.[1]

Integration. Soul-personality integration produces a world leader. Integration into the soul ashram occurs, a brotherhood of wise and enlightened beings. The words of power "I Assert the Fact" facilitate this process.

Mahatma Gandhi   *Abraham Lincoln*   *Joseph Stalin*

---

[1] Gathered from Bailey, Alice A. Esoteric Psychology II, 351-2

Integration Techniques
EPII 345-377

These are spiritual development formulas. They describe how the soul integrates and brings the personality ray into alignment with itself, prior to its fusion with the soul ray. The first part of the technique shatters the personality life; the second part applies the integrating aspect. Only integrated personalities should use the formulas.

The basis of this technique is the ACLRI process:

Alignment: personality alignment with the soul begins.

Crisis: life crises force the aspirant to turn to the soul.

Light: illuminating soul light enables the next step to be seen.

Revelation: the soul reveals that part of the Plan the aspirant can contribute to.

Integration: of soul and personality rays, of the disciple into his or her soul group.

Jewel
Diamond

Symbols
Crown
Diamond
Eagle
Flame
Hammer
Lightning Bolt
Lion
Mountain
Point within the Circle
Sickle
Spear
Straight Line
Sword
Volcano

Deviant Art

Love Types

Strengths

Attractive, compassionate, composed, empathetic, exquisite sensitivity, faithful, inclusive, loving, magnetic, patient, serene, sympathetic, tactful, tolerant, wise. Power to salvage, redeem and heal through love.

Weaknesses

Binds people through guilt because of an unrelenting need for love. Emotions expressed indiscriminately, excessive love of comfort, fearful, hypersensitive, impressionable, inferiority complex, non-assertive, over attachment, overprotective, self-pitying, vulnerable.

Wisdom types

Strengths

Clear perception and understanding, intelligence, power to teach, heal and illumine. Love of pure truth.

Weaknesses

Coldness, indifference, over absorbed in study, scorns mental limitation in others.

Famous Figures

Abraham Maslow, Albert Schweitzer, Alice Bailey, Buddha, Carl Jung, Christ, Mother Teresa, Plato, Pythagoras, Sigmund Freud.

RAY II: LOVE – WISDOM

Major ray: 2nd Aspect, 2nd Logos, solar fire, the colour indigo blue

Energy: an inclusive, enfolding, healing energy that embraces all. Its movement is spiral-cyclic. This second ray is pre-eminently the ray of applied consciousness and it builds forms for the use of spirit, so that the indwelling consciousness can evolve. It is the ray of the true psychic, of teachers, healers, scholars and lovers.

Some of the Names of the Lord of Ray Two: Displayer of Glory, Lord of Eternal Love, Cosmic Magnet, Giver of Wisdom, Master Builder, Great Geometrician, Radiance in the Form, The Cosmic Christ, The Conferrer of Names, The One who hides the Life, The Cosmic Mystery, The Light Bringer, The Son of God Incarnate.

Ray 2 Soul in control: the disciple loves wisely, understands people intuitively and directs Physical Plane activity with patience, tact and compassion. There are two psychological types: heart-centred and expressing love and intellectual and expressing wise understanding.

- Vocations: these require tact, foresight, personal magnetism, warmth and concern for others. They make excellent ambassadors, psychotherapists, teachers, healers and educators.
- Greatest contribution: wise and loving service given in health, education and spiritual guidance.
- Goals: to develop a deep intuitive loving-understanding of people to help them; or to become wise and knowledgeable in order to illumine people's minds.
- Most Joyous Activity: being in love; or the pursuit and distribution of intuitive understanding.
- Greatest Sense of sacred: divine love.
- Heart's desire: to be in love with all, one with all; or all knowingness and omniscience.

Ray 2 unregenerated personality: this personality uses charm and magnetism to manipulate people and get what it wants, to live in comfort. Fearful of being alone, oversensitive and timid, it binds people to its side through guilt and dependency. The "love" type needs to be popular, loved and it gets its way by being a suffering martyr. The "mental" type can be cold, indifferent, with contempt for mental limitations in others. Withdrawing into its private retreat, it leaves others to fend for themselves.

Ray 2 Mind: (uncommon, disciples only. Three disciples in Master DK's group had this field). These disciples are profoundly wise and knowledgeable. Natural academics that are intuitive and capable of clear abstract thought. Because thoughtforms may be soft-edged, not clear and precise, they may need to expend extra effort to ground thoughts clearly in the brain.

Ray 2 Astral Body: emotionally calm and affectionate, includes all and avoids causing harm. When prodded, it does not react with fire like the ray 6 field, but rather can dissolve for a while before it regroups. It tends to remain relatively calm and does not have great emotional displays. Fearful, it gives in more easily than passionate 6 types. It is a harmless emotional field and people instantly pick up on this and like them. It invites instant trust but can be a doormat.

Ray 2 Physical-Etheric Body: (uncommon - disciples only. One disciple in DK's group had this field). [1] A soft body, highly sensitive to pain, slow to action with love of ease and idleness. The ray 2 brain type would express ideas in a gentle and inclusive manner.

Ray 2 Soul-Personality Integration Technique - ACLRI Method

Signs
Gemini
Virgo
Pisces

Planets
Sun
Jupiter

Jewel
Sapphire

Symbols
All-Seeing Eye
Book of Wisdom
Chalice
Dove

Alignment. The ray 2 personality gets what it desires through "love", or selling "love". It gets material success and comfort by being nice to powerful people, relying on the efforts of others, such as marrying for social position. Wisdom types use knowledge for profit. This personality type cries:

> The love of love must dominate, not a love of being loved. The power to draw unto oneself must dominate..

Crisis. But one day, old "loves" no longer satisfy

> .. but into the worlds of form that power must someday fail to penetrate.
> .. Release thyself from all that stands around. For it has naught for thee..

A realisation comes eventually that it is time to detach from toxic relationships. This brings on a crisis and fear of being alone, of never finding love, of being unlovable. Depressed and discouraged an inner plea for assistance is made. Only then will the soul respond.

Light. Soul illumination broadens perception and highlights defects - fearfulness, the controlling need for material security, how the insatiable need to be loved triggers abandonment and rejection fears. Understanding dawns and purification work begins.

- Vices to eliminate: self-love, seeking approval from others, too attached to material things and relationships; or mentally cold.
- Virtues to cultivate: these are primarily independence and inner strength. Virtues for mind types are love, compassion and unselfishness.
- Use of the ray 2 integration word "Centralisation" to strengthen the character.

The aspirant is urged to develop "the love of that which is true, beautiful and good."

> .. look to me. I am the One who builds, sustains and draws thee on and up. Look unto me with eyes of love and seek the path that leads from the outer circle to the point. I, at the point, sustain. I, at the point, attract. I, at the point, direct and choose and dominate. I at the point, love all, drawing them into the centre and moving forward with the travelling points toward that great Centre where the One Point stands. What mean you by that Word? [2]

Even Armed Cross
Giving Hands
Mother and Child
Lotus
The Ocean
Owl
Radiant Heart
Rose
Sapphire
Shepherd's Crook
Spiral
The Sun

Revelation. Glimpses of the Solar Angel are seen. The disciple finds his or her part to play in the Spiritual Plan, a heart centred vocation, either healing, teaching or religion.

Integration. Eventually, integration of the threefold lower nature, of the Personality and Soul Rays takes place and alignment occurs with the One Central Point. The words of power "I See the Greatest Light", facilitates this process.

Marilyn Monroe *Bill Clinton* *Mother Teresa*

---

1 Based on the chart later in the section "Rays of the Tibetan's Disciples".
2 Gathered from Bailey, Alice A. Esoteric Psychology II, 355

RAY III: INTELLIGENT ACTIVITY

Major ray: 3rd Aspect, 3rd Logos, fire by friction, the colour green

Energy: the highly energetic force of substance that is adaptable and fertile. It gives that primeval and instinctual intelligence found in the form nature, which knows what it must do to survive and reproduce. It gives mental brilliance when working through man's mind.

Some of the Names of the Lord of Ray Three: The Keeper of the Records, The Lord of Memory, Unifier of the lower Four, Interpreter of That Which is seen, The Three-sided Triangle, Illuminator of the Lotus, The Forerunner of the Light, The One Who veils and yet reveals, Dispenser of Time, The Lord of Space, The Universal Mind, The Great Architect of the Universe.

Ray 3 Soul in control: the disciple is highly intelligent, energetic, resourceful and flexible. There are two types, one primarily expressing abstract thought and creative reasoning, the other is adaptable and very active physically.

- Vocations: those requiring excellent intellects, adaptability and resourcefulness. They make good tacticians, strategists, financial planners, business people, entrepreneurs and philosophers. They speak with the voice of reason and intelligence.
- Greatest contribution: stimulating the intellect and mental creativity of others. Creating plans that benefit humanity.
- Most Joyous Activity: mental and physical activity. To theorise, plan and then act on that plan.
- Greatest Sense of sacred: the appreciation of theories and proofs that explain the nature of things.
- Heart's desire: to plan along with God and manifest the Divine Plan.

Ray 3 unregenerated personality: it gets caught up in a multitude of plans, is over-active, restless, absent-minded, changeable and lacks continuity. Hypercritical and intellectually proud, it needs to be cleverest, one-step ahead "the early bird gets the worm" type. To this end, it could be deceitful, devious, manipulative, untruthful and bend the rules to suit itself. Whatever is required to win the day.

Ray 3 Mind: (uncommon, disciples only; two disciples in DK's group had this field). This combination gives a powerful and outstanding intellect. A wide-ranging type of mind that is weaving, incessantly active, fluid, versatile, highly verbal and communicative. It plans and strategises, is reasoning, resourceful, highly analytical, deductive, non-empirical, critical and loves abstract thought. Its weakness is that it is not concerned with accuracy, is generalising and can be absent-minded.

Ray 3 Astral Body: (uncommon, disciples only. No disciples in DK's group had this field - see the section "Rays of the Tibetan's Disciples"). Chaotic emotions, fluctuating desires and strong materialistic desires.

Ray 3 Physical-Etheric Body: a robust, stocky, strong, workhorse body, with high energy. It has a high pain threshold and is resistant to environmental pollutants. Very active it likes to keep on going and moving.

Comfortable in its skin it can be happy in an untidy environment or without an ordered routine. It likes spontaneity, to come and go as it pleases and resents having its activities curbed. If grace does not come from a higher ray, it plods firmly along, with graceless movements. The ray 3 brain type expresses ideas in a fluid, energetic, sometimes inaccurate manner.

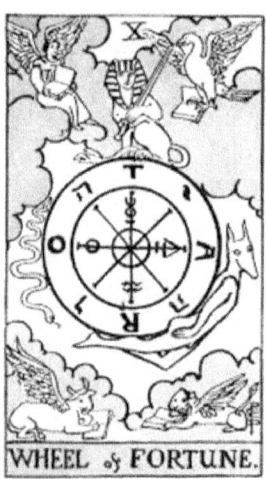

Strengths

Acute, creative, mentally fertile and powerful intellect capable of wide-ranging, philosophical and abstract thought: ability to plan, strategise, to understand and explain complex patterns, to theorise and speculate, apply rigorous analysis, skill with communication and facility with language. The power to manipulate for good or ill. Natural executive and business skill, good with money and philanthropic.

Weaknesses

Amoral and excessive materialism. Calculating, devious, dishonest, intellectual pride, manipulative, opportunistic. Excessive thought without practical action, scattered reasoning. Creating chaos disorderly, hyperactive, restless wasted motion, too busy.

Famous Figures

Albert Einstein, Aristotle, Bertrand Russel, Jack Nicholson, John D. Rockefeller, Machiavelli, Lucrezia Borgia, Shylock, St. Thomas Aquinas.

Ray 3 Soul-Personality Integration Technique - ACLRI Method

Alignment. The ray 3 personality covets money and is deceitful and manipulative in its efforts to get it. It spins webs, weaves many dreams and tries get-rich-quick schemes. Enmeshed in its own machinations, life becomes a confusing mess.

> Pulling the threads of Life, I stand, enmeshed within my self-created glamour. Surrounded I am by the fabric I have woven. I see naught else.

In time, the lack of direction, discipline and truthfulness, is seen as the cause of life chaos. The soul instruction is heard.

> The love of truth must dominate, not love for "my" own thoughts, or love of "my" ideas and forms; love of the ordered process must control, not love of "my" own wild activity.

Crisis. This creates a crisis. Soul illumination reveals the ugliness of the life, the manipulations and lies. Feeling empty, futile, unable to find life satisfaction, all outer life weavings stop. The person stands quiet. Alone, depressed and discouraged, only when a plea comes for assistance will the soul respond. Its instruction is:

> Be still. Learn to stand quiet, still and unafraid. I, at the centre, Am. Look up along the line and not along the many lines, which, in the space of aeons, you have woven. These hold thee prisoner. Be still. Rush not from point to point, nor be deluded by the outer forms and that which disappears.

Light. Going into a period of retreat, into stillness, a desire for change dawns and purification work begins.

- Vices to eliminate: disorganisation and an undisciplined life, inaccuracy, intellectual pride, criticalness, coldness, using mind power to manipulate people for personal gain and materialism. "Sexual excesses" [1] and "dogmatic, sectarian .. attitudes" [2].
- Virtues to cultivate: sympathy, tolerance, accuracy, common sense, stillness, right action and focus.
- Use of the ray 3 integration word *"stillness"* to bring inner quietness.

Revelation. The disciple finds his or her part to play in the Spiritual Plan, a heart centred vocation. For instance, manipulating ideas, money and systems to solve life problems and promote the greater good; training young minds to think clearly and rationally, to build right and good thoughtforms.

Integration. The words of power "Purpose itself Am I", facilitates this process. Eventually, guided by the soul - the "Weaver", soul-personality integration occurs.

> Behind the forms, the Weaver stands and silently he weaves. [3]

Timothy Leary *Albert Einstein* *Bill Gates*

Signs
Cancer
Libra
Capricorn

Planets
Saturn
Earth

Colour
Green

Jewel
Emerald

Symbols
Busy Hands
Busy Tongue
Communication, talking

Emerald
Fleur de Lis
Gold, money
Golden Coins
Hour Glass
Kaleidoscope
Labyrinth
Loom
Pen
Serpent
Spider and Web
Spinning Wheel
Tapestry
Triangle
Veil

---
1 Bailey, Alice A. Esoteric Healing, 62
2 Bailey, Alice A. Esoteric Psychology I, 349
3 Gathered from Bailey, Alice A. Esoteric Psychology II, 360

RAY IV: HARMONY THROUGH CONFLICT
Minor ray: soft line (feeling) ray with 2 and 6, the colour yellow

Energy: this force is related to the middle plane, the Buddhic. It oscillates and tries to bridge and reconcile opposites. Achieving a balanced central point results in harmony and beauty; otherwise, instability, conflict and trouble erupts. It is the ray of entertainers, artists, actors and warriors.

Some of the Names of the Lord of Ray Four: The Link Between the Three and Three, The Divine Intermediary, Hand of God, The Hidden One, The Seed that is the Flower, The Mountain whereon Form dies, The One Who marks the parting of the Way, Dweller in the Holy Place, The Corrector of the Form, The Master, Trumpet of the Lord, The Light within the Light, The Lower than the Three - the Highest of the Four.

Ray 4 Soul: "There are - except in the ranks of disciples - no 4th ray souls in incarnation" [1] [1936]. The disciple creates unity, peace, beauty and is someone to whom others come to be soothed, entertained and exposed to beauty.

- Vocations: careers that require spontaneity and creation of some form of beauty, colour and harmony. These are the natural actors, artists, musicians, writers and peacemakers.
- Greatest contribution: to help others harmonise and resolve conflict.
- Soul-inspired Aspiration: to bring divine harmony into every aspect of life, to express the exquisite and beautiful yet agonising and painful, drama of life in all its vibrancy.
- Most Joyous Activity: mixing, blending and harmonising to create beauty.
- Greatest Sense of sacred: beauty and perfect equilibrium.
- Heart's desire: to live in beauty forever and become beauty itself.

Ray 4 unregenerated personality: it lacks self-control, gets embroiled in personal dramas, has rapid mood changes, is inconsistent and unstable. Too ready to compromise, it fights with itself and others. It tries to assert its authority and control through exaggeration, by being the drama queen, or attacking - verbally or sometimes physically to try to force people to comply.

Ray 4 Mind: this intuitive mind is passionate and very intense. It is the conflicted mind, struggling, crisis-stressed, vacillating, ambivalent and indecisive. The ability to change the mind - back and forth, is a distinguishing feature. When you watch individuals with a ray four mind at work, you can often see their heads or features move from side to side. On one hand, this mind is aggressive, antagonistic and contradicting. Then it is the peacemaker, the "bridging" mind, linking, weighing, balancing, resolving, unifying, mediating and reconciling. Between the polarities it agonises - backwards and forwards, up and down, alternating between exhilaration and depression.

This mind is artistic, musical, literary, aesthetic, picture making. Non-rational, it sees in pictures, an outstanding trait. Grasping concepts and translating thoughts (pictures and colours) into words can be a struggle and often it communicates better through an artistic method. However, it is a pliable mind with a rapid grasp and recognition of mental truth. Quick and spontaneous, it likes to play. The undeveloped mind is vague and imprecise.

Ray 4 Astral Body: (uncommon. No disciples in DK's group had this field. See chart later in section). Hypothetically, constant struggle and conflict, emotional tides and changes, rapid emotional response to dissonance, excessive moodiness, highs and lows.

Strengths

Create harmony from conflict, grow spiritually and psychologically through crises and struggle. The warrior, fighting to resolve injustices. Natural peacemakers, they reconcile, negotiate, mediate.
They are also intuitive, imaginative, love beauty and creating beauty, with a love of colour. Dramatic and creative, they are spontaneous, musical, and have a natural ability to entertain and delight.

Weaknesses

Constant inner - outer conflict, extreme mood swings, self absorbed in suffering, worry and agitation, indecisive, procrastinating. The artistic temperament - emotional, exaggerating, dramatic, unpredictable and unstable. Moral cowardice, too eager for compromise, fight for sake of fighting.

Famous Figures

Ludwig van Beethoven, Claude Debussy, Fyodor Dostoyevsky, Isadora Duncan, Franz Schubert, Lawrence Olivier, Leonardo da Vinci, Lord Byron, Michelangelo, Wolfgang Mozart, Pablo Picasso, Richard Wagner, Robert Burns, Salvador Dali, Shakespeare, Vincent Van Gogh.

---

1 Bailey, Alice A. The Rays and the Initiations, 605

Ray 4 Physical-Etheric Body: (uncommon, disciples). No disciples in DK's group had this field). Hypothetically, physical agitation, a physical (sexual?) response to beauty, beauty of form, excellent proportions. The ray 4 brain type would express ideas in a vacillating, but also artistic manner.

Ray 4 Soul-Personality Integration Technique - ACLRI Method

Alignment. The ray 4 personality seeks peace and harmony - but on its terms and this brings war and separation. It seeks approval - but rejects, so is rejected. Endeavouring to create peace, it destroys because it is at war with itself. It cries:

> Midway I stand between the forces which oppose each other. Longing am I for harmony and peace and for the beauty which results from unity. I see the two. I see naught but forces ranged opposing and I, the one, who stands within the circle at the centre. Peace I demand. My mind is bent upon it. Oneness with all I seek, yet form divides. War upon every side I find and separation. Alone I stand and am. I know too much.

Eventually the desire nature begins to exhaust itself. Then, experiencing emptiness, futility and unable to find satisfaction, the person turns from the old life and hears the soul instruction:

> The love of unity must dominate and love of peace and harmony. Yet not that love, based on a longing for relief, for peace to self, for unity because it carries with it that which is pleasantness. Both sides are one. There is no war, no differences, no isolation. The warring forces seem to war from the point at which you stand. Move on a pace.

Crisis. Soul illumination reveals the ugliness of the life, the lack of true beauty. In crisis, alone, isolated and depressed, an inner call for assistance is made.

Light. In the ensuing quiet come the words of the soul:

> See truly with the opened eye of inner vision and you will find, not two but one; not war but peace; not isolation but a heart which rests upon the centre. Thus shall the beauty of the Lord shine forth. The hour is now. [1]

The pathway forward is seen and spiritual practises are applied.

- Vices to eliminate: undisciplined emotions, constant worrying, indolence, fighting for the sake of fighting, instability of emotions and life, "selfishness, dogmatism" [2].
- Virtues to cultivate: inner unity and harmony, serenity, confidence, purity, self-control, accuracy, mental and moral balance and steadfastness.
- Use of the ray 4 integration word *"Steadfastness"* to bring balance.

Revelation. The disciple finds his or her part to play in the Spiritual Plan, a heart centred vocation - creating beauty and peace on earth.

Integration. The words of power "Two Merge with One" facilitates soul-personality integration and the initiate becomes a centre of beauty and peace.

Angelina Jolie 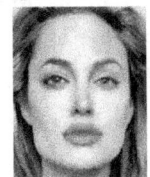   *Leonardo Da Vinci*    *William Shakespeare*

Signs
Taurus
Scorpio
Sagittarius

Planets
Mercury
Moon

Colour
Yellow
Jewel
Topaz

Symbols
Battlefields
Black + White
Bridge
Checker board
Comic
Mandalas
Musical Chords
Seesaws
Square
Tetrahedron
Tragic Masks
Vortexes
Warriors
Yin and Yang

---

[1] Gathered from Bailey, Alice A. Esoteric Psychology II, 363
[2] Bailey, Alice A. Esoteric Healing, 51

RAY V: CONCRETE MIND AND KNOWLEDGE

Minor ray: hard line (will-mind) ray with 1,3 and 7.
It is the "lower" mind ray, grounding ray 3. Its colour is orange

Energy: related to the Mental Plane this force enhances the mind and ability to discriminate, analyse, measure and find the truth. Consequently, scientists, analysts and technicians are often on this ray.

Some of the Names of the Lord of Ray Five: Revealer of the Truth, The Divine Intermediary, Crystalliser of Forms, The Three-fold Thinker, The Cloud upon the Mountain-top, The Dividing Sword, Winnower of the Chaff, The Fifth Great Judge, Rose of God, The Heavenly One, The Door into the Mind of God, The Initiating Energy, Ruler of the Third Heaven, Guardian of the Door, Dispenser of Knowledge, Keeper of the Secret, Beloved of the Logos, Brother from Sirius, Angel of the Flaming Sword, Master of the Hierophants.

Ray 5 Soul in control: The Ray 5 disciple has a keen intellect and excels in focused concentrated thinking, scientific analysis and is factually accurate, fair and just. There are two psychological types, one primarily expressing factual knowledge with great accuracy, the other demonstrating practical experimentation and technical inventiveness.

- Vocations: require a keen intellect and analytical accuracy. They make excellent scientists, electricians, engineers, analysts, data technicians and operating surgeons.
- Greatest contribution: to use the laser-like mental powers to discover new scientific truths, to advance truth and reject error.
- Soul-inspired Aspiration: to discover solutions to nature's mysteries through advanced scientific research and experimentation. To create inventions which uplift humanity.
- Most Joyous Activity: to discover what was previously hidden.
- Greatest Sense of sacred: the contemplation of the wonderful and intelligent design of Nature.
- Heart's desire: to "know" the mystery of life.

Ray 5 unregenerated personality: it focuses narrowly and exclusively on its own strictly mental, specialised and technical interests, at the expense of seeing and taking part in the larger picture. It tries to assert its authority and control people by being excessively rationalistic, by having all the facts to prove its position and that it is the expert. Separative, it can cut off its feelings and do things that a more compassionate type could not - for instance, the "hanging judge" type.

Ray 5 Mind: it is analytical, precise and scientific. Unbiased and unaffected by emotions, it is linear, rational, logical and very accurate. It finds mathematics easy. It is highly detailed but also lucid and clear. Irreverent and sceptical of the mystical, it is irreligious and dismissive of anything that cannot be proven scientifically. Taking time to think before speaking, it delivers words in monotone, emphasising the facts.

Ray 5 Astral Body: (uncommon, disciples only. No disciples in DK's group had this field. See chart "Rays of the Tibetan's Disciples" later in section). Hypothetically, a flat, colourless feeling response. The emotions would be easily controlled giving rise to extreme emotional detachment if there was not a compensating love aspect present.

Strengths

A fact based and scientific approach to life, facility with maths, technical expertise and mechanical ability. Enhances the mind's analytical powers so that it is lucid, keen, focused, intelligent, discriminating, accurate and precise in thought and action. Power to discover through research, investigation, experimentation. A mind that is impartial and that rejects nonsense.

Weaknesses

Excessive mental activity, over-analytical, rigid thought patterns, ultra-rational, over detailed, excessive objectivity. Narrow and prejudiced in thought, separative and judgmental. Wants to control through knowledge. Lack of intuitive sensitivity, of emotional responsiveness and magnetism. Social awkwardness.

Famous Figures

Charles Darwin, Galileo, Gregor Mendel, Isaac Newton, Louis Pasteur, Niels Bohr, Thomas Edison, Tim Berners-Lee, Wright Brothers.

Ray 5 Physical-Etheric Body: (uncommon, disciples only. No disciples in DK's group had this combination). Hypothetically, a hard, compact, rigid and awkward body. The ray 5 brain type would express ideas in a methodical and linear fashion.

Signs
Leo
Sagittarius
Aquarius

Planets
Venus

Colour
Orange

Jewel
Orange hued gems

Ray 5 Soul-Personality Integration Technique - ACLRI Method

Alignment. The ray 5 personality acquires knowledge and seeks respect through an invention, paper, discovery, or through technical expertise. It repudiates the mystical, is sceptical and irreverent. Seeing only the outer form, it cries:

> Towards me I draw the garment of my God. I see and know His form. I take that garment, piece by piece. I know its shape and colour, it's form and type, its parts component and its purpose and use. I stand amazed, I see naught else. I penetrate the mysteries of form, but not the Mystery. I see the garment of my god. I see naught else.

But, eluded by the ultimate prize or discovery and unable to find life satisfaction, the personality turns from the old life. This enables it to hear the soul instruction.

> Love of the form is good but only as the form is known for what it is - the veiling vase of life. Love of the form must never hide the Life which has its place behind, the One who brought the form into the light of day...

Crisis. Soul illumination reveals the aridness of the life, the damaged relationships caused by separativeness, the attachment to form. In crisis, suffering follows.

Light. The soul instructs the searcher to find truth within.

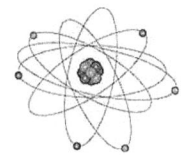

Symbols
Atom

Brain
Dictionary
Computer
Equation
Eye within the Ruler
Five Pointed Star
Laboratory
Laser
Magnifying Glass
Microscope
Pyramid
Scalpel
Telescope
Triangle

> Behind that form, I am. Know me. Cherish and know and understand the nature of the veils of life but know as well the One Who lives. Know me. Let not the forms of nature, their processes and powers prevent thy searching for the Mystery which brought the mysteries to thee. Know well the form, but leave it and search for Me.
>
> Detach thy thoughts from form and find Me waiting underneath the veils, the many-sided shapes, the glamours and the thoughtforms that hide my real Self. Be not deceived. Find Me. Know Me.

The search for higher self is approached scientifically.
- Vices to eliminate: narrow mental focus, materialism, separativeness.
- Virtues to cultivate: reverence, love, broad-mindedness, sympathy.
- Use of the integration word *"Detachment"* to free the mind from its rigidity.

Revelation. The disciple finds his or her part to play in the Spiritual Plan, a heart centred vocation - using science to reveal the usefulness of form.

> Then use the forms which then will neither veil nor hide the Self but will permit the nature of the self to penetrate the veils of life, revealing all the radiance of God, His power and magnetism; revealing all there is of form, of life, of beauty and usefulness.

Integration. The Personality and Soul Rays integrate and identification occurs with higher Mind. The words of power "Three Minds Unite", facilitates this process.

> The mind reveals the One. The mind can blend and fuse the form and life. Thou art the one. Though art the form. Thou art the mind. Know this. [1]

---
[1] Gathered from Bailey, Alice A. Esoteric Psychology II, 368-9

RAY VI: DEVOTION AND IDEALISM

Minor ray: soft line (feeling) ray with 2 and 4.
It is the "lower" love ray, grounding ray 2. Its colour is pale blue

Energy: related to the Astral Plane, this force is fiery and emotional and it feeds desire. Fostering an adoration of personal ideals and gurus, it is the ray of the devotee, the idealist and follower. It gives a passion for life and awe towards the macrocosm.

Some of the Names of the Lord of Ray Six: The Negator of Desire, The One Who sees the Right, Visioner of Reality, Divine Robber, The Hater of Forms, Sword Bearer of the Logos, Upholder of the Truth, Breaker of Stones, The Imperishable Flaming One, The One Whom Naught can turn, Warrior on the March, The Crucifier and the Crucified, Devotee of Life, Implacable Ruler, General on the Perfect Way.

Ray 6 Soul in control: the disciple wields ray 6 force with one-pointed devotion, reverence and loyalty. There is an outstanding ability to dedicate oneself totally, completely, passionately and without reservation, to a teacher or highest ideal. There are two psychological types, devotion or fiery aspiration and intense idealism.

- Vocations: those requiring devotion, dedication and selfless service. They make excellent preachers, orators, soldiers, nurses and personal secretaries.
- Greatest contribution: to inspire others to offer their lives to the highest ideal they can conceive.
- Soul-inspired Aspiration: devotion and adoration to the highest source of guidance and / or ardent and passionate commitment to the highest ideals.
- Most Joyous Activity: oneness with the object of devotion and / or joy in the fiery pursuit of an ideal.
- Greatest Sense of sacred: devotion to the Highest.
- Heart's desire: to love and be totally loved by the beloved and to perfectly express the highest ideals.

Ray 6 unregenerated personality: passionately involved in the one-pointed pursuit of its own desires, it is emotionally intense, extreme and fanatical. Preoccupied with the enthusiasm of the moment it draws attention to itself through acts of loyalty to its cause and guru. It tries to assert its authority and control people by urging them to follow behind the banner it is waving. Then, militant and unforgiving to its enemies, tries to force its beliefs on to those who are not drawn in, threatening "if you're not with me, you're against me."

Ray 6 Mind: (uncommon, disciples only. No disciples in DK's group had this field. See chart later in section "Rays of the Tibetan's Disciples"). Hypothetically, a mind that is fiery, inflexible. An unremitting one-pointed mental focus.

Ray 6 Astral Body: this is the most common emotional type. Fiery and passionate it is very reactive, defensive and emotional. Taking things personally, people with this field find it hard to rise above how they feel. Devoted to their current beloved, they burn with desire to be with the one they adore. They can be fanatical in the pursuit of their desires or ideals and jealous. This body is subject to glamour, the distortion of reality because of emotional bias. The refined field reacts promptly to suffering with compassion and forgiveness.

Strengths

Intense devotion, self-sacrificial ardour, transcendent idealism. One-pointed, single-minded, unflagging persistence. Receptive to spiritual guidance, to ecstasy and rapture. Earnest, sincere, loyal, unshakeable faith, undimmed optimism. Profound humility, purity, goodness, sainthood.

Weaknesses

Too emotional, rigid idealism, unreasoning devotion, ill considered loyalty, blind faith, unvarying one-pointedness in spite of evidence to contrary. Extreme, hyper-intense. Selfish and jealous, takes things personally, fanatical and militarism. Too dependent on others, superstitious, gullible, unrealistic, unwise susceptibility to guidance. Masochistic, it has a martyr-complex and is self abasing.

Famous Figures

Ayatollah Khomeini, Billy Graham, Florence Nightingale, Jane Fonda, Jerry Falwell, Jesse Jackson, Jesus of Nazareth, Jimmy Carter, Joan of Arc, Pete Seeger, Rev Martin Luther King, Ronald Reagan, Sir Galahad.

Ray 6 Physical-Etheric Body: (uncommon, disciples only. Two disciples in DK's group had this field). Hypothetically, there is a strong solar plexus emphasis, physical tenacity and persistence. Without wisdom, the ray 6 brain is one-pointed, narrow, inflexible and servant to the astral body.

Dreamstime

Signs
Virgo
Sagittarius
Pisces

Planets
Neptune
Mars

Colours
Silvery blue
Rose

Jewel
Ruby

Symbols
Bleeding Heart

Beacon
Burning Candle
Dog
Flag or Banner
Halo
Horse
Praying Hands
Pulpit Pyre
Rosy Cross
Torch

Ray 6 Soul-Personality Integration Technique - ACLRI Method

Alignment. The ray 6 personality is full of desire and lays its body on the altar of desire. It wants all that will satisfy its thirst and cries:

> I see a vision. It satisfies desire; it feeds and stimulates it's growth. I lay my life upon the altar of desire - the seen, the sensed, that which appeals to me, the satisfaction of my need - for that which is material, for that which feeds emotion, that satisfies the mind, that answers my demand for truth, for service and my vision of the goal. It is the vision which I see, the dream I dream, the truth I hold, the active form which meets my need, that which I grasp and understand. My truth, my peace, my satisfied desire, my dream, my vision of reality, my limited ideal, my finite thought of God; - for these I struggle, fight and die.

But gradually, after grasping all and still not satisfied and with the desire nature exhausted, all grasping stops. Then in the quiet, the voice of the soul is heard:

> Run not so straight.

Crisis. Soul illumination reveals the useless pursuit of idols that continually fall. This creates a crisis. Destitute of incentive, motive, sensation, lacking life purpose, feeling unappreciated and a fool, a crisis hits and it is severe.

Light. When the soul receives a plea for assistance, it throws down light and understanding so that the way ahead is seen. It instructs the aspirant to:

> Stand at the centre. Look on every side. Die not for outer forms. Forget not God, Who dwells behind the vision. Love more your fellow men. [1]

Understanding dawns and purification practises begin.
- Vices to eliminate: being too one-eyed, bound by separative and limiting truths, emotionalism; blindly worshipping gurus, creeds and causes; fanatical cruelty, sectarian.
- Virtues to cultivate: tolerance, serenity, balance and common sense.
- Use of the ray 6 integration words *"Restraint"* or *"Moderation"* to curb the blind emotional rushes.

Revelation. Purification reveals the part that the disciple can play in the Spiritual Plan. A heart centred vocation is found - to love and serve all.

Integration. The Personality and Soul Rays are fused and integration into the disciple's soul ashram takes place. The words of power "The Highest Light Controls", facilitates this process.

Billy Graham   *Ian Paisley*   *Martin Luther-King Jr.*

---

[1] Gathered from Bailey, Alice A. Esoteric Psychology II, 371-2

Strengths

Power to create order out of chaos, to plan and organise, to manifest and work on the material plane. Power to perfect form, to build and manage detail, to renovate and transform. Power to understand and implement the law. Power to coordinate groups, to synthesise. A keen sense of rhythm and timing, a natural ritualist, power to work as a magician, to work with devas and elementals.

Weaknesses

Rigid orderliness and formalism, subservience to habit, over concern with rules, laws, regulations, bigotry and sectarianism. Crystallisation, materialism, excessive perfectionism, snobbish, superficial judgement based on appearances. Pompous ritual, addiction to occult phenomena, perversion of the magical process.

RAY VII: CEREMONY, ORDER AND MAGIC

Minor ray: hard line (will-mind) ray with 1,3 and 5.
It is the "lower" power ray, grounding ray 1. Its colour is violet.

Energy: related to the Physical Plane this force gives power to bring order out of chaos, to organise people and forms so that they perfectly reflect an ideal, an idea or plan. It gives an ability to manifest through the hand that conceived in the mind. Ritualists, builders, architects, organisers and alchemists are often on this ray.

Some of the Names of the Lord of Ray Seven: The Unveiled Magician, Worker in the Magical Art, Creator of the Form, Manipulator of the Wand, The Watcher in the East, Custodian of the Seventh Plan, Keeper of the Magical Word, The Temple Guardian, The Representative of God, The Lord of Death, Builder of the Square, The One Who feeds the Sacred Fire, The Whirling Fire, The Divine Alchemical Worker.

Ray 7 Soul in control: the disciple expresses ray 7 energy courteously, with organisational, managerial and administrative prowess. A team player, physical plane activity is well planned, detailed and scheduled. There are three psychological types. The Order type is very formal and uses the will to preserve established forms and structures. The Ceremony type recreates and reorganises forms and structures. The third Magic type creates forms and structures easily, as if by magic. This latter type is drawn naturally to ritual and magical work.

- Vocations: those requiring practical efficiency, finesse, organisational skill and the ability to manifest ideas on the Physical Plane. Business people, organisers and ritualists.
- Greatest contribution: to help others organise their lives so thoroughly, their highest dreams manifest.
- Soul-inspired Aspiration: to bring order out of chaos, bring about the "New World Order" and invoke divine energies that relate spirit and matter according to the divine plan.
- Greatest Sense of sacred: contemplating forms (divine or man-made) that are a perfect embodiment of Universal Design.
- Heart's desire: to express the divine archetype in perfect form, to see tangible results of their thought and labour.

Ray 7 unregenerated personality: it is rigid and resistant to change and locks itself into its preferred personal routines, habits and customs. Preoccupied with and judging by appearances, its chief attention-getter is efficiency, being good and doing things the right way. It asserts its authority by insisting people follow the rules and do the right thing. There is a seven type that is unconventional and spurns the status quo. But there is a pattern to this behaviour as well.

Ray 7 Mind: (uncommon, disciples only). Highly organised, coordinating, synthesising, with an excellent memory.

Ray 7 Astral Body: (uncommon, disciples only). Hypothetically, a highly disciplined emotional body that desires a well ordered Physical Plane life. (No disciples had mind's or emotions on this ray. See chart later in section "Rays of the Tibetan's Disciples").

Ray 7 Physical-Etheric Body: it is refined, graceful, dignified and emphasises points with graceful hand movements. Moving in a measured and balanced way, it walks with grace. It prefers to live in an ordered environment and functions better with routine - for example, rising in the morning and eating meals at the same time each day. Sensitive, it has a low pain threshold. However, it can also be strong and trained in sports requiring strength and grace, like gymnastics. The ray 7 brain expresses ideas in an ordered manner.

Ray 7 Soul-Personality Integration Technique - ACLRI Method

Alignment. The personality is proud and seeks power. Efficient and ordered it tries to force its rules onto others. It cries:

> I, at the centre stand, the worker in the field of magic. I know some rules, some magical controls, some Words of Power, some forces which I can direct. What shall I do? Danger there is. The task which I have undertaken is not easy of accomplishment, yet I love power. I love to see the forms emerge, created by my mind and do the work, fulfil the plan and disappear. I can create. The rituals of the Temple of the Lord are known to me. How shall I work?

Crisis. Misuse of power creates a karmic backlash and a crisis. Soul illumination reveals the meaningless rituals and violations of the Law of Love. Chastised, all manipulations stop. In a quiet moment the words of the soul register:

> Love not the work. Let love of God's eternal plan control your life, your mind, your hand, your eye. Work towards the unity of plan and purpose which must find it's lasting place on earth.

Light. Understanding dawns. Reorientation and purification practises begin.
- ices to eliminate: placing importance on meaningless tasks, schedules and rituals. Pride in status, bigotry, judgment, "sectarian" [1]. Being addicted to phenomena and the wielding of power. "self-interest, pure selfishness, black magic".
- Virtues to cultivate: wide-mindedness, tolerance, humility, gentleness and love.
- Use of the ray 7 integration word *"Re-orientation"* to bring daily routines into line with divine rhythm.

Revelation. The disciple finds his or her part to play in the Spiritual Plan. A heart vocation is found - organising society so that life and people are brought into rhythm with the Plan of God.

> Work with the Plan; focus upon your share in that great work.

Integration. The Personality and Soul Rays integrate and entry into the soul group is made. From that high point, according to divine instruction, the Magician works. The words of power "The Highest and the Lowest Meet", facilitates this process.

> Stand in the centre of the pentagram, drawn upon that high place in the East within the light which ever shines. Stand steady in the midst. Then draw a line from that which is without to that which is within and see the Plan take form. [2]

Margot Fonteyn *Aleister Crowley* *"The Snob"*

---
1 Bailey, Alice A. Esoteric Psychology I, 211
2 Gathered from Bailey, Alice A. Esoteric Psychology II, 375-6

Famous Figures
Aleister Crowley, Audrey Hepburn, Benjamin Franklin, Jackie Onassis, Kofi Annan, Merlin, Sir Francis Bacon, Sir Francis Drake, Thomas Jefferson, Tony Blair.

Signs
Aries
Cancer
Capricorn

Planet
Uranus

Colour
Violet

Jewel
Amethyst

Symbols
Altar
Coat of Arms
Cornerstone
Crystal
Dancing hands
Lightning Rod
Official Seal
Peacock

Poised Graceful Rainbow
Sceptre
    Seven-pointed Star
Swastika
Talisman
Wand

Chart: The 7 Rays, Psychology and Disease

Ray	Disease pathology	Psychological keywords	Disease examples	Astrology
1	Ages, atrophies, contracts, cripples, crystallises, hardens, scars, stiffens.	Aggressive, controlling, egomania, hard, inflexible, inhibited, megalomania, obsessive, repressive, wilful.	Arthritis, atherosclerosis, blindness, cancer through repression, dementia, meningitis, multiple sclerosis, paralysis, scleroderma, stroke.	Pluto, Saturn, Uranus; Aries (and Mars), Leo, Capricorn.
2	Excessive growth and vitality, overdevelops, suffocates, too many atoms.	Amoral, excessive, gluttonous, greedy, impressionable, no emotional boundaries.	Blood disorders, cancer, heart disease, extra body parts, gluttony, tumours.	Sun, Jupiter; Gemini, Virgo, Pisces.
3	Diseases that are highly energetic, unstable, quick moving, subtly invasive, that trick the body.	Avarice, dishonesty, hyper-active, lying, manipulative, trickery, stealing, white collar crime, sociopathic.	Breathing troubles, certain brain disorders; gastric, stomach, intestinal disorders; sexually transmitted diseases.	Saturn, Earth, also Mercury; Cancer, Libra, Capricorn.
4	Constant conflict that devitalises and debilitates, opening the body up to disease.	Agonising, inner conflict, mental-emotional instability. mood swings.	Chronic fatigue, debilitation, epidemics such as influenza, susceptibility to indigenous diseases - cancer, tuberculosis, syphilis.	Moon, Mercury; Taurus, Scorpio, Sagittarius.
5	Builds barriers, separates, hardens, cleaves, splits apart.	Aloof, anti-social, cleavages, disassociates, divisive, many modern psychological disorders, separative.	Brain lesions, consciousness thread trouble, imbecilities. migraine.	Venus; Leo, Sagittarius, Aquarius.
6	Emotional or desire force out of control; violently expressed or repressed.	Emotional disorders: anger, delusion, fear, frustration, hurt, jealousy, reactive, sectarian, warped ideals.	Carcinogenicity, digestion problems, sexual diseases and perversions, viruses.	Mars, Neptune; Virgo, Sagittarius, Pisces.
7	Promiscuity at a cellular level leading to genetic mutations, germs and bacterial infections.	Perfectionism, regimenting, perverting, promiscuity.	Blood circulation problems, epidemics, sexually transmitted diseases, reproductive problems.	Uranus; Aries, Cancer, Capricorn.

Esoteric Healing 106-109, 298-304; plus other sources

2. THE RAY CHART

The rays govern each body. A Ray Chart or Seven Ray Personality Profile, is a list of the rays that govern the soul, personality, mind, emotional and physical-etheric bodies. It is a list of the energies and qualities that form our nature and that galvanise us into action. In this section we learn how to formulate ray charts.

Except for the soul ray and depending upon the need, disciples have their bodies on any ray, "to meet the emergency, the need or the service of a particular life". [1] All people below the rank of discipleship have their bodies on the following rays:

1. Soul ray: primarily 2, then any of the others, but unlikely to be 4 at this time.
2. Personality ray: it can be any of the seven but is different to the soul ray.
3. Mind ray: 4, 5 and sometimes 1.
4. Emotional ray: mostly 6, occasionally 2.
5. Physical ray: 3 and 7.

The desire nature is the controlling force in most people; their astral ray dominates them. But at this stage of our history, the focus is on mind development. As mind awakens, the Physical-Astral-Mind Rays begin a fusing process that eventually produces the personality ray.

This latter ray can be any of the seven. But it is a subray of the soul ray. This is possible because each ray carries all the other rays within itself. The soul ray colours the personality ray. For instance, a second ray personality will be more intense with a ray one soul, than it would be with a ray five soul.

Then the personality ray assumes power. When present it colours the outer appearance and influences how the personality will try to control its environment. Many people become famous through a driving and dominant personality ray. The hunger for power and wealth is so consuming, they allow nothing to stop the forward drive to their goal. Industrialists, corporate heads, chief executives, such as Kerry Packer and Rupert Murdoch, are outstanding examples. But later, when purified and positive, the personality ray is the soul's instrument for service in the world. This developmental process takes place over many lives.

Once the personality ray is alive and is assertive, the soul ray becomes more active and begins to clash with it for control. Eventually the aspirant becomes aware of the inner conflict and takes steps to straighten out the life. Purification of the physical appetites is marked by the 1st Initiation. The 2nd Initiation marks the purification of the emotional field. The 3rd Initiation occurs when the soul brings the entire lower nature under control.

> Gradually and increasingly, the soul ray begins to become more active. The personality ray and the egoic ray clash and then later a steady warfare is set up with the disciple as the onlooker—and dramatic participator. Arjuna emerges into the arena of the battlefield. Midway between the two forces he stands. Around him and in him and through him the energies of the two rays pour and conflict. Gradually, as the battle continues to rage, he becomes a more active factor and drops the attitude of the detached and uninterested onlooker. When he is definitely aware of the issues involved and definitely throws the weight of his influence, desires and mind on to the side of the soul, he can take the first initiation. When the ray of the soul focuses itself fully through him [he] takes the third initiation... a person whose powers are controlled by the dominant vibration of the soul ray and whose inner, sensitive mechanism is vibrating to the measure of that soul ray which—in its turn—is being itself reoriented to and controlled by, the monadic ray. [2]

Once the soul ray (egoic ray) is expressing through the lower nature, life focus is oriented to service and the higher good. After the 3rd Initiation, the Monadic Ray controls. It is that immortal spiritual fire aspect or ray that connects us with the Central Life. This ray is either 1, 2 or 3. The Monadic Ray absorbs the personality ray at the 3rd Initiation and the soul ray at the 5th.

---

1 Bailey, Alice A. Discipleship in the New Age I, 336
2 Bailey, Alice A. Esoteric Psychology II, 17-18

1. The Personal Ray Chart - Identifying your Rays

Start with the lower bodies first, then work your way inwards to the soul ray. Once you have your own chart, then observe yourself, your behaviours for as long as necessary to validate its accuracy.

1. Find the Physical-Etheric Ray first

Unless you are a disciple, this will be ray 3 (R3) or R7. Observe your physical nature and habits; complete the Physical Body Checklist chart in the Appendix.

Look at your body. Is it muscular, strong, stocky, active and busy (3), or more delicate (7)? Is it graceful when moving and dancing (7), or more vigorous and athletic, perhaps with poor timing (3)? Can the body be pushed to work long hours without nourishment, fall asleep anytime, anywhere (3)? Or, does it need regular meals, operating better with order and ritual (7) and a comfortable bed to fall into at the end of the day?

2. Find the Emotional (Astral) Ray

Unless you are a disciple, this will be R2 or R6. The odds are it will be R6. Observe your emotional displays; complete the Emotional Ray Checklist chart in the Appendix.

a. How is your emotional expression? Are you inclined to take things personally (6)? If betrayed by someone you love and trust, are you disappointed and deeply hurt, but otherwise quietly non-reactive (2)?

b. Or, are you intensely passionate, reactive, fiery, angry and jealous (6)? Have you been trying to transform your behaviour because fiery anger has got you into trouble in the past; but now you are more serene and can channel your fire serenely (6)?

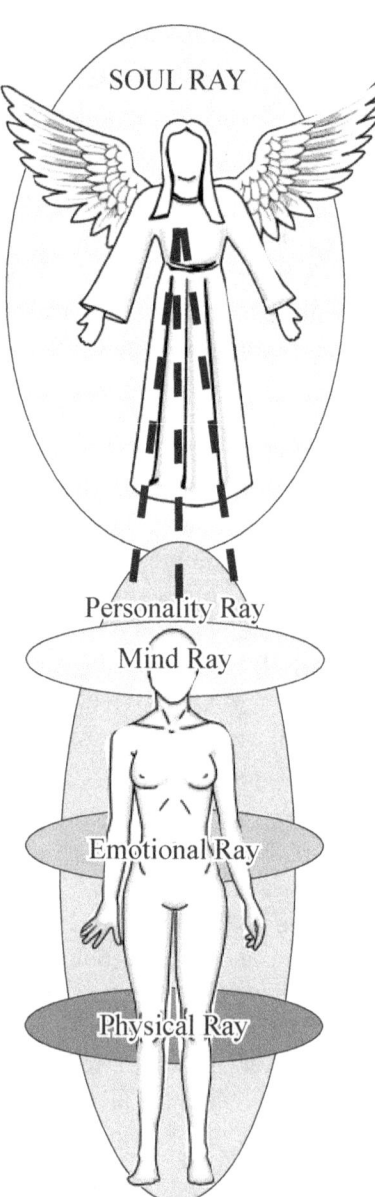

3. Find the Mind Ray

Unless you are a disciple, this will be R4, R5 or R1. Observe your thoughtform building processes; complete the Mind Ray checklist chart.

a. How do you solve problems? Analyse the method used to build thoughtforms, how words are delivered. Is the method left-brain mental: linear, logical, detailed, perhaps colourless and monotone focusing only on facts (5)?

b. Or is it right brain, entertaining, colourful, dramatic, intuitive, poetic, humorous and short on details (4)? Or do you jump to conclusions, go straight to the point and then defend your point of view arrogantly, beating your opponent down with power and assertion (1)?

c. Do you agonise over decisions and sometimes get emotional so you cannot think clearly (4). Or are you disciplined in problem solving and take a pragmatic and logical approach (5)? Do you summarise matters quickly and come swiftly to a synthetic conclusion (1)?

d. Or, does your mind process thoughts rapidly; drawing intelligently and coherently from all angles and then delivers these thoughts with speed and verbosity (3). (This latter ray is included for disciples)

4. Find the Personality Ray - any of the Seven Rays.

Complete the Personality Ray Checklist chart in the Appendix. It forms when the discriminatory powers of the mind develop and are used by the ego to control its world. Until then, there is no personality ray. If it is developing, careful analysis will find it. If it is fully formed and the soul ray is not yet controlling it, this ray will be a powerful "in-your-face" force and very easy to see. If illumination has occurred the personality ray positives will be easy to see.

a. Observe how the personality seeks to assert its authority. How does it go about fighting for its rights? Do you see hard line, pushy, mental (1, 3, 5, 7) or soft, cooperative, emotional (2, 4, 6)?

b. Go through all the rays and dismiss those that do not fit. Then focus on the others.

c. Identify outstanding negative traits. How does the ego try to get attention, to "big-note" itself? What traits have a destructive effect upon the life? These could indicate the personality ray.

d. Look at the career. A first career, or one which satisfies the ambitions but not the heart, could indicate the personality ray. A career that is fulfilling and that makes the heart sing, indicates the soul ray. No special career or many jobs may indicate the personality ray has not developed.

5. Find the Soul Ray - any of the Seven Rays

When working with someone else - start by determining whether you think the person is on the Path and is aspiring to that which is higher and finer. If not the person has a soul ray of either 4, 5, 6 or 7.

> Every human being, in the earlier stages of his development .. comes into incarnation upon one of the four Rays of Attribute, because these rays are peculiarly and uniquely related to the fourth kingdom in nature and therefore to the fourth Creative Hierarchy. [1]

Prior to the higher aspiring stage, this ray will be hard to find because the soul is not yet influential. As people reach the Path of Discipleship the soul begins to migrate onto one of the major rays of aspect 1, 2, 3.

> During the long, long cycle of the present fifth race .. individuals who had attained a certain state of consciousness transferred on to one of the three Rays of Aspect. [2]

The point of this is that, people on the Path will have a major ray as the soul ray (or be transferring to one) and because it is influential in the life it can be found. People at this stage are in vocations related to the soul ray or their heart pulls them in that direction. Note that the soul and personality will be on different rays.

Meditate upon the following questions, searching for answers in the heart.

a. What are my good qualities and my strengths? What special gifts or skills do I have?

b. Are there new qualities or strengths emerging? If so, what are they?

c. How would I most like to help the world? What are my highest aspirations? What vocation would most fulfil the need in my heart, to help people?

R1: My goal is to use my growing power and management and leadership ability - through government, politics or law, to strengthen and liberate others.

R2: My goal is to develop a deep intuitive loving-understanding of people to help alleviate suffering; or to become inclusive and wise so that I can teach and illumine others and alleviate suffering.

R3: My goal is to speak with the voice of reason and intelligence, to cultivate the intelligence of students and help them develop the powers of the mind. I wish to use my natural expertise in the world of business or economics to bring about the greatest good.

R4: My goal is to help others harmonise and resolve conflict in their lives, to beautify what was ugly, to express the exquisitely beautiful yet agonisingly painful drama of life in all its vibrancy.

R5: My goal is to use my scientific expertise and laser-like mental powers to discover new scientific truths to advance truth and reject error, to lead and direct others to bring about the greater good on earth (5 moving to 1).

R6: My goal is to use my growing love and wisdom to invoke crusades for the higher good, to inspire people to search for their highest ideals, to save the poor and suffering (6 moving to 2).

R7: My goal is to use my organising expertise and invoke divine energies to help organise the world so that it reflects the harmony and beauty of the divine plan.

---
1 Bailey, Alice A. The Rays and the Initiations, 558-9
2 Ibid, 559

Ask yourself, "what are my most joyous or sacred moments?"

R1: My most joyous activity is to discard all nonessentials and be in perfect freedom. My greatest sense of sacredness is to identify with the One Self and to stand exhilarated in the presence and the might and power of Deity. My heart's desire is "to be the One and only".

R2: My most joyous activity is "being in love" or pursuing wisdom and distributing understanding. My greatest sense of sacredness is divine love, or infinite inclusiveness and wholeness. My heart's desire is to be in love with all and one with all, or to achieve divine and complete wisdom and omniscience.

R3: My most joyous activity is mental and physical activity, to theorise, plan and then act on that plan. My greatest sense of sacredness is appreciation of those theories and proofs, which explain the nature of things. My heart's desire is "to plan along with God" and to manifest the Divine Plan.

R4: My most joyous activity is to create beauty and perfect equilibrium.

R5: My most joyous activity is to discover the previously hidden. My greatest sense of sacredness is contemplating the wonderfully intelligent design of nature. My heart's desire is to "know" the mystery of life.

R6: My most joyous activity is to be in the sacred presence of the one I adore and to love and be totally loved by the beloved, to have the freedom to pursue my highest ideal with fiery ardour and to express that ideal.

R7: My most joyous activity is to bring order out of chaos. My greatest sense of sacredness is to contemplate those forms (divinely created or man-made) which perfectly embody some aspect of the Universal Design. My heart's desire is to achieve a perfected expression of the divine archetype in form. [1]

2. Reading Ray Charts

Once the rays have been identified, the goal is to balance them, to bring the forces of the emotions, mind and personality into harmony and into right relation with the soul.

1. Example of a Ray Chart Reading - Carl Jung (1875-1961)

Brief biography: Jung was a theoretical psychologist and practicing clinician and became well known for his pioneering work in dream analysis. He also explored other areas including Eastern and Western philosophy, alchemy, astrology, sociology, as well as literature and the arts. Jung was obviously a very advanced human being, either a disciple or initiate. The hypothetical ray chart chosen for him, with justifications, is as follows.

Soul Ray II. Personality Ray 4. Mind Ray 3: Emotional Ray 6: Physical Ray 3

Soul - Ray 2 (R2) wisdom line. Jung's passion was healing and teaching, R2 vocations that point to a second ray soul. Souls on the wisdom line take ideas emanating from the Divine and make them attractive to the public. They train others to carry these ideas forth, to maximise the good that people can do with them. This was Jung's life. He lived to think, write and teach his ideas.

Personality - R4: Jung had a colourful personality, laughing and joking; his humour came across during his lectures and talks. He was also a talented artist - R4 gives a desire to produce art and beauty. When trying to assert his authority, he could go into battle. The conflict side of this ray was evident in the public animosities he had with Sigmund Freud, his former mentor and friend. He also struggled in the earlier part of his life to rise above depression, which is often associated with this ray.

Mind - R3: Jung demonstrated his advanced spiritual status through his forward-thinking ideas and the quality of his lectures, books and writings. He used the powers of his mind to explore the spiritual, the esoteric and the obscure and used what he learnt to help and heal. This wide ranging and philosophical approach on many subjects is typical of the third ray mind.

Emotional - R6: Jung was fiery and passionate in expression. Emotional battles point to a R6 astral field.

Physical - R3: his bulkiness points to a third ray physical nature - the "work horse" physical vehicle.

Analysis: Jung's R4 personality combined with his ray 6 astral, giving him his colourful appearance, artistic talent and passionate idealism and devotion. Once controlled, they were an avenue through which his R2 soul wisdom flowed. He used his mind to investigate spiritual, religious and esoteric philosophies. He was an outstanding representative of the R2 Ashram and with Freud, helped to pioneer the treatment of mental illness.

---
1 Information taken from Robbins, M; Tapestry of the Gods.

2. Ray reading for average person controlled by the emotions [5 - 6 - 3]

This is a chart for a person who is Atlantean in consciousness and controlled by the emotions. The soul ray is not evident nor is a personality ray, which has not yet formed. The R6 emotional field will be the problem, driving the person into hasty and fiery actions. The goal is to develop the R5 mind through study and work that develops scientific and research skills, then to use it to control the emotions. This will enable the personality ray to form and appear.

3. Ray reading for an advanced person controlled by the personality [II - 4 - 5 - 6 - 3]

A creative and colourful R4 personality, with an accurate scientific type of mind (R5). Because the personality dominates, ray talents are used selfishly and for personal profit and gain. But let us now suppose that a traumatic event occurs, so that the life is turned around (this is the way it always happens) and the higher search begins. The soul ray begins to have an effect and a new vocation will be sought on the R2 line. Practising the virtues for R4 such as mental and moral balance and by the constant sounding of the R4 integration word "steadfastness" will bring the personality into line with the soul.

4. Examples from Esoteric Psychology II, Alice Bailey (paraphrased)

(Example 1, pages 442-443) 1 - 4 - 3 - 6 - 1

The subject is an integrated personality. A first ray physical body and brain, dominated and controlled by a third ray mind gives capacity for varied intellectualism. A sixth ray emotional body that is idealistic and can be fanatical. A rapidly emerging fourth ray personality means the goal is to achieve harmony and unity through intense conflict. This is a person ambitious for power (1), but with right motive because of idealism in the nature (6). Will fight (4) intelligently (3), also fanatically (6) and put up a strong (1) fight.

(Example 2, pages 297-298) 1 - 2 - 5 - 6 - 2

The personality, astral and physical bodies are on the ray 2 line creating a psychological problem. The soul (1) and mental body (5) are along another line. This combination presents opportunity and difficulty.

The lower expression: it gives a person who is intensely sensitive, inclusive and self-willed (1). Emphasis will be upon material inclusiveness and tangible acquisition (prominence of ray 2). An exceedingly selfish and self-centred person who is not particularly intelligent, as only the fifth ray mental body relates the person directly to the mind aspect of Deity. However, he has the will to acquire what he wants (1).

Higher expression: when the evolutionary cycle has done its work - a sensitive, intuitive, inclusive disciple whose wisdom will flower and whose vehicles will be a channel for divine love.

3. Rays of the Tibetan's Disciples

The information contained in this chart is of great interest to students because it is the only credible public record of ray allocations. They were made by the Master Djwhal Khul (DK or The Tibetan), in the Alice Bailey books *Discipleship in the New Age* volumes I and II. DK was a master on the 2nd ray, which explains why most of the disciples on the list had R2 souls (23), then R1 souls (10), with a smattering of R3, R6 and R7.

1. Renowned author of the Psychosynthesis Psychology technique Roberto Assagioli was a student of DK's and is on the list as FCD. Here are extracts from correspondence sent to him.

   > You have .. the vices of your second ray virtues. You suffer from attachment and from a too rapid identification with other people. This can be handled if you stand steadfast as a soul and do not focus as a personality in dealing with people.. [1]

2. Here is a general comment about R1 Souls and Personalities.

   > In dealing with first ray egos .. or with those souls who are working through first ray personalities, I am faced always with the initial difficulty of their "isolated independence." It is not easy for such first ray types to cooperate, to fall into line with group suggestion, with group rhythm or group discipline [2]

---
1 Bailey, Alice A. Discipleship in the New Age I, 139
2 Ibid, 136

3. Most disciples had R6 personalities. This is advice given to BSD

> Your gift to this group of co-disciples is that fiery, dynamic, zealous aspiration which is the spiritual quality of the sixth ray, which governs your personality. [1]

4. Most disciples had R6 emotional bodies. BSD was advised in the following way.

> The astral or emotional body is conditioned by the sixth ray of devotion or of idealism, but this can be most easily transferred and transformed under the influence of the second ray of Love-Wisdom. Your task this life is to make this possible so that, in your next life, you can have an astral body conditioned by the second ray. [2]

5. There was a mixture of R3 and R7 physical bodies. Here are two quotes:

> [To J.W.K.P] Your physical body is on the seventh ray. Hence your Masonic opportunity and your ability to organise and to rule. I would remind you all that when the statement is made that the physical body is upon the seventh ray, it means that the atoms of the brain, in particular, are coloured and motivated by seventh ray energy. So it is with all the rays upon which a physical vehicle may be found. [3]

> [To R.V.B] Your physical body is on the third ray; it is here that your major problem lies. It is closely connected with your mental problem which is that of an increased dynamism. The dynamic power of your soul must pour through your fourth ray mind, galvanising it into a renewed, inclusive, loving, harmonising activity. Be more outgoing (as a part of your self-initiated training) to those, for instance, with whom your daily lot is cast. They need help. Give them of that help freely and fully. The 3rd Ray of Activity which governs your physical body is unduly quiescent and should be awakened by the soul to increased coordinated purpose. [4]

This completes this section of the work on the Seven Rays. Attention turns now to astrology and the signs and planets that carry the rays to our system, our planet and to us.

Rays of the Tibetan's Disciples

From Bailey's Discipleship in the New Age I

Disciple	Soul ray	Personality	Mind ray	Emotional	Physical	Page #
AAB	2	1				
BSD	3	6	5	6	3	105
BSW	1	7	4	6	7	621
CAC	1	2	4	6	1	203
CDP	2	6	5	6	6	504
DAO	7	1				278
DEI	2	1	2	1	3	497
DHB	2	6	1	1	7	416
DIJ	2	6	4	1	7	454
DLR	1	5	5	6	7	301
DPR	1	5	4	2	3	382
EES	7	6	4	6	1	645
FCD	2	4	1	2	7	138
GSS	7	6	1	6	3	406
HSD	6	1	1	6	7	571
IBS	1	6	4	6	3	235
ISGL	6	1	1	6	1	210
JSP	2	6	4	2	7	662
JWKP	1	2	4	2	7	157
KES	2		4	6	7	544
LDO	2	4	4	2	7	127
LFU	1	3	3	6	6	225
LTSK	1	6	5	1	3	2-724
LUT	2	1	4	6	3	471
OLRD	1	5	3	6	1	551
PDW	2	6	5	6	7	433
PGC	2	7	5	6	7	342
RAJ	2	7	4	6	2	173
RLU	2	4	5	6	3	531
RRR	2	1	4	6	1	649
RSU	2	3	1	1	7	355
RSW	2	7	4	2	7	637
RVB	2	4	4	2	3	263
SCP	1	6	2	6	1	321
SRD	2	6	4	1	3	560
SSP	2	5	4	6	3	189
WDS	2	1	2	1	3	375
WOI	2	5	4	6	7	441
WDB	2	4				291

---

1 Bailey, Alice A. Discipleship in the New Age I, 107
2 Ibid, 120
3 Ibid, 168
4 Ibid, 275

CHAPTER 5: ESOTERIC ASTROLOGY

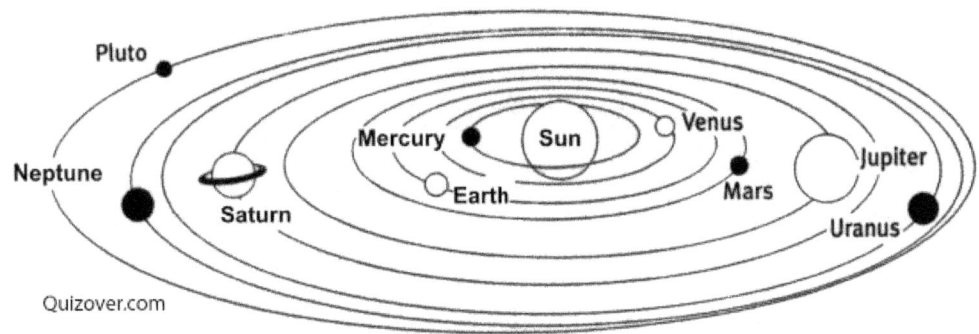

The science of astrology which is in many ways the science of sciences. [1]

---
[1] Bailey, Alice A. Discipleship in the New Age I, 437

INTRODUCTION

Astrology was born as a science in the ancient past when forward thinkers of the day - scholars and priests studied man's life and compared what they saw to the stars, to the universe and to space.

> The Ancient Wisdom teaches that "space is an entity." It is with the life of this entity and with the forces and energies, the impulses and the rhythms, the cycles and the times and seasons that esoteric astrology deals. [1]

At its highest, we are told that astrology is the purest presentation of occult truth in the world at this time because it deals with universal energies and forces that influence our solar system and earth.

> Astrology is essentially the purest presentation of occult truth in the world at this time, because it is the science which deals with those conditioning and governing energies and forces which play through and upon the whole field of space and all that is found within that field. [2]

In this book however, personal rather than cosmic astrology is studied. The goal is to gather information about the soul's plan for the current incarnation. This is the primary difference with Exoteric Astrology, which deals primarily with the personality life.

1. *Exoteric astrology:* it deals with the life of the personality, with the events, happenings, circumstances and the conditioning environment that appear in the personal horoscope. The heart of the exoteric chart is the Sun, which represents the personality.

2. *Esoteric astrology:* it concerns itself primarily with the unfoldment of consciousness that is awakened by the impact of the energies of the signs and rays. The heart of the esoteric chart is the Rising Sign.

3. *The Zodiac:* each of the twelve zodiac signs from Aries to Pisces, represent a stage in the evolution of consciousness from ignorance to enlightenment. Aries represents the birth of the mind and its early ignorance. Then each interim sign represents the unfoldment of a level of consciousness. But many cycles around the zodiac are required to achieve enlightenment. Round and round the zodiac we cycle under reincarnation. Gradually we develop the inner equipment needed to ascend in consciousness to the higher realms. It is an orderly process.

An important point to note is that, the status of a soul is not determined by the sign in which the Sun or ascendant sign is placed. For instance, if you were born in Pisces it does not mean that you are more evolved than people born in any other sign. Other people may have been around the Wheel of Life many more times and have a more advanced soul.

The Three Crosses

The evolutionary process occurs on three crosses or under the influence of three groups of signs. The twelve signs of the zodiac divide into three groups according to their mode or rate of vibration. Each group of four signs forms a "Cross". The signs of each cross work together collectively, releasing their forces through their ruling planets as a combined force to bring about required changes in consciousness.

1. The Mutable Cross and mutable signs collectively develop personality consciousness.
2. The Fixed Cross and fixed signs collectively develop soul consciousness.
3. The Cardinal Cross and cardinal signs collectively develop spiritual awareness.

Souls remain on one or other of the crosses for many incarnations until consciousness has learned all there is to learn. But while souls remain on one cross, experience is gained in all the signs. So, for instance a person's soul may be on any of the crosses, while the Sun Sign (the personality) cycles from life to life round the Mutable, Fixed and Cardinal Signs and Crosses.

---

1 Bailey, Alice A. Esoteric Astrology, 7
2 Ibid, 5

Quote

From point to point, stage to stage, and finally Cross to Cross, he fights for his spiritual life, in all the twelve houses and all the twelve constellations, subjected to countless combinations of forces and energies—ray, planetary, zodiacal and cosmic—until he is "made anew," is sensitive to the entire range of spiritual vibrations in our solar system and has achieved that detachment which will enable him to escape from the wheel of rebirth. He has accomplished this by mounting the three Crosses—the cross of the Personality or the changing form, the Cross of the Disciple or the eternal soul, and the Cross of the Spirit. This really means that he has passed through three momentous crises in his life cycle.[1]

The three crosses on Mount Golgotha were Biblical symbols of these three astrological crosses, the Common or Mutable Cross, the Fixed Cross and the Cardinal Cross.[2]

---
1 AAB; Esoteric Astrology 84
2 AAB, Esoteric Astrology, 82

1. The Mutable Cross

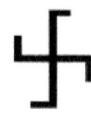

This cross is also known as the Common Cross and the Cross of the Hidden Christ. It turns in a clockwise direction. The young soul begins its journey on this cross. Here, blind to the larger picture, man suffers, agonises, desires and hungers.

The masses are on the Mutable Cross. Its effect on the personality when the Sun is in one of these signs, is fluidness. The spiritual goal is to develop and fuse the personality consciousness and to prepare for the 1st Initiation, taken in (Leo on the Fixed Cross).[1]

Gemini	Leads from instability to intelligent recognition of the soul.
Virgo	Leads from materialism to the birth of Christ awareness.
Sagittarius	Leads from gluttony to intelligent and inspired vision.
Pisces	Leads from impressionability to intelligent service.

Transition to the Fixed Cross occurs when people begin to aspire to something higher and finer. This means that they are responding to the esoteric forces pouring through the Mutable Cross. (Gemini is the primary influence on this cross).[2]

2. The Fixed Cross

This cross is also called the Cross of Discipleship and the Cross of the Crucified Christ. It turns anti-clockwise. The goal on this cross is to develop soul consciousness (group consciousness, love and wisdom) and control of the life by the soul. The esoteric planets rule those, whose souls are on this Cross. Its effect on the personality when the Sun is in one of these signs, is stubbornness.

> The Fixed Cross .. covers the period of the first three initiations.[3]

Taurus	Leads from desire to aspiration and love of the spiritual life.
Leo	Identification shifts eventually from the lower self to the soul.
Scorpio	Brings triumph over glamour. (Scorpio is the dominant arm for disciples, while Taurus is dominant for average man).[4]
Aquarius	Leads from personal desire to world service motivated by love.

3. The Cardinal Cross

This "Cross of the Risen Christ" turns in a clockwise direction. Its goal is to develop Monadic consciousness (spiritual will and power) and control of the life by the Monad. In the advanced beings on this cross, the lower life no longer controls and they live to serve the Plan and purpose of God. They stay on this cross until all levels of the solar system are mastered. It is the doorway to the stars. Its effect on the personality when the Sun is in one of these signs, is wilfulness.

Aries	Leads from sublimation of the personal will to the will of God.
Cancer	Leads from instinct to the will to serve the masses.
Libra	From unbalanced passion to the will to serve Higher Law.
Capricorn	Leads from personal ambition to the initiate who works with the Power of Love.

---
1 Gathered from Bailey, Alice A. Esoteric Astrology, 143
2 Gathered from Ibid, 345
3 Bailey, Alice A. The Rays and the Initiations, 693
4 Gathered from Bailey, Alice A. Esoteric Astrology, 381-2

1. THE SIGNS

The twelve signs or constellations embody twelve different aspects of soul expression. Collectively they develop all the qualities necessary to produce Masters of Wisdom and Compassion. Life after life they stimulate the soul conscious aspect within the form, producing inner activity that causes changes in outer personality expression and activity.

The twelve constellations might be regarded as embodying the soul aspect [1]

3. The signs condition consciousness

a. *The exoteric planetary rulers:* govern undeveloped or average man, distinguished by a weak, loose and unintegrated consciousness. Their task is to develop a strong and integrated personality.

b. *The esoteric rulers:* govern those who are on the Probationary and Discipleship Paths. Their task is to develop group consciousness and promote soul-personality fusion.

c. *The hierarchy rulers:* govern very advanced individuals. They fuse spirit, soul and personality into one blended unit, producing the universal consciousness distinctive of the initiate and Master of the Wisdom.

2. The Sun, Moon and Ascendant Signs

a. *Moon Sign:* the force flowing through the Moon indicates the past. It represents limitation, governs the physical body and shows where the "prison of the soul" is found. This "prison" is psychological, formed from negative and limiting thoughts and beliefs.

b. *The Sun Sign:* it is the primary representative for the personality. Related to the personality ray, it symbolises a person's responsiveness (or lack of) to the soul. It also symbolises the current level of personality integration, the present point of soul development and the present life quality. Initially the Sun Sign dominates the nature, but gradually this shifts to the soul as latent possibilities unfold.

c. *The Rising or Ascendant Sign:* it symbolises the spiritual goal and purpose for the immediate and succeeding incarnations. The energies of the rising sign will, if rightly used, lead to success. They evoke the unexpected, speed up the spiritual development process and unfoldment of the inner life.

Signs and Planet Rulers

SIGNS	Exoteric - Personality Level Rulers		Esoteric - Soul Level Rulers		Hierarchy - Spiritual Level Rulers	
♈ Aries	♂	Mars	☿	Mercury	♅	Uranus
♉ Taurus	♀	Venus	↓	Vulcan	↓	Vulcan
♊ Gemini	☿	Mercury	♀	Venus	⊕	Earth
♋ Cancer	☽	Moon	♆	Neptune	♆	Neptune
♌ Leo	☉	Sun	☉♆	Sun v Nep	☉♅	Sun v Uranus
♍ Virgo	☿	Mercury	☽↓	Moon v Vulcan	♃	Jupiter
♎ Libra	♀	Venus	♅	Uranus	♄	Saturn
♏ Scorpio	♂♇	Mars - Pluto	♂	Mars	☿	Mercury
♐ Sagittarius	♃	Jupiter	⊕	Earth	♂	Mars
♑ Capricorn	♄	Saturn	♄	Saturn	♀	Venus
♒ Aquarius	♅	Uranus	♃	Jupiter	☽♅	Moon v Uranus
♓ Pisces	♃♆	Jupiter - Nep	♇	Pluto	♇	Pluto

v = veiling

---
1 Bailey, Alice A. *Esoteric Astrology*, 28

Aries Soul Words: "I come forth and from the plane of mind I rule"

Personality Words: "Let form again be sought" [1]

Keynote: "Aries turns towards Capricorn" [2]

Spiritual Light: "The Light of Life Itself." [3] This is the searchlight or power of the Logos.

Hercules Labour in Aries: Capture of the man -eating mares.

The mares ravaged the land, killing everyone in their path and steadily breeding more evil horses. Hercules, with the assistance of his friend Abderis, successfully captured them. Hercules was so proud of his deed he instructed Abderis to herd the mares while he went off to brag. But Abderis was weak, the horses killed him and escaped. Grieving, Hercules completed the task alone.

The brood mares symbolise wrong speech and erroneous ideas. The aspirant must avoid using thoughts, words and actions that are harmful. Ideas should be fertilised from the spiritual realm. Hercules represents the soul and Abderis the personality, who, without the guidance of the soul, is too weak to cope with life's tests.

---

1 All Soul and Personality Words, Bailey, Alice A. (AAB). Esoteric Astrology, 653-4
2 All Keynotes Ibid, 332-3
3 All "Lights" Ibid, 329-30

ARIES

Keynotes: Creation - Being - Activity - Synthesis - Strife

The goal of the soul: to use the illumined mind to control the wild Arian personality, to direct the will intelligently in initiatives that benefit humanity.

Primary ray energies: ray 1 Will-Power gives pioneering and leadership skill. Ray 7 of Order and Ceremony gives ability to bring order out of chaos and to manifest and ground ideas.

- Unfoldment of Consciousness in Aries

a. **Mars**, God of War, influences the personality: at this level its effect can be likened to the impetuousness and immaturity of a teenager. Responding to the words "Let form again be sought" the inner fires feed an ardent desire for the many material advantages of physical incarnation. The lower self wants power, control and dominance.

Mars embodies sixth ray force, which leads to destructive fanaticism, struggle, strife and war.

b. **Mercury** carries the Soul's energy: and conveys the instruction "I come forth and from the plane of mind I rule". Its task is to illumine the mind, dispel illusion, transmute desire into aspiration and conflict into harmony, and teach the student to direct the life intelligently. The steps involved in personality and soul expression are:

- Express the will to be and do and to go out boldly into life.
- Unfold the power to manifest and develop the manifesting skills.
- Enter into battle for the Lord and fight for the principles.
- Arrive at unity through effort.

c. **Uranus** carries spiritual power: - its ray, the 7th, grounds the power of the 1st ray. Uranus rules the occult way and guides the student during the tests of the final stages of the Path. Initiates working through Aries initiate ideas and programs that serve the greater good. They are natural and strategic leaders. In the new World Order, many political and world leaders will be advanced Arian's.

- Rulers of Aries' Decanates.

Ordinary man: personality aggression (1. Mars) and a strong ego (2. Sun), results in the successful satisfaction of material ambition (3. Jupiter).

On the Reversed Wheel for Disciples: when wisdom (3. Jupiter) and self-control is evident (2. Sun), the disciple has triumphed in his fight (1. Mars) for spiritual awareness. [NB. The figures in the brackets refer to the sign decanates - "1" to the first 10 degrees decanate, "2" to the second 11-20 degrees, and "3" to the third decanate].

- Planets in Aries

a. **Sun**: is exalted. In the advanced man, it represents spirit that has come to full expression because of the evolutionary process. In undeveloped man it represents a full-blown ego.

b. **Venus**: in detriment. In the disciple, Venus' rays fade in the blazing potency of the Sun; the light of the personality fades as the light of the soul grows. On the Mutable Cross, lower desire dominates.

c. **Saturn**: this is a karmic position, indicating that individuals need to be responsible with their use of power.

TAURUS

Keynotes: Desire - Illumination - Will - Directed Purpose

The goal of the soul: is to control the lower appetites. This is achieved by transmuting desire into aspiration, impressing spiritual will on lower will and bringing Spiritual Light into the mind and life.

Primary ray energy: ray 4 Harmony through Conflict gives the Taurean the choice of either fighting or compromising, conflict or harmony, turmoil or serenity.

- Unfoldment of Consciousness in Taurus

a. **Venus** influences the personality: at this level, Venus represents the selfish desire nature of the personality. Stimulated by the conflict of ray 4 and responding to the words "Let struggle be undismayed", the personality takes, grasps and goes after that which is desired in a bull-headed, stubborn and destructive manner. Ruled by the passions, sexual and materialistic appetites control. Combative and conflict filled, life is unstable and filled with personal dramas.

Venus embodies 5th ray force, which enables Taurus people to detach themselves from the feelings of others.

b. **Vulcan** carries the Soul's energy: the soul wields Vulcan's 1st ray power like a hammer to fashion the lower self into an instrument fit for the expression of divine will. Under the stimulation of the cosmic Bull (Taurus) and responding to the words "I see and when the eye is opened, all is light", many fiery conflict-filled experiences follow to purify the nature. The goal is to remain aware of the lower impulses and not to give in to them. The result is a character of formidable inner strength and purpose.

The opened eye refers to the "third eye" of higher clairvoyance, which opens when lower sexual force is directed up, through and out, the throat centre.

c. **Vulcan** also carries spiritual power: initiates working with ray 1 are steadfast centres that others cling to, rocks who stabilise and strengthen any organisation to which they belong or work they do. They have endurance to complete any task, are reliable, loyal and unafraid to take on any battle or enter any fight that serves the greater good. They wield the higher light of wisdom.

- Rulers of Taurus' Decanates.

Ordinary man: when sensuousness (1 Venus), dominates the mind (2. Mercury), it results in conflict and karma (3. Saturn).

On the Reversed Wheel: when the struggling aspirant (3. Saturn), uses the mind intelligently (2, Mercury), intelligent love is the result (1. Venus).

- Planets in Taurus

a. **Moon**: exalted. Form life controls. As soul-fusion proceeds, unveiled Vulcan purifies, fashions and remoulds the form vehicles.

b. **Uranus**: it falls in this earth sign. This accentuates the wide divide between the lower appetites of the personality and the lighted soul, which is so marked in Taureans. Uranus awakens an inner response to the light, leading ultimately to full spiritual illumination.

c. **Mars**: in detriment. This adds to the warlike nature of Taurus but also gives the incentive to struggle towards light and understanding.

Soul words: "I see, and when the eye is opened, all is illumined"

Personality Words: "Let struggle be undismayed"

Keynote: "Taurus rushes blindly until Sagittarius directs"

Spiritual Light: "The penetrating Light of the Path." This is a beam of light streaming from Aries, the light of wisdom to be developed by the disciple.

Hercules Labour in Taurus: Capture of the Cretan Bull.

Hercules sought and eventually captured the bull in the maze of Minos on the island of Crete. He rode the bull back to a holy place on the mainland, using a gleaming star on the bull's forehead to light the way.

The desire nature (the bull), the aspirant's animal nature, is tested. The island symbolises the separated personality. The soul eventually controls and rides the passionate nature. Reaching the holy place on the mainland symbolises the integration or fusion of the personality with the soul.

Gemini Soul Words: "I recognise my other self and in the waning of that self I grow and glow"

Personality Words: "Let instability do its work"

Keynote: "Gemini moves towards Libra"

Spiritual Light: "The Light of Interplay." The dual light represents the interplay between spirit and form.

Hercules Labour in Gemini: Finding the Golden Apples.

In search of the apples, Hercules wandered here and there, forgetful of his task. He did not recognise his higher self who came several times to assist and give advice. He wrestled with the serpent of astral desire, eventually overpowering it. For aeons he was under the spell of Busiris, arch-deceiver, but eventually freed himself from illusion. Hercules was impatient to complete the task but could not ignore the suffering of Prometheus, and Atlas struggling under the weight of the world, so he stopped to assist them. Then three goddesses appeared before him, offering the apples. The labour was complete.

The aspirant wrestles with desire and illusion as he comes to an understanding of himself. Personal sacrifice are the actual goals of the labour, to forget oneself in service.

GEMINI

Keynotes: Fluidity - Recognition of Duality - Soul Control

The goal of the soul: this is to control the unstable nature of the personality by illuminating the mind and bringing it under soul control. This means developing discrimination, discernment and refining life values so that intelligent love is developed and expressed.

Primary ray energy: Ray 2 of Love-Wisdom gifts the nature with a love of truth, wise communication and harmlessness in thought and speech.

- Unfoldment of Consciousness in Gemini

a. **Mercury** influences the personality: it gives the gift of a clever mind and skilled communication but adds mental conflict (R4) and increases duality. The keynote at this level is "Let instability do its work". The personality is unstable, shallow, superficial and changeable. It plays games, drifts with the ebb and flow of life, is deceitful and can rationalise anything to justify its position. It is a chameleon.

b. **Venus** carries the Soul's energy: and conveys the instruction "I see my other self and in the waning of that self, I grow and glow". The task is to detach from the lower self, so that identification with the intelligence of the soul grows. Venus embodies 5th ray force and its gift to man is intelligent love. It symbolises everything fine, beautiful and of quintessential value which the soul has extracted from past lives. Under its influence, man develops right values to live by.

c. The **Earth** carries spiritual power: and provides a field for man to work out his spiritual destiny. Its ray is the very down-to-earth 3rd ray. These initiates are instruments for the Forces of Light, demonstrating intelligent love, perfect balance of intellect and heart and love in action. Their task is to oversee major changes in education and healing so these areas can better serve humanity. Others work in the material world, directing money and resources to higher causes.

- Rulers of Gemini's Decanates.

Ordinary man: materialism (1. Jupiter) and desire (2. Mars) are strong, feeding the ego (3. Sun). On the Reversed Wheel: true selfhood (3. Sun), is reached when the desire nature is defeated (2. Mars), bringing spiritual rewards and benefits (1. Jupiter).

- Planets in Gemini

In this sign, no planet falls or is exalted. The developmental goal is balance and to avoid all extremes.

If you have the Sun, Moon, Mercury, Venus, Mars, Saturn or Pluto in Gemini, strive to overcome negative Gemini traits - especially the superficial and shallow tendencies; replacing them with the higher, particularly balance. If it rules your ascendant, use the power of Venus to help you develop the higher qualities of Gemini and expand your soul light.

CANCER

Keynotes: Instinct - Intellect - Intuition

The goal of the soul: this is to develop the intellect and purify the emotional body, so they are no longer a playground for negative thoughts and emotions. When the mind is freed from illusion, it becomes a prism for the light and love of the soul.

Primary ray energies: ray 3 Active-Intelligence gives a versatile intellect. Ray 7 Ceremonial Order and Magic gives organising and executive skill and efficiency on the Physical Plane.

- Unfoldment of Consciousness in Cancer

a. The **Moon** influences the personality: responding to the words "Let isolation be the rule and yet the crowd exists," the defensive personality is emotionally isolated. Ultra-protective, volatile, unstable (R4) and highly sensitive to any slight or criticism, it is submerged and lost in the emotional waters of the masses. This is the Atlantean consciousness.

b. **Moon** and **Neptune** .. the Mother of all Forms and the God of the Waters .. a major synthesis of form and of desire-sensitivity and, consequently, a true statement of the stage of consciousness which we call Atlantean. Mass sensitivity and mass identification with form .. [is a Cancer trait]. [1]

c. **Neptune** carries the Soul's energy: and conveys the instruction "I build a lighted house and therein dwell." The task is to focus mentally and build a lighted consciousness. Neptune dissolves all blocks to love created through fear, it shows how emotional-desire can be transmuted into love-aspiration and gives a yearning to experience a state of oneness with all life. Through its higher 6th ray influence, it refines the lower nature, freeing it from illusion so that inclusive love is expressed.

Neptune also carries spiritual power: releasing disciples from the world of illusion, they are then free to save and lift mankind. This is the goal of advanced Cancer people. The magnetic pull of their souls saves many. They inspire (R6) the masses to strive towards the greater good.

- Rulers of Cancer's Decanates.

Ordinary man: desire (1. Venus), dominates the mind (2. Mercury), so that instinct (3. Moon), rules the consciousness.
On the Reversed Wheel: constant struggle (3. Moon), to free the mind (2. Mercury), from the lower instincts (Moon) and to develop the intelligence, results in an illumined mind (1. Venus).

- Planets in Cancer

a. **Venus**: in this sign, mind (Venus) is the servant of the personality. This is aided by the forces of the 3rd Ray of Active Intelligence.

b. **Jupiter** and **Neptune**: exalted. This gives the successful development and use of form and of psychic sensitivity, both at higher and lower levels.

c. **Saturn**: in detriment. "Cancer a place of symbolic imprisonment and emphasises the pains and penalties of wrong orientation." [2]

---

1 Bailey, Alice A. Esoteric Astrology, 321
2 Ibid, 342

Cancer Soul Words: "I build a lighted house and therein dwell"

Personality Words: "Let isolation be the rule and yet the crowd exists"

Keynote: "Cancer visions life in Leo"

Spiritual Light: "The Light within the form". The dark light of matter that awaits soul stimulation.

Hercules Labour in Cancer: Capture of the Doe.

Artemis (instincts) daughter of the Moon, and Diana (the intellect) daughter of the Sun, both laid claim to the doe and they tried to foil Hercules in his efforts to capture it. But capture it he did and he took it to the holy shrine of the Sun God.

The doe has various guises - the instinct, intellect and intuition. The development of the intuition (Sun God) subordinates the instincts (Artemis) and brings about the right use of the intellect (Diana), bringing true realisation.

Unveiled Neptune .. when a man is an initiate, he does not react to ordinary feeling .. eventually the watery life of emotional reaction is superseded by the life of true and of inclusive love. Soul control esoterically "obliterates" the Moon and all traces of Neptunian life. [1]

---

1 AAB. Esoteric Astrology, 322

Leo Soul Words: "I am That and That am I"

Personality Words: "Let other forms exist, I rule"

Keynote: "Leo seeks release in Scorpio"

Spiritual Light: "The Light of the Soul."

Hercules Labour in Leo: Slaying the Nemean Lion

The Nemean lion was devastating the population and Hercules was sent to kill it. The lion attacked but Hercules was too strong. The lion retreated and hid in a cave that had two entrances. Hercules blocked off one entrance so the lion could not escape and entering through the other, choked the lion to death with his bare hands.

The lion symbolises the personality running wild. It is not controlled as long as the emotional life is strong. Hercules, the soul illumined disciple, does not work with that lower aspect. He works through the intellect, enabling him to subdue the personality by choking off its energy and power.

> Leo .. In this sign, he undergoes preparation for the first initiation and takes it also in this sign. [1]

___
1 AAB. Esoteric Astrology, 143

LEO

Keynotes: Self Consciousness - Will to Know - Will to Rule

The goal of the soul: Leo represents the personality and the goal is to integrate the personality so that a self-conscious, self-empowered personality emerges. Then, to bring it under soul control so that creative power flows out for the good of the whole.

Primary ray energies: ray 1 Will Power gives leadership, managerial and executive skill. Ray 5 Concrete Mind gives a keen, focused intellect and highly developed powers of analysis and discrimination. Ray 2 Love-Wisdom stimulates kindness and compassion.

- Unfoldment of Consciousness in Leo

a. The **Sun** rules on three levels. It is the source of physical consciousness on the exoteric level. The Sun unveiling Neptune on the esoteric level is the source of soul awareness. The Sun unveiling Uranus on the hierarchy level, is the source of spiritual life.

b. The [physical] **Sun** influences the personality: and conveys the instruction "Let other forms exist, I rule because I am". Consequently, the personality is arrogant, selfish, autocratic and wants to control and make slaves of everyone in its domain. It stands proudly at the centre of its universe, consecrating all thought and time to its own well-being and personal interests. But psychologically it has a soft underbelly and is highly sensitive to any criticism - a consequence of the weakness of the 2nd ray, which the Sun embodies.

Neptune reveals the Soul's energy: it distributes divine love (the 2nd ray via the 6th ray) flowing from the Heart of the Sun. Under this influence, emotional desire transforms into love-aspiration and the emotional field becomes a clear channel for this divine energy. Responding to the soul instruction "I am That and That am I", consciousness identifies with the soul and the disciple steps forward as a wise and compassionate leader.

c. **Uranus** carries spiritual power: will and power (R1) flows from the Central Spiritual Sun and Uranus distributes its energy. Initiates working through Leo are electric and dynamic leaders. Pioneering, they are magnetic centres in their group and many advanced Leo leaders will lead man in the new World Order.

- Rulers of Leo's Decanates:

Ordinary man: the ego (1. Sun), is swollen (2. Jupiter) and the aggressive personality fights (3. Mars), to dominate the world.

On the Reversed Wheel: the struggle to be free (3. Mars), aided by wisdom (2. Jupiter), results eventually in self rule (1. Sun).

- Planets in Leo

No planet falls or is exalted in Leo. The advanced Leo is free from outside control, is king and ruler of the life. The power of Saturn and Uranus weaken in Leo, except in the case of the initiate who responds to the esoteric influence of Uranus.

a. **Uranus**: in detriment. The power of the mind symbolised by Uranus reduces. The mind is not in control. Instead, the soul uses and controls the mind.

b. **Saturn**: in detriment. Difficult karma awaits the man or woman who misuses power.

VIRGO

Keynotes: "Christ in you, the hope of glory"

The goal of the soul: this is to develop the mind power of discrimination and use it to bring about the purification of the physical, astral and mind bodies. This reveals the inner light, the Christ consciousness. The goal then, is service.

Primary ray energies: ray 2 Love-Wisdom gives a clear intelligence and ray 6 of Devotion and Idealism leads to selfless service.

- Unfoldment of Consciousness in Virgo

a. **Mercury** influences the personality: embodying the unstable 4th ray, at this lower level Mercury's versatile energy increases mental conflict and separativeness. Responding to the words "Let matter reign" the ego is materialistic and judgemental. Everything is criticised and found to be less than perfect.

b. **Moon** veiling **Vulcan** unveils the Soul's energy: the Moon rules the form and it is the will of God to manifest through the form. Virgo is the mother, the womb of matter, the form or personality life, which nurtures and then gives birth to the beauty of the soul, the Christ child. Virgo prepares the form so that this can take place.

The soul instruction "I am the mother and the child, I God, I matter am" is a direction to unite the three divine aspects of spirit (God), soul (child) and personality (mother). This enables the Christ Spirit to emerge. Vulcan's 1st ray gives aspirants the determination and will to persevere in this work.

c. **Jupiter** carries spiritual power: it gifts initiates with love and wisdom. Stepping forth as pure examples of "Christ in you, the hope of glory", they are generous servers who dedicate their lives to the upliftment of humanity, leading it into the ways of peace and progress. They oversee major changes in education and healing so that these areas can better serve humanity.

- Rulers of Virgo's Decanates.

Ordinary man: the instinctual mind (1. Venus and 2. Mercury), evolves and grows through the lessons of life experience and the consequences of karma (3. Saturn).

On the Reversed Wheel: through suffering and the seizing of opportunity to choose rightly (3. Saturn) and analyse correctly (2. Mercury), wisdom is developed (1. Venus).

- Planets in Virgo

a. **Mercury**: dignified. This strengthens the mind. Mercury reaches its full power in this sign because Virgo is intelligence and the hidden Christ is wisdom or pure reason.

b. **Venus**: falls. When materialism dominates the nature, then ignorance rules wisdom (Venus). Esoterically, wisdom disappears and vanishes into the darkness.

c. **Neptune**: in detriment. Sensitivity is not evident during the early stages of the Path when the personality nature, particularly lower mind, is being developed.

d. **Jupiter**: in detriment. Christ love is temporarily hidden in the depths of ignorance.

Virgo Soul Words: "I am the Mother and the Child. I, God, I matter am"

Personality Words: "Let matter reign"

Keynote: "Virgo hides the light which irradiates the world in Aquarius"

Spiritual Light: "The blended dual Light" (of form and of God).

Hercules Labour in Virgo - the Girdle of Hippolyte

Venus gave the girdle to Hippolyte the Amazon Queen. She was instructed to give it to Hercules but sought to keep it by using flattery to distract him. He ignored her, seized the girdle and killed her. But later repented and saved a maiden in distress.

The Amazons represent the lower aspects which keep the soul (girdle), imprisoned. Eventually the Father demands the return of the soul or son. The resistant personality is slain when the Christ Spirit births in the heart. The failure in this test is a warning to those who would try to achieve spiritual growth before they are ready. Hercules' redemption suggests that all evil deeds are exonerated in time, through loving service.

LIBRA

Keynotes: Balance - Equilibrium - Justice

Libra Soul Words: "I choose the way which leads between the two great lines of force"

Personality Words: "Let choice be made"

Keynote: "Libra relates the two in Gemini"

Spiritual Light: "The Light that moves to rest." This light oscillates until a point of balance is achieved.

Hercules Labour in Libra: Capture of the Erymanthian Boar

While searching for the boar in the mountains, Hercules met Pholos, a centaur. They drank wine which belonged to all the centaurs. This caused a fight and, in the battle, centaurs were killed. Although distressed, Hercules continued his search for the boar, captured it and drove it down the mountain by its hind legs. This was amusing to onlookers.

In Libra, the fires of pleasure and their consequences must be exhausted before the greater task of taming the personality (the capture of the boar) can begin. Hercules driving the boar by the hind legs symbolises the soul directing the ungainly personality. The amusement of bystanders is a reminder to balance the serious work of discipleship with a sense of humour..

The goal of the soul: this is to develop balance, moderation, right equilibrium between all opposites and express the will-to-good.

Primary ray energy: ray 3 Active-Intelligence develops the intellect and ability to think abstractly. It gives abundant mental and physical energy.

- Unfoldment of Consciousness in Libra

a. **Venus** influences the personality: at this level, Venus represents a mind that is yoked to the sensuousness of lower desire. Responding to the words "Let choice be made", this mind makes many wrong choices and is selfish, deceitful and dishonest. There is unbalanced fiery passion, sexual promiscuity, greed, morals which shift and change and denial of the truth. The personality swings to extremes and emphasis is on sex and the superficial.

b. **Uranus** carries the Soul's energy: and conveys the instruction "I choose the way which lies between the two great lines of force". Disciples strive for mental balance, an essential requirement to pass the three tests in Libra - honesty and integrity in the areas of justice, sex and money. Uranus embodies 7th ray force, which gives the ability to materialise ideas on the Physical Plane. This distinguishes Libra disciples from their less evolved brethren who procrastinate. The soul uses Uranus to shatter indecision, lethargy and limiting beliefs that keep it imprisoned in matter. It encourages independence, freedom and experimentation.

c. **Saturn** carries spiritual power: and gives initiates spiritual will and a wide intelligence (R3). Their task is to bring about balance and justice in society. In the New World Order, they will be involved in legislating fairer legal, financial and economic laws for the masses.

- Rulers of Libra's Decanates.

Ordinary man: self-indulgence (1. Jupiter), has karmic consequences (2. Saturn) and results in life conflict (3. Mercury).

On the Reversed Wheel: an illumined mind (3. Mercury), is the result when the lessons of adversity are learnt (2. Saturn), resulting in a beneficial life and rewards (1. Jupiter).

- Planets in Libra

a. **Saturn**: it is exalted. At the point of balance, people have an opportunity to use the intellect wisely, to make the right choice, or face negative karma.

b. **Mars**: in detriment. In this sign of interlude, the power of desire is lessened. This enables the mind to be developed.

c. The **Sun**: it falls. Neither personality nor soul dominate in the pure Libran. With balance achieved, esoterically they tune each other out. Unless there are other factors in the chart (in the psychology), this manifests as a life that is relatively conflict free.

If you have the Sun, Moon, Mercury, Venus, Mars, Saturn or Pluto in Libra, strive to overcome negative Libran traits replacing them with the higher. If it rules your ascendant, use the power of the Uranus and the Soul Words to help you develop the higher qualities of Libra and find balance between soul and personality.

SCORPIO

Keynotes: Struggle - Strength - Test - Trial - Triumph

The goal of the soul: this is to force the disciple to struggle, strive and to triumph over the illusions, rampant desires and deceit of the lower emotional life. This will reorient consciousness to the soul, readying it for initiation and tuning it into the spiritual Plan.

Scorpio, the sign of testing and of discipleship. [1]

Primary ray energies: only Ray 4 of Harmony through Conflict flows through Scorpio, producing a warrior. The Scorpio experience trains disciples to fight. They are being prepared for the greatest battle of their soul life- to fight against delusion until it is defeated.

- Unfoldment of Consciousness in Scorpio

a. **Mars**, God of War, influences the personality: it has a delusionary effect and its crusading 6th ray keeps the personality continuously embroiled in conflict. Responding to the words "Let maya flourish and let deception rule" self-deceit, rampant appetites and lower desires control. The unregenerated Scorpio personality is psychologically and sometimes physically, dangerous and vindictive.

b. **Mars** also carries the Soul's energy: at this higher level, a great battle takes place. Mars brings to the surface negative emotional patterns and habits that lurk deep in the psyche for destruction by the light of the soul. The Physical Plane tests are sex, love of comfort and money. Emotional Plane tests are fear, hatred and desire for power. Mental Plane tests are pride, separativeness and cruelty. Gradually, 6th ray desire is transmuted into spiritual aspiration and the light of the soul illumines the intellect. Then, responding to the instruction "Warrior I am and from the battle I emerge triumphant" the advanced Scorpio Warrior of Light emerges, one who fights for the higher good.

c. **Mercury** carries spiritual power: it gifts the mind with wisdom and the intuition so that intellectual warriors emerge. They fight with pen and word to destroy the shackles that bind souls to earth. In the New Order, many will be psychologists who use Mercury's 4th ray to relate the soul and personality.

- Rulers of Scorpio's Decanates.

Ordinary man: powerful and controlling desires (1. Mars), feed the lower appetites (2. Jupiter), so that the lower instincts rule (3. Moon).

On the Reversed Wheel: the struggle to overcome the lower instincts (3. Moon) and to act wisely (2. Jupiter), enables the disciple to fight and defeat (1. Mars), the lower nature.

- Planets in Scorpio

a. **Uranus** is exalted. It develops the scientific mind and enables the disciple to live the occult life and leave the mystic way behind.

b. **Venus** is in detriment. Eventually the Solar Angel (Venus), gives way to the spiritual Presence which it has previously hidden. Venus must wane and the Sun as a symbol of God, must wax.

c. The **Moon** falls. In the final victory in Scorpio, the instinctual life (the Moon), is entirely vanquished and defeated and desire killed.

---
1 Bailey, Alice A. Esoteric Astrology, 538

Scorpio Soul Words: "Warrior I am, and from the battle I emerge triumphant"

Personality Words: "Let maya flourish and let deception rule"

Keynote: "Scorpio stages the release of Leo"

Spiritual Light: "The Light of Day." This is the place where three lights meet - the light of form, the light of soul and the light of life. They meet, they blend, they rise.

Hercules Labour in Scorpio: Destroying the Lernaen Hydra.

The hydra lived in a swamp and had nine angry heads that breathed flames. Hercules attacked it, but two heads grew back for every one he severed. Hercules was being defeated. But then he had the inspiration to raise the hydra aloft and when its connection with the mud was broken, it died.

In the regions of the subconscious the shadow side of our nature lives. Discrimination is needed to expose it, patience to discover its lair, humility to bring its slimy fragments to the surface and expose them to the light of intelligent wisdom.

SAGITTARIUS

Keynotes: Aspiration - Orientation - Direction

Sagittarius Soul Words: "I see the goal, I reach that goal, and see another"

Personality Words: "Let food be sought"

Keynote: "Sagittarius, the disciple becomes the Saviour in Pisces"

Spiritual Light: "A beam of directed, focused Light." The point of light becomes the beam, revealing a greater light ahead and illuminating the way to the centre of that light.

Hercules Labour in Sagittarius: Killing the Stymphalian Birds.

Man-eating birds attacked and killed people. They lived and hid in the marshes. To bring them into the open, Hercules clashed cymbals together. When the birds rose in panic at the noise, Hercules mounted his winged horse and killed them with his arrows.

The marshes symbolise mind plus emotions. The birds uncontrolled words and thoughts, a devastating force. The words which do most harm are cruel gossip, selfish talk and the inappropriate release of knowledge to unprepared minds. These habits are destroyed by the light and power of the soul. The sound of the cymbals represents the 'word of the soul.

The goal of the soul: to develop harmlessness in thought and speech, to aspire towards the spiritual life and redirect the energies to new and more idealistic goals.

Primary ray energies: Ray 4 of Harmony gives a love of beauty and peace. Ray 5 Concrete Mind gives an acute intellect. Ray 6 gives higher idealism and fuels an aspiration to strive for the higher goal.

- Unfoldment of Consciousness in Sagittarius

a. **Jupiter** influences the personality: responding to the words "Let food again be sought" the personality indulges the lower desires and is a glutton for food, sex and money. It lacks discipline, is irresponsible, gossips and attacks others with cruel words.

b. The **Earth** carries the Soul's energy: and conveys the instruction "I see the goal, I reach that goal and then I see another". The Earth provides the field of experience and training, so that the reorientation to a new and higher life is achieved. Its ray is the 3rd of Intelligence and it teaches disciples to be more discerning and to develop harmlessness in thought and speech. Consequently, progress is fast along the Path. This is a sign of advanced discipleship.

c. **Mars** carries spiritual power: initiates wield Mars' idealistic force (R6) wisely and use their power to direct men and women to the Portal of Initiation. Coming from the heart, they are non-separative and are comfortable with both the elite and the common man. Many visionary thinkers in the New Order will be evolved Sagittarian's.

- Rulers of Sagittarius' Decanates.

Ordinary man: self-indulgence (1. Jupiter), of the desire nature (2. Mars), strengthens the power of the personality (3. Sun).

On the Reversed Wheel: when alignment with the soul (3. Sun) has been achieved and the struggle with the lower nature (2. Mars) is successful, then spiritual rewards come (3. Jupiter).

- Planets in Sagittarius

In Sagittarius, no planet is exalted and no planet falls. It is a sign of balance and has no extremes. Consequently, disciples under Sagittarius must learn to find balance and moderation.

No planet is exalted in Sagittarius and no planet falls. For this reason, Sagittarius is esoterically regarded as a sign of balance and of no extremes; there is no great fall and no exaltation. This fact indicates that the disciple must walk an even way between the pairs of opposites, uninfluenced by either the "power of exaltation or the potency of that which falls." Neither the valley nor heights produce any demonstrable effect. [1] Mercury: weakens. In time, wisdom supersedes the logical mind.

If you have the Sun, Moon, Mercury, Venus, Mars, Saturn or Pluto in Sagittarius, strive to overcome negative Sagittarius traits replacing them with the higher. If it rules your ascendant, use the power of the Lord of Earth and the Soul Words to help you develop the higher qualities of Sagittarius and to find your way to the heights.

---

[1] Bailey, Alice A. Esoteric Astrology, 191

CAPRICORN

Keynotes: Effort - Struggle - Strain - Initiation

The goal of the soul: this is to force man to overcome materialistic ambition (the Goat), kneel in humility before the Divine and offer the life in service.

Primary ray energies: the collective power of Rays 1 (Power), 3 (Intelligence) and 7 (Order), enables those born under Capricorn to be very successful in both a materialistic and spiritual sense. The test is one of choice. Will the Capricorn individual go the high or low way?

- Unfoldment of Consciousness in Capricorn

a. **Saturn** influences the personality: responding to the words "Let ambition rule and let the door stand wide", the appetite for power, influence and material wealth intensifies. The personality uses Saturn's 3rd ray of Intelligence to get what it wants. With guile, manipulation and calculation, it drives to its goal and there is no compassion for anyone in its way.

b. **Saturn** also carries the Soul's energy: under the stress of adversity, Saturn offers disciples the opportunity to use their intelligence wisely, to make correct decisions, bring the personality into line with divine law and to correct any imbalances of the past. This fulfils karma and enables disciples to respond to the higher instruction in Capricorn, "Lost am I in light supernal, yet on that light I turn my back". Ignoring personal advancement, these advanced men and women turn towards humanity and the light of love and compassion shines through their heart and onto those who need assistance.

c. **Venus** carries spiritual power: it gives initiates the gift of an acute mind (R5) and love. Politically influential, these initiates are highly organised leaders and pillars of strength who use their power for the higher good.

- Rulers of Capricorn's Decanates.

Ordinary man: karma dogs the man or woman (1. Saturn), who uses the gifts of mind (2. Venus), for selfish personal gain and self-aggrandisement (3. Sun).

On the Reversed Wheel: the disciple expresses soul illumination (3. Sun) and wisdom (2. Venus), enabling initiation to be taken (3. Saturn).

- Planets in Capricorn

a. **Mars** is exalted. In this earthly sign, the God of War and producer of conflict triumphs in the life of the undeveloped and average man. The ability to fight and to satisfy the lower ambitions is powerful. This most material of all the signs provides the battleground between the old established, covetous, habits and the new higher spiritual impulses.

b. **Saturn**: is dignified. It is potent in Capricorn. The intensified activity of the 3rd ray gives a powerful mind and intellect and power to manipulate life resources. When rightly employed it liberates the soul from form control. Otherwise, it attracts negative karma.

Capricorn Soul Words: "Lost am I in light supernal, yet on that light I turn my back"

Personality Words: "Let ambition rule and the door stand wide"

Keynote: "Capricorn consummates the work of Scorpio"

Spiritual Light: "The Light of Initiation." This is the light which clears the way to the mountain top of transfiguration.

Hercules Labour in Capricorn: Slaying Cerberus, Guardian of Hades.

Hercules travelled down into Hades, the underworld, to rescue Prometheus who was guarded by Cerberus. The dog had three heads. Hercules defeated it by choking it to death. He freed Prometheus who then gave man the gift of fire.

In this instance, Hades represents immersion in deepest materialism. The soul must come down into this world and challenge and defeat the personality. It is represented by Cerberus whose three heads symbolise sensation, desire and good intentions that come to naught - three aspects of the personality that must be overcome.

Aquarius Soul Words:
"Water of life am I, poured forth for thirsty men"

Personality Words: "Let desire in form be ruler"

Keynote: "Aquarius releases Virgo from her load"

Spiritual Light: "The Light that shines on Earth, across the sea." This is the light that always shines in the darkness, guiding pilgrims home.

Hercules Labour in Aquarius: Cleansing the Augean Stables

For thirty years, the great cattle stables of King Augeas had not been cleaned. The air was putrid and pestilence was sweeping the land. Hercules broke down a wall surrounding the stables and diverted two rivers through them, cleansing them within a day.

Breaking down barriers of separativeness needs to be done in the Aquarian Age. Then the healing waters of love and life can flow in.

The Moon is .. the hierarchical rule of Aquarius. [1]

The Moon which hides or veils Uranus [2]

AQUARIUS

Keynotes: Group Consciousness - World Service

The goal of the soul: this is to develop the scientific mind, to become more inclusive and group conscious and to develop the heart and intuition of a World Server. Then use these qualities in humanitarian interests to promote right human relations across the globe.

Primary ray: Ray 5 of Concrete Mind gives a keen, focused intellect and power to discover through investigation, research and experimentation.

- Unfoldment of Consciousness in Aquarius

a. **Uranus** influences the personality: its electric force gives quirky qualities to the personality, eccentricity, wilfulness and irresponsibility. Responding to the words "Let desire in form be ruler" attachment to Physical Plane gratification is strong. (Uranus' ray is the 7th and strengthens materialism at this level). The mind is awake, but its vision is narrow, fixed, rigid and driven by fear. The personality wants change and uses its will and intellect to destroy all that stands in its way.

b. **Jupiter** carries the Soul's energy: its expansive 2nd ray force unifies the heart and mind and the personality and soul. Transformed, the disciple responds fully to the instruction "Water of life am I, poured forth for thirsty men" and becomes a vessel for inclusive love and sensitive humanitarian awareness. Reformation of society for the highest good becomes the service goal.

c. **Moon** unveiling **Uranus**: initiates at this level and in this sign are World Servers who use power in world service and to reform planetary life. They have brilliant intellects and many are scientists who, motivated by their love of humanity and its welfare, invent new technologies and make scientific discoveries that improve people's lives.

- Rulers of Aquarius' Decanates.

Ordinary man: difficult conditions (1. Saturn) and conflict (2. Mercury), plus a mind that can think logically and scientifically, develops the powers of the mind (3. Venus). At this level, these powers are selfish.

On the Reversed Wheel: a new era of love-wisdom and of expressed brotherly relations (3. Venus), dawns because of soul illumination (2. Mercury) and making the right moral choices at critical testing moments (1. Saturn).

- Planets in Aquarius

No planet is exalted and no planet falls. This is because the Aquarian, who has worked through all the signs, has reached a point of balance and is no longer held by the pairs of opposites. He has surmounted all the tests of human life and stands free, distributing life, symbolised by the two wavy lines of the Aquarius symbol.

a. The **Sun** (the physical Sun) is in detriment. The personality (Sun) has its power lessened in this group conscious sign. When the 3rd initiation has been taken, the light of the personality is "put out" by the light of the subjective Sun (the soul or spiritual aspect).

---

1 AAB. Esoteric Astrology, 219
2 Ibid, 138

PISCES

Keynotes: Bondage - Detachment - Death

The goal of the soul in Pisces: to detach from the nonessentials in life and serve humanity with compassion, tolerance and understanding.

Primary ray energies: the love rays, Ray 2 of Love-Wisdom and Ray 6 of Devotion and Idealism, flow through Pisces. They give qualities of compassion, unconditional love and dedication to a life of service.

- Unfoldment of Consciousness in Pisces

a. **Jupiter** and **Neptune** influence the personality: their expansive (R2) and boundless (R6) forces in this watery sign, create a personality that is very fluid and hypersensitive. With no boundaries, it is subject to delusion and fantasy. Ungrounded, it tries to escape the perceived harshness of physical life through avoidance, denial, alcohol and drugs. Until corrected, Piscean's respond to the command "Go forth into matter" and remain bound to the Wheel of Rebirth.

b. **Pluto** carries the Soul's energy: this is the force of the 1st ray, which destroys all ties that bind the soul to earth. Pluto destroys all snares from the past, closes all chapters and purges all obstacles to love. It drags negative subconscious patterns to the surface, destroying them and releasing the soul from the prison that holds it captive. Then, responding to Piscean compassion and the instruction "I leave the Father's house and turning back, I save", the disciple serves unselfishly.

c. **Pluto** also carries spiritual power: the 1st ray gives initiates the power to make major radical changes in human society and culture for the greater good. They serve selflessly and sacrificially. Many oversee major changes in religion and health so that these areas can better serve humanity. The lighted glow of spiritual love flows through them drawing people in for guidance, healing and love. They are shepherds of men, in the manner of the Christ and are on the Path of the World Saviour.

- Rulers of Pisces' Decanates.

Ordinary man: lacking central control (1. Jupiter), the instincts control (2. Moon) and life is ruled by the desire nature (3. Mars).

On the Reversed Wheel: battling through all the challenges (3. Mars) that life presents and by purifying the form nature (2. Moon), brings spiritual success. Wisdom rules. (1. Jupiter).

- Planets in Pisces

a. **Venus** is exalted. The two fishes joined together symbolise the captivity of the soul in form. Pluto cuts the thread which binds them and then Venus reunites the severed lives, but on a much higher level. Eventually, the Sons of God - who are also the sons of Mind, rise into glory through the crucifixion experience, having learned to love.

b. **Mercury** falls. In ordinary man, the power of mind weakens in the ocean of the emotions. After the 4th initiation when the initiate links directly with the Monad and has full spiritual awareness, the power of the mind ends. It is no longer required. Intuition takes its place.

Pisces Soul Words: "I leave the Father's Home and turning back, I save"

Personality Words: "Go forth into matter"

Keynote: "Pisces takes from all the signs"

Spiritual Light: "The Light of the World." This is the light which reveals the light of life itself. It ends forever the darkness of matter.

Hercules Labour in Pisces: Capture of the Red Cattle of Geryon.

In a golden cup, Hercules sailed to the island of Erytheia where Geryon, a monster with three bodies in one, was holding red cattle unlawfully. Hercules killed a two-headed dog guarding the cattle but spared the shepherd Orthrus. He shot Geryon in the side, with an arrow that pierced all three bodies at once, killing him. He sailed with the cattle and Orthrus back to the mainland and offered them to Athena, Goddess of Wisdom.

The golden cup is the Holy Grail, the pure, revealed soul. The red cattle symbolise the lower desires, the two-headed dog the material and psychic natures. The shepherd who was spared represents the mind. Geryon symbolises the three aspects of the personality. The task of the World Saviour in Pisces, is to lift humanity up into heaven.

2. THE PLANETS

The planets are the bodies of great lives called Planet Logoi or Lords. The planets carry the energies of the rays and signs.

Each of these seven rays is transmitted into our solar system through the medium of three constellations and their ruling planets. [1]

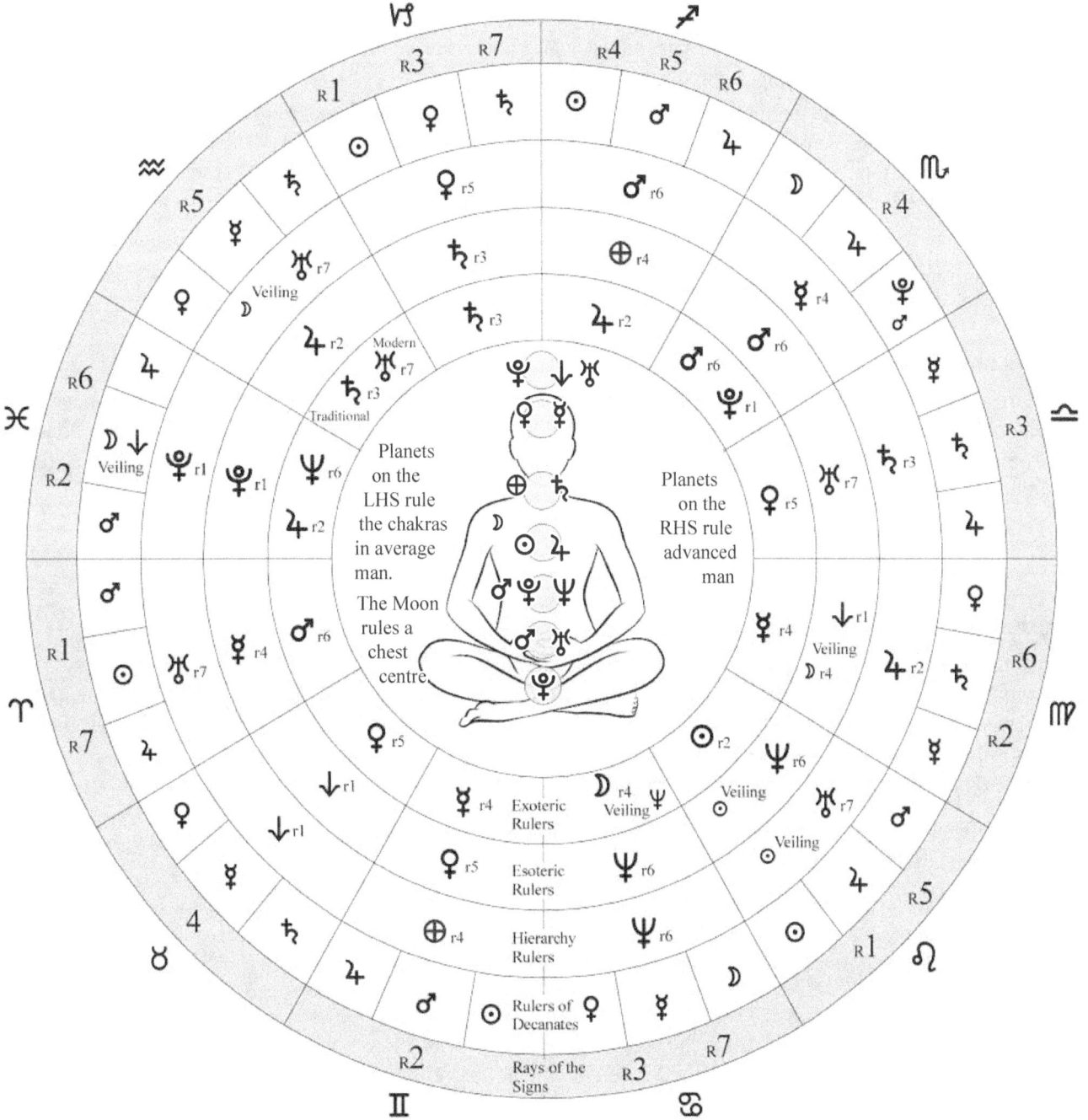

---
1   Bailey, Alice A. Esoteric Astrology, 423

The forces of the planets - more correctly, of the rays that use the planets as their means of distribution; their impact upon us drives us forward on the Path of Evolution.

> The twelve planets... their influence, plus inherited karmic conditions, produces those environing states and those circumstances which give opportunity for the development and eventually the control of the form side of life. [1]

1. The Exoteric, Esoteric and Hierarchy Planets Rule Consciousness

a. Firstly, the rays of the exoteric planets dominate, developing personality consciousness. Over lives they develop our qualities and strengths step by step. The goal is to bring about a powerful and dominant ego who is master of the lower forces in his nature and who uses these forces and powers to dominate the environment around him. The primary symbol for this stage is the Leo lion.

b. Then as a person steps onto the Path, the rays of the esoteric planets develop soul consciousness. They create within us a yearning for higher and finer things in life and drive us on to seek out and find new and higher pathways and interests. Sagittarius directs us to this higher way.

c. Then the rays flowing via the hierarchy planet rulers begin to dominate. They bring about the final destruction of any shred of lower control that may still exist and develop within us higher spiritual or global awareness. The truly international citizen is born who sees all men and women as his "family". Aquarius that represents universal brotherhood and which is the opposite sign to egotistical Leo, represents this stage.

d. Once a person is on the Path, the rays flowing through the signs supersede the forces of the planets.

> The moment that a man becomes aware of his own soul and is endeavouring to control his own "path in life," the influence of the planets weakens and steadily becomes less and less.[2]

2. Sacred and Non-sacred Planets

It is interesting to note that the Planet Lords tread an evolutionary path just as we do. The more advanced have stepped onto the cosmic Path of Discipleship. Their bodies or planets are called "sacred", their rays are finer and support the soul's influence. Less advanced Lords are on the cosmic Probationary Path. "Non-sacred", their forces strengthen the personality.

Sacred Planets, Vulcan, Jupiter, Saturn, Mercury, Venus, Neptune and Uranus.

Non-sacred planets: the Sun, Moon, Earth, Mars and Pluto.

3. The Sun and Moon "Veil" Planets

The average person is unable to receive high-vibrational energies represented by Vulcan, Neptune and Uranus. These forces would over-stimulate unprepared nervous systems. To prevent this, their forces are veiled or blocked by the coarseness of the lower nature, which is represented by the Sun and Moon. But, from the moment that the soul becomes influential, the Sun and Moon unveil or release these energies.

a. For aspirants, the Sun and Moon unveil Vulcan's ray 1 force.

b. For disciples, the Sun and Moon unveil Neptune's ray 6 force.

c. For initiates, the Sun and Moon unveil Uranus' ray 7 force.

Example of "Veiling": Carl Jung had the Sun in Leo and the Moon in Taurus. Let us suppose he was a disciple. This would mean that the Sun and Moon unveiled Neptune's ray 6 force. As a Leo personality he would be very idealistic (he was) and his Taurus moon would unveil a devotional aspect (it did).

Two other points to note:

> Virgo .. The Moon (Vulcan).—This is the esoteric ruler. [3].
>
> [The hierarchy ruler of Aquarius is] .. the Moon which hides or veils Uranus. [4]

---

[1] Ibid, 51
[2] Ibid, 16
[3] Ibid, 263
[4] Ibid, 138

THE SUN - the will and power of the personality

The provides man with an opportunity to develop a strong identity.

- A non-sacred planet that strengthens the personality
- Ray 2 Love and Wisdom
- The Physical Sun is the exoteric ruler of Leo
  The Heart of the Sun is the esoteric ruler of Leo, veiling Neptune
  The Central Spiritual Sun is the hierarchy ruler of Leo, veiling Uranus
- Rules the heart chakra in average man

At the lower level, the Sun Sign symbolises the personality, the ego, the little "I" and the vitality and energy of personal will, power and authority. It symbolises the *present* level of personality integration, its power and strength and its responsiveness (or lack of) to the soul.

The initial task for aspirants is to integrate and strengthen the personality. To do this the mind (Mercury) must be developed and used to implement personal will. This is a necessary developmental step prior to soul-personality alignment. Then at a higher level, the task is to bring personality force under soul control. Ultimately, the Sun represents Deity.

THE MOON - the "prison of the soul"

The Moon provides man with an opportunity to break old emotional patterns.

- A non-sacred planet that strengthens the personality
- Ray 4 Harmony through Conflict
- Exoteric ruler of Cancer
  Esoteric ruler of Virgo (veiling Vulcan)
  Hierarchy ruler of Aquarius (veiling Uranus)
- Rules no major chakra
- Co-rules the 3rd Initiation (veiling a sacred planet), with Mars

In exoteric astrology, the Moon represents the emotions and all things to do with mother, women, family, domesticity and the home.

Esoterically, the Moon is a dead planet and rules the instinctual form or body nature. It symbolises that which is *past*, the instincts and negative emotional responses and habits that imprison the soul. When the Moon is strong in the chart, in the psyche, it means that these negative and unconscious thoughts and impulses dominate the conscious mind.

Its sign and position show where the soul will have conflict in the environment as it battles to overcome these ancient automatic impulses, or in modern terminology, negative core beliefs.

THE ASCENDANT OR RISING SIGN

- Exoterically, the ascendant represents the image and approach to life.
- Esoterically the ascendant indicates the spiritual goal and purpose for the immediate incarnation. It presents those energies and qualities which, when rightly used, unfold the inner life and lead to spiritual life success.

> The ascendant or rising sign .. represents the sattvic or harmony aspect of life and can produce right relationship between soul and personality in any one incarnation. It thus points the way to the recognition of the force of the soul [1]

> The horoscope built up around the rising sign, with the esoteric planets ruling, will convey the destiny of the disciple. [2]

---

1 Bailey, Alice A. Esoteric Astrology, 18-19
2 Ibid, 513-514

The "Physical" Sun is a non-sacred planet. But the higher aspects of the Sun are very sacred.

The purpose of this solar system is the unfoldment of consciousness .. the Sun .. is the source of physical consciousness (exoteric and symbolic of the personality), of soul awareness (esoteric), and of spiritual life (hierarchical) [1]

The moon is a dead planet from which all the principles are gone [2]

The Moon brings about the inclination to create these conditions which lead to the critical transformations of instinct into intellect. [3]

The rising sign .. concerns itself with the struggle of the spiritual man "to carry on" from the point achieved so that when the life energy is temporarily exhausted and the "death of the personality" takes place, the man finds himself "nearer the centre of his life, closer to the centre of his group and approaching the centre of divine life [4]

---

1 AAB. Esoteric Astrology 294
2 Ibid, 665
3 Ibid, 139
4 Ibid, 17

Mercury, who is the illuminating principle which releases the mind, directs the way of man through life and enables him to become aware of the divine Plan which underlies all his fiery experience. [1]

Mercury, the star of conflict [2]

The light of intuition (Mercury) [3]

Vulcan stands for the glorification, through purification and detachment, of matter [4]

Vulcan .. fashioning the instruments of war when war and conflict are the only means whereby liberation can come, though woe betide those through whom wars come. [5]

Persistence, endurance and continuity of effort ... characteristics imparted or stimulated by energies pouring from Vulcan. [6]

---

1. AAB. Esoteric Astrology, 96
2. Ibid, 357
3. Ibid, 323
4. Ibid, 126
5. Ibid, 386
6. Ibid, 274

MERCURY - brings "Illumination"

Mercury provides man with an opportunity to develop and illumine his mind and connect with the soul and higher spiritual levels.

- A sacred planet that supports the purpose of the soul
- Ray 4 Harmony through Conflict
- Exoteric ruler of Gemini and Virgo
- Esoteric ruler of Aries
- Hierarchy ruler of Scorpio
- Is related to the brow chakra
- Co-rules the Path of Discipleship and the 4th Initiation with Saturn.

Exoterically, the Messenger of the Gods represents the mind generally and human communication in its many forms, commerce, networking, etc.

Esoterically, Mercury has several tasks. Firstly, with Venus, it develops the logical and intelligent mind and transforms it from being conflict-filled and warlike to being serene and wise.

Secondly, Mercury develops the antahkarana, the communication bridge between the personality and the soul. Then, it carries messages between the personality and soul and later to the Monad.

Finally, Mercury dispels illusion and illumines the mind with the light of the intuition. This enables the spiritual man to communicate with the cosmos.

VULCAN - glorification through purification

Vulcan provides man with an opportunity to purify his nature and transform desire into spiritual will.

- A sacred planet that supports the purpose of the soul
- Ray 1 Will and Power
- Exoteric ruler of no sign
- Esoteric ruler of Taurus and of Virgo
- Hierarchy ruler of Taurus
- Co-rules the head chakra
- Co-rules the 1st Initiation with Pluto and the 4th Initiation

Vulcan does not rule on an exoteric level, which explains why it is "undiscovered". It will be "found" when a certain proportion of human's step onto the Path of Purification.

In mythology, Vulcan is the forge of the gods who fashions beautiful and powerful instruments for their use. He plunges base metal into fire, then with his hammer beats it into shape. Here is the connection with the myth and the purification work done in the human being. Vulcan symbolises the "grip of the soul" on the personality and its place in the chart represents the fiery experiences the soul takes the lower self through as it beats, purifies and burnishes it into a high state of brilliance. An analogy is the shaping, grinding and cutting a jeweller does to transform a rough gem into a beautiful diamond.

With Pluto, Vulcan expresses the powerful 1st Ray of Will. Vulcan carries the higher spiritual will and this only begins to manifest upon the Path of Discipleship. This is why Vulcan does not rule at the personality level. The Sun and Moon, representing the dense vibration of unpurified bodies, block its force.

At present, there is not a valid ephemeris for this planet. An option is to place it between natal Sun and Mercury and over the natal Moon.

VENUS - intelligent love, the Human Soul, the Solar Angel

Venus provides man with an opportunity to develop intelligent love.

- A sacred planet that supports the purpose of the soul
- Ray 5 Concrete Mind and Knowledge
- Exoteric ruler of Taurus and Libra
- Esoteric ruler of Gemini
- Hierarchy ruler of Capricorn
- Rules the brow chakra
- Co-rules the 2nd Initiation with Jupiter and Neptune

Exoterically, Venus rules personal love, affection, money, the arts, femininity, beauty, young women etc.

Paradoxically, Venus, which has always been associated with earthly love, transmits the 5th Ray of Concrete Mind. This ray awakens the mind and then Venus transforms it into a vessel of love. True love is unable to flow through a mind that is filled with thoughts of hate and spite, hence the importance of Venus' work.

In the chart, Venus is the socialising planet and represents relationship lessons required to transform our minds into instruments of intelligent love. It points out where we must beautify relationships with wisdom and kindness, establish right human relations and express love-wisdom. True love is not sentimental affection:

> True love or wisdom sees with perfect clarity the deficiencies of any form and bends every effort to aid the indwelling life to liberate itself from trammels. It wisely recognises those that need help and those that need not its attention. It hears with precision and sees the thought of the heart and seeks ever to blend into one whole the workers in the field of the world. This it achieves not by blindness, but by discrimination and wisdom [1]

Venus is the symbol of the human soul, symbolising everything fine, beautiful and of quintessential value which the soul has extracted from past life experiences. It also represents the Solar Angel, man's mentor and guide.

THE EARTH - the sphere of experience leading to growth

The Earth provides man with a field of experience on which to evolve and develop group skills.

- A non-sacred planet that strengthens the personality
- Ray 3 Intelligent Activity
- Exoteric ruler of no sign
- Esoteric ruler of Sagittarius
- Hierarchy ruler of Gemini
- Has a relationship with the base chakra

The Earth only has an individual effect when people are on the Path. Its general effect is to provide a field of experience for the masses on which to evolve and learn to use the mind - the Earth's ray is the 3rd of Intelligence.

In the charts of the spiritually oriented, it represents the physical location of a person's duty or dharma. It points to the need for a practical, grounded and intelligent approach, in daily affairs. The sign the Earth is in represents those qualities that counterbalance personality selfishness (represented by the Sun Sign) and that develop group awareness. Good aspects to the Earth indicate that man has freedom to roam the earth at will.

Through Venus— under the power of mind, transmuted into wisdom through the instrumentality of love. [1]

Venus, pure love wisdom. [2]

The nervous system is ruled by Venus. [3]

Through the Earth— under the influence of planetary experience (which is different to individual experience) .. [he comes] .. in order to transmute his personal consciousness into group awareness. [4]

Our Earth, being a non-sacred planet, is in process of becoming a sacred planet. This means an interim of upheaval, chaos and of difficulty. [5]

The sacral centre and the spleen are primarily connected with the planetary emanation of the Earth itself. [6]

---

1 Bailey, Alice A. Letters on Occult Meditation, 285

1 AAB. Esoteric Astrology, 127
2 Ibid, 281
3 AAB. Esoteric Healing, 143
4 AAB. Esoteric Astrology, 127
5 Ibid, 519
6 Ibid, 80

Through the fiery processes of war and strife, brought through Mars, the God of War, a needed purification takes place. [1]

The tests in Scorpio and the activity of Mars are potent to arouse the entire lower nature and bring about its final rebellion and the last stand .. of the personality against the soul. It is Mars who brings the world Arjuna into the active fight. The whole man is then engaged and the "quarrel of the sexes" is resolved in its highest aspect through the battle between the highly developed personality or form nature and the soul [2]

Head and heart, of mind and love, and of will and wisdom, the work of Jupiter is to develop these two qualities and bring them into synthetic interplay. [3]

Jupiter .. the way of love-wisdom (2nd ray) is the way for humanity to go. [4]

---

1 AAB. Esoteric Astrology, 95-96
2 Ibid, 211
3 Ibid, 126
4 Ibid, 127

MARS - the desire nature

Mars provides man with an opportunity to transmute desire into spiritual aspiration.

- A non-sacred planet that strengthens the personality
- Ray 6 Devotion and Idealism
- Exoteric ruler of Aries and Scorpio
- Esoteric ruler of Scorpio
- Hierarchy ruler of Sagittarius
- Rules the solar plexus chakra and is related to the sacral
- Co-rules the 3rd Initiation with the Moon

Mars is the God of War and represents desire, passion, physical drive and war. At the lower level, this combination gives rise to destructive fanatical types when this planet is strong in the chart.

> Mars is definitely the planet which rules and controls the physical vehicle... is closely related to sex ... vitalise(s) the blood stream .. governs the senses. [1]

Esoterically, Mars governs the desire nature and its energy is that of the 6th ray. In the chart, it shows the nature of this desire, where it plays out in the life and what to do to refine and control it. In short, what needs to be done to impose the higher will over the lower.

Although its fiery power can thwart the soul, Mars establishes relations between opposites, between opposing, warring forces. This is positive and the first step towards reconciliation. On the higher level, Mars symbolises the aspiration and will of the soul-inspired man, to fight delusion.

Bailey gave Mars as the exoteric ruler of Scorpio. However, "Mars is the alter ego of Pluto" [2] and the latter does have influence in Scorpio.

JUPITER - expands, fuses and synthesises

Jupiter provides man with an opportunity to develop wisdom and brotherly love.

- A sacred planet that supports the purpose of the soul
- Ray 2 Love and Wisdom
- Exoteric ruler of Sagittarius and Pisces
- Esoteric ruler of Aquarius
- Hierarchy ruler of Virgo
- Rules the heart chakra in advanced man
- Co-rules the 2nd Initiation with Venus and Neptune and 5th with Uranus

Generally, Jupiter represents expansion, success, rewards and good fortune; and those larger than life and exaggerated behaviours such as excess, boastfulness and gambling. It inspires long distance journeys and quests in search of greater understanding.

Esoterically, transmitting the 2nd ray, Jupiter symbolises open-hearted and magnanimous love that magnetically attracts to itself, that which is desired for the good of the whole.

In the chart, it indicates the method by which the soul will expand one's vision, broaden perspective and promote the synthesis of head and heart, of mind and love and of will and wisdom.

It represents the wise teacher who will find the student when he or she is ready for higher instruction.

---

1 Gathered from Bailey, Alice A. Esoteric Astrology, 210-215
2 Ibid, 507

SATURN - Lord of Karma offers opportunity

Saturn provides man with an opportunity to live within the greater law of love.

- A sacred planet that supports the purpose of the soul
- Ray 3 Intelligent Activity
- Exoteric Ruler of Capricorn and co-ruler of Aquarius
- Esoteric Ruler of Capricorn
- Hierarchy Ruler of Libra
- Rules the throat chakra
- Co-rules the Path of Discipleship and the 4th Initiation with Mercury.

Exoterically Saturn brings misfortune and loss. Esoterically, its method of coercion *is* the Law of Karma. What we give out comes back to us. Evil attracts evil and good attracts good. Saturn is teaching us to live within the Law of Love. It tests us with adversity, difficult situations and crises and encourages an intelligent assessment of life experience (its ray is the 3rd of Intelligence), giving us the opportunity to demonstrate wise choice and correct decision. Then it grades us and gives us what we have earned.

Saturn guards the Gate of Initiation. It tests our fitness or readiness to step onto the Path of Initiation, to progress along that path and to receive spiritual power and influence. It points out where we need to comply with divine law, correct imbalances of the past and fulfil karmic obligations.

> Saturn is the Lord of Karma, the imposer of retribution and the one who demands full payment of all debts and who therefore condemns us to the struggle for existence, both from the form side and from the soul side. Saturn, therefore, "fell" when man fell into generation. He "followed the sons of men down into their low place". [1]

URANUS - awakens the sleeping consciousness

Uranus provides man with an opportunity to awaken to our spiritual life.

- A sacred planet that supports the purpose of the soul
- Ray 7 Ceremony, Order and Magic
- Exoteric co-ruler of Aquarius
- Esoteric ruler of Libra
- Hierarchy ruler of Aries and Aquarius
- Rules the sacral chakra
- Co-rules the 5th Initiation with Jupiter.

On an exoteric level, Uranus represents that which is odd or different, the unorthodox and unpredictable, the new and modern. It gives individuals the sense that they are unique and can have an independent existence.

Esoterically, Uranus is the Awakener and, in the chart, indicates the power of the soul to shatter life confinements with the lightning power of new vision. It shows where we must open things up and experiment, where we can most rapidly cut away old patterns and revolutionise our approach to life, where we can initiate a new order of life and conditions and be free.

Uranus' ray is the 7th, the force which relates spirit and matter. It thus ensures all sons of God reach their "heavenly father", that is, become spiritually aware. It rules the "final burning ground", the flaming heat of tests and trials that the initiate passes through to destroy all final impurities. Uranus equips the disciple, with the necessary skills to pass through this fire - the scientific mind and the ability to think clearly and abstractly.

---

1 Bailey, Alice A. Esoteric Astrology, 105

Saturn's power is completely ended and his work accomplished when man (the spiritual man) has freed himself from Karma and from the power of the two Crosses—the Common and the Fixed. Esoterically, Saturn cannot follow man on to the Cardinal Cross. [1]

Saturn .. conditions primarily the point in evolution where choice definitely becomes possible, where rejection of opportunity or its acceptance can consciously be undertaken, and the shouldering of personal responsibility becomes a recognised fact in a planned and ordered life. [2]

Uranus gives innate spontaneous activity and this produces evolutionary development—both natural and spiritual. It is the urge to better conditions... Uranus causes the great transference in the human consciousness from intellectual perception to intuitive knowledge. [3]

---

1 AAB. Esoteric Astrology 105
2 Ibid, 19-20
3 Ibid, 139

Neptune—Mystical consciousness or that innate sensitivity which leads unerringly to the higher vision [1]

Neptune .. the Initiator. .. the great Teacher of the West and the present world Initiator, Christ, is spoken of as Neptune, Who rules the ocean, whose trident and astrological symbol signifies the Trinity in manifestation [2]

Pluto is a deity with the attributes of the serpent. He is a healer, a giver of health, spiritual and physical and of enlightenment. [3]

The destructive power of the first ray, focussed in Pluto, brings change, darkness and death. [4]

.. The Great Releaser, which shatters the forms which are bringing death to that which is embodied. [5]

Pluto drags to the surface and destroys all that hinders in these lower regions. [6]

---

1. AAB. Esoteric Astrology, 306
2. Ibid, 219
3. Ibid, 667
4. Ibid, 187
5. Ibid, 545
6. Ibid, 70

NEPTUNE - the Christ Consciousness

Neptune provides man with an opportunity to refine his emotional expression.
- A sacred planet that supports the purpose of the soul
- Ray 6 Devotion and Idealism
- Exoteric ruler of Pisces
- Esoteric and Hierarchy Ruler of Cancer
- Co-rules the solar plexus chakra with Mars
- Co-rules the 2nd Initiation with Venus and Jupiter and is involved with the transference of solar plexus energy to the heart centre. Candidates who are approaching this initiation should have Neptune prominent in the chart.

On an exoteric level, Neptune represents mysticism, dreams, fantasies, ideals, service and compassion. In psychology, it symbolises delusion and escapism.

Esoterically, the Sun unveils and uses Neptune to transmit love-wisdom from the Heart of the Sun, that is, from the Heart of God. The effect of this energy refines the astral nature, so that emotional-desire transforms into love aspiration. Neptune dissolves all blocks to soul influence, allowing love and compassion to enter the personal life. It stimulates higher visions and ideals and an aspiration to experience a state of oneness with all life.

In the chart, it shows where to develop greater sensitivity to oneself, to others, to life; and where to forgive and extend compassion.

PLUTO - the Arrow of Death

Pluto provides man the opportunity to eliminate limitation.
- A non-sacred planet that strengthens the personality
- Ray 1 Will and Power
- Exoteric co-ruler of Scorpio with Mars
- Esoteric and Hierarchy ruler of Pisces
- Rules the head chakra in average man and the base chakra
- Co-rules the 1st Initiation with Vulcan

On an exoteric level, Pluto represents large monopolies and pressure groups, mega-power and control, manipulation, death and radical transformation. Esoterically, Pluto only affects individuals who are on the Path.

> Pluto at present only evokes response from groups or from those disciples who are enough evolved rightly to respond. [1]

Then, Pluto's fire begins a purifying process.

> (Pluto) .. becomes active in the life of the man who is "becoming alive in the higher sense, his lower nature passes into the smoke and darkness of Pluto, who governs the lesser burning ground, in order that the man may live in truth in the higher land of light." [2]

The soul fires Pluto, the Arrow of God, to destroy the snares of the past, to close old chapters and to purge all obstacles to soul-fusion. Pluto "pierces the heart and death takes place." In aspirants and disciples, its place in the chart represents an aspect of the nature that needs transforming.

When Pluto has done its work, lower will is in alignment with higher will. Now the soul can radiate its power directly into life, without interference from the personality.

> Esoterically speaking, Mars is the alter ego of Pluto. [3]

---

1. Bailey, Alice A. Esoteric Astrology, 509
2. Ibid, 78
3. Ibid, 507

3. THE HOUSES

The houses provide a range of experiences designed to awaken us spiritually. But they are prisons for younger souls who accept their lot and cling to conditions that surround them at birth.

> all the twelve .. [houses] .. indicate limitation or that which withholds the Dweller in the mansion from expanding his consciousness, if he permits himself to be imprisoned by them. On the other hand, they offer opportunity if he is oriented towards the higher life. [1]

1. Personality attitude to a house is represented by the exoteric planet, which rules the sign on the house cusp.
2. Soul purpose, the endeavour to promote growth in that life area, is represented by the esoteric ruler.

First House

Exoteric Keywords
- Physical body
- Appearance, mask worn to get approval
- The head
- Approach to life, personal interests
- Mannerisms

Esoteric Keywords
- The causal body of the soul [2]
- The emergence of the soul
- The head centre
- Soul activities, purpose and expression
- Ray types and qualities

The 1st house (1H) represents birth in a physical body, which is coloured by planets in the 1st house and the sign on the ascendant. In young souls, consciousness identifies completely with its physical form. Then, because feedback from the world is hostile it creates a mask to hide behind, a perfect image to show the world to gain acceptance and approval. If the personality (the Sun) is weak, consciousness identifies with this manufactured image. The approach to life is fearful, personal activities narrow. On the Path, the soul ray begins to shine through consciousness and soul qualities appear. The 1H approach to the world will either block the soul or open the door to its entry.

Second House

Exoteric Keywords
- Possessions, personal resources
- Energy
- Losses
- Gains
- Personal money and business
- Material values

Esoteric Keywords
- Control of the form
- Prana and use of spiritual energy
- Withdrawal from matter
- Acquisition of spiritual powers
- Spiritual resources to use in service
- Spiritual values to live by

Planets in the 2H and the sign on the cusp colour values and attitudes to possessions. The exoteric ruler represents the values of the personality. It covets material things and struggles to surround itself with wealth and possessions to be secure against the dangers of life. With its identity merged with its acquisitions, it defends them against loss as it would its own life. It is possessed. The esoteric ruler represents spiritual values to develop. The 2H also represents resources available for selfless service.

Third House

Exoteric Keywords
- Close environment, neighbours
- Communication and networking
- Schools, siblings, relatives
- Short journeys, commerce, trade

Esoteric Keywords
- Daily interaction with souls in the environment
- 1st stage of the Antahkarana, mental telepathy
- Outer esoteric schools, soul brothers and sisters
- Search to find the Path

---

1 Bailey, Alice A. Esoteric Astrology, 508
2 Ibid, 511

Planets in the 3H and the sign on the cusp, colour our attitude to the local environment, our neighbourhood, schools, siblings and relatives; and all contacts and experiences that educate the mind and develop communication skills. The exoteric ruler influences the way lower mind communicates. Unchecked, it makes many superficial contacts and communications. The esoteric ruler represents experiences that develop wise contact with others. When the spiritual Path is approached, a search for knowledge and understanding begins, self-development courses are taken and connections are made with brothers and sisters in spirit who share similar ideas. In time the mind learns to be discerning, communication becomes harmless and the initial stage of the antahkarana begins to be constructed.

Fourth House

Exoteric Keywords
- Family, mother, home
- Inherited roots
- Unhealed psychological patterns
- Life endings

Esoteric Keywords
- Mother Earth, Nature, one's spiritual family or ashram
- Opportunity to be grounded in the physical body
- Inherited family-national karma
- Opportunity to cut all karmic links with the past

Planets in the 4H and the sign on the cusp colour our perception of home, mother and family. The exoteric ruler of the fourth represents how the personality copes with family life. If the family is dysfunctional, the home and parent's hostile, deep wounds occur and psychological wounds cripple confidence, causing low self-esteem. Then in adult life, the traumatised adult-child will look for mother or father in other figures, still searching for acceptance and emotional security. The esoteric ruler represents the experiences that develop healthy family attitudes and life roots. On the world stage, the 4H symbolises Mother Earth, home to the family of man and family, racial and national karma. It also represents our spiritual family.

Fifth House

Exoteric Keywords
- Creative activities
- Children
- Romance and lovers
- Hobbies, sports, pleasure
- The creative personality

Esoteric Keywords
- Soul-inspired creative projects
- Younger brothers and sisters on the Path
- Unconditional love
- Soul energy expressed joyfully in creative projects
- The causal body [1] and creativity of the soul.

Planets in the 5H and the sign on the cusp colour our creative spirit and attitudes to sex and pleasure. The exoteric ruler represents things that the personality likes to do. Sacral energy pours into hobbies, sports, sex, romance, risky adventures, pleasure and making children. The esoteric ruler represents experiences that redirect the use of sacral sexual energy into higher and more creative areas, so that the 1st Initiation - control of the physical appetites, is taken. This gives abundant creativity to pour into projects, especially those where children or younger souls are involved.

Sixth House

Exoteric Keywords
- Service, work, co-workers
- Skills
- Health and crises
- Small animals

Esoteric Keywords
- Service, soul group co-workers
- Development of skills to serve the Plan
- Purification of blocks to the flow of soul energy
- Service to the Animal Kingdom

Planets in the 6th house and the sign on the cusp colour our attitude to work and health. The exoteric ruler of the sixth represents the way the personality copes with working life. It gets a job, develops skills, learns a trade and builds relations with co-workers. If there are insecurities then stress levels rise and if not dealt with positively, then health issues occur. If there are blocks to soul energy in the system, the soul may use ill health to draw the eyes of the personality to that part of the body, so that healing on both physical and metaphysical levels can take place. The sign on the cusp, the exoteric ruler and planets in the house indicate these illnesses.

The 6th house is the link between the personal houses 1 to 6 and less personal 7 - 12, symbolising the adjustment needed to pass from the Mutable Cross (exclusive consciousness) to the Fixed Cross (group consciousness). At this level, it represents those many life adjustments needed to integrate harmoniously with the environment. The esoteric ruler represents work and service opportunities and skills to develop and use in our chosen area of service.

---
1 Bailey, Alice A. Esoteric Astrology, 509

Seventh House

Exoteric Keywords
- Partners, relationships
- Formal partnerships, marriage
- Others, one-on-one unions
- Open enemies,
- Legal matters

Esoteric Keywords
- Souls from the same soul group - soul mates
- Soul-personality fusion, true spiritual partnerships
- People from other soul groups, soul to soul bonding
- People who mirror back personal glamour and illusion
- Karmic Law

Planets in the 7H and the sign on the cusp colour our attitude to formal relationships and one-on-one partnerships. The exoteric ruler represents how the personality copes. Many have insecurities in this area and are dysfunctional. Some fear abandonment and seek either a partner that they can control or avoid commitment by moving casually from one relation to another. People generally are attracted to those who have the same energy pattern, the same fears and insecurities, a mirror of the self. Some project their "stuff" onto the partner, seeing only what they expect to see. The esoteric fact is, if individuals remain separated consciously from their souls, the source of true love, relationships will end in disillusionment.

The esoteric ruler represents the experiences that develop spiritually mature and wise relationship skills. The key is to be intelligent in relationships and in the selection of partners, to be compassionate, forgiving and loving. This will attract partners who are similarly compassionate and loving. It will also attract soul mates from the same soul-group, for both personal and formal relationships. At a more advanced stage, the Dweller on the Threshold (the complete negative personality) makes its appearance to challenge the soul. This house prepares us for this battle.

Eighth House

Exoteric Keywords
- Death, rebirth
- Others people's money, legacies
- Sex, transformation
- Occult groups

Esoteric Keywords
- Death of the personality, birth of the soul in the heart
- Resources of the group
- Desire, emotional purification and the 2nd Initiation
- The Path of Discipleship, Esoteric Psychology

Planets in the 8H and the sign on the cusp, these influence how we face major life challenges. For instance, sex issues, shared resources, money, death, inheritances and the struggle to change. The exoteric ruler represents how the personality copes. For many, transformation goes no further than the momentary enjoyment and loss of self, experienced with an orgasm. Life disappointments and impotency drive others to seek psychological help. To find answers some investigate the occult. A few gain knowledges in the evil-arts and become black magicians.

The esoteric ruler represents experiences that bring psychological and life transformations. Contact is made with an esoteric group, knowledge of the mysteries is gained and spiritual disciplines are applied. Disciples prepare for the 2nd Initiation, the purification and control of the astral nature. As major crises arise, the disciple is confronted with those aspects of the Dweller in himself, which need to be held in the light. When negative patterns begin to die and solar plexus energy is transferring up to the heart centre, the 2nd Initiation is taken.

Ninth House

Exoteric Keywords
- Collective mind, beliefs
- Long distance travel
- Foreign lands, people, cultures
- Higher study, religion, philosophy

Esoteric Keywords
- Higher abstract mind, Universal Mind, Truth
- The spiritual Path or quest, the Antahkarana
- Higher spiritual realms
- Esoteric colleges, Wisdom Teachings, spiritual Teachers

Planets in the 9H and the sign on the cusp colour our attitude to religion, higher learning, foreign affairs and people and the spiritual Path. The exoteric ruler of the 9H represents the personality perspective of that area. Long distance travel, contact with foreign cultures and study of higher philosophies may broaden the consciousness somewhat. But if the personality controls the lower mind, inner growth is limited.

In the 9H, the disciple travels fast upon the Path. Setting off on a voyage of discovery, an earnest search for truth and understanding begins. The esoteric ruler represents experiences that expand consciousness. Esoteric teachings are studied and the abstract mind develops. The construction of the antahkarana completes, linking the mind directly to the Spiritual Triad. Opportunities to teach wisdom arise

10th House

Exoteric Keywords
- Father, authority figures
- Career, professional life, ambitions
- Status, public recognition
- Government

Esoteric Keywords
- The Monad, Masters, the Triad
- The Master's work
- Initiation
- Shamballa, the Hierarchy

Planets in the 10H and the sign on the cusp colour our attitude to a vocation or profession. The exoteric ruler represents the personality's search for power and glory. As it matures, it conforms to the rules of society and through a career or other means, tries to get the power, status and respect it sees that others have and wants for itself. If it fails, it could feel the weight of the law or gain notoriety. Those who reject society turn to friends for consolation and the disenchanted may become revolutionaries (the 11H).

The esoteric ruler represents vocational opportunities that serve the greater good. Important life goals revolve around work that furthers the Plan. Although not sought, status and recognition come to those who serve selflessly. The disciple begins to scale the mountain and prepare for the 3rd Initiation where the integrated and powerful personality (Dweller on the Threshold) is annihilated by the Angel of the Presence. From that point on he or she is an integral part of the Master's group, the Hierarchy and Shamballa.

Eleventh House

Exoteric Keywords
- Friends
- Groups and organisations
- Social reform, politics, revolution
- Hopes and wishes

Esoteric Keywords
- True spiritual brotherhood
- Ashram group, New Group of World Servers
- Humanitarian groups and social reformation
- Spiritual vision, creative visualisation

Planets in the 11H and the sign on the cusp colour our attitude to friendships, social activities, group relations and activities. The exoteric ruler represents the way the personality seeks social intercourse. It joins groups, organisations and makes friends with people who share the same ideals. If it did not achieve status in the 10H, it rebels and becomes the revolutionary. Hopes and wishes remain personality based.

The esoteric ruler represents the experiences that develop group skills and sensitivity, the experiences we have with groups and where to find our soul group and an organisation to serve world need.

Twelfth House

Exoteric Keywords
- Self-undoing, karma
- Confinement, prisons, large institutions
- Retreats and sanctuaries
- Hidden enemies
- The hidden, the universe, the unknown
- Service

Esoteric Keywords
- Subconscious sabotaging patterns
- Karma, glamour, illusion which binds the soul
- Inner work, meditation
- The Dweller prior to its emergence
- The Absolute Reality, the greater cosmos
- Selfless service, work of the Christ

Planets in the 12H and the sign on the cusp colour our attitude to suffering, serious illness, things we want to hide from others and matters that are outside our control. It also represents how easy it is (or not), to let go and flow when life imposes its will upon us. This house represents times we leave the main stream and go into a more introspective phase. This may be caused by illness, work, a self-initiated search for understanding, or we may be incarcerated by force for a perceived cultural violation. This period then, provides an opportunity to self-analyse and identify any habits, patterns of thought, or actions and activities in our outer life that are self-sabotaging. At an unconscious level, the sum of these negative thoughts and feelings constitute the Dweller on the Threshold, or negative collective "stuff". The exoteric ruler of the twelfth represents how the personality copes when matters are overwhelming.

The esoteric ruler represents the experiences that will bring negative core beliefs into the light for healing and how to grow in love and understanding even in the most adverse of circumstances. For some it may point to outstanding karmic debts that require payment. These experiences help us to develop compassion, understanding and to give universally to others. 12H disciples are the quiet servers, healers, therapists, counsellors and spiritual advisors, who work with the imprisoned, sick and disadvantaged.

4. Planets in Signs and Houses

4a. Planets in Signs

The Sun

☉ *The Sun symbolises the personality, the ego. The sign the Sun is in colours the personality and represents wilful negative traits that need to be controlled and positive qualities to be cultivated and expressed. The ray of the Sun is the 2nd Ray of Love and Wisdom. Its spiritual task is to develop the personality and infuse it with love and wisdom. But at first, it is the 1st ray of Leo that is most influential, bringing forth the ego.*

Sun in Aries: the personality "ram" is warlike, aggressive, unthinking, childish and destructive. It acts before thinking and is foolish in its courage and daring.

Bringing the "ram" under intelligent control is the transformational goal. In other words, acquire knowledge, develop the intellect, control the lower will and rein in the aggressive emotional impulses. This enables the natural leadership qualities to flourish without the distorting effects of emotionalism and anger. The wisdom-infused Aries personality is distinguished by fiery but balanced power, tremendous courage and the power to stand alone if necessary. Intelligent and pioneering, they destroy the shackles that bind.

Sun in Taurus: the personality "bull" is conflicted and driven by lower desire. It is obstinate, destructive, unimaginative, lazy and greedy.

"Riding the bull" is the transformational goal - control of desire. Aspirants must develop dispassion and use the higher will to control the impulsive nature. The wise Taurus personality has steadfast strength and power and the ability to stand firm for its principles; like a mountain against a storm. There is an artistic and creative side and power to create beauty and harmony.

Sun in Gemini: the unregulated personality is symbolised by the twins, a dual and two-faced ego. It is unstable, has a superficial thought life and is gossipy, deceitful and restless.

Stabilising the over-fluid mind and curbing its restlessness is the transformational goal. This is achieved through daily meditation and the appreciation and expression of beauty. The wisdom-infused Gemini personality has a lighted intelligence and is a distinguished and witty communicator, brilliant with the pen and influencing many with the power of the word.

Sun in Cancer: the personality "crab" has moods and lives in the past, hanging on to old things and dead relationships.

Stepping free from the defensive shell is the transformational goal, developing the intellect and using it to free the consciousness from emotional control. This is achieved by refusing to give in to emotional moods but instead, learning how to deal with negative emotions in an intelligent and healthy manner. A nurturing spirit, kindness and compassion distinguish the wisdom-infused Cancer personality. People feel protected and nourished in its presence.

Sun in Leo: the personality "lion" is arrogant, vain, over-indulged and lazy. Over-dramatic and posturing, it continually draws attention to itself.

Controlling the "lion" is the transformational goal, bringing the lower will and mind into line with the wisdom of the soul. This is achieved through daily meditation and the practise of selflessness, which develops soul sensitivity. The soul-infused Leo personality has radiant power and magnetism and many are attracted by this light and warmth. Wise and intelligent, he or she is a benevolent leader and teacher.

Sun in Virgo: the personality has natural intelligence and superb teaching and communication skills. But unregulated, it is insecure, hypercritical and small-minded. With a narrow focus and an irritating perfectionism, materialism rules the life.

Purifying the mind of its negativity is the transformational goal. In time, this will give birth to the Christ consciousness, the love-intelligence aspect. The wisdom-infused Virgo personality is distinguished by a clear and direct intelligence, brilliant craftsmanship and dedicated service to the poor and suffering. Harmless in word and deed, many benefit from the quiet goodness and expertise given by these souls.

Sun in Libra: the unregulated personality lacks balance; it is indecisive, procrastinates, is promiscuous and dishonest. Vain and concerned with appearances, it takes advantage of others with its charm and attractiveness.

"Balancing the scales" is the transformational goal, bringing the life into balance and order. Spiritual discipline and the ongoing practise of honesty and integrity is required. The wisdom-infused Libra personality is distinguished by a brilliant intellect, a judicial mind that is creative and powerful and which helps many find peace and harmony.

Sun in Scorpio: the personality is symbolised by the lethal scorpion that is dangerous, vindictive, revengeful, holds grudges and is emotionally conflicted. Self-delusion rules.

Extinguishing the power and sting of the "scorpion" - overcoming self-deception; is the transformational goal. This is achieved through esoteric meditation, which teaches the student to hold the mind steady in the light of intelligence and the practise of dispassion to control the emotional life. The wisdom-infused Scorpio personality is an intelligent and strategic warrior and is distinguished by an aura that radiates power and strength. They go into places (physically, emotionally or mentally) where other people fear to tread. Feeling safe in their presence, others follow.

Sun in Sagittarius: the personality "centaur" loves "wine, women and song" and carelessly wounds others with thoughtless words and gossip. It is extravagant and boastful, a wasteful gambler who squanders life's gifts and opportunities.

Curbing the appetites of the "centaur", one-pointedness and harmlessness in speech and action, are the transformational goals. This is achieved through meditation and self-discipline. The wisdom-infused Sagittarius personality is distinguished by an aura that radiates warmth, joy and confidence and that immediately lifts the spirits of all who come into his or her presence. Creative and artistic, burning with devotion and love for the spiritual teachings and Teachers, many are inspired to follow.

Sun in Capricorn: the personality "goat" is avaricious, Machiavellian, the true materialist. It is ruthless and calculating in its quest for power and control.

Controlling the ambitions of the "goat" and the development of true humility are the transformational goals. But this will not happen until the hunger for the material life is exhausted. When the work is done, the wisdom-infused Capricorn personality is a force to be reckoned with. Distinguished by an aura that radiates the success of a powerful and influential executive, many are drawn to discover its source. Intelligent and kind, these skills are used to benefit the greater good.

Sun in Aquarius: the unregulated personality uses its mental powers to be "superior", but is unstable, volatile, dogmatic and mentally rigid. It separates itself from humanity behind walls of illusory and impenetrable thoughtforms, living there in aloof solitude, weaving impractical schemes.

Bringing the mind and heart into balance and reconnecting with humanity at a feeling level, is the transformational goal. This is achieved by studying the Wisdom Teachings and by following a scientific self-development path. The wisdom-infused Aquarius personality is distinguished by an acute intelligence and an aura that flows with friendliness and inclusiveness. They use the power of the scientific mind and the flow of love to benefit humanity.

Sun in Pisces: the restless personality swims through life without clear direction and lives in a fantasy world of its own creation. Hypersensitive, impressionable and naive, it sees itself as a victim. It is also cunning, controlling others through guilt, false obligation and passive aggression.

Emerging consciously from the ocean of the emotions is the transformational goal. This means developing the intellect and using it to develop a clearer sense of self and to be independent and less reliant on others. The ruthless pruning of interests and relationships that are not core or vital is essential. The wisdom-infused Pisces personality is a distinguished server of mankind. Following in the footsteps of the Master, they are born to save and alleviate suffering.

The Moon

☽ *The ray of the Moon is the 4th Ray of Harmony through Conflict. The sign it is in represents the unconscious negative mind patterns and emotional habits that cause conflict with others and with the soul. The spiritual task of the Moon is to present these "prison of the soul patterns" to the self-aware person, for their purification. When working with aspirants, pencil Vulcan over the Moon. It shows what needs purification. Or use Neptune for disciples and Uranus for initiates.*

> (Instead of working with the moon) let them work with Vulcan when dealing with the undeveloped or average man and with Uranus when considering the highly developed man.[1]

Moon in Aries: the problem pattern is one of fast, unthinking and aggressive emotional reactions. The ego is hot-headed and selfish. It acts with blind and unthinking aggression and throws tantrums if anything or anyone blocks its way.

"I come forth and from the plane of mind, I rule" is the corrective instruction. The goal is to develop the intellect and use it to control the rash emotional impulses. Success releases the positive strengths of Aries - intelligent leadership and the power to build forms (personal relationships and life structures) that are dynamic and full of life.

---

1 Bailey, Alice A. Esoteric Astrology, 13

Moon in Taurus: the problem is uncontrolled emotional and sexual desire. The "bull" goes after what it wants in a stubborn and destructive manner, creating chaos.

The developmental instruction is "I see and when the eye is opened, all is light". Concentrated mind light is used to investigate the inner state and then steps are taken to eliminate the undesirable. Success releases the positive strengths of Taurus - the power to stand strong and steadfast in the face of opposition and to build personal relationships that are light-filled, stable and beautiful.

Moon in Gemini: the problem pattern is a restless mind that fills itself with trivia. The ego is shallow and changeable. Lacking empathy, it plays games and deceives people.

"I see my other self and in the waning of that self, I grow and glow" is the corrective instruction. The task is to learn to hold the mind steady in the light of the intellect and then use it to observe the lower self and resist its negative impulses. Success releases the positive strengths of Gemini - oratorical, communication and networking skills oriented to the higher good; and wisdom to build personal relationships filled with love and light.

Moon in Cancer: the problem is extreme defensiveness that leads to emotional isolation.

"I build a lighted house and therein dwell" is the soul's instruction. The task is to develop healthy emotional expression and build a clear and lighted consciousness. Success releases the positive strengths of Cancer - power to reach out to people with love and sensitivity and to build light filled and nurturing personal relationships.

Moon in Leo: the binding pattern is that of having a too powerful and pride filled ego, which is arrogant, self-absorbed and controlling.

"I am That and That am I" is the corrective instruction. The task is to lift the eyes from the little self to the higher (the "That"), thereby expanding consciousness and eliminating the pattern. Success releases the positive strengths of Leo - the power to rule and lead with strength and loving sensitivity and to build personal relationships filled with fiery love and warmth.

Moon in Virgo: the negative pattern is a life focus that is too narrow and that concentrates on acquiring material possessions. This narrowness also extends to the mind, which is tight and hypercritical. It wants perfection in this imperfect world.

The alignment mantram is "Christ in you the hope of glory". The task is to make a conscious connection with the soul (through meditation), enabling Christ love to shine through and dissolve negative impulses and limitations. Success releases the positive strengths of Virgo - an intelligence enhanced with wisdom and power to build personal relationships and life structures that are useful, practical and nurturing.

Moon in Libra: the problem is unbalanced fiery passion and shallow, frivolous living that results in procrastination, promiscuity and dishonesty.

"I choose the way which lies between the two great lines of force" is the soul's corrective instruction. A balanced mind and moderate life approach is needed. Success releases the positive strengths of Libra - intelligent experimentation in personal relationships until the right harmonious combination is found. Purified Libra has the intelligent power to build forms and life structures that are new and beautiful.

Moon in Scorpio: the repressive pattern is delusion because powerful emotions distort reality. The ego sees only what it wants to see. It has voracious desires and is stealthy, ruthless and relentless when seeking satisfaction or revenge.

The developmental instruction is "Warrior I am and from the battle I emerge triumphant". The battle is to learn to hold the mind steady in the light of the soul and face reality as it is - to face the dark, face all fears and see the truth. Success releases the positive strengths of Scorpio - courage and warriorship enhanced with a clear and insightful intelligence and the power to build relationships that are deep, authentic and truthful.

Moon in Sagittarius: being driven blindly by the appetites is the problem. There is a too powerful desire for excessive consumption - food, drink, sex, wealth, power, experience and life generally. Also a tendency to gossip and wound through speech.

"I see the goal, I reach that goal and then I see another" is the instruction for appropriate change. The task is to discipline the energies and focus them on higher and more aspirational goals. Success releases the positive strengths of Sagittarius - a natural ability to inspire people to search for their highest truth and the power to build relationships that are founded on true friendship and shared ideals.

Moon in Capricorn: the problem here is a relentless hunger for power and wealth. The personality is ruthless, calculating and cunning in its efforts to get what it wants.

The developmental guide is "Lost am I in light supernal, yet on that light I turn my back". The task is to turn the back on avarice and follow a higher way; for those who are ready this means walking the Spiritual Path and taking initiation. Success releases the positive strengths of Capricorn - success in any profession or ability to reach any goal through fair means and the power to build personal relationships that are founded on a rock of integrity and trust.

Moon in Aquarius: the problem is being too mental, individualistic and isolated from feelings and human intimacy, resulting in separativeness.

"Water of life am I, poured forth for thirsty men" is the soul's instruction. Isolation is overcome by learning to connect with others from the heart and to think with the heart. Success releases the positive strengths of Aquarius - the ability to make friends anywhere and at any level of society and the power to build personal relationships founded on a deep friendship and inclusive kindness and love.

Moon in Pisces: the problem pattern is emotionalism, a consciousness that is too fluid and ungrounded; and a too powerful attachment to life comforts.

"I leave the Father's house and turning back, I save" is to be followed. On a personality level, the task is to bring the focus back from its many outer life interests and to centralise and ground it in the wisdom of the soul. To achieve this, the intellect needs to be developed and healthy emotional boundaries constructed. Success releases the positive strengths of Pisces - a natural ability to connect spiritually and emotionally with people and the power to build relationships that are founded on openhearted trust and unconditional love.

Ascendant: Represents soul purpose

The ascendant sign and its rays represent the purpose of the soul - the inner work that is required to expand consciousness. In this section, the esoteric planet rulers of the ascendant are included. They rule the chart spiritually and are the primary representatives of soul purpose. Their signs and houses show how and where soul purpose will work out.

Aries ascendant: the personality approaches life with a fire for battle and an ardent desire for lower satisfaction. But it changes direction when the soul words "I come forth and from the plane of mind I rule" register. The instruction is to develop the intellect, use it to rein in the undisciplined impulses and bring the lower life under rule and control.

The qualities to develop through Aries rays are: intelligent leadership (ray 1), organising skills (7), higher aspiration (6, Mars), mind control and peacemaking skills (4, Mercury).

Esoteric ruler is Mercury. Its sign shows the state of the mind and where (house) and how (sign and aspects) to develop and use it.

Soul Purpose is to control the mind and life and to step forward boldly into life as a pioneer, leading the fight for the higher good.

Taurus ascendant: when the Bull of Desire rules the approach to life, the thirst for sensuous experience and materialism is consuming. But life changes when the soul words "I see and when the eye is opened, all is light" register. The instruction is to discipline the mind through meditation so that it fills with the light of wisdom. Then, transmute desire for materialism into an aspiration for the spiritual life. This will fill the nature with blissful light, opening the third eye.

The qualities to develop through Taurus' ray are: dispassion and balance (4), wisdom (5, Venus) and alignment of the lower will with the higher (1, Vulcan). These are necessary to control the bull.

Esoteric ruler is Vulcan. The Sun and Moon reveal Vulcan's power. The signs these two planets are in show traits needing purification and their houses, where to do this.

Soul Purpose is to align consciousness with the higher will, control the desire nature; then stand like a rock for higher principles and be a creator of beauty and harmony.

Gemini ascendant: with an unstable and superficial approach, the personality moves through life randomly in whichever direction the winds of fate happen to be blowing at the time. But it pauses and listens when the soul words "I see my other self and in the waning of that self, I grow and glow" register. The instruction is to observe the lower nature and use the disciplined mind to control it. This will fill the consciousness with light and enable the soul to take back its power from the ego.

Develop the qualities of Gemini's rays: mind stability (4, Mercury), wisdom (5, Venus) and love through life experience (2).

Esoteric ruler is Venus: in the chart, it represents the ability to love and the state of the mind that either contaminates or beautifies relationships. It house shows where to develop and express intelligent love.

Soul Purpose is to stabilise and beautify the mind and step forward into life as a "Messenger of the Gods", one who speaks and teaches higher truths.

Cancer ascendant: life is a lonely place, when the defensive heart of the personality does not know how to let people in.

But when the soul words "I build a lighted house and therein dwell" are heard, the aspirant knows what to do for a better future. The instruction is to purify the emotions through spiritual practises, so that soul light permeates the nature. This dissolves emotional negativity and isolation and fills the consciousness with the light and love of the soul.

The qualities to develop through Cancer's rays are: the intelligence (3), being grounded and ordered in life (7), balanced (4, Moon) and refined (6, Neptune) emotions. These are necessary developments for emotional control.

Esoteric ruler is Neptune: it represents delusions

that spoil relationships and shows how and where they should be dissolved; and where to cultivate openhearted love and compassion.

Soul Purpose is to walk freely in the world of illusion as a Light Bearer, a prism of love and wisdom, nurturing the masses in their attempts to grow spiritually.

Leo ascendant: approaching life under the banner of "Let other forms exist, I rule", the ego struts life's stage puffed up with its own glory. But forward momentum comes to a halt when the soul words "I am That and That am I" register. The instruction is clearly heard - to bring about identification and alignment with the "That", the soul, through meditation. Success leads to the 1st initiation (control of the physical appetites).

Develop the qualities of Leo's rays: wisdom (2, Sun) and sensitivity (6, Neptune) to others, a mind that can walk in the shoes of others (5), spiritual will (7, Uranus) and power used for the greater good (1).

Esoteric ruler is the Sun: it unveils Neptune's force, which refines the astral nature. The Sun's sign (and also Neptune's) shows negative traits to dissolve and strengths to develop.

Soul Purpose is to align with the light and power of the soul, to radiate the power of love and fight to uphold the highest principles and greater Law.

Virgo ascendant: when life approach is coloured by the personality words "Let matter reign", the desire for form life and love of material things is strong. But life direction changes when the soul words "I am the Mother and the Child, I God, I matter am" register. The instruction is to purify the lower nature so that the birth of the Christ spirit in the heart occurs.

Virgo qualities to develop through its rays are: wisdom through life experience (2), an aspiration for the spiritual life (6), a balanced mind (4, Mercury) and leadership skill (1, Vulcan). Collectively, these qualities and attributes foster the emergence of love and wisdom.

Esoteric ruler is the Moon unveiling Vulcan: the Moon Sign indicates the particular earthly attachments needing purification and its house shows where.

Soul Purpose is to give birth to the Christ spirit and to approach life in a wise and intelligent manner, serving humanity with skill and expertise.

Libra ascendant: an unbalanced and unstable life approach leads to procrastination, unwise choices and the emphasising of appearance to the detriment of character. But life direction changes when the soul words "I choose the way which lies between the two great lines of force" register. The instruction essentially is to balance the mind.

Libra qualities to develop through its rays are: a wide-ranging and discriminating intelligence that is poised and balanced (3 and 5 Venus) and an orientation to a new and higher way of life (7, Uranus). This brings the mind into alignment with Universal Mind.

Esoteric ruler is Uranus: it brings radical change to the life and awakens consciousness to new and higher truths and interests.

Soul Purpose is to walk "The Noble Middle Path" and be a harmonising and peace-making influence in life; to awaken people to humanitarian causes that are just and fair.

Scorpio ascendant: when life is coloured by the personality words "Let deception rule", emotional bias distorts perception, truth fades and life is conflicted. But life direction changes radically when the soul words "Warrior I am and from the battle I emerge triumphant" register. The instruction is to fight against and eliminate self-delusion. Specifically, those delusionary attitudes concerning sex, love of comfort and money; fear, hatred and desire for power, pride, separativeness and cruelty.

Psychological strength that is steadfast and stable (4) and the inner strength to fight any battle until victory is achieved (6, Mars) are the qualities to develop in Scorpio.

Esoteric ruler is Mars: it rules on both the exoteric and esoteric levels, indicating the ferocity of the battle fought between the personality and soul. Its house shows where the battle will primarily play out and where the blood-rushes of Mars should be curbed.

Soul Purpose is to stand in the light of wisdom and soar through life like an eagle, above the illusion of the lower emotional life; to be a warrior who fights to the death until justice prevails and truth unfolds.

Sagittarius ascendant: if the words "Let food again be sought" dictate the life approach, then excess, exaggeration and waste will follow. That is, until the soul words "I see the goal, I reach that goal and then I see another" are heard with the inner ear. This is a clear instruction to change life direction and aim for higher goals.

Qualities to develop through the rays are: balanced appetites (4), knowledge of the higher teachings (5), brotherliness through world travel (3, the Earth) and an aspiration for the Path (6). These qualities redirect the Archer's aim to the higher goal.

Esoteric ruler is the Earth: its house shows where to develop group understanding and group skills.

Soul Purpose is to move in a gradually ascending arc as a teacher, a prophet and as a director of men.

Capricorn ascendant: influenced by the note "Let ambition rule and let the door stand wide", life is driven by an insatiable desire for power and wealth. But under the weight of karma, this momentum halts. Only then, will the soul words "Lost am I in light supernal, yet on that light I turn my back" register. Practically applied, it is a command to turn away from the glamour of outer worldly ambition and find and follow a path that leads to greater Spiritual Light.

Capricorn qualities to develop through its rays are: an intelligence imbued with the light and wisdom of the soul (3), managerial and administrative skills (1 and 7), true humility before God (1) and ultimately, a love of all mankind (4, Venus). These qualities are vital to find and tread the higher Path.

Esoteric ruler is Saturn: its sign and house indicates where karma is met, where rank ambition should be avoided and where to give selflessly.

Soul Purpose is simply to serve the Plan - the greater good of humanity, with all the resources that one has.

Aquarius ascendant: when "Let desire in form be ruler" colours the personality approach to life, desire for material life is consuming and manifests in a variety of unusual ways. But when the soul words "Water of life am I, poured forth for thirsty men" registers in the heart, life direction changes radically. The aspiration to pour love ("water of life" is love) over the troubled waters of the world births in the heart, taking the aspirant in a higher direction.

A unified mind and heart (2 Jupiter and 5), scientific knowledge (7, Uranus) used for the good of those who still struggle (4, Moon), are the Aquarian qualities to develop.

Esoteric ruler is Jupiter: its sign and house shows where to find a teacher and develop wisdom.

Soul Purpose is to become an agent for the love and wisdom pouring from the Water Bearer, to be a benefactor and reformer of society for the higher good.

Pisces ascendant: at the lower level, the personality drifts with the wind and waves of the ocean of the emotions so that life is fluid and easy. But the whole nature is galvanised and life direction changes radically, when the soul words "I leave the Father's house and turning back, I save" are felt in the heart. The call to serve registers and the man or woman emerges from the world of illusion into truth.

The qualities to develop through Pisces' rays are: wisdom (2), inner strength and self-awareness (1, Pluto).

Esoteric ruler is Pluto. Its task is to destroy all that stands between the soul and its spiritual freedom. Its sign shows the negative traits and attachments needing elimination and its house shows where.

Soul Purpose is to emerge from illusion into truth and follow in the footsteps of the Master.

Vulcan

Vulcan's ray is the 1st Ray of Power. It gives aspirants the will they need to struggle free from the lower life. Pencil it in over the Sun and Moon.

Vulcan in Aries: the soul wants to break the power of the wilful "stallion" aspect of the personality and free the soul. It is a battle of wills, but eventually the soul will prevail. Success results in a powerful spiritual will that is oriented to the higher good, clear thought before action and superb leadership skills.

Vulcan in Taurus: the goal is to eliminate materialistic tendencies and bring the physical appetites into balance. Vulcan's power clashes with the "bull" aspect of the personality, creating conflict as the higher and lower battle for supremacy. Success brings soul illumination and a character of formidable inner strength and purpose, dedicated to the higher good.

Vulcan in Gemini: Vulcan has an electrifying and centralising effect upon the personality. It stops the restless personality oscillations so that the soul gains control of the mind, turning it to the pursuit of higher interests. The exterior presentation remains charming, but behind it, the steely will of the soul begins to come through.

Vulcan in Cancer: the electrifying force of Vulcan's light reveals the unsatisfactory state of the life, the slavery of the mind controlled by unstable emotions. The shock of this drives the aspirant "onto dry land", freeing consciousness from lower emotional control. Success results in greater soul will and autonomy and an intellect that operates independently of the emotions.

Vulcan in Leo: there is a battle of wills between the soul and the "lion" aspect of the personality. When the aspirant intelligently assists the soul in the struggle, the lower nature is brought under soul control. Success opens the heart to forces flowing from the Heart of the Sun, adding pure love to the magnificent spiritual power radiating from the Leo aspirant.

Vulcan in Virgo: the lower nature must be purified to prepare for the birth of the Christ (soul consciousness). Vulcan's fiery ray cuts through the mental thicket of little thoughts imprisoning consciousness, giving breadth, a glimpse of the spiritual heights and the work needed to reach this elevated level. Then it strengthens the aspirant's will to continue with the necessary spiritual disciplines until transformation occurs.

Vulcan in Libra: Vulcan brings crises through money matters, issues of integrity and relationships. The soul drives the personality out of its procrastination and forces it to make a choice between the old and new and eliminate deceit and game playing. Success results in the birth of a powerful intelligence oriented to the higher good and the will to bring life and all relationships into correct balance.

Vulcan in Scorpio: the struggle to the death between the soul and personality spans incarnations. The aspirant needs to stand steady, focused in the intellect, take refuge in the truth, under the illuminating light of the soul. Success creates a warrior of light, one who can walk free and untainted by the world of illusion.

Vulcan in Sagittarius: light reveals excessive and irresponsible behaviour and gluttony. It strengthens the will to clean up the life, lifting the eyes to the heights, instilling an urge to pursue that goal instead. When this is successful, the *Archer on the White Horse* travels fast across "the plains" - fast upon the Path, drawing others along as well.

Vulcan in Capricorn: the battle is long and hard before the lower will is broken and the Capricorn goat (ego) kneels in humility before the divine. This is a defining moment for those about to climb the mountain of spirituality. Success brings the highly developed managerial skills and expertise in the material world, under the control of the soul.

Vulcan in Aquarius: Vulcan's power shatters the ivory tower of rigid thoughtforms so that light and wisdom from the soul pours through. When this flow reaches the heart, life changes forever. The mind empties of dogma and fills with soul wisdom. A powerful advocate of truth emerges, a highly intelligent and wise fighter for social justice and reform.

Vulcan in Pisces: the will of the soul brings the aimless swimming in the ocean of emotionalism to a halt, so that an advanced man emerges. Piscean disciples easily align their hearts with the central pool of divine love, but Vulcan adds the necessary characteristics of leadership, will, power and strength. Pisces is the sign of the Messiah and representatives must have love and will in balance. Then the ocean of Pisces is the sea of selfless service.

Mercury

☿ *Mercury is known as the Star of Conflict and its ray is the 4th Ray of Harmony through Conflict. Its task is to transform the mind from an instrument of conflict, into an agent of harmony.*

Mercury in Aries: hot-headed and aggressive, the personality uses lower mind to attack without discrimination. Judgment is poor because the lower emotional impulses are stronger than mental control. Mind battles are fought.

As the soul asserts its power, it illumines the substance of the mind and the disciple achieves mental control. Later, Mercury unfolds the intuition, the all-knowing faculty. This illumined mind is innovative, it sees the broad picture and is a peace-making and harmonising instrument. Communicating its messages upon the power ray, those who hear obey and follow.

Mercury in Taurus: the double ray 4 (Taurus and Mercury) produces tremendous mental conflict and a tendency to agonise. Lower mind is a blunt club used to fight and bash the opposition.

On the Path, Vulcan's fiery force purifies the mind's substance, cleansing it, so that vision becomes clear and the light of understanding shines through. The mind balances and begins to relate with other minds more harmoniously. When the intuitive faculty starts to unfold, mind transforms into an instrument of light and wisdom. The illumined Taurus mind conveys soul messages in a powerful, creative and practical way.

Mercury in Gemini: restless and superficial, lower mind moves incessantly to touch the new, the interesting, the next unknown thing, etc. It plays at life, bringing it into conflict with other minds.

When soul illumination begins to illumine the mind and purification practises are applied, the mind expands and deeper truths are touched. Thought life becomes more harmonious. As the intuition unfolds, mind transforms into an instrument that communicates divine thought. Fully developed, this mind is intelligent, wise, loving and understanding. Used by the soul, it conveys higher truths and inspirational messages. Many great spiritual teachers and orators have this combination.

Mercury in Cancer: easily disturbed by the emotions, lower mind is vague and has difficulty building clear thoughtforms. This brings it into conflict with others because it "the truth" is obscured by emotionalism.

But when the intelligence unfolds and self-control is applied, mind lifts from its astral focus and fills with soul light. This lights the way ahead so that thoughts and actions are wiser. The illumined Cancer mind is an intelligent and lighted "house". It is sensitive and thoughtful, nurturing others with kind thoughts and words. When the intuition comes into play the soul has a very effect instrument for world use. This is the nurturing and compassionate mind.

Mercury in Leo: arrogant, controlling, over-dramatic and attention seeking, lower mind continually tells itself and others that it has a divine right to rule. This brings it into conflict with other powerful egos and humiliation when its pomposity exposed.

As soul illumination shines through, ego sensitivity dissolves and the mind identifies with gradually increasing larger wholes. As the intuition unfolds, the soul has a superb mental instrument for leadership use. Communicating its messages upon the 1st Ray of Power, those who hear obey and follow.

Mercury in Virgo: lower mind operates within a very narrow perspective, focused on material acquisition. It is judgmental, querulous and makes a fuss over unimportant details. This brings it into conflict with other minds that retaliate, finding *its* imperfections.

As soul illumination floods the mind, its boundaries broaden so that it has greater vision and wisdom. Relationships become more harmonious. Then, as the intuition unfolds, this mind works to its greatest potential. Virgo is intelligence and the hidden Christ that is associated with this sign, is the intuition or pure reason.

Mercury in Libra: unstable, over busy and restless, lower mind swings to extremes. Lacking depth, it procrastinates, frets, dwelling upon that which is frivolous, sensuous and superficial. This brings it into conflict with other duplicitous minds.

When steadied by the soul a discerning and judicious mind demonstrates its potential. Wise communications result in harmonious and peaceful exchanges. As the intuition unfolds and the abstract reasoning powers are applied, the Libran mind gives the soul a superb instrument for legal, counselling and diplomatic work.

Mercury in Scorpio: seeing people and life as a battleground, lower mind is ultra-defensive, reactive and lethal on attack with cruel thoughts and words. Self-deluding and unstable, it oscillates between emotional highs and lows. This brings it into conflict with other hostile and unstable minds.

As soul light permeates the mind, it lifts above astral domination and begins to stabilise. Spiritual practise clears it of negativity and mind becomes more peaceful. As the intuition unfolds, a delver of life's mysteries, a revealer of the truth, reveals itself. The soul then has a superb warrior-mind that is harmless in the spiritual sense and fights with pen and word.

Mercury in Sagittarius: careless with facts, lower mind verbalises loudly, trumpeting its presence to all who will listen. It harms, wounding others by targeting their "sins" and self-justifying with the claim of "speaking the truth". This brings it into conflict with other minds that sit in judgement of its sins.

As the light of the soul begins to permeate, faults correct and a higher direction is followed. The mind becomes more sensitive to the points of view of others. As the intuition unfolds, it evolves into a philosophical and reasoning instrument. Wise, creative, intuitive and visionary, this Sagittarius mind draws many to the Path.

Mercury in Capricorn: hungering after material power, lower mind is coercive, calculates, plots, deceives and connives to satisfy ambition. This brings it into conflict with other minds that are just as ambitious and cunning.

On the Path, a vision of the higher way unfolds. The mind begins to search for this greater truth and to find and practise the spiritual disciplines necessary to take initiation. Mind exchanges become transparent and inclusive. As the intuition unfolds, this mind communicates with the power of truth and others listen and obey. Systematic and efficient it knows how to bring about the best for all.

Mercury in Aquarius: lower mind is intelligent and likes to demonstrate its superiority. Detached from the emotions, judgmental and dogmatic, it is not sensitive to people's feelings. This brings it into conflict with other minds that are just as judgmental in their assessments.

Then, as soul radiance permeates the mind-stuff, right-relations are gradually restored between mind and heart. Exchanges become harmonious. Later, as the intuition unfolds, love and wisdom flows through and the beauty of the higher mind reveals itself. The combination of intelligence, wisdom and an awakened intuition gives one of the finest minds possible. In Aquarius, the soul can think the Plan of God into existence.

Mercury in Pisces: vague, deluded and confused, lower mind has difficulty building clear thoughtforms. It promises all but there is little follow up. It is easily distracted as something else more interesting captures its attention. This brings it into conflict with other minds that are just as delusional.

As soul light permeates the mind, consciousness frees itself from astral influence and the mind thinks clearly. Now promises are kept and exchanges with others are truthful and reality based. Through the harmonious Pisces mind, the soul communicates Christ's loving words to alleviate the suffering of man.

Venus

♀ *Venus represents the ability that we have (or lack of), to build loving unions. This is determined by the level of development of our minds. Venus' ray is the 5th Ray of Concrete Mind. Its task is to beautify the mind and bring it into right relation with the heart. This transforms the mind into an instrument of love.*

Venus in Aries: personality affections are ardent, passionate and expressed selfishly and immaturely. Love is sex and sensuous gratification.

As soul light begins to permeate the mind, the aspirant begins to appreciate the benefits of equal sharing, cooperation and to value higher and finer things in life. Love-intelligence expressed through Aries results in relationships that are a balance of ardent fire and cooperative sharing. Through Aries, the soul directs with the power of love.

Venus in Taurus: at the lower level, the "bull of desire" drives love and the personality focuses on physical desire and sex. Love and relationships are a battle.

When the light of the soul begins to permeate the mind and Vulcan's fire purifies the emotions, lower desire transforms into an aspiration for the spiritual life. Simultaneously, the quality of all unions becomes higher and finer. Love-intelligence expressed through Taurus results in relationships based on loyalty and trust. They are also intensely powerful, creative and filled with beauty and colour. In Taurus, the soul loves to create tangible demonstrations of beauty.

Venus in Gemini: personality affections are a mind game and love is superficial, irresponsible, non-committal and ephemeral. There is no depth of true feeling or ability to love intimately.

As soul radiance begins to permeate the mind, then gradually mental integrity unfolds and honesty in relationships. This brings greater depth to all unions. Love-intelligence expressed through Gemini results in relationships based on kind thoughts and words and an all-embracing appreciation of the value of others. In Gemini, the soul loves to communicate wisdom to beautify the minds and hearts of all.

Venus in Cancer: love at the personality level is needy, clingy, with many oscillating highs and lows. Fearful and glamoured imaginings cause the defensive crab to isolate itself. An impenetrable wall of fear prevents love from being expressed or received.

As the refining light of the soul permeates the mind, relationships are seen in a truer light and communication is truthful, beautifying all unions. Love-intelligence expressed through Cancer results in relationships based on an exquisite sensitivity and appreciation of the value of others. In Cancer, the soul loves to light the way home for the masses.

Venus in Leo: at the personality level, love is narcissistic, needing constant approval, appreciation and adoration. All must revolve around it and supply its needs.

As soul radiance begins to permeate the mind, gradually a more inclusive love of the whole replaces the egocentric focus. Love-intelligence expressed through Leo results in relationships that are a balance of fiery power and sensitivity to the needs of others. Through Leo, the soul loves to provide intelligent, wise and loving leadership.

Venus in Virgo: at the personality level the critical mind kills love, like a heavy frost burns and withers spring buds. Love is cold, with an accountant-like mentality governing and rationing affection.

Over time, the penetrating light of the soul permeates the mind and Vulcan's purifying action cleanses its negative contents. Consequently, there is a deeper appreciation of the value and worth of others and loving relationships blossom. Love-intelligence expressed through Virgo gives all that it has and does it all that it can to help others. Through Virgo, the soul loves to serve and assist the helpless and needy victims of life.

Venus in Libra: the personality is restless and seeks excitement and diversions, turning love into a sensual game, with many partners and deceit.

Gradually, the soul's radiance steadies the mind and life brings challenging experiences awakening a desire for change and a yearning for higher forms of love - unconditional and true friendship. Gradually, new and more loving unions form. Love-intelligence expressed through Libra conducts relationships intelligently and judiciously, with consideration for the points of view of all concerned. Through Libra, the soul loves to bring opposites into perfect union.

Venus in Scorpio: personality affections have a devouring intensity and there is a desire to control partners. Possessiveness, deceit, jealousy and threats, tarnish relationships.

Holding the mind in the light of the soul frees consciousness from illusion. Relationships are clearer and communications and actions are kinder, reflecting the growing capacity to love as a soul. All unions improve. Love-intelligence expressed through Scorpio results in relationships that are a balance of intense power and depth, but that also appreciate the boundaries and rights of others. Integrity, truth and honesty are highly valued. Through Scorpio, the warrior soul loves to go to war on behalf of those who suffer.

Venus in Sagittarius: personality love is like a wild untameable horse, which demands freedom and avoids responsibility and commitment. When it wants, it wants all. When it has had enough, it leaves without looking back.

As soul wisdom permeates the mind, consciousness becomes more inclusive and the old impulses fade. Love-intelligence expressed through Sagittarius results in relationships that are built upon a deep friendship, which are honest, direct and have a foundation of transparent integrity. There is often shared love of spiritual or philosophical teachings. Through Sagittarius, the soul loves to beautify the hearts and minds of others by teaching inspiring philosophy and the Ageless Wisdom.

Venus in Capricorn: ambition turns love into a commodity, as barter and a means to gain material benefit. The personality affections are controlled and lack warmth.

Through adversity and loss, gradually the lesson is learnt that love is more important than power and money. Then, as soul radiance begins to permeate the mind, the warmth of Christ love melts the ice, freeing and opening the heart. The mind transforms into an instrument that appreciates the value of love and of loving unions. Love-intelligence expressed through Capricorn forms relationships based on mutual respect, friendship and considerate communications. Through Capricorn, the soul loves to shoulder heavy responsibilities that lighten the load for humanity.

Venus in Aquarius: captive to lower mind, separativeness and judgment blights love. Relationships are less important than the desire for freedom and independence.

As soul-radiance begins to permeate the mind, a new perception of the value of people at a deep and non-material level dawns. Loving and inclusive relationships form, based on a union of mind and heart and a love of the truth. Love-intelligence expressed through Aquarius results in wisdom and an appreciation of the whole of humanity in all its shades and colours. Through Aquarius, the soul loves to pour the healing waters of love.

Venus in Pisces: personality love is like the waves of the ocean that flow here or there depending upon the way the wind is blowing. Childlike and avoiding responsibility, dependent upon others, this love plays the victim and binds people through guilt.

When soul radiance begins to permeate the mind, illusion strips away and the cold light of truth reveals the way life has been lived and wasted. The will to eliminate the old ways arises and transformation is rapid. Love-intelligence expressed through Pisces flows like an ocean of inclusive and compassionate love that inspires, lifts, heals and saves. Through Pisces, the soul loves to serve humanity with compassion, in a very selfless Christ-like way.

The Earth

The Earth's ray is the 3rd of Intelligent Activity. It provides a field of experience for humanity and helps the development of intelligent action through the experience of reincarnation. Opposite the Sun, its sign qualities when adopted help to balance the ego. The Earth has an individual effect only on people who are on the Path.

Earth in Aries: leadership and spokesperson roles both at work and in the personal life and the experience and knowledge gained, balances Libran personality procrastination. This combination gives the potential to bring peace and harmony to troubled souls, by using the power of thought to shatter chains that enslave consciousness.

Earth in Taurus: taking a practical and dispassionate approach to life balances and grounds Scorpio aggression. At work and in service, choose leadership roles and conduct affairs in a thoughtful and practical way. This combination gives the potential to fight against injustice and to work creatively.

Earth in Gemini: thinking intelligently about problems before reacting, balances and redirects Sagittarius force more wisely. In the world at large, make the effort to communicate with others intelligently and with consideration. This combination gives the potential to be heard around the globe, because information and knowledge is conveyed with simplicity and is easy to understand.

Earth in Cancer: being more sensitive and inclusive of the feelings of others balances Capricorn personality rigidity. In the professional life and at home, always consider the emotional impact of decisions on others. This combination gives the potential to express executive and management power through structures and ways that are nurturing to the majority.

Earth in Leo: a more inclusive and loving approach balances Aquarian mental rigidity and opens the heart. In both work and the social life, always consider the emotional affects that decisions have on others and if necessary, change plans and ideas that are harmful. This combination gives the potential to express the love and wisdom of the Water Bearer, in very creative and effective ways.

Earth in Virgo: using the mind intelligently and thinking through issues before responding, balances Pisces emotional instability and brings structure to the life. In life generally, take a no-nonsense approach. This combination gives the potential to radiate love and wisdom in technical and practical ways.

Earth in Libra: being cooperative and fair, balances Aries impulsiveness and lack of consideration. In all relationships, talk, negotiate and come to some consensus, before acting. This combination gives the potential to shatter indecision and procrastination, through the power of new ideas and strong leadership.

Earth in Scorpio: holding the mind steady in the light of truth and not giving in to emotionalism balances and checks Taurus "bullish" personality desires. In all meaningful situations and in life generally, the high goal is to fight for the higher truth and principle. This combination gives the potential to stand steadfast in the face of great threat or danger and to come out the other end victorious, if battle-scarred.

Earth in Sagittarius: refocusing and redirecting life energies into a new and higher direction balances Gemini mind instability. In all areas, search for the higher ideal or principle and aim for that. This combination gives the potential to communicate the Wisdom Teachings to the world at large.

Earth in Capricorn: being more business-like and structured in life, balances Cancer emotionalism and defensiveness. At work and home, be professional and intelligent in presentation. This combination gives the potential to build structures through which the nurturing flow of spiritual love can reach man.

Earth in Aquarius: being more inclusive and group-minded, balances Leo personality arrogance and individualism and fosters a more cooperative approach. In both work and the social life, engage with others with a sense that you all belong to a universal brotherhood. This combination gives the potential to express leadership power wisely, through a team, to benefit society.

Earth in Pisces: opening the heart and mind to the troubles of humanity balances Virgo perfectionism and stimulates heart expression. In whatever area of service, be compassionate and empathetic in all communications and dealings. This combination gives the potential to heal and save the masses, through practical knowledge and expertise.

Mars

♂ *Mars' ray is the 6th Ray of Devotion and Idealism. It represents whatever a person is devoted to, the nature of the desire life, ideals and beliefs. Mars therefore represents what men fight and die for, battles fought and how we engage with others who have different ideals and beliefs. Mars presents us with an opportunity to control the astral nature and transmute desire into aspiration for higher and finer things in life.*

Mars in Aries: lower will is powerful and the hot and passionate desire nature has urgent and selfish needs. It is reactive and warlike. Demanding immediate satisfaction, it batters its way through life trying to satisfy its cravings. There are contests for control and leadership, jealousy, retaliation and aggression.

As the inner life starts to have an effect, then gradually desire transmutes into fiery spiritual aspiration. With this adjustment, the soul has an astral field through which it can inspire the best in others. In Aries, the aspirant fights to overcome blind and forceful desire in his own nature. When successful, he or she steps forward as an intelligent and assertive leader who fights with fiery power for the higher good.

Mars in Taurus: with immovable will, volatile and explosive, the desire nature swings from the heights of exhilaration to the depths of despair. Driven by the "bull of desire" the appetites are voracious.

Over time, Vulcan's purifying force scours the astral field and it fills with light. Desire transmutes into spiritual aspiration. Now the soul has a stable and lighted vessel through which to direct its power. In Taurus, the aspirant fights to release himself from the hold of lower desire and emerges as a warrior of light.

Mars in Gemini: this combination links the astral nature and mind so that there is mental combativeness, hot and angry thoughts, volatile verbal outbursts and a lot of talk.

Gradually Venus (esoteric ruler of Gemini) refines the astral field and it fills with light, transforming desire into aspiration. Now the soul has a clear vessel that does not distort its ideas, but instead sends them forth with fire. In Gemini, the aspirant fights to overcome wasted restless motion within the mind and when successful, emerges as a warrior of the pen and thought.

Mars in Cancer: emotional power is strong. There are moods and wallowing incessantly in past hurts and grievances. The unpurified desire nature harbours resentment, jealousy and throws tantrums. The emotions boil and erupt in hot torrents, venting themselves on the closest target.

As Neptune refines the emotional life it lifts energy from the lower chakras up to the heart and desire transmutes into spiritual aspiration. Now the soul has a clear and intuitive vessel that responds with kind action. In Cancer, the aspirant fights to free himself from bondage to the emotions and when successful, fights to free the masses from this slavery as well.

Mars in Leo: the will and power of the ego is immense. Hot and reactive, the unpurified desire nature wears its sense of superiority with swollen pride and arrogance. There are explosions, anger, sulks, hurt feelings and much dismissing of people from the royal presence.

Gradually the refining action of Neptune clears the astral nature so that the heart centre begins to open and consciousness becomes more sensitive to the soul. Desire transmutes into spiritual aspiration and the soul has a clear path through which to radiate spiritual fire. In Leo, the aspirant fights to displace the selfish ego from the seat of control and bring it into line with the soul. When successful, a warrior-leader filled with the power and glory of the Sun emerges.

Mars in Virgo: there is expertise with machinery and technology. But when this extends to people, when the exacting mind tries to force its will on those who are not "perfect", then trouble arises. Conversely, sometimes the emotions are suppressed, resulting in passive aggression and spiteful actions carried out in secret.

As the Path is approached, Vulcan's fiery force burns out impurities and desire transmute into spiritual aspiration. The astral field fills with light so that response to the world is kinder. In Virgo, the aspirant fights to overcome a conflicted mind controlled by the emotions and when successful fights to free humanity from servitude to materialism and the drudgery of human life.

Mars in Libra: Mars heats up the sacral centre, the sensuous nature and drives the man or woman out to find satisfaction. Searching for passion and excitement, it creates conflict and leaves behind a trail of failed relationships. There is a warlike touch to the mind so that mental barbs can be acute, if subtle, creating disharmony.

Over time, Uranus (esoteric ruler of Libra) begins to shatter the old habits. The emotions purify and desire transmutes into spiritual aspiration. Then the soul has a clear and balanced astral field through which to work. In Libra, the aspirant fights for equilibrium within his own nature, then strives to bring peace and harmony to the world.

Mars in Scorpio: lower will and bias distort reality, giving rise to churning emotions that are dark, aggressive, retaliatory and revengeful. They are exhausting for their owner, who continually fights battles "to the death" with all, sundry and himself.

Across lives, the illumined mind gradually disperses the darkness and desire transmutes into spiritual aspiration. Now the soul has a purified astral field that is steady and clear, a lighted vessel that responds intelligently to life stress. In Scorpio, the aspirant fights the darkness in his own nature and then fights the darkness in humanity.

Mars in Sagittarius: the freedom loving desire nature is fiery, reactive, with an enormous appetite for sensuous and physical pleasure. Blunt, insensitive and gossipy, verbal attacks harm others.

Gradually illumination refines the astral field so that it clears and becomes a lighted vessel through which higher inspiration flows. With desire transmuted into spiritual aspiration, the traveller directs his search towards the higher ideal. In Sagittarius, the aspirant fights for release from the hold of matter, then directs humanity onto the higher way so that others can do the same.

Mars in Capricorn: the power of ambition drives the personality and it fights to destroy all who blocks its way to life success, money and power. But karma awaits those who violate the Law of Love and in time, the soul breaks the lower will through humiliating experiences and adversity, forcing the personality to its knees.

Gradually the astral field fills with light and ambition is transmuted into an aspiration to climb the spiritual mountain. In Capricorn, the aspirant fights to release himself from the slavery of material ambition and strives for executive power to serve with power, the Plan of God.

Mars in Aquarius: the power to enforce one's intellectual superiority is strong and so is the desire to be "right" and to defeat all opposition with facts and pointed argument. Beliefs are aggressively defended and expressed. The ego uses intellectual power to get what it wants.

Over time, the mind lightens and inner changes occur. The astral field clears and lower desire transmutes into aspiration. The astral field becomes a clear vessel through which the soul can inspire people to reach out in friendship and love to all humanity. In Aquarius, the aspirant fights to break free from the prison of illusion and then uses the power of clear argument to do the same for humanity.

Mars in Pisces: Mars' fire weakens in this watery sign leading to lethargy, confusion, blunted ambition and feelings of impotency. Unacknowledged or undealt with emotions bubble beneath the surface, manifesting as confused resentment and passive aggression.

Then at the portals of the Path, soul light purifies the astral field and desire transmutes into spiritual aspiration. Quiet and light-filled, it is now a perfect and clear vessel for the distribution of kind action, love and compassion. In Pisces, the aspirant fights to free himself from drowning in the astral waters and when successful, fights to save humanity from its suffering.

Jupiter

Jupiter's ray is the 2nd Ray of Love and Wisdom. Its task is to open the heart chakra and infuse consciousness with love-wisdom.

Jupiter in Aries: the hot-blooded personality traits of the "ram" expand in ordinary man. But on the Path, the prophetic words "I come forth and from the plane of mind, I rule" inspires the aspirant to go on a search for knowledge and understanding. A Teacher appears and if the student heeds advice, spiritual practises divert energy from the solar plexus chakra to the Heart, which blossoms. When the prophecy fulfils a wise Aries leader emerges, a director of men who inspires followers to reach for the "Light of Life", the power of God.

Jupiter in Taurus: the appetites of the "bull", the lust driven personality expands in ordinary man. It rushes blindly, to satisfy the lower cravings. For those on the Path, the prophetic words "I see and when the eye is opened" inspires a search for understanding. A Teacher appears and if the student responds wisely, purification programs divert energy from the lower appetites up to the heart, so that the "eye of the soul" opens. A wise, Taurus prophet emerges; teaching fundamental truths, students are inspired to search for the lighted Path that leads to greater wisdom.

Jupiter in Gemini: uncontrolled fluidity, instability and shallowness expand in ordinary man. There are huge dreams, many ideas, a lot of talking, but without practical application. But increasing soul sensitivity enables a few to hear the prophetic words "I see my other self and in the waning of that self, I grow and glow". Inspired, the student goes on a search for the beauty and truth of the soul. A Teacher appears and spiritual practises expand heart-mind wisdom. Eventually a wise Gemini prophet-teacher emerges, a master of the Light of Interplay, of the power that plays between spirit and form. Students are instructed to overcome the problems of duality so that they in turn become teachers.

Jupiter in Cancer: emotional confusion and neediness expands. But when the prophetic words "I build a lighted house and therein dwell" are received by the inner ear, the aspirant is inspired to emerge from the conflicted emotional waters and strive towards the light. A Teacher appears and in time, spiritual practises develop knowledge, understanding and the heart centre opens. A wise Cancer Light-bearer emerges. Radiating wisdom to students like a lighthouse piercing dark and dangerous waters, those who are lost are guided home.

Jupiter in Leo: the arrogance of the lion, the selfish all-powerful personality expands in ordinary man. Full of itself and proud, it is puffed up with its glory and wonderfulness. Then on the Path, the prophetic words "I am That and That Am I" reveal the glory of the Higher Self and in comparison, the ridiculous state of the ego is seen. This causes a life reversal. A Teacher appears and if the student responds wisely, spiritual practises open the heart chakra, expanding its aura. A wise Leo leader emerges, charismatic and powerful, whose directions to others are like rays emanating from the Sun to warm the earth.

Jupiter in Virgo: the nit-picking negatives of the mind may be somewhat blunted, but acquisitiveness and love of trivia expands. It is only upon the Path that the prophetic words "Christ in you the hope of glory" register, revealing the radiance of the soul to the inner eye. The impact is strong and life direction reverses. A Teacher appears and if the student responds wisely, purification practises bring the mind and heart into balance. The student evolves into wise Virgo teacher, whose illuminating discourses and instructions are practical, clear and transformative.

Jupiter in Libra: there is an abundance of failed relationships, indecisiveness and procrastination. Then, when the prophetic words "I choose the way which lies between the two great lines of force" register, they make a powerful impact. The cause of troubled relationships is seen - unwise decisions and a life not in balance. Seeking change, a Teacher appears and spiritual practises and wiser choices bring the life into balance. A wise Libra mediator emerges; with a finely-honed intellect, legal and judicial powers, he or she has the Wisdom of Solomon.

Jupiter in Scorpio: in young souls, desire and emotional delusion expands and consciousness is blind. Then upon the Path, the prophetic words "Warrior I am and from the battle I emerge triumphant" inspires the student to begin the long struggle to climb out of the swamp of lower emotional control and strive towards the Light. A Teacher appears and if the student perseveres, the practise of esoteric techniques frees the consciousness from astral control. The heart centre opens and a wise Scorpio warrior emerges; strong and courageous he or she fights evil with words of light and wisdom.

Jupiter in Sagittarius: appetites are huge in young souls and the desire to consume something, anything, dominates. But in time, physical and psychic congestion brings a halt to the old ways and a reversal begins. Now on the Path, the prophetic words "I see the goal, I reach that goal and then I see another" reveals the life and the inner work to be done. A Teacher appears and points to the higher way. In time the heart centre unfolds and a wise Sagittarius prophet-teacher emerges. Dispensing wisdom like the rays of the Sun, many are drawn to listen and follow.

Jupiter in Capricorn: the ambitions expand and the Capricorn goat doggedly climbs the mountain of materiality. But those who are more advanced hear the prophetic words "Lost am I in light supernal, yet on that light I turn my back" and they have a major impact upon life direction. Light reveals the glamour of the material life and a new direction is sought. A Teacher appears and if the student responds wisely, initiation is taken and ascension begins on the spiritual mountain. When the prophecy fulfils, a wise Capricorn leader emerges, one who is ablaze with the "Light of the Intuition", the light that clears the way to the mountaintop and that produces transfiguration. Steadily he or she shines this light into dark places so that searchers can find their way to the Source.

Jupiter in Aquarius: the ego is puffed up with a desire for knowledge and control. There is a lot of dreaming and many ideas, but little practical action taken to manifest anything substantial. Then upon the Path, the prophetic words "Water of life am I, poured forth for thirsty men" inspires the aspirant to become such a person, a fountain of wisdom to help reform society. A Teacher appears and if the student responds wisely, higher knowledge is absorbed and the heart and mind come into balance. In time, a wise Aquarius Water Bearer emerges, one who distributes love and wisdom to the masses and who radiates the light that ever shines in the dark.

Jupiter in Pisces: the desire for new emotional satisfactions, expand in ordinary man. Consciousness is fluid and the lower psychic instincts dominate. Within a few, the prophetic words "I leave my Father's house and turning back, I save" make an impact upon the heart and the aspirant is inspired to follow in the footsteps of a Master and serve humanity. A Teacher appears and over time, spiritual practises free the consciousness from lower control. A wise Pisces prophet-teacher emerges, a true representative of the World Saviour. Serving selflessly, he or she shines the light of love and compassion out into the darkness of human ignorance, so that people can see and find their way "home".

Saturn

♄ *Saturn represents the Lord of Karma and it offers us the opportunity to advance spiritually through adversity. Its ray is the 3rd Ray of Intelligent Activity. Karma is the result of the thoughts we think and words we speak. Saturn asks us to be more intelligent about the choices we make so that we do not violate the Law of Love. Keep in mind that most of out karma originates from a previous life.*

Saturn in Aries. Negative karma arises when the Law of Love is violated. For example: hard authority figures riding roughshod over our feelings, being unfairly blocked from promotion or advancement, damage to the head or brain. Saturn in Aries can lead to a fear of taking risks, of initiating new projects or failing as a leader.

To neutralise hard karma, practise meditation mind disciplines to bring the mind under control and use it to rein in impulsiveness. Use power wisely and develop kindness. Positive karma is being respected as a wise and intelligent leader, for having a commanding presence that draws admiration and respect, being a highly respected pioneer in one's field of interest.

Saturn in Taurus. Negative karma arises when lower desire or greed guides decision-making. Some examples are being deprived of possessions, bankruptcy, being unfairly disrespected and devalued, sex difficulties and physical and emotional disorders. Saturn in Taurus fears never having enough, losing all one's money or possessions and being perceived as being dumb.

To neutralise hard karma, curb lower desire and live moderately. Give generously. Good karma comes as steady prosperity, marked success in the chosen profession or work, becoming a highly respected authority or artist.

Saturn in Gemini. Harsh and critical words attract karma. Some examples are receiving hard and insensitive communications from authority figures, denied fair right of response, being the subject of scandal, having opinions ignored or disrespected, speech or psychological disorders, physical ailments with the throat, tongue or breathing apparatus. This combination can lead to being afraid to speak out or not being heard, a fear of not being clever enough, being afraid of life.

Balance karma by being disciplined with what you think and say and stop gossiping. Meditate so that you learn to develop greater depth in whatever you do. Every day think kind thoughts and say nice things to others. Positive Saturn will give a strong and solid intelligence, accuracy in thought, wisdom that brings respect from others, success in the profession or chosen area of work, respect for being a wise and loving teacher.

Saturn in Cancer. Building emotional, defensive walls attracts karma, such as rejection, being denied emotional and physical nurturing, ending up being isolated and alone, depression and anxiety. Saturn in Cancer gives a fear of rejection, being alone and lonely, thinking one is unlovable and will never find love.

Karma can be offset through meditation and learning how to open the heart and to trust in love again. Every day take a risk by trusting someone and be forgiving if people fail. Find someone or something to love and cherish. Positive Saturn gives emotional stability, inner strength, trust in oneself and in one's ability to handle life and all it brings, nurturing relationships, ability to build lighted forms (thoughtforms, life structures), being a Light-Bearer (carrier of wisdom).

Saturn in Leo. We attract karma when the Law of Love is violated, such as being subject to harsh and heartless treatment by powerful authority figures, being publicly humiliated and denied children or problems with them. Associated health disorders are those that affect the heart, blood and circulation. Associated fears are a fear of not being in control, having no personal power, disrespected or humiliated.

To offset hard karma, stop misusing power professionally and personally. Every day, "walk in the shoes" of those who suffer and give assistance to those in need. Positive Saturn rewards us with respect for being a wise and intelligent leader, professional success, a regal presence that naturally draws respect, being loved and obeyed, the love and respect of children, a strong heart.

Saturn in Virgo. Negative karma arises when the critical ego rules decision making. For instance, being ruled by a mean-spirited perfectionist, being subject to vindictive gossip, deprived of emotional warmth, loss of possessions, forced to work long hours in miserly conditions for a pittance or digestive disorders. Saturn in Virgo fears never being able to achieve the desired standard, of losing one's possessions or money.

Hard karma can be mitigated by following a spiritual teaching that helps to overcome materialism. Cultivate kindness and refuse to judge and criticise. Every day think kinds thoughts and find something nice to say about someone you dislike. Positive karma can come as success in the chosen profession or work, recognition and respect for one's artisanship or technical skills, scientific expertise, accolades for selfless service.

Saturn in Libra. Dishonesty in relationships attracts negative karma, such as difficulties in personal or sexual relations, attracting partners who are venal or cold, being unfairly judged, bankruptcy and kidney problems. Saturn in Libra fears intimacy, being controlled by partners, making decisions, being harshly judged.

To overcome karma, meditate to cultivate a serene and balanced mind, stop unhealthy sexual imaginings. Every day be fair and endeavour to be scrupulously honest in what you think and say. Saturn positively expressed in this sign gives personal qualities such as a judicial mind and profound insight and wisdom, success and respect in the legal profession or in any area that requires compromise or counselling and loving personal and professional relationships.

Saturn in Scorpio. Negative karma arises when the dark side of the nature guides decision-making. Some examples are: sexual or emotional abuse, being stalked or attacked by unscrupulous, jealous or criminal people; sex-related diseases or disorders in the sexual region; unpleasant psychic occurrences and psychological disorders. Saturn in Scorpio can give a fear of retribution, of losing control, of sexual dysfunction, fear of the dark and of the supernatural, a fear of oneself.

Beat karma by meditating every day in order to learn how to hold your mind steady in the light of the soul and to see reality as it is. Take steps to develop a healthy sex life and stop unhealthy sexual imaginings. Stop trying to control others. Every day, forgive someone who has hurt you. Saturn rewards us with positive qualities such as emotional stability and a solid intelligence that can delve to the root of a problem. Other positives are good psychological strength and the ability to fight against evil, being a highly respected authority and practitioner in metaphysics, the occult, healing, psychology, or other esoteric field.

Saturn in Sagittarius. We attract negative karma when greed guides decision-making or when thoughtless words wound people. For instance, being harshly judged or verbally attacked, being treated shabbily and "ripped off", being the subject of scandal, difficulties with religion or cults, having one's freedom curbed and excesses exposed. Saturn in Sagittarius gives a fear of loss of freedom, mistrust of foreigners.

Meditating regularly upon your highest ideals and aspirations, on any positive or sacred subject helps to neutralise hard karma. Practise moderation and being responsible in life and with others. Every day, say something generous and kind. Positive karma can come: as being gifted with a powerful and discerning intelligence, respect and success for being a wise authority in academia, in philosophy, religion, or on the Ancient Mysteries.

Saturn in Capricorn. We attract hard karma when the Law of Love is violated for the sake of ambition. Some examples are: being controlled by hard and uncompromising authorities, bankruptcy, having one's dishonest dealings exposed, being humiliated, loss of status and power, losing all, incarcerated in prison or other institution. Saturn in Capricorn can lead to a mistrust of authority figures, fear of taking reasonable risks in business, a fear of love and life or of not being lovable or likeable.

Meditating regularly on a positive or sacred topic helps to make karma your friend. Be generous. Be open and fair in all dealings. Every day, do or say something loving. Positive Saturn can come as prosperity and success in life and business, becoming a wise and beloved leader, being lovable and taking initiation.

Saturn in Aquarius. Negative karma follows when we are separative and judgmental, such as being exposed for intellectual errors or theft of intellectual property, harshly judged by rigid-minded authority figures, rejected by friends, being a victim of rebellious action. Karmic health examples are problems with the ankles, nerves, circulation or accidents. Saturn in Aquarius can lead to a fear of expressing one's thoughts, rejection by friends, of not measuring up intellectually.

To mitigate hard karma be inclusive in thought and action and sensitive to the feelings of others. Every day give generously (time, ideas, assistance and money). Positive Saturn gifts us with an exceptional intelligence, a scientific mind balanced with wisdom, success and respect in the chosen profession or work, solid friendships, finding one's soul group.

Saturn in Pisces. Negative karma flows our way when we lack compassion and kindness. For instance: developing a chronic illness or an emotional disorder, being incarcerated - harshly treated or taken advantage of, becoming a vagrant, having to carry heavy responsibilities without recognition or reward, unfairly forced to sacrifice the life for others. Saturn in Pisces can lead to a fear of the unknown, not trusting the processes of life, or that one will become a victim of others and life.

Hard karma can be neutralised by meditating on sacred topics, by developing discrimination and making wiser choices. If you are working with lower psychism, stop such practices. Ground yourself in reality, be honest and use your common sense. Volunteer your time in service. Positive Saturn rewards us with emotional stability, inner strength and self-confidence, being respected and recognised as a teacher, healer and spiritual leader.

Uranus

♅ *Uranus' ray is the 7th Ray of Order, Ceremony and Magic. This ray relates us with our spiritual source and this is Uranus' ultimate task - to awaken consciousness and bring it into alignment with spirit.*

Uranus in Aries: this is a generation of wilful individuals. Emotions and actions are impulsive and erratic, behaviour is selfish and thoughtless actions create conflict and chaos with friends and groups.

At the portals of the Path, a shock awaits the ego. The lightning flash of the intuition reveals the lower life and the ancient pattern and lower control shatters. Later, on the higher burning ground, Uranus develops the scientific mind and esoteric work unfolds the spiritual gifts of Aries. For example: intuitive leadership brilliance and expertise, the will and power to change things for the better, power to manifest the divine Plan.

Uranus in Taurus: this is a generation filled with stubborn and conflict-creating individuals. The lower will and rebellious nature is strong and desires are powerful and sometimes bizarre. They form self-indulgent and hedonistic groups.

On the Path, the ego clashes with the soul who throws an intuitive flash of truth into the mind. Clear sight reveals the "bull" and the control it has on consciousness shatters. Esoteric work unfolds the spiritual gifts of Taurus. For example: the opened third eye, the higher intuition, creative brilliance, the will to create harmony and beauty, a steely will and the power to stand in the light and destroy darkness.

Uranus in Gemini: the minds of this generation en masse, are shallow, unreliable and behaviour is superficial and erratic. Hot and rebellious thoughts cause trouble and there is a lot of talk about revolution. Friends are argumentative and there is trouble in groups.

On the Path, the soul confronts the ego and Uranus' flash of intuition reveals the shallowness and superficiality of the life, shattering ancient control. When duality has been resolved and consciousness is aglow with wisdom, the scientific mind develops and esoteric work unfolds the spiritual gifts of Gemini. For example, intellectual and intuitive brilliance, in tune with universal wisdom and having the power to teach it, a "Messenger of the Gods" teaching esoteric truths in a clear, scientific manner, radically transforming minds.

Uranus in Cancer: home life is transient and chaotic for this generation. Unpredictable mood swings, explosive emotional eruptions and rebellious outbursts, destabilise and disrupt family and emotional life.

On the Path, Uranus' intuitive flash shatters ancient habits, awakening the aspirant who "steps onto dry land" (rises above emotionalism). When the student is ready, Uranus unfolds the scientific mind and the spiritual gifts of Cancer appear. For example: the will to bring Light into the darkness, the intuitive Light Bearer who can radiate the brilliant light of the soul, to transform and improve the conditions of the family of man

Uranus in Leo: the personality "lion" roars out its arrogance and pride in this generation. They rebel against authority, demanding that all should look to them for leadership and rule. They are troublemakers in groups.

On the Path, Uranus throws a bolt of lightning into the mind, a flash of intuitive insight, so that the thinker sees the ridiculous state of the ego. Ancient control and personality power shatters. As the heart centre opens, Uranus develops the scientific mind and esoteric work unfolds the spiritual gifts of Leo. For example: intuitive leadership brilliance, the will to rule and direct, the glory of divine spiritual will, heart power that lifts and enfolds, charismatic magnetism that draws in many followers.

Uranus in Virgo: this generation uses ingenious methods to acquire material possessions. They are rebellious in thought and word and repelled by imposed duty and responsibilities.

On the Path, the light of the intuition radiating from the soul reveals the selfishness of the life, the littleness of focus, how the so-called perfect life is just a surface fascination with no true depth. Under this unrelenting blaze, the ancient ways and material control shatter and the Christ spirit births in the heart. Later, on the higher reaches of the Path, Uranus develops the scientific mind and esoteric work unfolds the spiritual gifts of Virgo. For example: the functioning intuition, intellectual brilliance and technological and teaching expertise, especially in health and education; the will and power to raise the health or work conditions and standards in humanity and the power to unfold the Christ Spirit in others.

Uranus in Libra: in this generation, friendships, unions and groups are chaotic and unstable. Playing games, they enter bizarre or unorthodox relationships and impulsive decisions cause trouble.

The intuition (the soul's brilliant light) reaches those on the Path. It reveals in stark clarity the shallowness of the life and deceit, shattering the ancient ways and habits. Later, Uranus unfolds the scientific mind and esoteric training produces the spiritual gifts of Libra. For example, intuitive and intellectual brilliance, the will to balance and harmonise, judicial power to establish just and humanitarian laws and resolve the problem of sex.

Uranus in Scorpio: this generation is secretive and they like to hide in the swamp, the lower emotional life. Intense sensual urges take some in a dark direction.

There is stealth, stalking and even violence at times. Friends can become prey.

But for those on the Path, the blazing fire of intuition streaming from Uranus, lights the darkness. Seeing the hydra in all its ugliness, the disciple uses that light to destroy its power and shatter its ancient control. This enables the disciple to fight his way from the darkness of illusion into the light of day. Then, on the greater burning ground of trial and testing, Uranus develops the scientific mind and the spiritual gifts of Scorpio unfold. For example, the intuitive powers of the White Magician who wields Spiritual Light (words, actions) to destroy evil and darkness and the will to unite and harmonise.

Uranus in Sagittarius: the "centaur" influences this generation, the animal appetites are strong. Coveting their freedom and independence to do what they will, life is adventurous but irresponsible. There are many friends to carouse with who similarly over-indulge, wild living, risk taking, rebellion, chaos and trouble.

On the Path Uranian intuition reveals the higher Way and the promise of a new adventure. The ancient shackles shatter when inspired aspirants swerve to follow the higher path. On that higher way, the scientific mind develops and esoteric training unfolds the spiritual gifts of Sagittarius. For example: a brilliant teacher of the wisdom and a true intuitive prophet. The will and power to radiate truths that inspire and elevate. Becoming the Archer whose arrows of Spiritual Light always hit their target, a beam of directed, focused Light.

Uranus in Capricorn: this generation rebel against authority and any restriction of their freedom. They demand to live by their own laws and dictates and try to enforce these onto others. They use ingenious methods to manifest their ambitions. Friends are used to further their plans.

When we find the Path, the intuition reveals the aridness of the life and this shatters the chains of ancient material control. The disciple turns towards the lighted mountain peak and begins to climb again. Esoteric training develops the scientific mind, initiation is taken and the spiritual gifts of Capricorn unfold. For example: brilliant statesmanship, intuitive leadership and organising power, influence and power in the financial, business and spiritual worlds. In this sign, Uranus gives the will and power to manifest the Plan of God on earth.

Uranus in Aquarius: this generation is a group of independent individuals, who refuse to conform to the "ordinary or boring". With rigid and bizarre opinions, they are rebellious, unpredictable and find like-minded souls with whom to plot revolution. But with narrow and self-serving goals, chaos is the result.

When the Path is found, Uranus' light (the power of the intuition) shatters the wall of rigid thought and illusion. Uranus develops the scientific mind; the heart opens and disciples find the Path of Initiation. Esoteric work unfolds the spiritual gifts of Aquarius. For example: intellectual and scientific brilliance, the will to know and reveal the truth, the intuitive powers of a true World Server, of a Water Bearer, with power to get things done on a global scale. One who has the will to raise humanity up through science and esotericism.

Uranus in Pisces: this generation has unstable emotions and seek sensual "spiritual" experiences that excite the lower nature. With confused outlook and distorted view, they follow cults or join strange groups. There are odd friendships and confused rebelliousness. Illusion distorts reality.

For those on the Path, Uranus' brilliant light permeates the emotional waters, clearing the way for intuitive thought to reach the mind. Instantly, the confused life is seen for what it is, ancient control shatters and the soul begins to swim towards the light. Later, towards the end of the journey on the greater burning ground, Uranus develops the scientific mind and the spiritual gifts of Pisces unfold. For example: an intuitive heart radiating the compassion of Deity, the pulsing heart of a World Saviour, power to comfort the suffering, the will and power to save humanity.

Neptune

♆ *Neptune's ray is the 6th Ray of Devotion and Idealism. Related to the Emotional Plane, this ray creates glamour (the mind's distortion of reality through emotional bias) in the unenlightened mind. Neptune's task is to refine the emotional nature so that the truth is seen, to inspire idealism and develop compassion and empathy.*

Neptune in Aries: (1862-1876, 2025-2039). Delusion in Aries manifests as a belief that one and one's group or country is the best, the strongest and bravest. Religious fanaticism flourishes along with the emergence of messiahs - true and false.

Many structures in society dissolve under this transit and new idealistic leaders arise. The higher goal is to bring about spiritual rebirth or renewal. Evolved souls who respond to Neptune's call to the heights lead humanity into higher ways. Demanding higher standards and ethics in business and politics, they create new spiritual and religious organisations that serve the needs of the people, rather than the power hungry. Genuine spiritual leaders emerge from amongst the fanatics. For aspirants, the task is to see through illusion and stand in the truth.

Neptune in Taurus: (1876-1890, 2039-2050). Values are confused and the glamoured masses feel entitled to take as much as they can under this transit.

Neptune's task is to dissolve man's attachment to the material life and to refine his values. In the process, old selfish attitudes and financial and business structures that do not serve the greater collective good dissolve and new ones arise. So do new ideas and practical systems that allow for a freer flow of money and resources into areas of need. Artists, musicians and other creative workers all help in the higher task of spiritualising and beautifying humanity. For aspirants, the task is to resist the lure of the "bull".

Neptune in Gemini: (1889-1902, 2050-2065). Delusion in Gemini manifests as communication confusion, misinformation and misunderstandings. Fanatics, who incite hate and evil, coat their words in a glamorous facade so they appeal to man's lower nature. Examples of this type are Nazis Hitler, Herman Goering and Heinrich Himmler.

Neptune's task is to dissolve old ideas and methods of communication. In the process, guidelines shaping civilisation dissolve and new ideals and ideas about how things should be, arise. The higher ideal is to enlighten minds through inspired or spiritual communications. Whenever Neptune is in this sign, a deluge of inspired writings - both high and low pours forth and a new generation of idealistic and intuitive thinkers is born. For aspirants, the task is to overcome illusion and hold the mind in the clear light of reality.

Neptune in Cancer: (1916-1928, 2065-2080). Delusion in Cancer manifests as separativeness and feelings of entitlement about family, property and land. World War I was fought during this cycle, started by Germany trying to expand its boundaries.

Neptune's primary task in Cancer is to refine and illumine man's astral nature, transmuting desire for material possessions into a sense of inclusiveness for all. As a result, old habits that shape family life and class boundaries dissolve as new and inclusive ideals arise. This happened in Great Britain in the aftermath of WW1. When Neptune returns in 2065, evolved souls will respond by bringing in more light - greater transparency, integrity, loving care and concern, in domestic and family affairs. For aspirants, the task is to overcome glamour and hold the mind in the clear light of truth.

Neptune in Leo: (1915-1928, 2080-2092). The deluded in this transit believe they have the right of Gods to do and take what they want. The 1st World War ended during the last cycle. But illusion remained and Fascism flourished, igniting World War II when Neptune was in the materialistic Virgo.

Neptune's primary task in Leo is bring forward leaders who inspire people to follow their highest ideals. But at man's current level, leaders who glamorise greed also rise. When Neptune re-enters Leo in 2080, a greater number of evolved souls will seek high office and use their power to benefit the masses. For aspirants, the task is to be more sensitive to their souls and to others.

Neptune in Virgo: (1928-1942, 2092-2106). The glamoured yearn to increase what they have and find reasons to justify their greed. World War II started when the Nazis took possession of other countries.

Neptune's task is to illumine the substance of the lower nature, particularly the mind, so that the Christ spirit (the soul) births through the heart. In the process, attitudes regarding material possessions dissolve and new ideals arise. Work-place constraints change and liberal conditions are implemented. When Neptune re-enters Virgo at the latter part of this century, evolved souls will advance health and work conditions for the masses. Spiritual healing will become more credible in the mainstream and scientists will prove the existence of the human soul. For aspirants, the task is to dissolve material attachments.

Neptune in Libra: (1942-1956, 2106-). Delusion in Libra manifests as confusion about human relations and the law. Old laws change, relationship boundaries dissolve and new ideals about marriage and sex arise. In the recent cycle, World War II quickly finished, the Nazi trials were held at Nuremberg and the United Nations was created.

Neptune's higher task in Libra is to refine and harmonise relationships, especially sexual. Other goals are to spiritualise the justice system so that it can better meet the needs of the masses and to liberalise and bring balance to society generally. For aspirants, the task is to refine and balance relationships.

Neptune in Scorpio: (1956-1970). Neptune's light has a distorting effect upon the perception of unawakened souls. Twisted idealism and delusionary visions that feed and empower the dark side of man's nature arise.

The task for Neptune in Scorpio is to spiritualise or bring light to darkness, primarily the darkness that lies within the psyche of man. In the process, civilised constraints that protect man from his darker side dissolve, so that monstrous things happen. In the last cycle, segregation was introduced in South Africa, nuclear weapons flourished, the drug thalidomide wreaked havoc and the Kennedy brothers and Martin Luther King were assassinated. With the darker side thus exposed, healing and remedial work can begin as humanity searches for answers. This comes through inspired actions, writings and oratory. For example: Martin Luther King with his "I have a dream" speech. It inspired the civil rights movement. For aspirants, the task is to refine the astral nature and overcome illusion.

Neptune in Sagittarius: (1807-1828, 1970-1984). In the masses, Neptune's intense light results in religious fanaticism, confused goals and the idealising of a hedonistic and self-indulgent lifestyle.

Neptune's task is to refine man's animal appetites and foster an aspiration for the higher and finer. In the process, collective beliefs about religion and life dissolve and new ideals about how to grow in mind and spirit, arise. Neptune illuminates the Path to the mountaintop and inspires a new generation to search for truth, to follow their highest ideals, to seek out their Holy Grail, on whatever level that is. For aspirants, the task is to reach for their highest ideals.

Neptune in Capricorn: (1821-1834, 1984-1998). Neptune's positive effect weakens so that materialism flourishes. In its 19th century cycle, Capitalism began. In the recent cycle, materially inspired politicians dissolved regulations that curbed unfair profiteering. Greed flourishes under unregulated Capitalism.

Neptune's higher task is to dissolve the attachment to material life that currently controls the masses. The higher goal is to foster an ambition to find the higher rewards and treasure of the spiritual life, to develop compassion and to appreciate the intrinsic value of human souls. Under this transit, many mystics will find their way to the Occult Path that leads to the mountaintop of spiritual enlightenment. For aspirants, the task is to dissolve lower ambition.

Neptune in Aquarius: (1835-1848, 1998-2012). 1835-1848, 1998-2012). Aquarius is related to science and a result of the recent transit was the deliberate confusing of scientific facts for profit and gain - as seen in the tobacco industry and climate change debate. A positive effect is the dissolving of rigid concepts and old science

Fostering universal brotherhood, the effect of this combination was clearly seen in 2003, when people worldwide protested the proposed USA attack on Iraq. USA went ahead with its crusade, but a precedent for universal protest against violations of human rights, was established. This combination encourages mystics to step from the Path of the Heart onto the Occult Path, to pursue spirituality intelligently. Many spiritually inspired scientists are born in this period. For aspirants, the task is to bring the heart and mind into union.

Neptune in Pisces: (1848-1858, 2012-2025). With Neptune in this sign, on the mass level truth is easy to distort as common-sense dissolves. This enables the unscrupulous to get mass support for ideas and issues that are counterproductive for the greater good.

Neptune's task is to free humanity from its materialistic focus and hasten spiritual development. In the interim, this transit brings to the fore the current state of man's lower desire, so it can be dealt with. This is occurring now in the current cycle. Pluto (the esoteric ruler of Pisces) brought to light the greed of profiteering bankers and other money manipulators in the share market crash of 2008, causing outrage and demand for change. Materialists fight those who are trying to free the soul from bondage in the lower worlds, but radical change is inevitable. For aspirants, the task is to overcome delusion and emotionalism.

Pluto

Pluto's ray is the 1st Ray of Will and Power. Its task is to destroy all obstacles that prevent the soul from finding its spiritual freedom. It has a mass effect on humanity, but man's response to its force will be more intelligent than in the past now that Aryan (intelligent) consciousness is growing.

Pluto in Aries (1824-1853, 2068-2097). This cycle purges rigid thoughts and political institutions that are obstacles to man's spiritual expansion. Militarism is stimulated and groups and nations become fanatical and attack each other. We hope that man can respond more positively when Pluto returns later this century. When carnage is extreme, the masses demand that their political leaders find cooperative ways to deal with disputes. Pluto in Aries empowers leaders, whether their intention is good or ill. The challenge for aspirants is to purge emotional impulses that cloud good judgement and to think before acting.

Pluto in Taurus (1853-1884, 2097-2127). This cycle purges greed and avarice. In the process, materialism is stimulated, giving rise to disputes over property and territory. When the masses begin to suffer dearly because of the profligate and excessive appetites of the rich and privileged, a demand will rise for greater checks and accountability in finance and business. Pluto in Taurus clears the way for higher values to emerge. The challenge for aspirants is to purify lower desire and demonstrate moderation and balance.

Pluto in Gemini (1883-1914, 2127-). This cycle purges evil thought and speech life of the race. Communications that whip up hatred and prejudice become extreme, such as murderous rhetoric inciting violence. Nazi Adolf Hitler began his rise to power in this period. The positive side is the mass revulsion to the harm done and the demand for change. Pluto in Gemini clears the way for inspiring communications that benefit the collective good. The challenge for aspirants is to purify the quality of their thought life and to write and teach goodwill.

Pluto in Cancer (1914-1939, 2158-). This cycle purges aggressive nationalism. Fears about security, family and property arise and an urge to reach out and take what belongs to others. This period spanned World War I and the beginning of WWII, which were fights over land and territory. In the aftermath of the wars, the masses, revolted by human-rights abuses demanded greater protection for the rights of all people. Pluto in Cancer clears the way for Light bearers, the wise and intelligent who work to uplift the masses. The challenge for aspirants is to eliminate emotional control and stand in the light.

Pluto in Leo (1939-1957, 2183-). This cycle purges megalomaniacs from the ranks of world leaders and generally, arrogance and aggression from humanity. Pluto stimulates a sense of being entitled to take whatever one wants and can get. Rulers driven by this impulse arise. They preach a message of being superior, a "master race," urging their followers to commit violations en masse. World War II taught man to put steps in place to curb the ambitions of dictators and warmongers such as Hitler and Tito. Pluto in Leo empowers leaders and rulers, both high and low. The challenge for aspirants is to develop self-awareness and positive self-rulership.

Pluto in Virgo (1957-1971, 2202-). This cycle purges humanity of rank materialism. An obsessive need to acquire material possessions and financial gain is stimulated. The recent transit gave rise to the Consumer Age, the "I want to be a millionaire by age 30" attitude. Between 1998 and 2008 when this generation started making their mark, the number of millionaires doubled. Greed will be purged when the masses become intelligent and united enough to enforce the demand for fair treatment. Pluto in Virgo empowers intelligent and hardworking souls who seek no glory, wishing only to serve. The challenge for aspirants is to be more spiritual and less material in attitude.

Pluto in Libra (1971-1984, 2217-). This cycle purges human rights abuses and rids the judicial system of bad laws and practises. But first it intensifies evil tendencies hidden in man's psyche such as violence in marriage, sexual exploitation, prostitution, masochism and paedophilia, bringing them to the surface for elimination. This brings a mass demand for greater legal rights and protection for victims. Pluto in Libra empowers legislators, diplomats and moderators who fight for fairness and justice. The challenge for aspirants is to find balance in their lives and to be fair with others.

Pluto in Scorpio (1984-1995, 2230-). This cycle purges dark and evil tendencies in the human psyche, such as paedophilia, prostitution, violence and torture. It brings them up into the light of day, into public awareness, so that a tremendous cry for change will arise. Pluto in Scorpio empowers healers, psychologists and anyone generally who fights for the sick, weak and helpless. The challenge for aspirants is to fight for their own spiritual freedom, then help others to do the same.

Pluto in Sagittarius (1995-2009, 2242-). This cycle purges humanity of greed. But first, excess is stimulated: for instance, greediness in business and banking, laziness and gluttony. Change will come when revulsion at the excess is widespread, then humanity will change. This cycle began noticeably in 2008 when a major global financial meltdown began. With the firing of the "Arrow of Death" radical change in the commercial world is inevitable. Pluto in Sagittarius empowers inspirational and creative teachers and visionaries who point humanity in the right direction. The challenge for aspirants is to do the inner work and become such visionaries.

Pluto in Capricorn (2009-2024, 2255-). This cycle purges depravity and greed from governments and corporations. In the meantime, corruption becomes brazen so that it is easily seen causing the masses to rise up and demand greater accountability and responsibility. Pluto in Capricorn empowers executives and leaders of both the higher and lower types. The challenge for aspirants and disciples is to bring in the needed changes and many will take initiation in this period.

Pluto in Aquarius (2024-2044). This cycle purges separativeness in society. First it intensifies selfish materialism that prevents fair and equitable distribution of goods and services in the community. For instance, the ideology of Capitalism born in the 18th century cycle has been manipulated by the clever and greedy for selfish gain. These selfish ideas and systems will be purged when the masses, revolted by material excess rise up and demand change. Pluto in Aquarius empowers groups who promote radical ideas, whether high or low. The challenge for aspirants is to respond to the cry of the masses, destroy the old and work together to initiate a freer flow of resources and appropriate reforms.

Pluto in Pisces (2044-2068). This cycle purges all that stands between the soul of man and his spiritual freedom. At a lower level, materialism is stimulated and the desire by religious and business leaders to gain greater control over people and resources. These impulses will be purged from humanity when the masses, revolted by excess and violations that occur under the banner of "God is with me", or "this is just business", demand radical change. Pluto in Pisces empowers the masses, who without wise leadership, can turn into unruly mobs. The challenge for aspirants is to provide wise leadership and to guide the destruction and reformation of outdated institutions and religions that no longer serve the common good.

One complete cycle of Pluto and of all the planets, is not sufficient to bring all to enlightenment. The planets continue to cycle around the Zodiac until every last individual soul in humanity is enlightened.

4b. Planets in Houses

The Sun in Houses

 The Sun's house is where effort should be made to develop and integrate the personality and to express its power.

1: Express yourself strongly and openly. Face life honestly, without a mask. Be you, up front, a presenter and leader. Set an example for others.

2: Distinguish yourself by being a person who lives by a higher set of values and be true to your principles. Use power to attract and manage resources and possessions, but do not be ruled by them.

3: Distinguish yourself by developing excellent communication skills and use them to broadcast your truth to others, powerfully and confidently. Find an esoteric school and study with soul brothers and sisters.

4: Becoming the heart of the family, a centre of strength that family respect and look up to, will bring distinction. (For some, this will be the family of man.) This will create a solid and healthy foundation to life.

5: You can distinguish yourself by developing your creative, outdoor, or artistic skills and talents and find a field to excel in. Another option is to express the power of love through work, with children and younger souls.

6: Developing and using skills to become a centre of strength that co-workers or clients turn to, will bring distinction. Build a successful career and strong physical and psychological health.

7: You can gain distinction in your important formal and intimate partnerships - personal and professional, by becoming a centre of strength and love that others can cling to and rely upon.

8: Develop a strong mind and personality by facing life challenges intelligently and courageously and by fighting your way to psychological health and life success. Study the occult. Embrace change.

9: Distinguish yourself as a centre of knowledge, authority, power and influence, in an area of higher learning, religion or spirituality; or overseas with foreign nations, people or trade. Search for self-understanding and wisdom.

10: Distinguish yourself in a vocation, so that people look to you for guidance, authority and inspiration. You are destined to shine in life. Do the Master's work.

11: Distinguish yourself in your circle of friends, or in your group or organisation, by becoming a centre of love and authority that others can rely upon, one who brings joy and inspiration.

12: Develop inner strength and psychological health and strive to be who you really are at a deep, authentic level. This will help you to overcome low self-esteem. Reach out for help if overwhelmed. Do the Christ's work by helping those in need.

The Moon in Houses

☽ *The Moon's house represents the primary life area that imprisons the soul and therefore where aspirants must fight to free themselves from destructive and unconscious habits and behaviours.*

1: The negative pattern is fear of life and it is overcome by facing life honestly, without a mask or playing games. The key is to approach life with a clear awareness of self and motive, free of conditioning and denial.

2: The pattern is believing that we need money or material things and possessions to be safe and secure. Learn to live by higher spiritual values. Use resources, prana and spiritual energy in service.

3: The negative pattern concerns improper communication with acquaintances and relatives. Learn to relate in a more loving way. Find an esoteric school and study with soul brothers and sisters.

4: The limiting pattern is one of being too dependent upon a parent or the security of a family. Complete unfinished business with family, grow up emotionally and psychologically "leave home". Find your spiritual family.

5: The lunar pattern concerns the selfish pursuit of pleasure and avoidance of life difficulties and responsibilities. Complete unfinished business with children and lovers and develop healthier relationships. Express the love and joy of the soul in creative soul-inspired projects.

6: The debilitating pattern is being too busy so there is no time for spiritual growth; or avoiding life through invoking illness. Complete unfinished business with co-workers. Develop skills and use them in service. Keep thoughts on health positive.

7: The limiting pattern is being too reliant on the approval of partners. Change negative relationship patterns. Complete unfinished and karmic business with partners and move on. Do not stay in a "dead" relationship for fear of being alone.

8: The negative pattern consists of uncontrolled emotionalism, sensuality, self-torment and fear. Study spiritual psychology to understand how to minimise harm inflicted by negative thoughts and dark impulses. Detach from addictions and unhealthy habits.

9: The old pattern concerns running from life, judging and criticising others for their moral ineptitude, relying unwisely on a "higher" authority. Develop a comprehensive and loving understanding of all peoples of the world. Study the Ageless Wisdom and apply it to yourself and your life.

10: A limiting pattern of being driven to succeed and to shine in the vocation to compensate for low self-esteem binds the soul. There is a need for approval from the father or other authority figure. Complete unfinished business and move on.

11: The old and binding pattern is being too dependent upon the support of old friends or groups that have become toxic. Form new and healthier friendships. Develop group consciousness by working with an inclusive and soul-inspired group.

12: The debilitating pattern is an uncontrollable urge to hide away from life and reality. Reverse this tendency. Deliberately choose to rejoin life by building healthy social connections and tangible relationships.

Vulcan in Houses

In Vulcan's house you need to purify your attitudes and actions.

1: Purify your body (healthy diet and lifestyle) so that your soul ray qualities can flow through. Stand alone, rely on your own strength, do not wear a mask. Be a leader of integrity and power.

2: Burn out materialistic values and attitudes, so that higher spiritual values emerge. Live simply without ostentation, focus on needs and not wants. Then, your quiet strength and goodness will be magnetic, attracting the resources needed to help those in need.

3: Purify daily communication with acquaintances and relatives so that more thoughtful and kind thoughts and words can emerge. Be circumspect with your speech so that you do not hurt others with what you say. Say what you mean and mean what you say.

4: Purify the foundations of your life: burn away the past so that you have a solid base on which to found a healthy family life. This will enable the true steel of your character to emerge, enabling you to deal confidently with difficult situations in the future.

5: Purify the way you use your creative energy, balance your sexual and creative sides. Give your love simply and patiently. Then your quiet strength and goodness will enable you to create beautiful works of art - children, love affairs, or artistic endeavours.

6: Learn to be self-reliant, decisive and strong under stress. Face life simply, counting your blessings as you go. Then your quiet strength and goodness will enable you to step forward as a leader, give you healing potency, good health and a positive attitude to life.

7: Burn out negative habits and attitudes that sabotage otherwise healthy relationships. Then your quiet strength will enable you to go into relationships without dragging along baggage from the past. Express your goodness and connect with people at a deep level of integrity and truth.

8: Purify your emotional nature and any dark attitudes that you may have carried forward from your previous life. Then your steely inner strength and integrity will enable you to face down evil and lead those who have been "lost in the darkness", into the light.

9: Purify beliefs and morals. Burn out any separative and judgmental attitudes, so you are receptive to higher truths. Do not to rely on others to tell you what to think but find your own truth. Then your ability to convey higher spiritual truths with simplicity and clarity will inspire many to search for their own truth.

10: Purify selfish ambition and focus on serving the greater good. In a roundabout way, this will bring you what you want. When you place the greater good above personal ambitions, you will be rewarded with life success and greater responsibility in the Master's work.

11: Purify your group life. Be discerning in your choice of friends. Look for organisations that operate with truth and integrity. Place the wellbeing of group endeavours above personal agendas. Be a group leader.

12: Free yourself from negative patterns, old fears and limitations that undermine your ability to form healthy relationships with people and life. Appreciate the simple blessings in life. Seek assistance from a strong spiritual counsellor. Your quiet strength will enable you to find and heal those who suffer.

Mercury in Houses

 Mercury's house represents a life area where you are required to develop mind wisdom and where to focus your thought life and communication.

1: Endeavour to think before you act. Develop good communication skills and use them to achieve soul purpose, in soul activities.

2: Study life values and develop higher values to live by. Communicate what you believe, your truth with power and network to distribute resources in service.

3: Improve communication with relatives and the environment generally. Develop the mind by studying, teaching and writing. Build the antahkarana.

4: Improve communication with parents and family. Use the mind to understand and heal deep inner wounds. Learn and teach from home.

5: Improve communication with children and younger souls. Be mentally creative in soul-inspired projects and in joyful pastimes.

6: Improve communication with co-workers. Develop

the mind and communication skills and use them in service. Identify and understand the mental and emotional causes underlying illness.

7: Improve communication with close partners. Develop counselling skills and use these to heal divisions and conflict in relationships.

8: Study the deeper issues in life, the occult teachings and use these to transform negative thinking patterns, unhealthy imaginings and personal glamours.

9: Travel far, study and teach the Ageless Wisdom. Build the Antahkarana. Expand consciousness and detach the mind from crystallised beliefs.

10: Improve communication with authority figures and the father. Develop communication skills to benefit your vocation and get your message out.

11: Develop harmlessness in thought and speech with your friends and groups. Become a communicator, a networker in your organisation. Study and teach humanitarian issues.

12: Improve communication with your inner self. Take time out of the mainstream to reflect and meditate. Quietly study self-defeating patterns and use positive thought to overcome them.

Venus in Houses

Venus' house represents the primary life area needing beautification. Be intelligent and kind in all interactions occurring in this life area.

1: Beautify your nature by learning to love yourself and radiate this to the world. Use your intelligence, beauty and artistry creatively. Share these with the world.

2: Beautify your nature by refining your values and honouring your principles. Love and appreciate life's bounties and prosperity and share with others.

3: Beautify your nature and life by learning to communicate with love and wisdom. Express kindness in your environment and with the extended family. Value your siblings, soul brothers and sisters.

4: Appreciate your parents and family and beautify your home life. Turn it into a place of serenity and love so all who come feel blessed. Express intelligent love with family and with the world.

5: Appreciate and value children, younger souls and lovers. Fill these relationships with beauty. Express the artistry of the soul in creative soul-inspired projects.

6: Beautify your workplace and relations with co-workers. Be intelligent and kind with your words and actions. Build a healthy body. Value service work and express the artistry of your soul and wisdom at work.

7: Express the loving artistry of your soul through one-on-one relationships. Beautify important unions by being intelligent and kind with your words and actions. Refine your relationship skills.

8: Overcome glamour and emotionalism. Do this intelligently, following a structured esoteric approach. Beautify your nature. Love intelligently and kindly.

9: Beautify your nature by learning to love and value the Wisdom Teachings, other cultures, countries and all people of the world. Share what you learn.

10: Value father and authority figures. Express the beauty and artistry of your soul in your career. Radiate wisdom to the world. Love the Master's work.

11: Beautify your group life and develop goodwill skills, by being intelligent and kind with your words and actions. Show your friends you value and appreciate them. Express the beauty and artistry of your soul through humanitarian organisations.

12: Use your intelligence to rise above negative thoughts. Seek the assistance of your soul and a loving counsellor or mentor when needed. Find your real self. Seek counselling and meditate to achieve this. Love and value that self. Love nature, love Life, love God.

The Earth in Houses

The house the Earth is in shows where to be practical and "down to earth".

1: Develop a simple approach to life. Be unafraid to show to the world the simplicity of who you really are. Endeavour to be fair and balanced in your approach to relationships.

2: Be practical and down-to-earth in your use of money and resources. Develop a value system that is straightforward and uncomplicated, which is transparent, basic and honest. Use your resources to benefit others.

3: Be knowledgeable about life and learn to relate to people in the environment, your neighbours and extended family, in a straightforward and honest manner. Say what you think and mean what you say.

4: Use the experiences that you gain in your outer and professional life to develop a simple, honest and practical approach to family affairs. Be grounded in your physical body.

5: Develop a simple, kind and honest approach in the way you relate with those you love, with children and younger souls. Demonstrate your personal creativity in tangible and practical ways.

6: Be open, honest and straightforward in your work or service life and cooperative with co-workers. Pay attention to physical exercise and diet to keep your mind and body healthy.

7: Balance your independent and assertive side with a simple, honest and transparent approach in one-on-one and formal partnerships.

8: Approach personal transformation and the way you handle personal crises in a down to earth and straightforward manner. Call a spade a spade. Be honest in your business life and financial dealings.

9: Whatever education you receive in your early life, ground it solidly in life experience by for instance, studying higher teachings and travelling the world. Make real contact with real people.

10: Use the experience gained from your family background and roots, to develop a simple and honest approach in your career, when aiming for higher goals and when doing the Master's work.

11: Use the experience and expertise gained through work with children, or from your hobbies and pastimes, to develop a simple and honest approach in your relations with friends and groups.

12: Use the experience gained through illness, work and service, to develop a simple and down-to-earth approach to life. Celebrate the oneness of nature and of spiritual unity.

Mars in Houses

♂ *Mars' house represents a life area of major conflict, where the rebellious personality is very strong and therefore where the aspirant must guard against unintelligent emotional impulses.*

1: Discipline any desire to attack - yourself, others, or life. Stop fighting. Harness and direct your passionate energies to achieve your soul purpose. Focus on soul-inspired activities.

2: Discipline any desire to possess everything and everyone, to fight for money and gain. Replace lower selfish values with higher ones. Use energies for the greater good.

3: Think before you speak, especially with siblings or others in the environment. Stop fighting relatives. Use energy and enthusiasm to study and communicate the Wisdom Teachings.

4: Discipline any desire to project anger onto the family. Stop fighting with them. Use physical energies to heal family relationships, to build and maintain a home, a community or spiritual ashram.

5: Projecting anger onto children, younger souls, or onto lovers will ruin your relationships. Use excess energy in physical sports or adventures. Find non-competitive and pleasurable physical activities that you can share with loved ones.

6: Discipline any desire to project anger onto co-workers, or to blame others for ill health. Purify and heal anger patterns or you could have surgery from related illnesses. Develop practical physical skills and use them in service.

7: Discipline any desire to project anger onto partners. Avoid controlling patterns. Use energy and enthusiasm to learn how to be cooperative in relationships. Stop fighting others.

8: Purify and transform your desire nature. Overcome selfish use of power and develop cooperative values. Put energy and enthusiasm into walking the Path of Discipleship.

9: Aspire to walk the spiritual Path, study the Wisdom Teachings and build the Antahkarana. Divert your energies, from fighting your teachers or hating those who are different, to expanding your understanding and knowledge.

10: Discipline any desire to project anger onto a parent, authority figures or society. Aspire to serve the Masters, take initiation and achieve spiritual goals. Put energy and enthusiasm into doing the Master's work.

11: Discipline any desire to project anger onto friends and groups. Learn to work cooperatively in groups. Put energy and enthusiasm into humanitarian causes.

12: Become aware of subconscious anger patterns that you direct against yourself. Bring these and any incidents of covert abuse into the light. Express buried anger. Direct your energies into "behind the scenes" projects that benefit people.

Jupiter in Houses

 Jupiter's life area is where we find unconditional support, abundance, fellowship and a wise teacher.

1: Use personal freedom to follow your soul purpose. Be generous and loving in your approach to life and radiate wisdom liberally to others. Blessings flow back to those who give generously.

2: You have a lucky touch with money and resources. Use the gifts of abundance and any spiritual powers you have, to bless and assist others. This will bring abundance flowing back to you.

3: Be generous and loving with siblings and generally in the way you communicate in your close environment. Communicate with love and people will speak kindly of you in return. Study, communicate, write, teach and publish the Ageless Wisdom.

4: Be generous with your family and make your home a warm, light-filled place. Share any family wealth and prosperity with others and your home and family will receive blessings as a result.

5: Be generous and loving with children and younger souls and cultivate their talents. Use your creative gifts to bring joy and love to others and love will flow back to you with abundance.

6: Be generous with your co-workers and your working will life will be a source of joy and fulfillment. Avoid over eating and drinking and being sedentary; moderation is the key to good health. If you are drawn to healing or teaching, you will be a very wise and loved teacher and healer.

7: Use your wisdom to counsel and help others and be generous and loving with partners. You will attract loving and wise partners - both professional and personal, because of your generosity.

8: You have freedom to walk the Path of Discipleship and transform your nature and life. You could become a teacher of metaphysics or psychology. Use your gifts to help others transform their lives as you have changed yours. Abundance will flow to you through business and legacies.

9: You have freedom to walk the spiritual Path of your choosing, or to roam the world at will. Life will support whatever choices you make or direction you take. You will do well in the academic or spiritual life, receiving blessings because of the generous way you share your understanding and wisdom.

10: You will prosper in any career you choose. Use personal success and freedom to reach your spiritual goals, to take initiation and do the Master's work. Spiritual blessings and public recognition will flow with abundance if you share your wisdom generously.

11: Use your wisdom and prosperity to benefit friends, your chosen group or organisation and humanitarian causes. Spiritual blessings will flow to you because of your generosity and the joy and fellowship you bring to your group work.

12: You will be given freedom to take time out from mainstream life if that is what you want. Life will support your endeavours so use the opportunities wisely. If you selflessly and generously use your gifts to help others, blessings will flow to you from hidden sources.

Saturn in Houses

♄ *Saturn shows the life area where karma will be met and so where we should be careful and intelligent in our responses - restraint should be applied and forgiveness extended. This is where we need to shoulder responsibilities without complaint.*

1: Karma affects your approach to life, your range of influence and your physical body. Be disciplined and responsible, but also learn to be flexible in your approach. Stop judging yourself and others. Avoid wearing a rigid psychological mask. Relax.

2: Karma affects your resources. Be disciplined and responsible with money. Learn to be flexible and more generous with what you have. Overcome fears about poverty and deprivation. Develop higher values. Stop judging the way other people use their resources.

3: Karma affects your relationships with relatives and the way you communicate in your environment. Be disciplined and responsible with what you say, but also learn to be flexible in thought and speech. Speak only the truth, but kindly. Support your neighbours.

4: Karma affects your relationships with your parents, family and roots. Be responsible but also flexible in these areas. Understand, heal and master your inner fears. Build your life foundation on truth. Be prepared to take on family leadership and responsibility.

5: Karma affects your relationships with your children, lovers and pleasure activities. Be disciplined, responsible but also learn to be flexible in these relationships and how you use your creativity. At some time or other you will be called on to take on responsibility for a child or children.

6: Karma affects your work and health. Be disciplined, responsible but also flexible. Rigid mind equals a rigid body. Do not judge the work performance of others but be a quiet and a solid support for those in need.

7: Be disciplined and responsible in partnerships and marriage, but also learn to be flexible. Understand, heal and master a fear of partnerships or of rejection. Do not try to control or judge others. At times you may feel you are carrying extra responsibility, but that is your karma.

8: Be disciplined and responsible in your use of sexual energy, metaphysical knowledge and with other people's money. Use power wisely and manage the resources of others with impeccable integrity.

9: Be disciplined and responsible in your use of knowledge. Heal any fears about "foreigners". Teach the Ageless Wisdom. Resist the urge to put yourself up as the expert, the one who knows everything.

10: Karma affects your career and status. Learn to be humble. Be disciplined and responsible in the use of power and with life success. Understand and heal a fear of public failure.

11: Karma affects your relationships with your friends and groups. Be disciplined, responsible but also flexible and forgiving. Understand and heal a fear of feeling inadequate in groups.

12: Take time to locate, understand and heal subconscious feelings of inadequacy and low self-esteem. Quietly meet all karmic debts. Be a rock for souls who are lost, a centre of support and quiet responsibility.

Uranus in Houses

Uranus' house is where we are required to make all things new. This is also the area in which to take risks and experiment.

1: Be daring and develop a new approach to life, a new image. Use your initiative and scientific mind to walk the occult path, to focus on soul purpose and soul activities. Like-minded fellows will join you.

2: Develop new spiritual attitudes and values towards resources and money. Use your initiative to manifest resources to serve the Plan. You will draw new friends to you as you change your values.

3: Be independent in thought and speech with relatives and neighbours. Study, teach, write and communicate in a way that awakens people's minds to the truth. Siblings and students will be friends.

4: Develop an independent relationship with family, parents and roots and leave your roots behind if there is abuse. There will be many changes in this area, use this to your advantage. Build a spiritual ashram; hold occult or scientific discussions with friends, at home.

5: Be independent, unorthodox in relationships with younger souls and children. Use your unique creative talents to awaken young minds to higher truths and understandings. Lovers and children will be friends.

6: Be daring and more independent at work. Try the new, the occult, the scientific and the alternative. Develop skills in science, with new technology and in alternative areas. Co-workers will be friends.

7: Change the way your normally relate with partners and in your choice of partners. Be more independent, aim for someone higher or different. Relate in a new and more healthy and intelligent way. Walk the Occult Path with soul mates. Partners will be best friends.

8: Walk the Path of Discipleship and radically transform attitudes to sex, death and business. Use your occult or scientific knowledge and power, for the higher good. Choose different types of friends

9: Be independent and daring when you express your concepts and beliefs. Study, teach, write and communicate, the new, the alternative, the Wisdom Teachings. You may choose "foreign" type friends.

10: Be daring and alternative in your choice of career. Look for unique opportunities where you can use your initiative. Communicate the Master's work to the world. Take initiation. Authority figures will be friends.

11: Be more independent and daring in your choice of friends and groups until you find a humanitarian group that focuses on the higher good. Use your unique talents to lead your group in a higher direction.

12: Free yourself from subconscious fears and mystical nonsense. Bring these to light and destroy them with the power of scientific and rational thought. You will have many hidden friends.

Neptune in Houses

Neptune's house represents a life area where we should refine our emotional life and search for and express our higher ideals.

1: Avoid being naive in your approach to life, deluding yourself that all is well when it is not. Be realistic, clear and honest. Radiate soul love openly, but intelligently.

2: Overcome naivety or dishonesty with money and possessions by being more realistic and honest. Give your resources selflessly but be wise in your giving.

3: Overcome any tendency to lie, especially by omission and speak the truth. Train your mind to think clearly. You have a gift of being able to communicate in a most loving and creative way. Give voice to your compassion.

4: Overcome any naivety, confusion or dishonesty in family matters, by being realistic, clear and honest in what you say and do. Bring abuse into the light. Be wise when you give to the family or spiritual ashram.

5: Learn to be more realistic, clear and honest in your relations with children, lovers and the way you use creative energy. Be forgiving. Give your creative gifts freely to others.

6: Overcome any confusion at work or in health matters by being more realistic, clear and honest in your communications. Give of yourself selflessly and wisely.

7: Learn to be more realistic, clear and honest with people generally. If you are grounded and clear you will form truly beautiful relationships. Otherwise, you will attract the confused, deceitful, weak and needy.

8: Overcome any naivety or confusion in sex or business matters, by being more realistic, clear and honest in these areas. Use your metaphysical gifts selflessly, but wisely. Choose very carefully the occult teachings to follow. Stay on the lighted Path.

9: Avoid a spiritual path, teacher or guru, whose message insults your intelligence, or which flatters your pride. Study the Wisdom Teachings then endeavour to become a wise and selfless spiritual teacher.

10: You are best suited to careers that are selfless, artistic or spiritual, so choose your life work carefully. It may take some time and many attempts to find what it is you were born to do.

11: Overcome naivety or confusion in your relations with friends or group members, by being more realistic, clear and honest in communication. Give selflessly in these areas and wisely.

12: If you seem to be a victim of life, be realistic, clear and honest in assessing the way you think and act and where you need to establish clearer boundaries. Work with a compassionate or spiritual counsellor to do this. Give selflessly to life's victims.

Pluto in Houses

 Pluto's house is where an old and obsessive habit or behaviour must die.

1: You have power and radiate strength, but your approach to life needs transforming. Let your spiritual will guide you rather than the selfish personal will. Be more flexible, detached, less controlling and obsessive.

2: Be vigilant and transform any controlling attitudes or values, or obsessions over money and possessions. Do not use wealth to manipulate others. Use your higher will to develop spiritual values to live by.

3: Speak with power but ensure your communications with relatives and neighbours is not manipulative. Be assertive but also harmless, in thought and speech. Otherwise, there could be unfortunate repercussions.

4: Observe family dynamics and use your higher will to transform any manipulative or controlling patterns. Do not put up with abuse and permanently sever ties with family or your "roots" if matters are toxic or it is out of your power to change things.

5: Observe the way you relate with younger souls, children and lovers and use your higher will to transform any misuse of your power. Be more inclusive, gentle and loving. Sever ties if things do not improve.

6: Do not put up with abuse at work, or be abusive, or your health will be seriously at threat. Be assertive but also inclusive in attitude. Change jobs if necessary.

7: There are manipulative patterns in your partnership area - either in yourself or in others. Use your higher will to transform any need to control partners. Be assertive but also inclusive. Avoid dangerous and controlling partners and leave if threats start.

8: Use your higher will to transform any obsessive and inflexible patterns. Be assertive but also discerning in the way you use your sexuality, vital energies and power. You have talent in detection and occult work. Stay away from dangerous people and on the right path.

9: You will meet powerful teachers and gurus who will radically change your life. But do not give your power away. Use it to transform any obsessive and inflexible beliefs and concepts you hold and be a force for good. Be assertive but also inclusive.

10: You are destined to have managers who are powerful and some will be abusive. Use the experience to develop your own confidence and power and assertive but fair managerial skills. Change careers if necessary.

11: In your earlier life, you are likely to attract dangerous or criminal friends. Learn what you can and leave before things go too far. Use your power to change things for the better - in groups and with friends and organisations.

12: Avoid becoming a secretive manipulator. If you find yourself confined or ill, be honest about the cause. Transform the way you relate to yourself and to life.

4c. Reading Houses on Exoteric and Esoteric levels

The exoteric planet that rules a sign on a house cusp, represents the attitude of the personality towards that house or life area. Soul purpose is represented by the esoteric ruler.

1H: Approach to life: Aquarius. (Personality ruler Uranus, soul ruler Jupiter).

Jung's personality approached life with mental alertness, but its ideas and beliefs were fixed (Aquarius) and self-serving (Uranus in Leo). An unwillingness to compromise in close one-on-one relationships caused disruption and separations (Uranus in Leo 7H).

Jung's soul purpose was to develop an inclusive and universal approach to life, to become a World Server (Aquarius). The heart needed to open and wisdom cultivated (Jupiter, the esoteric ruler of Aquarius); mental flexibility and life balance (esoteric ruler Jupiter, in Libra). This required a program of esoteric study and discipline to make the transformation (Jupiter 8H). The eighth house rules occult lore, psychology and Jung specialised in both.

2H Values: Pisces. (Personality ruler Jupiter and Neptune; soul ruler Pluto).

The personality's values were loose, lacked discrimination, which extended to finance (Pisces). There was a taste for luxury (Neptune in Taurus 2H) and money spent on indulging and enjoying (Jupiter) sensual activities (8H).

Jung needed to develop higher and more spiritually inclusive (Pisces) values and use his resources differently (2H). To achieve this old values and old desires had to die (Pluto in Taurus). Jung had to free himself from the thought life and values of his extended family (3H). The Jewish values Jung was raised with were limiting for his higher purpose.

3H Communication: Taurus. (Personality ruler Venus, soul ruler Vulcan; both in Cancer 6H)

The personality would direct mind power and communication (3H) into work (6H) that brought personal profit and gain (Venus) and benefit to the family (Cancer).

Soul wanted Jung to use his communication skills in service (6H), to be a purifying and healing force (Vulcan in 6H). Specifically, for the career that Jung chose for himself: to destroy (Vulcan) people's delusions (Venus as the deluded mind), to purify (Vulcan) thoughts (Venus) that lead to ill health (6H); to try new (ray 1 via Vulcan) techniques to heal the ills of humanity.

4H Home and family: also Taurus.

Taurus rules both the 3rd and 4th Houses. With Vulcan carrying the soul's influence, a planet symbolising death and rebuilding through its 1st ray force, old and limiting patterns of thought (3H) that were steeped in family tradition and obligations (4H), needed to die. This would free Jung to pursue his soul work.

5H Pleasure and creativity: Gemini. (Personality ruler Mercury, soul ruler Venus; both in Cancer 6H).

The personality would use creative power (5H) to benefit the family, in the family trade (Mercury in Cancer). Instead, Jung used his creative talent to benefit the family of man (Cancer), to beautify the minds (Venus) and lives of those who came for healing (6H).

6H Work and health: Cancer. (Personality ruler the Moon, soul ruler Neptune, both in Taurus 3H).

Cancer rules the sixth house and as previously mentioned, Cancer rules "the family" and in Jung's case, the family of man. He had a choice to go into the family work (being a Rabbi) but decided otherwise.

Both ruling planets are in Taurus in the third house. The thoughts he communicated about his work would be in line with either his lower desire nature (Moon in Taurus), or his spiritual aspiration (Neptune in Taurus). We know he expressed the latter.

7H Close partnerships and marriage: Leo. (Personality ruler the Sun; soul ruler Sun unveiling Neptune,

The personality wanted to be the dominant partner (Leo on 7H and Sun in Leo 7H), to rule and control. The soul wanted increased sensitivity and compassion demonstrated in close unions and for Jung to form partnerships with true ashramic soul mates (Neptune unveiled by Sun, is soul ruler of 7H). This house represents the close partnership Jung had with Freud. Although they were both probably ray 2 souls on the wisdom line and therefore soul-mates, the union eventually ended in divorce. (Uranus, the divorce planet is in this house).

8H Transformation and other people's values and money: Virgo. (Personality ruler Mercury in Cancer 6H, soul ruler Moon unveiling Vulcan, in Taurus 3H).

The approach either way would be detailed and meticulous. The personality would work (6H) meticulously to increase the family fortune (8H) and to have funds to spend on pleasure activities (Mercury rules fifth house),

The higher goal was firstly to be meticulous with his personal transformation (8H) and cultivate the Christ spirit within (Virgo). Then, to build a form (his counselling practise) to which the public had access (the Moon) and through which he could direct his radically new (1st ray) ideas (3H). Other interpretations are, to purify negative attitudes using esoteric knowledge (8H) and soul power (Vulcan); to teach this new esoteric knowledge and his values (Taurus) to humanity (Moon).

9H Beliefs and 10H Profession: both ruled by Scorpio. (Personality and soul ruler, Mars 11H).

These two houses "beliefs" and "profession" have the warrior sign Scorpio on the cusp. Jung would be called on to fight (former) friends, groups and organisations (Mars 11H); for his beliefs and for his professional life. The soul wanted Jung to fight for his beliefs, ideas and ideals (9H and 6th ray) and to win (Scorpio).

The very public battle between the two professionals (10H) Freud and Jung was one of belief (9H). Jung disagreed with Freud's theory of sexuality. Each man had his own group (11H) of followers that supported his convictions. Jung inspired his friends to help him in his battle (Mars), to be pro-active in promoting his new psychological (Scorpio) theories.

11H Friends and groups: Sagittarius. (Personality ruler Jupiter, soul ruler the Earth).

The personality was adventurous, liked a good time (Jupiter) and sex (Mars 11H, Jupiter 8H). His soul wanted him to choose friends that would help him ground his soul purpose (Earth conjunct ascendant) and fulfill his role in world service (Aquarius ascendant).

12H Hidden things, Capricorn. (Personality and soul ruler is Saturn).

The 12H was an important house for Jung, because it represents the unconscious. His work required him to delve into the unconscious minds of people who were mentally troubled, to free them from irrational beliefs. With the ruler of the unconscious in the first house (Saturn in 1), either the unconscious would dominate the conscious mind, or self-awareness would dominate the unconscious. Throughout his life, Jung went through periods of doubt and anxiety (Saturn), but his struggles to stay sane and in control provided experiences that were of benefit to him in his professional life.

This concludes this brief example of houses, read on the esoteric and esoteric levels.

4d. Vocations

Vocations by the Rays

Ray 1 of Will or Power: leader, manager, supervisor, politician, occultist, explorer, executive and dictator. The forces. Any career that requires great will power, strength and stamina, the ability to stand firm in the face of all obstruction, the ability to destroy if required.

Ray 2 of Love Wisdom: vocations that require tact, foresight, personal magnetism, warmth and concern for others. For example: ambassador, psychotherapist, teacher, healer, educator, sage, scholar and humanist.

Ray 3 of Active Intelligence: third ray vocations require mental dexterity and adaptability, a clear intellect, ability to speak with the voice of reason and intelligence and resourcefulness. For example: tactician, strategist, financial planner, business person, entrepreneur, philosopher, astrologer, economist and historian.

Ray 4 of Harmony through Conflict: fourth ray vocations require spontaneity and the creation of some form of beauty, colour or harmony. For example: actor, artist, musician, writer, mediator, poet and counsellor.

Ray 5 of Concrete Science: fifth ray vocations require a keen intellect, accuracy with details, scientific and research skills. For example: scientist, electrician, engineer, analyst, data technician, operating surgeon, researcher, alchemist, inventor and technician.

Ray 6 of Devotion and Idealism: sixth ray vocations require devotion, dedication and unselfish service. For example: minister, mystic, missionary, devotee, preacher, orator, soldier, nurse, personal secretary, philanthropist and crusader.

Ray 7 of Ceremonial Order: vocations requiring practical efficiency and finesse, organisational skills, an ability to create order and the ability to manifest ideas on the Physical Plane. For example: business person, organiser, judge, legal worker, architect, builder, administrator, designer, revolutionary, magician and esotericist.

Vocations associated with Signs and Houses

Aries and 1H: careers that require initiative, ideas, mental and physical dexterity and drive. For example: manager, leader, supervisor, soldier, politician, activist and surgeon. Other Aries vocations involve machinery, engineering, metals, tools and sports. Esoteric careers: those that fight against evil for the higher collective good, pioneering programs to benefit humanity, initiating programs that communicate wisdom.

Taurus and 2H: careers that require reliability, practical application and commitment. For example: finance, banking, business and farming. Also, the arts and beautification of the earth. Esoteric careers: those that bring illumination and light to earth, which fight against evil and for the higher collective good.

Gemini and 3H: any career in the communication or information industries. For example: education in schools and universities or reporting on the world situation through social or political commentary. Esoteric careers: communicating the Ageless Wisdom, those that train and beautify the mind of man, the academic and training aspects of the esoteric arts and science, especially as it involves fusion of soul and personality.

Cancer and 4H: careers that involve nurturing, healing, female issues, service industries, working with the public generally, taking on organising and administrative positions in any area of service. Esoteric careers: those that involve metaphysics, spiritual healing, emotional healing, astral purification, cultivating and training the intellect, nurturing the Christ spirit and improving civilisation generally.

Leo: and 5H this is a sign of leadership: manager, leader, supervisor and self-employment and those who are the heart of an organisation or who work with hearts. For example, a heart surgeon or care of children or younger souls. Leo also rules creative areas - art, theatre, acting and dance. Esoteric careers: fighting for human rights and better conditions for the masses, fighting against evil and for the higher collective good, leading with kindness and compassion.

Virgo and 6H: careers in education, health, technology and that require attention to detail. For example: teacher, analyst, researcher, scientist, technician, librarian, administrator. Esoteric careers: work to develop the soul or Christ consciousness.

Libra and 7H: careers in the legal service and those that involve mediation, such as the diplomatic service, counselling, conflict resolution and relationship counselling. Esoteric careers: communicating the Ageless Wisdom, the cultivation of intellectual brilliance and soul personality balance and alignment.

Scorpio and 8H: those careers involving death, sex, surgery, the military, birth, the underworld, sanitation, subterfuge, the stock-market, investments, unions and politics. Scorpio is connected to healing and psychology, via Pluto. Esoteric careers: study of the occult, personal transformation, transformational or esoteric healer /

psychologist, fighting against evil and for the higher collective good.

Sagittarius and 9H: careers that involve travel and expansion:- physically, mentally or spiritually. For example: philosophy, teaching, religion, academia, libraries, publishing, vocations involving foreign countries and people. Esoteric careers: teaching the Ageless Wisdom, lifting the gaze of man up to that which is higher.

Capricorn and 10H: in this leadership sign career examples are: manager, leader, chief executive, politician, the law, large service organisations and big business. Also, vocations connected with the land, real estate, mining, minerals, death and time. Esoteric careers: doing the Master's work - that is, improving civilisation generally by managing and overseeing humanitarian projects, teaching the laws and methodology of initiation.

Aquarius and 11H: covers those careers that concern science, new technology, the modern, new and alternative. Also, careers that improve civilisation generally, such as the welfare, salvaging, reformation and upliftment of humanity. The United Nations. Esoteric careers: researching, writing and teaching, the occult sciences.

Pisces and 12H: any area of service, particularly in health, religion, spirituality and education. Pluto's esoteric rulership covers vocations that bring about the destruction of all that hinders good health and spiritual wellbeing.

Vocations associated with Planets

The Sun: all leadership careers, such as manager, authority figure, president, organiser, ruler, dignitary, magistrate and banker. Esoterically, leading others wisely and lovingly, especially children and younger souls.

The Moon (unveiling Vulcan, Neptune or Uranus): a nurturing leader, all the care and healing vocations, metaphysical worker, spiritual work, astral purification, art and music in healing, politician and reformer.

Vulcan: all leadership roles in any area of service and those involving politics and the military, fighting against evil and corruption, purification of the physical appetites and life generally.

Mercury: all vocations in communication and sharing ideas. For example, interpreter, publisher, writer, orator, satirist, journalist, reporter, linguist, educator, mediator, counsellor and conflict resolver.

Venus: governs vocations in the arts, finance, law, diplomacy, counselling and mediating. Esoterically, careers that bring about the improvement and beautification of the mind, which express intelligent love and soul alignment.

Earth: all vocations that involve practical service delivered intelligently and that promote group harmony. The third ray includes careers in business, the world of ideas, cultivation of the intellect and philosophy.

Mars: vocations connected with the improvement of the physical body, such as, body-worker, surgeon, physical activities, athletic and sports coach. Those that use the warriorship of Mars for the higher good such as, leadership in the military to fight against global evil and corruption. Also, careers that utilise the engineering skill of Mars to benefit civilisation.

Jupiter: vocations in higher education, healing, religion and that promote brotherliness, wisdom, universality and oneness. For example: spiritual leader, preacher, teacher, moraliser, charity worker, philanthropist and philosopher.

Saturn: executive positions, particularly in government, authority bodies and in law and order. Careers that are concerned with making practical improvements to the conditions of the elderly and incarcerated and that build structures to improve civilisation generally. The third ray aspect of Saturn brings in vocations that cultivate the intellect and intellectual brilliance.

Uranus: careers related to science and technology and that are pioneering and new and that improve and reform civilisation in practical ways. For example: radio, television, computers, the internet, electricity, inventing, aviation, astrology, metaphysics, the human sciences and cosmology.

Neptune: all service and care vocations, health, religion and spirituality. For example: careers that create a yearning for the higher and finer and promote higher ideals, which refine the astral nature, which promote a healthy imagination through music, dance, poetry, theatre, photography and film.

Pluto: powerful positions and rulership in any area of service, but particularly in politics, military, the law, research, detection and psychology. Also, fighting against evil and bringing that which is corrupt into the light, into the public consciousness, for destruction and healing.

5. ASTROLOGY READINGS

LIFE PLAN READINGS

> Every disciple has a life plan and some chosen field of service. If he has not such a field, he is not a disciple. [1]
>
> The only truly self-conscious person is the man who is aware of purpose, of a self-directed life and of a developed and definite life plan and programme. Where these are present, the inference is that there is mental perception and some measure of integration. To be motivated only by emotion and actuated by desire is no indication of true self-consciousness. [2]

The distinguishing feature of esoteric counselling is that it lays emphasis upon the inner life and the necessity to bring about a closer alignment with the soul. Life direction readings using only the Seven Rays are very useful. Astrology adds detail about the purpose of the soul.

1. Determine the spiritual status of the person.

If you are working as a professional, you could ask "Why have you come to see me?" Otherwise, "What is it you would most like for yourself in this world", or "Are you interested in spiritual matters?" If the response is purely personal assume the person is not yet on the Path. If however, there is an interest in life direction, an aspiration for something higher and finer, then place the person on the Path of Spiritual Development.

2. Readings for people not yet on the Path

a. Atlantean man: emotions rule the mind and important decisions are made based on emotional need. There is little discrimination being demonstrated, an inability to complete plans and a lack of personality integration is demonstrated.

   The personality ray is not developed and is not evident. Do not try to identify it - clients will be confused and so will you. The soul ray is not making its presence felt so cannot be seen. The high spiritual goal is to develop the mind and integrate the personality.

   Readings: work with the physical, emotional and mind rays; and exoteric astrology. Include esoteric astrology if and where appropriate.
   - Give an overview of the hypothetical spiritual status, what it means.
   - Physical, Emotional and Mental Rays: the personal equipment.
   - Moon Sign: negative core beliefs constituting the "prison of the soul" pattern.
   - Sun Sign: emphasise the integration and strengthening of the personality (integration of the positive Sun sign qualities), as the high spiritual goal.

b. Aryan man, personalities: they are intelligent, strong, forceful, motivated, assertive and selfish. They want money, success and power and are taking steps to get what they want. They are making their mark on life and are not interested in spiritual matters.

   Readings: work with the personality ray and exoteric astrology. Include esoteric astrology if and where appropriate.
   - Give an overview of the hypothetical spiritual status, what it means.
   - Moon Sign: negative core beliefs constituting the "prison of the soul" pattern.
   - Sun Sign working with the personality ray: emphasise the Sun Sign and personality ray qualities, their integration and strengthening, as the high spiritual goal.

---
1 Bailey, Alice A. Glamour a World Problem 62-63
2 Bailey, Alice A. Esoteric Astrology 288-289

3. Readings for people on the Path

a. Aspirants: they are aspirational, are seeking life direction and they have not yet settled on one spiritual path or have developed a daily routine of spiritual practise. Their distinguishing task is to discipline the physical appetites because they are being prepared for the 1st initiation.

Readings: work with the personality and soul rays and both exoteric and esoteric astrology.

- Give an overview of the hypothetical spiritual status, what it means.
- Give an overview of the 1st Initiation, what needs to be done.
- Moon Sign: negative core beliefs constituting the "prison of the soul" pattern; Personality Words. The major purification work to be done, Soul Words.
- Sun Sign with the personality ray: identify the negatives to overcome - the Personality Words; emphasise the positives to strengthen via the Soul Words.
- Ascendant Sign with the soul ray: identify the positive ray qualities to strengthen using that sign's Soul Words. Include vocations related to this sign and its rays.

b. Disciples: they are steadfast in their spiritual orientation and service work and are applying emotional purification disciplines. This group is approaching the 2nd initiation. Reading format is the same as for aspirants, excepting status is a "disciple working towards the 2nd Initiation".

c. Initiates and Masters: they no longer have independent personalities. The personality is now just an extension of the soul. Read the chart in terms of their world service work. Include hierarchy planet rulers.

4 Astrology aspects to include by non-astrologer counsellors

Non-astrologers should include an astrology component in readings. Start with the Moon Sign - patterns from the past to clear up. Then the Sun Sign, what to develop and express. For those on the Path, include the ascendant sign for soul purpose. Build around the "words" or instructions for each sign; the personality word traits need to be overcome and the soul word qualities cultivated.

Aries	Personality words: "Let form again be sought", desire for physical plane gratification. Acting without thought. Soul words: "I come forth and from the plane of mind, I rule". Think before acting. Gain distinction by leading intelligently, using the initiative, being pioneering.
Taurus.	Personality words: "Let struggle be undismayed", emotional struggle, inner and life conflict. Soul words: "I see and when the eye is opened, all is illumined". Be aware of how energy is used. Strive for balance and life stability. Gain distinction in creative work.
Gemini	Personality words: "Let instability do its work". This is mind and life instability, duality. Soul words: "I recognise my other self and in the waning of that self I grow and glow". Observe the lower unstable self in action, while identifying with the quietness within. Cultivate a quiet mind. Gain distinction by communicating or in communications that are intelligent and wise.
Cancer.	Personality words: "Let isolation be the rule and yet the crowd exists". Emotional isolation and defensiveness. Soul words: "I build a lighted house and therein dwell". Cultivate the mind and clear thought uncontaminated by the emotions. Gain distinction by nurturing others.
Leo.	Personality words: "Let other forms exist, I rule". Arrogance and control. Soul words: "I am That and That am I". Identify with the highest light, the goodness within. Be more sensitive to the needs of others. Gain distinction by leading wisely.
Virgo.	Personality words: "Let matter reign". Too concerned with material success; too critical. Soul words: "I am the Mother and the Child. I, God, I matter am". Identify with the nurturing and healing wisdom within. Cultivate kindness and compassion. Gain distinction by using intelligence and craftsmanship to build a career that meets the needs of others.
Libra	Personality words: "Let choice be made". Mind instability and procrastination. Soul words: "I choose the way that leads between the two great lines of force". Balance and moderation. Gain distinction by creating harmony within one's own life and others.
Scorpio.	Personality words: "Let maya flourish and let deception rule". A mind that builds images about people that are false or flawed because the emotions (and emotional distortions) are controlling the mind. Soul words: "Warrior I am and from the battle I emerge triumphant". Learn to hold the mind high in the light of truth. Gain distinction by being a warrior who fights for truth and good.

Sagittarius Personality words: "Let food be sought". Control the lower appetites, wasting energy and talents. Soul words: "I see the goal. I reach the goal and see another". Practise self-control and concentration. Gain distinction by reaching the heights of one's career or spiritual aspiration.

Capricorn Personality words: "Let ambition rule and the door stand wide". Being ruled by ambition and materialism. Balance the ambitions, appreciate people more. Soul words: "Lost am I in light supernal, yet on that light I turn my back". On the lower level, avoid being controlled by the light of ambition. Gain distinction by achieving professional success with integrity. For those on the Path - strive to climb the Mountain of Spirituality. World service.

Aquarius Personality words: "Let desire in form be ruler". Using the powers of the mind to satisfy lower desire. Soul words: "Water of life am I, poured forth for thirsty men". Be involved in the reformation of society for the greater and wider good. Gain distinction with wise counsel.

Pisces Personality words: "Go forth into matter". Being lost in the emotions, in a life that meanders without clear life direction. Soul words: "I leave the Father's Home and turning back, I save". First save oneself from emotional control and establishing healthy emotional and life boundaries. Then save others. Gain distinction in selfless service.

5. Reading structure for astrologer counsellors

Moon Sign - Negative unconscious pattern to clear

Begin by emphasising that you are addressing the "Prison of the Soul Pattern", the primary unconscious negative pattern requiring elimination. Give an overview of the Moon pattern in the chart, sign, house and aspects. Include the negatives of this sign and the Personality Words. Explain the importance for its elimination. Then focus on remedial work. Give the Soul Words, which are a spiritual direction for self-improvement. Encourage the cultivation of the positive qualities of the Moon Sign and of the esoteric planet ruler - sign, house and aspects. Include the Soul Words for the Moon Sign and for the sign the esoteric ruler is in.

Personality Ray and Sun Sign - The Nature of the Personality

Emphasise that you are addressing the personality nature, negatives to discipline and positives to strengthen. Give an overview of the negatives: the personality ray that plays through the Sun Sign, the Personality Words, where the personality is strong - house and aspects. Include the exoteric Ruler of the Sun Sign, its sign, Personality Words, house and aspects. Then give advice about how to build a strong and positive personality: the personality ray and Sun Sign positives. The Soul Words of the Sun Sign and of the esoteric planet ruler, sign, house and aspects.

The Soul Ray and Ascendant Sign - Soul Purpose

Begin by emphasising that you are addressing the soul purpose for the life.

a. From the ascendant sign, give the primary qualities to develop and suitable soul vocations. Include the Soul Words for the sign. If you are working with the soul ray, include its qualities and vocations.

b. Then focus on the esoteric ruling planet of the ascendant: the qualities of this planet and its ray, its house and aspects. Soul Words for the sign it is in and qualities to develop and express.

Summarise: close the reading with a summary of important points, for instance

Self-realisation is an important part of gaining control over the lower nature. Study how you express your force from this point on, striving for balance.

a. Eliminate the Lunar Pattern.
b. Develop your personality strengths.
c. Develop your soul qualities, laying emphasis on these.
d. Find a soul vocation to serve in.

> **NB. You do not have to be an expert or have a counselling degree to offer esoteric advice and assistance. Esoteric counselling is based on a solid understanding of esoteric principles, of the constitution of man and of the soul and of the latter's activities that underlie the various disorders and problems of life. Simply respond as a good friend would to someone who is troubled or who seeks guidance. However, counselling training would be beneficial.**

Example 1: Life Plan Reading for Barack Obama
4 August 1961, 19:24, Honolulu Hawaii, Placidus.

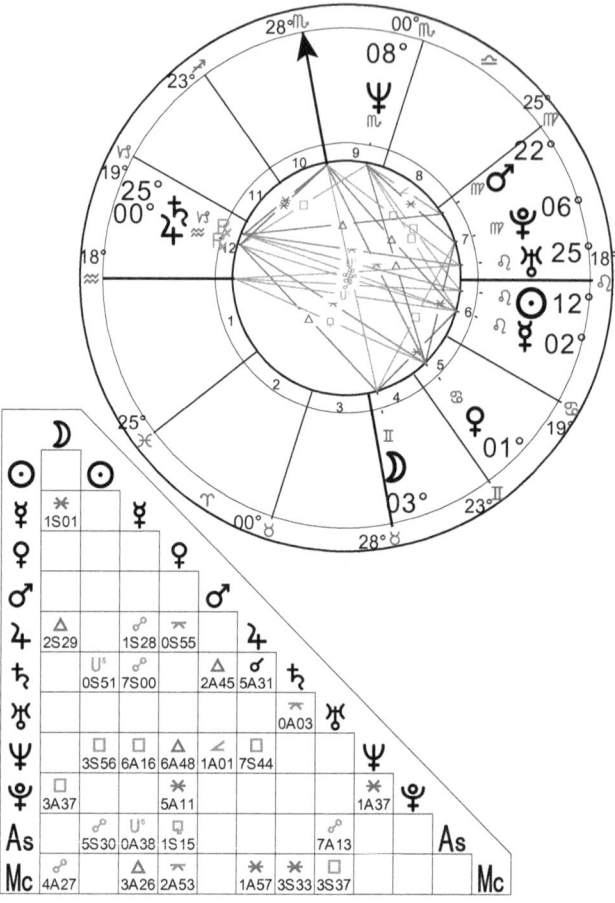

1. Spiritual status

Analysis: Obama is highly intelligent, integrated, effective and able to sway others with the force of his personality. This means he is an integrated and powerful personality. There also appears to be a great measure of soul fusion. There is enough evidence in the public domain that points to the fact that he is motivated by goodwill and seeks to work with people and groups to resolve problems. This means he is group conscious and a disciple. Add to this the fact that he influential on the world stage, a world leader, it opens to the possibility that he could also be an initiate. Aquarius is one of the signs that represent this higher level and Obama has an Aquarius ascendant. An initiate has universal consciousness and identifies with all humanity; while soul consciousness identifies with groups but has not yet become universal.

2. Soul and Personality Rays

Vocations of advanced souls are related to the soul ray. Obama is a political leader, giving him a ray 1 soul. His personality ray modifies the potential 1st ray roughness. He is dignified, cooperative and a team player - hypothetically a 7th Ray Personality.

3. Gemini Moon Sign, the "Prison of the Soul Pattern"

Traits and Personality Words for Gemini: the Personality Words for Gemini are "Let instability do its work". The unconscious pattern is instability, of the mind and in the life. Obama would not have become USA President if unstable instincts still controlled him. However, for educational purposes, the nature of an undisciplined pattern is covered.

The pattern is one of restless mind fluctuations and unstable emotions. At this level, the mind tends to be superficial and skim on the surface of life, seeking ever-new sensations and experiences. It avoids emotional entanglements, lacks empathy, views "heavy" relationships as obstacles to a free and enjoyable life. Preoccupied with its own concerns, it is self-centred. To avoid difficulty or unpleasantness, it will play games with people, telling them what they think they want to hear, or simply lie. Consequently, life and relationships are shallow and unstable. If this unconscious pattern should control the conscious life, there will be many interesting experiences but without depth or deeper meaning.

a. *Soul Words for Gemini:* the key to the pattern's purification is "I recognise my other self and in the waning of that self, I grow and glow". This is an instruction to develop mental focus and to practise the technique of right-detachment - to observe the lower fluctuations, without reaction. This causes the lower impulse to gradually wither and die. The purified Moon pattern produces "Messengers of God", those who communicate wise truths that uplift those that hear. Obama is an inspirational orator and is remarkably poised and balanced, indicating that he is responding to the higher aspect of Gemini.

b. *Esoteric ruler Venus:* the nature of the higher aspect is Venus. This gives Obama 5th ray mental acuteness and the radiance of Venusian glow and charm.

4. Leo Sun Sign: the nature of the Personality

The 7th Ray Personality is modified by Leo. Obama is a leonine statesman who is courteous, dignified and a team player. He does not demonstrate to any noticeable degree the negative traits of the personality ray, which wants to force a rigid set of rules onto people. Nor does he display the Leo personality negative of "Let other forms exist, I rule, because I am". The unregenerated personality with this combination would be proud, arrogant and very controlling, enforcing edicts with a heavy hand. Since he has been in the public eye, Obama has not demonstrated these traits although political opponents may disagree. Rather, he is responding to higher Leo, to the Soul Words - "I am That and That am I". Higher Leo's have identified with the "That", the soul and are being guided by the will and wisdom of the soul. One of the benefits of having the 7th ray is that you get things done. Obama's passage of his Health Care Package into reality and law in 2012, is due to his 7th ray manifesting skills.

- Esoteric ruler of the Sun Sign is unveiled Neptune expressing the 6th ray. Neptune instils an aspiration to serve one's highest ideals and to become more heart-centred, sensitive and compassionate. Obama has made the connection and has demonstrated his compassion for the suffering in public.

5. Aquarius Ascendant Sign. Soul Purpose

With a 1st ray soul, Obama is motivated by the "will to do good" and he expresses this will in a friendly Aquarian way. Aquarius represents the World Server and universal brotherhood. Obama is already a disciple and group conscious. Now (hypothetically) his task is to develop the global consciousness of the higher Aquarian. In other words, to consider himself one with the family of man irrespective of race or nation and work for the good of the whole.

This is reinforced by the Soul Words of Aquarius, one could say the mission statement for this sign - "Water of life am I, poured forth for thirsty men". When global concern is developed, then Obama becomes a "Water-Bearer". "Water" is all that nurtures; food, water, shelter, protection, guidance, wisdom and love. This is the goal for Obama, his soul purpose - to nurture not only the people of the USA, but all humanity.

The rays of Aquarius are repetitions of rays flowing through him from other sources. The 2nd ray (of Jupiter gives him an inclusive wisdom, the 7th ray of Uranus gives him power to manifest, the 5th ray of Aquarius gives him a mind that excels in detail and research. A University of Harvard graduate, Obama is renowned for his intellect.

Esoteric Ruler

The esoteric ruler of the ascendant sign represents the second part of soul purpose for disciples - this is Jupiter. It carries the love-wisdom ray and when the Aquarian man functions at this higher level, it points to the fact that the mind and heart have been synchronised. (Jupiter is also in Aquarius but retrograde in the 12th house of hidden things). Transit Jupiter turned direct and crossed Obama's ascendant before he was one years old. His mission on earth began at that early age.

If Obama is an initiate, then the Hierarchy Ruler of Aquarius, the Moon unveiling Uranus, represents his world mission. The Moon (the masses) is in Gemini in the 4th House of humanity. This seems apt and fits with the previous statement "to nurture .. all humanity".

6. In summary

a. Obama has natural leadership gifts thanks to his ray 1 soul and because his personality is in Leo. Because he has achieved a measure of soul-personality alignment, he is releasing this power sensitively.
b. He is highly intelligent thanks to his Leo Sun and Aquarius ascendant, which carry the 5th ray; and Venus (5th ray) which rules Gemini esoterically.
c. Wisdom flows from Jupiter esoteric ruler of Aquarius and from Venus.
d. The Hierarchy ruler of his Gemini Moon (Hierarchy Ruler of the ascendant) is the Earth and it is in Aquarius conjunct the soul purpose point, the ascendant.
e. Obama is a man of destiny who was born to serve the greater good.

Obama's soul purpose via his Aquarius ascendant is to pour out all he has in service to humanity.

Example 2: Life Plan Reading for Carl Jung

26 July Kesswil Switzerland, 19:29. Placidus.

1. Spiritual Status and Initiation

Carl Jung was a mature, intelligent and self-directed personality, indicating he had at least reached the zenith of the Mutable Cross experience. This means he was an integrated personality.

Very creative, Jung served humanity through his revolutionary healing approach with the mentally ill. These are indicators of a Fixed Cross level of consciousness. This means he was at least a disciple and early in his life was approaching the 2nd Initiation. The evidence for this was the emotional struggles he had in childhood life, which he seemed to rise above.

It is unlikely that Jung took the 4th initiation because his life did not reflect the total destruction and sacrifice of the life, which is symbolic of this very advanced stage. The Dalai Lama is probably the best living example of this level. It appears that Jung's developmental goal was to take the 2nd and perhaps the 3rd Initiations.

a. 2nd Initiation

Jupiter, Neptune and Venus are strong in Jung's natal chart. They rule the 2nd Initiation, supporting the view that he was to take the 2nd - purification and control of the emotional body. Their positions in the 4th, 6th and 9th houses indicate that the tests and challenges of this initiation would be found in the home, work and in his beliefs. To take the initiation he would need to learn to respond intelligently and inclusively in these areas, rather than react emotionally.

Young Carl was insecure and had health problems (sixth house [6H]). Dominated by Mother (4H) he was expected to become a Rabbi (9H). But as he approached University level, there was a definite stiffening of his character. The 2nd initiation could have been taken in that period.

b. 3rd Initiation

Bailey said that the 3rd can be taken in the same life as the 2nd.[1] Its goal is purification of the personality and its infusion by the soul. People, who have reached this level have a major influence on humanity.

Jung, along with other notables like Sigmund Freud, established the revolutionary science of psychology.

The notion that Jung took this initiation is supported by the astrology. The rulers of the 3rd initiation, Mars and the Moon (unveiling Uranus), are strong. The Moon is exalted or very strong in Taurus and Mars is the most exalted planet in the chart. They symbolise the strength of the Dweller on the Threshold, the unregenerated personality that emerges fully at the 3rd initiation to challenge the soul. The challenges came via his group associates (Mars in 11H) and a dispute over ideas (Moon in 3H). He had a very public and bitter dispute with Freud, because of their different viewpoints on psychology. This may have been the public face of this inner struggle.

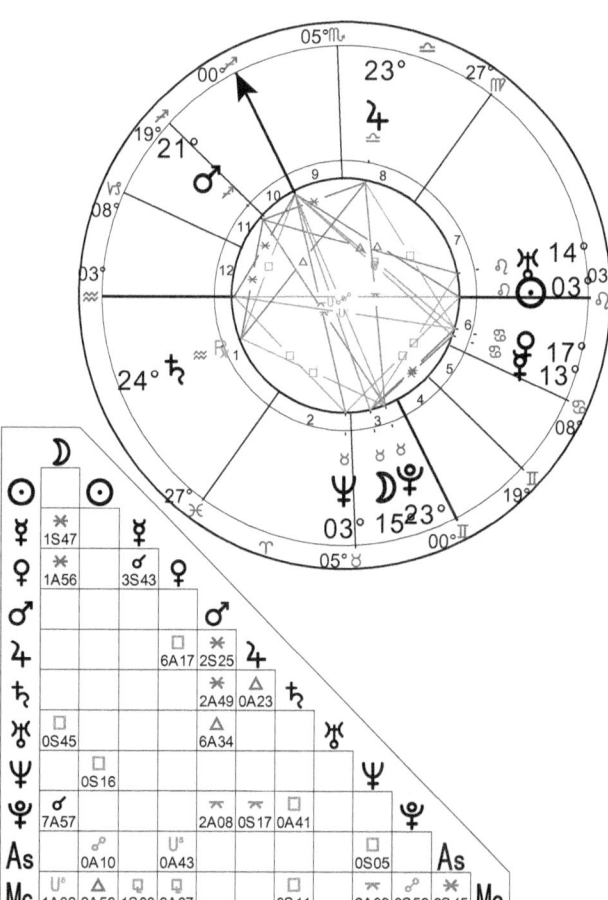

---

[1] Gathered from AAB. *Initiation Human and Solar*, 85

2. Identify the Soul and Personality Rays

a. Soul Ray 2 (wisdom line)

This ray was selected because Jung was a healer, thinker, writer and educator. These are 2nd ray vocations. As such, his task was to help initiate and promote new ideas in his field and to educate the public. He chose also to be a healer and utilised his knowledge in a hands-on healing practise.

b. Personality Ray 4 (Harmony through Conflict)

The 4th ray was selected as the personality ray because Jung had a very colourful personality, was jovial and a talented and creative artist and sculptor. He was also often embroiled in conflict, a common 4th ray trait. This was probably Jung's "problem ray", the energy that most needed to be balanced. The 4th ray flows through the Moon, so it strengthens the power of the "prison-of-the-soul" pattern.

Minor rays: a ray three mind (wide ranging intelligence), six emotional (reactive and retaliatory) and three physical (husky and robust body in adulthood).

The Astrology Chart

1. Taurus Moon Sign: elimination of the "Prison of the Soul Pattern"

The Personality Words are "Let struggle be undismayed". The moon is exalted in Taurus, strengthening the pattern - being bull-headed, stubborn and destructive in pursuing lower desires.

a. Elimination of the Pattern:

There are two major challenges to the Moon pattern - from Uranus and Pluto, indicating necessary purification work. Pluto is conjunct the Moon, in Taurus, in the 3rd house. The Moon is square Uranus in the 7th house.

Pluto is the "Arrow of Death" and whenever it is involved, it targets a pattern for elimination. Pluto affected Jung's family life and mother (Moon). Maternal nurturing was not available because Jung's mother did not find it easy to provide the emotional support that young Carl desired. Thrown back on his own resources he learnt to be emotionally independent. Another casualty was Jung's Jewish family traditions. He came from a line of Rabbis but rejected this to practise psychology. This took considerable courage but it was inevitable with Pluto's influence.

Uranus awakens people to the "new". Jung was attracted to people with unconventional and new ideas who challenged the old traditions that kept him bound to the past. This helped him to cut away past habits that were obstacles to soul growth.

The Moon's conjunction with Pluto in the third house, made it inevitable that Jung would cut links with his extended family and old community.

b. Remedial Work for Taurus

- There are two important soul instructions regarding the Moon in Taurus pattern:
    - The Soul Words for Taurus are "I see and when the eye is opened, all is illumined".
    - The Soul Words of Cancer (because Vulcan is in this sign) are "I build a lighted house and therein dwell".
- The goal was to become aware of the limiting pattern, through self-analysis. Then make changes, emotional and mind purification. This allowed the light of intuition to permeate his mind.
- This work and goal is emphasised by Vulcan - the esoteric ruler of Taurus. This planet of purification is in Cancer, ruled by the Moon.
- With the purification of the prison-pattern, Jung was able to channel the lighted intuitive power of Taurus, into his healing work.
- The spiritually mature Jung tuned intuitively, mentally and emotionally into the needs and requirements of his patients.

2. Leo Sun Sign: Personality Positives to Strengthen and Weaknesses to balance

Jung expressed his Leo personality confidently. He was sunny and magnetised people into his orbit. With the Sun dignified in its own sign and in an angular house, his personality was strong but could also be warlike and a troublemaker. (His 4th ray Personality worked through the Leo Sun).

a. Personality Negatives

Leo negatives are legendary, as the Personality Words for Leo highlight - "Let other forms exist - I rule". Leo's can be arrogant and controlling. Jung had a major glamour to deal with in his personality (Sun square Neptune 2H in Taurus). His sense of truth and reality could become confused when his Taurus desire nature was triggered, when money or desire was involved.

Jung's personality was strategically placed in opposition to the soul, challenging it for control of the life (Sun opposite the ascendant). This fits with the notion that Jung took the 3rd Initiation, soul control of the personality. The summarised ego - the Dweller on the Threshold is the opponent. What an almighty battle that would have been.

b. Personality Strengths to Reinforce

The spiritual direction for Leo personalities is "I am That and That am I". The task is to continually lift the consciousness upwards and identify with soul wisdom and inclusiveness, with the "That". This brings the Leo ego to heel. There is a need to render the personality more sensitive to others, through kindness and compassion. (The astrology symbols for this are the Sun unveiling Neptune and the force streaming from Leo's opposite sign, Aquarius). The dominant lion must eventually transform itself into the group conscious world-server.

As Jung moved from the 2nd to the 3rd initiation (perhaps later in his life), the force of the Hierarchy Ruler Uranus was unveiled, giving him the gift of spiritual will and power.

Advanced Leo's are very powerful. The unveiled Sun opens the door to soul and spiritual force and Jung seems to have achieved this level. He radiated solar power.

3. Aquarius Ascendant Sign: Soul Purpose

Jung's 2nd ray Soul worked through Aquarius, the sign of the World Server, symbolising his soul mission and purpose. His soul instruction was "Water of Life am I poured forth for thirsty men", to love and nurture humanity. Because he was a 2nd ray soul he chose to do this through health and education.

Jupiter - Esoteric Ruler of the Ascendant and of the Chart

Jupiter indicates specific work Jung would need to do to fulfill his soul purpose, in his case develop the consciousness of a World Server. Jupiter fuses the heart and mind, so that people love with the mind and think with the heart. Jupiter is in Libra, the sign of balance. Jung had to bring harmony and balance between his personality and soul and between himself and others. The Libra Soul Words are "I choose the way that lies between the two great lines of force".

As a symbol of soul service, the eighth house represents death, rebirth and transformation. It also rules psychology and healing as vocations (the influence of Scorpio, the natural ruler of the 8H). Jung rescued and healed people who were lost in astral realms (Jupiter opposite Chiron conjunct Neptune, a ruler of astralism); helped them to find balance and equilibrium. Much of his work focused on interpreting dreams (Neptune).

The eighth house also rules the occult. Jung investigated many esoteric philosophies and wrote widely about his investigations. He was a source of wisdom in many areas and wrote liberally on a wide variety of occult topics.

> ***Jung's high spiritual goal was to develop the qualities of universal brotherhood and become a World Server. The gains that Jung made and the knowledge he acquired because of his spiritual, psychological and physical struggles, he used to help heal those who were psychologically ill. This was his profession and his work and along with other pioneers such as Freud, he had a major global impact upon the field of health. He served humanity and achieved his soul purpose.***

CHAPTER 6: SPIRITUAL PRACTISES

As birds fly together to summer realms, so souls unite in flight. Passing through the gate they thus alight before the throne of God. [1]

---

[1] Bailey, Alice A. Discipleship in the New Age I, 291

1. MEDITATION

1. The Object of Esoteric Meditation

The aim of esoteric or eastern meditation is to facilitate union with the Divine, to develop and merge consciousness with Universal Mind. The primary factor in man that determines evolutionary status is the state of the MIND

Mind is vital. The mind is an instrument for illumination and esoteric meditation is a strictly mental process, scientifically designed to train the mind to observe eternal states. Through this type of transformed mind, the soul or Self can transmit wisdom to the physical brain.

To the outer world, individuals who have achieved this state appear to be very wise, loving and compassionate. People are drawn like filings to a magnet because of the fineness and sacredness of their aura. This transformative task lies before all human beings. There is no choice. All return to the sacred Source. The only factor that individuals can influence is the timing. Steady and regular meditation accelerates progress.

Ordinary men and women focused in their physical or emotional natures will not feel the urge to meditate. Even when the mental body is active, no urge arises. The reason for this and why such people appear on the surface sometimes to be without soul or inner wisdom, is because they are not yet receiving adequate spiritual inspiration. There is a gap in consciousness. This gap lies between the concrete mind and soul and spirit, on the higher Mental Plane. Technically, this gap lies between the first and fourth subplanes of the Mental Plane. But over many lives, a connection or bridge forms. The eastern name for this bridge of light is "the antahkarana".

Only when the cup of pleasure and pain is tasted and life lived entirely for the lower self is found unsatisfying, will the inner attraction be strong enough so that an urge to meditate arises. Then man becomes the spiritual seeker and turns his thoughts to higher things, seeking the source from where he came. Through meditation, consciousness fills with the inner light of love and wisdom. This occurs gradually and stage by stage.

1. Through meditation we discover our relation to the universe, that our physical body and vital energies are part of the outer garment of Deity or Universal Mind.

2. Through meditation we find that our ability to love and feel puts us in touch with the love that pulses at the heart of all creation.

3. Through meditation we discover that the mind is the key that unlocks the door of wisdom and when enlightened, it enables us to enter the purposes and plans of Deity.

4. Through meditation we eventually arrive at the Source of all. Knowing that we are divine, we find that the whole is equally divine.

5. Through meditation, the powers of the soul unfold, new states of consciousness register and a new phenomenal world is seen.

6. Through meditation we transform from being a selfish and unhappy person who is attached to outer material life, into a blissful, free and spiritually powerful soul.

2. Occult Meditation

In this section, an overview of occult or Eastern Raja Yoga meditation method is given. Each of the five steps leads sequentially to the next. Keep these five steps in mind and endeavour to practise them in meditation and in the daily life.

> Now comes to all of you the most important series of lives to which the previous points of culmination were but stepping stones. In the lives immediately ahead of those upon the Path will come final achievement through the instrumentality of the ordered occult meditation, based on law. For some few may come attainment in this life or the next; for others, shortly in other lives. [1]

1. **Concentration**: this is the act of concentrating, focusing and quietening the mind.
2. **Meditation**: this is the prolonged focussing and steady holding of the mind on a desired idea, analysing and gathering information about that idea. The chosen idea is the "seed-thought".
3. **Contemplation**: this is the perceiving activity of the soul or higher wisdom when it is detached from the mind and the latter is in a state of quietness.
4. **Illumination**: this occurs towards the end of the meditation period when the mind sweeps into activity in an attempt to register the information streaming in from the soul.
5. **Inspiration**: conclusions and insights are grounded in the brain consciousness, inspiring students to follow the higher way and help others.

- Preparation
    a. Try to meditate in a quiet spot. The same spot used daily will build a shell of protection.
    b. Early morning is best time for meditation.
    c. Make your meditation space beautiful and fragrant. Use incense, flowers, a photograph or statue of an enlightened Master.
    d. Burn a candle, to purify the atmosphere.
    e. Sit comfortably, spine erect, on a chair or floor, hands gently clasped together in your lap. Balance your head comfortably on your neck, the chin slightly down and ensure there is no tension in your jaw or body. Breathe two or three breaths, relaxing as you out-breathe. The goal is to forget about your body during meditation.
    f. Eyes are normally closed, though may be opened slightly (looking downwards) to help stay alert.
    g. For beginners, fifteen minutes is ample time to meditate. The point is not how long you meditate, but whether the practice brings a certain state of mindfulness and presence. Five minutes of wakeful alertness is of far greater value than twenty minutes dozing.
    h. Deep meditation only occurs when the physical, emotional and lower mind bodies are quiet and at peace. It is very difficult to meditate when emotionally upset. Then, even if the physical body is comfortable and the emotional body serene, the mind is easily distracted. In Occult Meditation, the mind is being trained to be quiet when required and to think clearly when required. The "Basic Alignment" method is a good way to start meditation. It helps to bring the lower bodies under control.

- Basic Alignment
    a. Prepare for meditation.
    b. Go within. Disconnect attention from the outer world and focus high in the head. Hold focus there through the meditation.
    c. Purify and align the bodies
        Visualise the physical vehicle. Softly, breathe a purifying OM through it.
        Visualise the emotional vehicle. Softly, breathe a purifying OM through it.
        Visualise the mind body. Softly, breathe a purifying OM through it.
    d. Refocus in your head.
    e. Briefly, visualise your soul's presence above you, its radiance permeating the upper part of the body.
    f. Sound an OM, bringing your mind into alignment with the love and wisdom of the soul.

---
1 Bailey, Alice A. *Letters on Occult Meditation*, 12

Stage 1. Concentration

Average man does most things unconsciously. He eats unconsciously, drinks unconsciously and talks unconsciously. He is completely unaware of the afflictions (negative thoughts) rampaging through his mind, influencing everything that he does. Aspirants must learn to stay focused in the present moment. This starts with concentration.

Concentration is the power to focus the mind on a given subject and to hold it there as long as desired. The mind's true function is to be an intermediary between the soul and brain, to transmit to the brain that which the soul has become aware of. This starts with concentration.

The best way to harness the mind's attention is to become really interested and focused on whatever is being done in the moment. This will make the mind one-pointed. Avoid daydreaming and that half-alert state of mind when the mind is allowed to drift. In daily life, focus steadily on what you are doing and saying.

Recommended meditation format

There are certain meditations such as observing the breath and mindfulness when walking, which quieten the mind as well as develop concentration. Practise these. Following a simple meditation format also helps concentration. A recommended meditation format is:

1. Preparation
2. Basic alignment
3. Establish a motive for doing the meditation, for instance "to alleviate suffering".
4. The Meditation
5. Dedicate all the positive energy generated in the meditation, to some high purpose.
6. Sound the Great Invocation.

- Use of the Sequential Thinking process in Analytical Meditation.

Analytical meditation is the investigative analysis of a seed thought. To avoid mind distraction, to keep the mind focused on the seed thought, use the sequential thinking technique.

Method: start by concentrating on the seed-thought. Then move your mind to the next thought that has arisen from the seed and concentrate on that. Then move your mind to the next thought that has arisen from the previous thought and concentrate on that. Move your mind forward like this in a sequential manner, concentrating intensely, linking the next thought with the previous thought. You are laying a pathway of thoughts, neatly strung together. Be alert as you come to the end of a thought and before you connect with the next thought. This is when the mind is most likely to try to resume its restless ramblings.

The following example of sequential thinking comes from Alice A. Bailey's "From Intellect to Intuition" page 330. It starts with the seed-thought "Thou God seest me."

> Thou God seest me.
> This God is the divine in me, the indwelling Christ, the soul.
> For long ages, this soul has perceived and observed me.
> Now for the first time I am in a position to see God.
> Until now, I have been negative to this divine Reality.
> The positive relation is becoming possible.
> But — this seems to involve the idea of duality.
> But I and God are one.
> I am God and have been all the time.
> Therefore I have been seen by my Self.
> I am that Self, That Self am I.

Using a topic you find interesting, practise the technique. In the beginning, it may help to write your thoughts down. If you take the time to train your mind to follow the sequential thinking method, it will greatly benefit your meditation work.

Another variation of this technique is useful when saying prayers or affirmations that you know well. Especially if your mind tends to drift elsewhere, while your mouth keeps reciting the words by rote. Concentrate on just one word at a time, as you move your mind along. This technique will help build a thoughtform making process that is intelligent, clear and concise.

Stage 2. Meditation

Meditation is extended concentration. The only difference is the time factor. The focussing and steady holding of the mind on any desired idea, analysing and gathering information about that idea, is meditation.

- Meditation with Seed

Method: commit the seed-thought to memory and close your eyes. Thoroughly investigate the seed idea, using the sequential thinking method. Then, after having amassed various thoughts and concepts and assembling them into order, synthesis and coherency, turn your attention upwards and prepare for contemplation.

Be alert always in meditation. Do not daydream or space out so that at the end of the meditation period you feel good but cannot remember what happened. If the mind wanders say "I am observing" and this will help restore concentration. Or, open your eyes slightly, looking downwards.

Another important point concerns the selection of a seed-thought. Only choose positive seed thoughts that are inspiring, uplifting and that connect you with sacred and holy energies.

Stage 3. Contemplation

A point will come in meditation, when you decide you have analysed the seed-thought enough in that meditation period. Then, when

> ... the mind .. positive, alert and well-controlled .. held steady at the highest attainable point .. in a waiting attitude, whilst the consciousness of the thinker shifts into a new state of awareness and he becomes identified with the true inner and spiritual man. [1]

> [Then the Soul contemplates] .. The human consciousness ceases its activity and the man becomes what he is in reality — a soul, a fragment of divinity, conscious of its essential oneness with Deity. [2]

A definition for contemplation is the intuitive apprehension of realisations that one knows are true.

> through the part, the Whole is contacted and an expansion of consciousness takes place, involving bliss or joy. Beatitude always follows upon realisation of the unity of the part with the Whole. [3]

Method: having completed meditation, imagine you are going beyond mind into the contemplative stage. Attempt to visualise and feel with your mind. Open your consciousness for Divine inspiration. Expect a soul inspired thought or symbol to drop into your consciousness. This may not happen at once but persevere and it will. Keep this period brief to avoid spacing out.

Stage 4. Illumination or Samadhi

> I would define illumination as an overwhelming sense of oneness with The Whole. [4]

Towards the end of the contemplation stage, when successful, there is a synthetic flash of understanding or illumination. With the contemplative stage at an end, the soul endeavours to impress its wisdom upon the mind, which then sweeps into activity to register information streaming in from the soul.

Method: recall any insights, summarise and ground them in your memory.

At first, illumination received and absorbed will only be brief. A flash of intuitive perception and then all is gone. The vision is lost. But with persistence, the doorway will gradually remain open longer, with subsequence illumination and upliftment of consciousness.

Stage 5. Inspiration

Successful occult meditation results in a life inspired by higher spiritual ideals.

Method: incorporate the gains of meditation into daily life.

---

1 Bailey, Alice A. From Intellect to Intuition, 135
2 Ibid, 137
3 Bailey, Alice A. Light of the Soul, 34
4 Bailey, Alice A. From Intellect to Intuition, 153

3. Dangers of Meditation

Take care when meditating. The activity takes place takes place on the Mental Plane and the energies of that plane are fast and of a high vibration. Flooding the unaccustomed system with this "fire" is dangerous.

1. A common problem is over-stimulation of the nervous system. Early signs are excitability, an inability to relax, increased irritability, twitching, depression and low vitality. In the early stages, keep meditation under 15 minutes to avoid this problem.
2. Raising kundalini fire. Violent meditation or focusing on the chakras to stimulate progress may cause kundalini fire to rise too soon. If so, body tissue damage will impede occult work for several lives.

    > When meditation is forced, or is pursued too violently, before the alignment between the higher and lower bodies via the emotional is completed, this fire may act on the fire latent at the base of the spine (that fire called kundalini) and may cause it to circulate too early. This will produce disruption and destruction instead of vivification and stimulation of the higher centres. [1]

3. The atrophying of the emotional or physical body. Selfishness accompanied with a too intense mental focus can atrophy the emotional body so that there is no feeling or empathy for others. If the physical body is starved of energy because it is being poured into the emotional life, death could occur. If these problems occur, it results in a useless life for the soul. The remedy is to make mental aspiration factual on the Physical Plane.
4. Emotional and sexual overstimulation. Keep yourself alert. Do not space out, that is, wander vaguely in lower astral realms. Aim to maintain emotional balance and to be receptive only to spirit. Watch and guard the lower vehicles to ensure positivity is maintained. To ensure the sexual nature is not being overstimulated, avoid meditating immediately after sexual intercourse.

- To overcome problems

Stop meditating immediately. Take steps to strengthen the bodies: the physical body through exercise, sunshine and bathing the etheric body with violet light. Nourish the emotional body with inspirational music, beauty in nature and by thinking positive thoughts. Strengthen the mind with mental exercises and concentration. Do not meditate again until health is restored and the mind is alert, strong and able to focus. Observe the following points.

  a. Be clear about your limitations and your strengths.
  b. Proceed slowly and with caution.
  c. Study effects, realising that eternity is long and that which is slowly but soundly built, endures.
  d. Aim for regularity.
  e. Realise always that the true spiritual effects are seen in the exoteric life of service.
  f. Realise that psychic phenomena is a backward step and is not an indication of successful meditation.

4. Use of the Sacred Word "OM" and Great Invocation

The OM is part of the original sound of the Most High, which created the worlds. It is the sound or word of the soul. When correctly sounded, it attracts finer matter into the various fields, casts out that which is coarse and releases the soul from its entanglement with the world of glamour. It assists alignment with the soul and helps to hold the lower bodies steady.

To gain maximum benefit, sound the OM inaudibly within the head, then hear it reverberate there recognising that this sound is part of the original Sound of the Most High. The Sound is the name of the One in Whom we live and move and have our being and when it is the dominating note, the initiate is identifying with the Whole. [2]

- The Great Invocation

This is a potent invocation designed to bring about needed spiritual adjustments in humanity. Its evocative power is increasingly attracting the forces of Light, Love and spiritual Power into humanity. (Find the Invocation in the example meditation at the Full Moon).

---
1 Bailey, Alice A. Letters on Occult Meditation, 103
2 Gathered from AAB. The Rays and the Initiations, 52-53

5. Meditation at the Full Moon Period

At each full moon, the power of the Sun representing spirit overshadows the Moon, which represents the forces of evil. To take advantage of this, the Masters hold spiritual rituals to channel cosmic energies into the earth-space for planetary healing. Each astrology sign sends its own quality and vibration. Aries, Taurus and Gemini are the major festivals and build the divine qualities of Will, Love and Abstract Intelligence into the collective consciousness.

- The three major festivals

Festival in Aries: Easter, Festival of the Risen Christ. Keynote: "I come forth and from the plane of mind - I rule". In this festival, the forces of restoration flowing from the Mind of God stimulate the mind of man, inspiring him to initiate a new and higher World Order based on Christ's principles. These energies affect governments and politics in particular.

Festival in Taurus: Wesak, Festival of the Buddha. Keynote: "I see and when the eye is opened, all is light". Forces of enlightenment flowing from the Heart of God stimulate hearts and minds, urging man to develop a wiser understanding of all men and women.

Festival in Gemini: Goodwill Festival, World Invocation Day. Keynote: "I see my other self and in the waning of that self, I grow and glow". This is the festival of the Spirit of Humanity aspiring towards God. Christ, standing before the assembled Hierarchy and representing humanity, "preaches again .. the last sermon of the Buddha".[1] This invokes the forces of reconstruction and promotes world unity and peace.

- The nine minor festivals

Festival in Cancer: Keynote "I build a lighted house and therein dwell." This festival cleanses the collective mind of man of negativity, emotionalism and separativeness. See dark clouds of fear dissolving under spiritual force and the mind of man becoming radiant and translucent. Vision the one family of man.

Festival in Leo: Keynote "I am That and That am I." This festival helps to integrate the various nations and races into a unified whole and brings humanity under the influence of the Spiritual Hierarchy. See humanity respond to love flowing from the Hierarchy and will-to-good permeating political and power institutions.

Festival in Virgo: Keynote "I am the mother and the child, I God, I matter am." Virgo symbolises the birth of the Christ child (soul). This festival purifies the lower nature so that the beauty of the soul can shine through. See human consciousness evolving into Christ (group) consciousness.

Festival in Libra: Keynote "I choose the way which lies between the two great lines of force." This festival helps to restore balance in all departments of human life, but particularly in relations between people, groups and nations. See spiritual order and right human relations manifest throughout the world.

Festival in Scorpio: Keynote "Warrior I am and from the battle I emerge triumphant." This festival urges man to fight the dark side of his nature. See light destroying hatred, separativeness and cruelty in all human departments. See the human spirit soaring victoriously, like an eagle.

Festival in Sagittarius: Keynote "I see the goal, I reach that goal and then I see another." This festival inspires man to use his energies to reach for his ideals and to search for higher understanding. See humanity re-orienting itself towards higher ideals such as peace and goodwill.

Festival in Capricorn: Keynote "Lost am I in light supernal, yet on that light I turn my back." This festival urges man to give his resources and sacrifice his life for the greater good. See governments, power institutions and leaders, transformed by Spiritual Light and serving the needs of the masses.

Festival in Aquarius: Keynote "Water of life am I, poured forth for thirsty men." This festival promotes universal brotherhood and the urge to give where the need is greatest. See spiritual love and light wash away prejudice from the collective consciousness, stimulating cooperation between all nations.

Festival in Pisces: Keynote "I leave my Father's house and turning back, I save." This festival promotes an urge to help the suffering. See the collective consciousness imbued with Christ light, all suffering alleviated and humanity saved and light-filled.

---

1 Bailey, Alice A. *The Externalisation of the Hierarchy*, 480

Example: Solar Meditation at the time of the Scorpio Full Moon

1. Motivation

Our motive for doing this meditation, is to invoke the spiritual energies of
Scorpio and use them to increase Spiritual Light, love and power, on earth.

2. Alignment

- <u>Do the Basic Alignment</u>
- Say together, the Group Mantram:
    I am one with my group brothers and sisters and all that I have is theirs;
    May the love which is in my soul pour forth to them,
    May the strength which is in me lift and aid them,
    May the thoughts which my soul creates, reach and encourage them.
- Above the group, visualise the Star of Christ, the Spiritual Hierarchy.
    With an OM, send a line of light to the Hierarchy and to the Christ at the heart of Hierarchy.
    Extend this light to the Centre Where the Will of God is Known. OM.
    Take a few moments to stabilise the group energies to this higher vibration.

3. Higher Interlude (say the following, pausing between sentences where appropriate)

In the heavens, see the constellation Scorpio shining bright with its millions of stars; and from its heart, spiritual energy stream into our Sun - the 4th ray energy of Harmony through Conflict; and flowing on to earth via Mercury, reinforcing the 4th ray and via Mars, picking up the 6th Devotion and Idealism Ray. Meditate on the Scorpio seed-thought "Warrior am I and from the battle I emerge triumphant." See humanity rise up as a warrior, to fight against injustice.

4. Lower Interlude. Refocus as a group within Hierarchy ... silently affirm:

In the centre of all love I stand. From that centre, I the soul will outward move.
From that centre I, the one who serves will work.
May the love of the divine Self be shed abroad,
In my heart, through my group and throughout the world.

5. Distribution:

Seal this work by sounding the Great Invocation. Simultaneously visualise Light, Love and Power pour through the five planetary inlets (London, Darjeeling, New York, Geneva, Tokyo) irradiating the entire consciousness of the human race.

   THE GREAT INVOCATION

   From the point of Light within the Mind of God,
   Let Light stream forth into the minds of men,
   Let Light descend on earth.

   From the point of Love within the Heart of God,
   Let Love stream forth into the hearts of men,
   May Christ return to earth.

   From the centre where the Will of God is known,
   Let purpose guide the little wills of men,
   The purpose which the Masters know and serve.

   From the centre which we call the race of men,
   Let the Plan of Love and Light work out,
   And may it seal the door where evil dwells.

   Let Light and Love and Power restore the Plan on earth.

   OM ... OM ... OM

6. Creative Meditations and Affirmations

Esoteric Meditation, visualising beauty and sounding sacred mantrams serves to impress light, love and wisdom on the mindstream. By constantly impressing the mind with positive thoughts, consciousness transforms. The reason negative patterns are so hard to change is that they are repeated across lives, becoming powerful. They also infect millions of people and when we try to change other people may reinforce the ancient pattern. For a lasting effect, this work must be regular or the old habits will reassert themselves. Consciously invoking soul assistance enhances the effect. Start each meditation with the Basic Alignment, given in the Occult Meditation section.

1. Balance the Chakras

This is an exercise to tone up the seven major chakras, to bring them into right relation with each other and under the influence of the soul. Start from the base chakra and work down the list - working up the chakras. Choose one colour system to work with. The technique can also be used for the initial alignment prior to meditation.

Chakra	Option 1	Rays
base	red	red
sacral	orange	violet
solar plexus	yellow	pale blue
heart	green	indigo blue
throat	pale blue	green
brow	indigo blue	orange
crown	violet or white	red or white

Align with your soul. OM

From the level of the soul, look down at the base chakra.

1. Breathe in,
2. On the out-breath, sound an OM, sending an energy stream through the chakra.
3. Simultaneously, colour that stream a beautiful clear red, fading it out to pure white.
4. See the chakra healthy and vibrant.
5. Repeat for all other chakras and colours.

2. Meditation on Silence

When we quieten the restless chatter of the mind, the subtle messages of the soul can be heard.

Basic alignment.

1. Visualise you entering an ornate doorway in the heart of a busy and noisy city.
2. Immediately, you step into a far distant spiritual temple, located high on a sacred mountain. It is silent. The view before you is of mountaintops. There is no one else present. You sit in silent contemplation, looking at the view. Rejoicing in the silence, you listen to what silence sounds like.
3. Then you move your awareness inwards - imagining that you are moving ever deeper into the Spiritual Light and Silence within.
4. When you have completed the meditation, send a blessing of peace and goodwill to the world.

3. Advanced meditation to open the Heart

Do the Basic Alignment then link with the Monad, the "Greatest Light".

1. See a clear cool stream of spiritual love, flow from the Monad into the love petals of the egoic lotus, energising and opening them.
2. into the astral body, energising all astral matter; then briefly
3. into the solar plexus, purifying and energising it, then up to the heart centre.
4. See and feel the heart centre expand and radiate love through your whole being.
5. Radiate spiritual love to the world.

4. Master in the Heart Meditation

Basic alignment.

1. Focus in your heart centre and see within it, a golden lotus that is closed. (The heart centre is between the shoulder blades, outside the spine).
2. Silently sound OM. Simultaneously see the lotus slowly open and, in the centre, a radiating whirlpool of electric blue-golden light.
3. In the centre of that light, build a tiny replica of your Master in etheric, emotional and mental matter.
4. When the image is fully built, hear your Master sound an OM, which vibrates through all your fields. You feel wonderful.
5. Do all this very slowly, gradually, maintaining an attitude of perfect peace and calm.

5. Cutting Ties that Bind

Basic alignment.

1. See yourself sit in one half of a horizontal figure 8 force field, a band of circulating golden light.
2. See the person you wish to disconnect from (X), sitting in the other half of the figure 8. You are in the presence of X and yet you are not. The circulating yellow light separates you.
3. Speak kindly soul to soul; say all those things you need to say to bring the relationship to a final and spiritually clear end. Ask X for forgiveness for any karmic debts you have with him/ her. Offer forgiveness for any debts X has with you.
4. See X do the same for you.
5. Visualise the psychic ties that bind you to that person as ties of coloured light - from solar plexus to solar plexus and from sacral to sacral.
6. Silently say "I now cut the ties that bind us". See the psychic ties dissolve. Sound an OM to reinforce the work and white light washing through both your bodies, healing old wounds.
7. Say, "I now release you X, to continue your life journey and I now release myself to continue my life journey." Hear the other person say the same.
8. See the 8 dissolve into two separate circles and the person being carried away.
9. Give thanks for the healing you have received.

6. Building the antahkarana

Basic alignment.

1. Visualise the antahkarana already built, connecting your brain to your spiritual Triad. The primary colours are those of your Soul and Personality Rays if you know them. Otherwise, use indigo blue as the primary colour amongst all colours of the rainbow.
2. Breathe in. On the out-breath sound an OM. Direct the energy of the OM and the breath up the antahkarana to your spiritual Self. Colour that OM-stream with your soul ray colour or if unknown, indigo blue. Use the words of power for the soul ray, found in the Rays section.
3. See the antahkarana filled with light, connecting your mind with the soul and Monad. Do this daily.

8. Mantrams

a. "OM Mane Padme Hum"

Sound this sacred mantram daily. It means "the jewel in the lotus", or the spirit that resides within. It is "the most sacred of all the Eastern mantrams given out as yet.

b. The Gayatri

This is at widely used mantram that greets Deity and is a plea for enlightenment.

Oh Thou, Who givest sustenance to the universe.
From whom all things proceed,
to whom all things return.
Unveil to me the face of the true spiritual Sun,   Hidden by a disk of golden light.
That I may know the truth and do my whole duty, as I journey to Thy sacred feet.

c. Noon Mantram

O Lord of Light and Love,
I know about the need;
Touch my heart anew with love,
That I too may love and give.

d. 5pm Mantram

May the Power of the One Life
Pour through the group of all true servers;
May the love of the One Soul,
Characterise the lives of all
Who seek to aid the great ones.
May I fulfil my part in the one work,
Through self-forgetfulness,
Harmlessness, and right speech.

d. Group Bonding

I am one with my group brothers and sisters,
And all that I have is theirs;
May the love which is in my soul
pour forth to them,
May the strength which is in me
lift and aid them,
May the thoughts which my soul creates
Reach and encourage them.

2. THE PRACTISE OF RIGHT DETACHMENT

The Wisdom Teachings tell us that we are beings in this world, but not of it. We are dual. We have a spiritual Self and a lower self. Previous chapters have described the way the personality distorts reality and lives in self-deception. Karmically, this brings suffering. All unenlightened beings live in suffering to some degree.

The vital task for all those on the Path is to free the mind so that it lives in truth. This takes considerable effort, consistency and the application of the scientific process of detachment. Success brings the cessation of suffering and a mind that dwells in peace, joy and bliss. The Buddha stated this simply in The Four Noble Truths.

1. The Four Noble Truths

a. The world is full of suffering. Old age, sickness and death, separation from a loved one, vainly struggling to satisfy one's needs, is suffering. Life that is not free from desire and passion always involves pain.

b. The cause of suffering is attachment to our human passions and thirsts. These are rooted in the desires of the physical body and instincts.

c. Suffering is overcome by detaching from lower desire. If these desires that lie at the root of all human passion are removed, then passion dies out and human suffering ends.

d. Success results in happiness, cessation of pain and release from the Wheel of Rebirth.

To start this process, we must learn to observe the way the negative patterns operate within us and accept what we see without shame and judgement. We are facing an extremely sensitive and reactive part of our nature. Few people can do this, but for those committed to the path of Self-Realisation, there is no other way.

Do the Basic Meditation Alignment, emphasising your alignment with the soul and send while light through your fields. Affirm to yourself that the soul is guiding and assisting you through this process. Briefly recall an incident that disturbed you and how you reacted in that situation. Then as an impartial observer, review your reaction. The point of the exercise and the goal - is to remain impartial and avoid being an active participant; that is, losing your detached point of view and be sucked back into the drama. As you practise, do not try to change what you did, do not judge or criticise. Just observe as if you are witnessing someone else in action. In the beginning, it is difficult to acquire a neutral attitude, but this is the goal. Until we adopt an attitude of indifference, we cannot see ourselves as we really are or change things.

Apply the technique in daily life as negative patterns arise. If someone is trying to hurt you with words, just observe what is going on inside you. Do not search for reasons or respond, simply observe. Do you have fears? Simply name them and observe how they start and fade. Are you emotional? Name the emotion, which will focus attention in the mind and bring about a certain detachment from the emotion. As you apply the technique, you will notice that you will begin to stop automatically identifying with your emotional states or thoughts. You will see that emotional upheavals are only the result of unhappy or angry thoughts. You will start to feel release from the constant dramas of your lower nature and joy will begin to enter.

2. Practise this Simple Detachment Meditation

a. In your mind's eye, observe your physical body. Sound the OM through it as you silently affirm, "I have a body but I am not my body".

b. Observe your emotional body. Sound the OM through it as you silently affirm, "I have emotions but I am not those emotions." Feel emotional peace.

c. Observe your mental body. Sound the OM through it as you silently affirm, "I have thoughts but I am not those thoughts." Feel mental stillness.

d. Affirm "I am that Self, the Soul."

3. Detachment from the mental nature

The emotional world is like the ocean and the mind is like the atmosphere above. Any motion in one affects the other. Men move in the direction of their thoughts. If thoughts are greedy, a person becomes greedier. An impure mind surrounds itself with impure things, a pure mind with pure things. Once we have begun emotional purification, extending this to the mental level is the next step.

Do not let your mind run free. Practise mind control. Select one area to start with, perhaps sexual imaginings, or angry thoughts. Every time you find your mind starting to think those thoughts, think an opposite, positive or healthier thought.

Make a castle of your mind. Decorate it with thoughts that are good, beautiful and true. Fiercely guard your mind and protect it against evil or coarse thoughts.

Take responsibility for the consequences of your actions. An empowered person does not act like a victim and blame others. Do not make choices based on fear. Choose to be a student of life.

Train yourself to think only good about others, even in the face of adversity, temptation and abuse. Choose words with care, for you will affect people by what you say - for good or ill. Never speak ill of others. Speak truth with harmlessness and kindness.

Energy follows thought. Constantly visualise your mind as being soul illumined and your thoughts loving, generous and kind.

4. Think an "opposite" thought

"As a man thinketh so is he." A person becomes whatever dominates his thought life. Raja Yoga creator, Patanjali, recommended many ways to correct wrong thinking and quiet the constant restlessness of mind. One of the most important techniques is to replace a negative thought with an opposite positive thought.

For example: "hate" - opposite positive thought "love"; "fear' - opposite thought "confidence".

Another version is to use the same image and / or affirmation in every circumstance. Use the 2nd ray image of the sun and Words of power "I see the greatest light". Lift the consciousness high, visualise the sun and sound the words. Finish with an OM.

5. Creative Visualisation

Another valuable technique that will become more popular in the future is creative visualisation.

> The capacity.. to act "as if", holds the solution to the problem. By the use of the creative imagination, the bridge between the lower aspect and higher can be built and constructed. "As a man thinketh, hopeth and willeth" so is he. [1]

6. Other things to do to support this process:

a. Practise sympathy, tenderness, steadiness of purpose; dispassion towards pleasure or pain, to all forms of good or evil.
b. Meditate on Light and Radiance.
c. Purify the lower nature and stop indulging the lower desires. This will stabilize the mind stuff.
d. Maintain perfect discrimination. This will free you from bondage to the mind.
e. Continually flood your emotional body with beauty - of nature, art, classical music, the wisdom teachings, etc.
f. Practise selflessness and harmlessness.
g. Enter into stillness.

---

1 Bailey, Alice A. Esoteric Psychology II, 428

3. THE MASTERS AND SERVICE

At the end of it all, our higher spiritual task is to develop our talents, expand our consciousness and find our way to our soul ashram and into the service of the Master of that ashram.

1. The Masters train students to be Esotericists

The Master's prepare their students for this work. They are esotericists and train their disciples to live a life that is in tune with the inner sacred realities and to use their energies to manifest the Divine Plan of Goodwill. The Masters are light-bearers (carriers of wisdom, truth and love) and are training their disciples to become light-bearers as well. To become an esotericist or light-bearer, students must step from the mystical world into the thinking world of the occultist and of energies.

- Mystics walk the Path of Love

Mysticism is a normal and natural stage in man's evolution. Mystics concentrate on the subjective and sometimes overlook the value of the outer life. A sense of duality distinguishes them. They concentrate on God, their Master or saint "without". Such Lovers of God feel, sense, love and adore. Sometimes the desire to be one with God is so intense, they become delusionary and impractical dreamers, useless to themselves and others. They pour all their energies into the astral field, into yearning for the "beloved" and the physical body suffers. Mystics must become occultists. They must learn to value the form and bring the whole nature under rule. They must work on the mental body, study life intelligently and become knowledgeable and informed.

- Occultists walk the Path of Mind

The words *occultist* and *esotericist* are used inter-changeably in the sense that they both refer to the intelligent use and manipulation of energies that lie beyond the normal range of human comprehension. Would-be esotericists need to learn to work with the powers of the mind, this is the instrument of energy manipulation that is of concern. With the mind alive, in their search for understanding, occultists analyse and study each level of nature. Exhausting each topic, they go to a deeper level, layer after layer, body after body. They meditate upon form until the form is lost sight of and the creator of the form is all that is seen.

Occultists are powerful and effective people and they know it. The dangers that may befall them are pride, selfishness and using force for personal gain. To achieve a balanced state, occultists should first be mystics and then occultists, balancing the mind and heart.

In this work, occultists / esotericists must become sensitive to and understand the nature of those energies seeking to condition and work through them. They must discard those energies that are harmful and work with those of the soul. By walking the Occult Path intelligently, students can become effective workers in the ranks of the White Brotherhood, the Spiritual Hierarchy.

2. Stages of the Master-Pupil Relationship [1]

Past karma, old association, a student's ray and the need of the hour; this governs the choice of a pupil by a Master. Entry into the Master's ashram hastens if the student has needed skills. The Master's attention is drawn to the student by the brilliance of the indwelling light. When the bodies are sufficiently refined, the aura a certain hue, the vibration raised and the life sounds an occult note it attracts the Master's attention.

The Master makes a small image of the probationer composed of emotional and mental matter that shows all the fluctuations of the nature. The Master works with the image to stimulate the pupil's bodies. For instance, applying a higher vibration to step up the student's vibration in readiness for the 1st initiation and gradually to the vibration of the Master. This takes place mostly at night when the student is out of the physical body, or during meditation. Other concerns of the Master are to expand the consciousness of the pupil, vivify the centres and their correct awakening and develop the capacity of the pupil to work in group formation.

---

[1] Gathered from AAB. Letters on Occult Meditation, 278

Finally comes a time when on inspection of the image, the Master sees that the needed rate of vibration is held, the required eliminations have been made and a certain depth of colour has been attained. Then he takes the risk and admits the probationer into his aura. Consequently, the disciple becomes an "accepted disciple".

3. Students should follow the Rules of the Road

The Road is trodden in the full light of day, thrown upon the Path by Those Who know and lead. Naught can then be hidden and at each turn upon that Road a man must face himself.

Upon the Road the hidden stands revealed. Each sees and knows the villainy of each. And yet there is, with that great revelation, no turning back, no spurning of each other, no shakiness upon the Road. The Road goes forward into day.

Upon the Road one wanders not alone. There is no rush, no hurry. And yet there is no time to lose. Each pilgrim, knowing this, presses his footsteps forward and finds himself surrounded by his fellow men. Some move ahead; he follows after. Some move behind; he sets the pace. He travels not alone.

Three things the Pilgrim must avoid. The wearing of a hood, a veil which hides his face from others; the carrying of a water pot which only holds enough for his own wants; the shouldering of a staff without a crook to hold. Each pilgrim on the Road must carry with him what he needs: a pot of fire, to warm his fellow-men; a lamp, to cast its rays upon his heart and shew his fellowmen the nature of his hidden life; a purse of gold, which he scatters not upon the Road, but shares with others; a sealed vase, wherein he carries all his aspiration to cast before the feet of Him Who waits to greet him at the gate - a sealed vase.

The Pilgrim, as he walks upon the Road, must have the open ear, the giving hand, the silent tongue, the chastened heart, the golden voice, the rapid foot and the open eye which sees the light. He knows he travels not alone. [1]

4. It all ends with Service

True service is a spontaneous heart-felt response with no thought of personal gain.

Disciples evolve into true servers by firstly doing the inner work. They use the physical body wisely to avoid ill health, so as to be available for the Master's work. Cultivating emotional stability and serenity, they have a sense of secure dependence on Divine law. Training the mind to function scientifically, they equip it with information, knowledge and facts. Simultaneously they cultivate the qualities of selflessness, harmlessness and right speech.

Then, skilled and prepared, discriminating, intelligent and accurate, they step forward to meet the need of the moment. True servers understand the need in the world and channel all resources to meet that need. Finding their niche in the general scheme, they use their capabilities to fill that niche. Adaptable, they step up into a higher position or aside, if someone better equipped comes along, to ensure that need is met in the best way possible. They are dispassionate and self-forgetful, do not waste time looking backwards in regret; but steadily press forward to the accomplishment of the next duty. The ultimate sacrifice and act of love is service to alleviate suffering. To this task all True Servers are called.

> **Once we expand our consciousness from ignorance to enlightenment and gain entry into the 5th Kingdom of Souls, service is our task. In this we follow in the footsteps of the Great Ones.**
>
> **The One Central Life is in service and sacrifice to all lives in the universe so that they find liberation from the trammels of matter.**
>
> **Similarly, the Solar Logos and Heavenly Men are in service, to all lives in all kingdoms within their sphere.**
>
> **Lord Maitreya the Christ, all the ascended Masters, Deva Lords, the 5th Kingdom, all deva workers and countless others, are in service to man as he seeks spiritual liberation.**
>
> **Our great test, but also ultimately our greatest joy, is to serve in return, to give compassionately and willingly to all who suffer.**
>
> **On the note of service, I draw this book - the Journey of the Soul, to a conclusion. I hope it has been useful for you.**
>
> **Leoni Hodgson for the Master**

---

[1] Bailey, Alice A. Discipleship in the New Age I, 583-4

A FEW FINAL WORDS FROM THE TIBETAN MASTER DJWHAL KHUL

That the Angel of the Presence may make His nearness felt and inspire you to pass courageously through the fires of the burning ground is my earnest prayer; that the fact of the Presence may be sensed by you and lead you to greater activity - once the burning ground is passed - is my deepest wish for you; and that the light may shine upon your way and bring a certain and assured consummation of all the travail and struggle which has characterised your way of life is my heart's desire for you. To more active and steady enterprise I call you. The Tibetan. [1]

---

[1] Bailey, Alice A. *Glamour: A World Problem*, 271-272

APPENDIX

1. GLOSSARY

Agni	The Lord of Fire in the Vedas, the oldest and most revered of the Gods in India.
Agnishvattas	Fire Angels - as of Agni. Deva Lords of Flame or Solar Angels
Antahkarana	A bridge of mental essence between the higher and lower minds, which serves as a medium of communication between the two. When the higher reach of this bridge is constructed, man has access to his spiritual nature (the Spiritual Triad) and is aware as a spiritual man.
Arhat	One who has taken the 4th initiation and renounced the personal life for the larger whole; who is freed from the lower worlds and aligned directly with the Monad.
Asc	The ascendant in astrology. It forms the cusp of the first house.
Ashram	A spiritual group or centre, to which the Master gathers his students for personal instruction.
Aspirants	Those who are beginning to tire of material life, who aspire to a higher and finer life and who have reached the portals of the Path of Spiritual Development.
Atlantis	The continent that was submerged in the Atlantic ocean, according to occult teaching. Atlantis was the home of the Fourth Root Race, the Atlanteans.
Atma	Universal Spirit, the seventh Principle, or aspect of truth to be developed by man.
Atomic Subplane	Matter of the solar system is divided into seven planes. The highest subplane of each seventh plane, is called the atomic subplane. On the atomic subplane of the Atmic, Buddhic, Mental, Astral and Physical Planes, man's permanent atoms are located.
Aura	A subtle invisible essence or fluid which emanates from all living things.
Bodhisattva	See Christ. Bodhisattvas need one more incarnation to become a perfect Buddha.
Buddha	A Buddha is one who is enlightened (to the Monadic level in esoteric terms) and has attained the highest degree of knowledge and wisdom possible for man in this solar system. The term is commonly applied to Gautama Buddha, born in India about B.C. 621.
Buddhi	Buddhi is a synonym for the intuition.[1] The Universal Soul aspect in man. It is pure, all knowing consciousness, the Sixth Principle as Atma or Spirit is the Seventh Principle.
Cadent houses	These are the 3rd, 6th, 9th and 12th houses. They are related more so to the Mental Plane, to the mind, and planets located in them are not considered strong physically. The 6th and 12th being related to health, any planets located here warn of potential health trouble.
Causal Body	See Egoic Lotus
Chohan	Lord, Master, a Chief. Those Adepts who have gone on and taken the 6th initiation.
Christ	Christ and Bodhisattva are synonymous terms for the office of World Teacher, which is at present occupied by Lord Maitreya - the Christ. He is the Head of all the religions of the world, the Master of all Masters and of the angels.
Deva (Angel)	The deva life stream runs parallel with the Human life stream. The higher devas are called celestial beings, angels, or Greater Builders. The lower unconscious devas are the elementals of substance in all kingdoms and are called Lesser or Lunar Builders, fairies and goblins. There are many grades of semi-intelligent devas between these two extremes.

---

1 Gathered from AAB. Discipleship in the New Age I, 69

Disciple	One who is pledged to a Master and to co-operate with the plan of the Great Ones as best he may. The personal task is to take initiation and become enlightened
Dhyan Chohans	*Dhyana*: Sanskrit, meditation. *Chohan*: Tibetan, lord. Lords of Meditation.
Ego	The Thinker. A capital "E" (Ego), signifies a higher thinker such as the soul or spirit. A small "e" (ego) signifies the thinking personality or lower self.
Egoic Lotus	The Causal Body. It is the centre of human or soul consciousness and is formed from the conjunction of buddhic and manasic essence. All knowledge and wisdom accumulated throughout a series of incarnations is stored in the lotus. It shatters at the 4th initiation when man is spiritually aware.
Elementals	Lower devas, the unconscious creatures of the four kingdoms, the elementals of Earth, Air, Fire and Water. They build and are the bodies. For instance, man's physical body is built by physical elementals from physical deva substance and it is called the physical elemental. The same applies for the other bodies.
Enlightenment	Generally, to infuse consciousness with love and wisdom. In Bailey's work, enlightenment is associated with the 3rd initiation of Transfiguration, symbolised by Jesus on the mountaintop when he was flooded with spiritual light. In Buddhism, it seems to equal Monadic awareness, or esoterically, the 6th Initiation.
Esoteric	The words "esoteric" and "occult" signify "that which is hidden". They indicate that which lies behind the outer form, the causes which produce appearance and effects. They refer to the subtler world of energies. Esotericism is the scientific study and intelligent use of energies. An esotericist uses energies intelligently.
Etheric body	(Etheric double or web.) Man's physical body has two parts. The dense physical body, formed of matter of the lowest three subplanes of the Physical Plane and the etheric body formed of the four higher etheric subplanes of the Physical Plane. The etheric body is the blueprint for the physical and it receives and distributes energy.
Fohat	Primordial light. The name given to cosmic electricity or fire, the synthesis of the many forms of electrical phenomena. It is the universal propelling force that drives all lives along their various paths in the universe, the ceaseless destructive and formative power.
Glamour	A psychology problem affecting the emotional: reality is distorted because of emotional bias
God	That sumtotal of manifestation which can be called Nature, or God and which is the aggregate of all the states of consciousness.
Guru	A Teacher of Master in metaphysical and ethical doctrines.
Hierarchy	Myriad groups of lives, both high and intelligent, semi-intelligent, or low and unconscious. Each hierarchy cooperates with other hierarchies to control the evolutionary processes. The Spiritual Hierarchy on earth is formed of Chohans, adepts and initiates, working through their disciples in the world. Christ is the head of this hierarchy.
Holy Grail	The object of evolution in the human family is to bring Christ force into full manifestation upon the physical plane through his lower three bodies. "This triple sheath is the Holy Grail, the cup which is the receiver and container of the life of God." [1]
Illusion	A psychology problem affecting intellectuals. Reality is distorted because of lower mind bias
Initiate	Higher than a disciple in consciousness, but beneath an Arhat and Master. One in whom soul and personality have fused and who rules the human worlds. He is a spiritual man, a blend of scientific and religious training, who is guided by the Monad.
Initiation	The Path of Initiation is the final stages of the path of evolution trodden by man. Initiations are expansions of consciousness. Each initiation enables an individual to function consciously on a higher level than before and to express a greater proportion of wisdom.
Kalpa	In Hindu and Buddhist tradition, an immense period, reckoned as 4,320 million human years and considered to be the length of a single cycle of the cosmos (or 'day of Brahma') from creation to dissolution.

---

[1] Bailey, Alice A. *Light of the Soul*, 227

Karma	The law of cause and effect. It is the power that controls the behaviour of all things.
Kumaras	The seven highest self-conscious beings in the solar system. They manifest through the medium of a planetary scheme in the same way as a human being manifests through the physical body. They are the sum-total of intelligence and of wisdom.
Kundalini	The power of Life. One of the forces of nature. It is centred in the base chakra and rises up the spine when man connects consciously with his spiritual nature.
Lemuria	The name given to a continent that, according to Blavatsky's *The Secret Doctrine*, preceded Atlantis. It was the home of the third root race.
Light	"Divinity is .. radiance and pure white light". [1] In the Bible Christ said "I am the Light of the World". [2] "From light to light we pass, from revelation to revelation until we pass out of the realm of light into the realm of life which is, as yet to us, pure darkness." [3] These lights are varied: 1. The light of matter itself, found in every atom of substance. 2. The light of the vital or etheric vehicle. 3. The light of the instinct. 4. The light of the intellect or the light of knowledge. 5. The light of the soul. 6. The light of the intuition. 7. The light of Divinity.
Logos	Gk: "word", in Greek and Hebrew metaphysics, the unifying principle of the world linking God and man. Theology: the divine word or reason incarnate. The divine Life behind the Sun is called the solar Logos. Plural: Logoi.
Macrocosm	That which is larger than the microcosm. Can be applied flexibly. Generally, applies to the universe in relation to the contents of the universe. Or the solar Logos and solar system in relation to earth and man. Similarly, God or the Monad is the macrocosm for man, the microcosm.
Manas	Or manasic principle. Literally the mind, the mental faculty. The individualising principle that enables man to know that he exists, feels and knows.
Mantrams	A set of words or syllables rhythmically arranged so that when sounded, a vibration of a certain note is generated.
Manu	Sanskrit: man. Name of the great Being Who is Ruler and primal progenitor of the human race.
Manvantara	A great period of activity as opposed to a period of rest (pralaya).
Master	One who has taken five initiations and is master over the five lower planes of the system. Through meditation and service, he has expanded his consciousness to include the plane of spirit.
Maya	Sanskrit: *illusion*. Physical Plane activity directed by the deluded mind or glamoured emotions.
MC	The midheaven, medium-coeli, or highest point of the chart. It represents our professional life, our highest life goals, status, power and rulership.
Monad	The One. It often means the unified triad—Atma, Buddhi, Manas. It is that part of man that reincarnates through the lower kingdoms to man and thence through the higher kingdoms back to the Source of Life.
Mystic	One who senses divine realities from the heights of aspiration. Who contacts the mystical vision through prayer, adoration and worship, then longs ceaselessly for the constant repetition of the achieved ecstatic state. The mystic must eventually become an occultist.
NGWS	The New Group of World Servers. All men and women who reach a certain level of harmlessness and who are selflessly serving humanity, are spiritually linked to this group. The distinguishing feature of all members is an attitude of goodwill.

---

[1] Bailey, Alice A. From Bethlehem to Calvary, 55
[2] Bible, John 8:12
[3] Bailey, Alice A. Glamour: A World Problem, 205

	Every man and woman who is working to heal the breaches between people, evoke the sense of brotherliness, foster the sense of mutual inter-relation and who sees no racial, national or religious barriers, is a member of the NGWS. These people belong to all parties, religions and races on earth.
Occult	"This term concerns the hidden forces of being and those springs of conduct which produce the objective manifestation". [1] This is the world of energies. Occultism is the manipulation of energies. Occultists are concerned with the manipulation of those energies and forces which all outer forms veil and hide. The Occult Path is the path of mind the manipulation energies.
OM	A sacred word, sound or vibration. The word of the 2nd aspect, of the soul.
Permanent atom	There are five, one on each of the five planes of human evolution. The Monad appropriates them for the purposes of manifestation. Around them the various sheaths or bodies are built. They are small force centres in a sense carry the "DNA" of a person's bodies from life to life.
Planetary Logos	The highest planetary spirit working through any globe or planet.
Pralaya	The cosmic heaven of rest. A period of quiescence, commonly used to describe the periods between activity on various globes in a planetary scheme.
Prana	The Life Principle, the breath of Life.
Raja Yoga	The Royal Science of the Mind. Union with the divine through mind. It involves the exercise, regulation and concentration of thought.
Ray	One of the seven energy streams of force of the Logos.
Root Race	One of the seven races of man which evolve upon a planet during the great cycle of planetary existence. This cycle is called a world period. The Aryan root race is the fifth.
Shamballa	City of the Gods, sacred island in the Gobi Desert. The seat of world spiritual government, headed by Sanat Kumara.
Solar Angel	Also called the Lords of Flame. One of the great Hierarchies of spiritual beings who guide the solar system. They took control of the evolution of humanity upon this planet about 18 million years ago, during the middle of the Lemurian, or third root race. From their own essence, they planted the seed of intelligence in animal man - the great act of "individualisation". Through millions of years, they hover over the developing egoic lotus in the causal body, fanning the expanding solar fire. At man's 4th initiation they return to their source - the Sun.
Solar Logos	The ensouling life of the solar system.
Soul	The consciousness aspect in all living things. The human soul body (egoic lotus or causal body) is the storehouse of man's expanding soul knowledge, love and wisdom.
Triad	The expression of the Monad, the Spiritual Man: Atma - Buddhi - Manas.
Universal Mind	The collective hosts of the higher creative Dhyan Chohans. The divine intelligences charged with the supervision of the Kosmos.
Wesak	Buddha's birthday. A festival in the Himalayan Wesak Valley at the full moon of May attended by all members of the Hierarchy. Buddha is present for a brief period renewing his touch and association with the work of our planet.

---

1 Bailey, Alice A. A Treatise on White Magic, 10

2. SEVEN RAYS QUESTIONNAIRE AND CHARTS

Please be strictly honest in the sections where you are asked to look at your weaknesses. Everybody has these and if you are honest, it will make it easier to identify the ray and traits which imprison your soul. Otherwise, you deepen delusion. Select no more than two options in each section and only one if one is outstanding. Only the rays that are available to aspirants are presented. Disciples however can have their bodies on any rays.

1. Find the Soul Ray

A. What is your highest aspiration?

1. a. I aspire to be a leader that makes dynamic and effective changes for good.
   b. I aspire to liberate people from all forms of bondage and oppression, to free them from servitude.
2. a. I aspire to completely love, heal and include people, to save them from suffering so they are happy.
   b. I aspire to be completely wise and knowledgeable so I can teach people how to find their highest potential, avoid suffering and find enlightenment.
3. a. I aspire to use my mental agility and resourcefulness in intellectually challenging enterprises to solve pressing or unsolvable problems that impede the greater good.
   b. I aspire to arrive at Truth through the power of wide, deep thinking and careful reasoning.
4. a. I aspire for inner harmony and to bring harmony and peace to the lives of others.
   b. I aspire to use colour and art to create beauty, to beautify the lives of others, to bring them joy.
5. a. I aspire to use scientific research to solve problems and unlock the secrets of hidden mysteries.
   b. I aspire to invent technology that will greatly improve the quality of human life.
6. a. I aspire to strive towards my highest ideals, towards the right and true, with passion and fiery zeal.
   b. I aspire to serve my God or teacher with complete faith and utter devotion.
7. a. I aspire to bring order out of chaos through perfect organisation, to help people achieve their highest goals.
   b. I aspire to build forms that perfectly reflect spiritual archetypes, so that people can connect with spirit on earth.
   c. I aspire to manifest spiritual reality through ritual, metaphysical and magical practises.

   1st Choice ....   2nd Choice ....   Other ....

B. My greatest sense of the sacred is ....

1. Identification with the One Self, exhilaration at being in the presence of the might and power of Deity.
2. Being in the presence of Divine Love; or in the presence of omniscient wisdom.
3. Appreciating the Mind which created the Universe, the theories, proofs which explain the nature of things.
4. Being in the presence of true beauty and becoming beauty itself.
5. Contemplation of the wonderful and intelligent design of nature, the way things fit together.
6. Absolute and yearning adoration for the object of my devotion.
7. Forms or structures that perfectly reflect an aspect of the divine; or, reverence of the sacred rhythms of life which create perfect order throughout the universe.

   1st Choice ....   2nd Choice ....   Other ....

C. Soul vocations, careers that are deeply fulfilling

1. Any career which requires great will power, strength and stamina, the ability to stand firm in the face of obstruction, the ability to destroy and rebuild if required. Leader, manager, supervisor, politician, occultist, explorer, executive, manager and dictator. The armed forces and law and order.

2. Vocations that require wisdom, tact, foresight, personal magnetism, warmth and concern for others, which convey truth in simple terms (2b). Ambassador, psychotherapist, teacher, healer, educator, academic, sage, scholar and humanist.

3. Positions that use the broad and sweeping intellect, voice of reason and resourcefulness. Strategists, orators, higher mathematics, philosophy, theorist, metaphysician, cosmologist, communicator, interpreter, teaching people to think, business magnate, entrepreneur.

4. Vocations requiring spontaneity and the creation of some form of beauty and colour. Actor, artist, musician, writer, poet. Those, which bring unity, harmony, peace and at-one-ment. Mediator, diplomat, human resources, negotiator and counsellor.

5. Vocations requiring a keen intellect, accuracy with details, scientific and research skills. Scientist, electrician, engineer, analyst, data technician, operating surgeon, researcher, alchemist, inventor, technician, detective, psychologist, astrologer.

6. Vocations requiring devotion, dedication, idealism and unselfish service. Minister, mystic, missionary, devotee, preacher, orator, soldier, nurse, personal secretary, philanthropist, crusader, spiritual healer, religious server, caring services, spiritual warriors inspiring orator.

7. Vocations that bring order and structure, organising people and cities so there is greater flow and design. Initiating and grounding processes so human living can be conducted in greater harmony and rhythmic flow. Business person, organiser, judge, legal worker, architect, builder, administrator, designer, revolutionary, magician, esotericist, ritualist, Freemason.

   1st Choice .... 2nd Choice .... Other ....

D. Work/ profession you have been in/ done - in the past/ now?

Past employment ....

....

Current employment ....

What you would like to do ....

2. Find the Personality Ray

A. What major self-defeating pattern would you like to change or have already changed?

1. Wanting to control everyone and everything, arrogant, ruthless, destructive, hard, cruel, insensitive, bossy.

2. a. Too fearful, weak, non-assertive, playing the victim, over concerned with personal comfort, over protective, binding others through emotional blackmail so you won't be alone.

   b. Cold, indifferent, scorning mental limitation in others, over absorbed in study, isolating yourself in study/ books.

3. Uses superior intellect to manipulate, trick, play games, escape commitment. Being superficial, inaccurate, excessively busy.

4. Wildly fluctuating emotional highs and lows, continually agonising about life, the artistic temperament, fighting oneself and others.

5. Too judgmental, hypercritical, ultra-rational, too mental and unfeeling, rigid thought patterns, irreverent towards the beliefs of others.

6. Being fanatical, one-eyed, so intensely emotional the truth is distorted, continually putting people on pedestals then devastated when they fall, jealous, takes things too personally.

7. Too intolerant and concerned with appearances, rules and orders; being a perfectionist.

   1st Choice .... 2nd Choice .... Other ....

B. When you started "getting your act together" and gaining recognition, was it through ...

1. a. An increased and fearless ability to control, direct and lead
   b. Being highly independent with a clear, simple and synthetic approach to life, unafraid to be alone or stand alone if necessary.
2. a. Your magnetic attraction, being warm and likeable; healing talent.
   b. Because of a clear, quiet and simple approach to life and ability to teach.
3. a. Intellectual power and resourcefulness, mental accuracy, power to influence people, to change their minds by weaving ideas and thoughts.
   b. Indefatigable energy, ability to strategise and adapt.
4. Your fighting spirit and courage to confront people, to move forward until you win; or your artistic talent and ability to create beauty or harmony.
5. By becoming recognised as an expert in your field, able to master facts, figures and data.
6. Your unselfish devotion, enthusiasm, dedication and sacrificial service, to a higher cause, person or ideal.
7. Your team-playing ability and unfailing courtesy; your efficient organising skill that brings order to chaos; your ability to do things as if by magic.

   1st Choice ....   2nd Choice ....   Other ....

C. How does your personality crave attention and want others to see it?

1. As being strong and independent, to be left alone.
2. As being kind and loving or wise and knowledgeable.
3. As being brilliant and clever.
4. As being creative, delightful and entertaining.
5. As being knowledgeable and expert.
6. As being self-sacrificing, devoted and loyal.
7. As being well-organised, efficient; well-groomed and classy; skilled in ritual and working with magic.

   1st Choice ....   2nd Choice ....   Other ....

D. How do you fail to respond to that inner call to achieve something finer/ higher/ greater?

1. By being too proud of yourself/ life/ power/ position, independence, to obey it.
2. By being too timid, placid, fearful, comfort loving, to be stirred by it.
3. By being too busy, hyperactive, or preoccupied and therefore exhausted, to take time for it.
4. By being too worried, torn, fighting (inwardly or externally), or emotionally troubled to respond to it.
5. By being too sceptical, critical, scientific, irreverent, smug in being a rationalist, to be inspired by it.
6. By being too one-pointedly devoted to your own guru or exciting goals to change direction.
7. By being too self-satisfied with your personal habits, procedures and daily routines to reschedule your life for it.

   1st Choice ....   2nd Choice ....   Other ....

3. Find the Mind, Emotional and Physical Rays

A. How does your mind process information?

1. Your mind is fast, brief, synthetic, direct, easily grasping essentials. You are a person of few words, but blunt, going straight to the point. You can be verbally aggressive or assertive, can speak with power, can annihilate with words. You may punch the air with one finger to emphasise a point.

3. Does your mind process thoughts rapidly, think faster than others; draws ideas from all directions and then delivers these thoughts intelligently and coherently with speed and wordiness. (This ray is included for disciples)

4. Your mind is weaving, creative, colourful, intuitive and poetic. When at school, you could not think as quickly as other kids with more scientific minds, was not so good at maths. If you shone at all, it was because of your creativity. You have a mind that agonises, a contrary mind that shuttles back and forth between alternatives, a moody mind easily affected by the emotions. If pushed, you can be mentally or verbally aggressive, but are usually immediately sorry after an outburst. You tend to think in pictures and express thoughts better through art and writing, rather than through speech. You punctuate what you say with humour and colour and this enables you to communicate brilliantly if your mind is also intelligent and well organised and has overcome the previous mentioned vacillations.

5. You have a technical mind, logical, practical, scientific and you are good with facts and figures. You take pride in getting your facts right and like to look for the flaw in other people's arguments. You amass myriad facts in decision making and demand rational and verifiable answers from others. You can be cynical, irreverent, judgmental and a sceptic.

1st Choice .... 2nd Choice .... Other ....

B. Describe your emotional reactions

NB. Those on the Path are going through a process of emotional purification. If this is you, then think back to how you expressed yourself emotionally before you achieved balance.

1. Emotionally suppressed and isolated, fear of emotional attachment, super cold, super intense, emotional rigidity interspersed with powerful and overwhelming emotional expression and explosions. (This ray is included for disciples)

2. Emotionally quiet, inclusive, affectionate, serene, patient and nonreactive. But also, fearful, non-assertive, unable to say "no" appropriately, a victim. Slower to fall in love, but more selective and relationships are often smoother. Quietly uses emotional blackmail and guilt to get what it wants.

6. Emotionally fiery, enthusiastic and intense. Falls in love quickly and passionately and is devastated if rejected. However, when it's over, "it's over" and moves on quickly to the next pursuit. Wears rose - coloured glasses, full of idealism, devotion and is very loyal. Highly reactive, jealous, takes things too personally.

1st Choice .... 2nd Choice .... Other ....

C. Your physical body

3. Your body is strong, broad, stocky. Like a workhorse, you can work long hours without a break and without meals. Always on the go, your body is busy, restless and highly active. You probably excelled in and loved sports or other physical activities at some time in your life and you dance with vigour. Your brain is often busy with a jumble of things that need doing and happily does whatever it wants to.

7. You body is rather fine boned and more sensitive to impact than other types. It does better with an orderly routine - regular meal breaks, bedtime, exercise. It is graceful in dancing, glides when moving and hand movements are expressive and graceful. But it can also be tough, like a gymnast. Your brain tries to prioritise things which need to be done and is overwhelmed by disorder.

1st Choice .... 2nd Choice .... Other ....

Checklist for Soul Ray

	The Experience	Contribution	Soul-inspired aspiration	Heart's desire:	Vocations
1	A dynamic charge of spiritual will and power.	To strengthen and liberate people, to impel them to find the courage to "be".	To be a dynamic, powerful, benevolent leader; to free people from oppression.	To be the One and Only.	Leaders, managers, controllers, politics, armed forces, law.
2	a. An inflow of loving inclusiveness or b. An inflow of expansive wisdom.	To lovingly and wisely teach and help people to achieve their potential and become whole.	To develop an intuitive loving understanding of people. To help people achieve self-realisation and illumination.	To be in love with all - one with all. To live a quiet and simple life.	Health, education, religion. Study and dissemination of the Wisdom Teachings.
3	An inflow of creative, versatile and acute intelligence.	To stimulate the intellect and mental creativity of others. To solve unsolvable puzzles.	To create a philosophy explaining the truth of reality. To apply the intellectual powers to challenging enterprises	To plan along with God. To manifest the Plan.	Thinker, teacher, scientist, philosopher, philanthropist, business and finance.
4	An inflow of creative artistry. An urge to create beauty or to harmonise chaos.	To help others harmonise and resolve conflict. To beautify what was ugly. To fight for the higher good.	To harmonise every aspect of life. To express the exquisitely beautiful yet agonisingly painful drama of life in all its vibrancy.	To live in beauty forever and to become beauty itself.	Actors, artists, musicians, writers, entertainers, fighters for good, protectors of the weak, peace-makers
5	An inflow of crystal clear and logical thought that unravels life mysteries.	To discover new scientific truths and technology, that empowers man.	To find solutions to problems through advanced scientific research. An urge to reveal life's mysteries.	To know the truth as expressed through form.	Science, research, technology, finding the truth.
6	An inflow of dynamic idealism, or heart-felt devotion to a master or teaching.	To inspire people to devote their lives to their highest ideals. To serve and sacrifice the life for the beloved Teacher.	To surrender in complete faith, devotion, adoration to the highest guidance. Loyalty to the highest ideals.	To express the highest and most sacred ideals	Care and service industries, inspiring people to find their true Path or Teacher.
7	A dynamic surge of power and urge to bring order out of chaos, to manifest ideas in perfect form.	To help people manage and organise their lives so they realise their dreams.	To bring order out of chaos. To provide leadership and organisation skills in order to help people bring their lives into line with divine law.	To achieve perfection in form	Managers, designers, builders, architects, organisers. Ceremonialists, workers in magic.

Tick any boxes you relate to, then add up your score in each row.

Personality Ray Dynamics

	Nature of the ego	How the ego misses the call of the soul	How the ego limits expansion	Selfish demands of the ego	How the ego self-references
1	Proud, dominating, self-assured; too determined to do things entirely on its own, exactly as it chooses.	Preoccupied with bossing others around, getting its own way, protecting its power, place and position.	Refuse to accept the value of what others have to offer. Do things its way. Isolates itself.	Demands to be "number one." Is aloof and separative.	By exaggerating its importance, always self-referencing, taking charge noticeably.
2	Too weak, timid, fearful, accepting, tolerant, permissive, inclusive; too attached to its relationships and life comforts.	Preoccupied with personal comfort and attached to things that bring personal happiness. Giving-in to inertia.	Weak, too sensitive, lethargic, too fearful to seize the moment or upset others in case it is rejected.	Demands to be popular, loved, appreciated. Will compromise its integrity to this end.	By self-pitying, its suffering, the sacrifices it must make; or as being a wise and learned person
3	Too busy, active, critical, vague and impractical, devious, untruthful, manipulative and entangled	Preoccupation with a multitude of plans, scattered projects and extraneous activities	Through excessive changeability, disjointedness and busyness, lack of continuity.	Demands to be the cleverest and most astute. Uses its intelligence selfishly. It is separative	Pride in its superior mentality, to cleverly turn any situation to its advantage, skill in living, working hard.
4	Lacks self-control, too temperamental, inconsistent, unstable, emotional, filled with conflict, combative.	Preoccupied with one's personal dramas, crises and battles; mood swings and emotional suffering.	By repeatedly fighting and struggling with themselves and others.	Demands self-expression without discipline and ignoring social constraints.	By calling attention to its suffering, or to its artistic and entertaining talent.
5	Narrow exclusive focus on its own mental and technical interests at the expense of the larger picture.	Preoccupation with 'foreground' considerations.	By an overly mental, rationalistic approach to life.	Demands to examine all life experiences and other people's lives, with clinical objectivity.	By putting itself up as the expert who has all the facts and who knows more than anyone else.
6	Fanatical, extreme, emotional, rigid and narrow, too convinced of the rightness of its point of view.	Preoccupation with the "enthusiasm of the moment." Being too intensely "caught up"	Through narrowness of vision, rigidly held.	Demands the right to find and follow the "one true path" and insists that others follow the same path as well.	Claims to be one of the chosen and special one, following the true teacher, God, better than others.
7	Rigid and resistant to change, too caught up in externals, methods, rules; too locked into personal routines and habits.	Preoccupied with appearances or routines, too busy with mundane chores to hear the soul call.	By being superficial, too rigidly formal, its tendency to judge by appearances.	Demand that others note and follow its superior methods of work.	By doing things properly, by finding flaws in others, showing how perfect and proper it is, by being different.

Tick any boxes you relate to, then add up your score in each row.

Note that transformational work will bring out the positive qualities and if the soul ray is expressing, it will modify the personality ray. EG. R1 will strengthen it and R2 will soften a hard-line ray.

Checklist for Mind Ray
(From Tapestry of the Gods, Michael Robbins)

Ray One Mind	Ray Four Mind	Ray Five Mind	Ray Three Mind
The occult mind.	The intuitive mind	The scientific mind	The intellectual and philosophical mind
Fast, moves rapidly in a straight line, like an arrow seeking its mark.	Can be fast, but when making decision, oscillates, weighing things, before deciding.	Slow, careful and deliberate mind, moving step by step towards a conclusion.	Sinuous weaving motion, looping out then returning to the centre. Can be rapid.
Thoughts are clear cut, hard edged, sharp and trenchant.	Accuracy is often sacrificed for exaggeration and dramatic effect.	Highly accurate thoughts, sharply delineated. Avoids inaccuracy at all costs.	Clear, precise when dealing with abstract issues. Less accurate when dealing with details.
Firm, decisive, one-pointed, holds its point of view against all opponents. Can be rigid.	Indecisive mind constantly subject to change, holds its position with difficulty.	Firm mind that holds its position by giving "the facts", "the truth".	Can hold its position thru reasoned argument or manoeuvre into a more advantageous position.
Can be inflexible or jump rapidly to a new conclusion if it wills it to be so.	Flexible and pliable mind that gives way under strong impression, only to correct itself later.	Can be inflexible unless facts determine its position to be erroneous.	Most flexible mind that easily changes position.
Synthetic mind, decisive, arrives at conclusions quickly	Capable of synthesis and analysis. Indecisive, vacillating, oscillating, ambivalent	Specialist mind, minutely analytical, prolonged decision making to ensure the facts are correct	Highly analytical, weaving, dealing with too many threads can paralyse decision making.
Large minded, prefers to manage the larger picture than deal with details.	Dislikes having to deal with details unless related to the creation of beauty.	Thrives on dealing with detail.	Wide views, attentive to fine points but can ignore mundane details.
Brief, trenchant in speech. Straight to the point.	Can be direct or indirect. Likes to communicate thoughts through art or writing, colourful ideas and speech.	Proceeds cautiously to marshal evidence to prove the point. Sticks to the facts but goes on and on to explain them.	Most verbal of all the rays. Can be extremely indirect, avoiding clarity and directness when it wants to.
Can be abstract, intuitive, or concrete. A sensible realistic mind.	Intuitive, abstract, creative. Power to imagine, feel and create beauty. Sees in pictures and colour.	Most concrete mind interpreting literally what it sees, reasoning its way to a conclusion.	Highly creative mind, abstract and articulate. Highly rational, reasoning its way to conclusions.
Excellent organising, prioritising mind.	Not well ordered but has an ordered sense of colour and proportion.	Very orderly, logical, sequential mind.	Good at organising if it avoids complexity.
Makes assumptions without checking facts, can be aggressive.	Mind easily overwhelmed when emotional, vague and struggles to build clear thoughts.	Hyper-critical mind, narrow, too sure of its "rightness", can be rigid.	Devious, slippery, can entangle itself like a spider in a web.

Tick any boxes you relate to, then add up your score in each column.

Note that transformational work will bring out the positive qualities. Higher rays will modify the way the mind works. If the soul or personality rays are active, expect the mind to demonstrate their traits at times.

Checklist for Emotional and Physical Body Rays

Ray Two Emotional Field	Ray Six Emotional Field
Selfish, personal love, binds others through manipulation and by playing the helpless victim. Selfish unselfishness.	Selfish, personal love is coloured with burning desire, ardent pursuit of loved ones to possess them. Plays the martyr. Honesty and loyalty is important.
Emotional force is cooler, calm, patient, non-reactive. Easily overwhelmed by circumstances.	Emotional force is intense, hot, urgent, very reactive. Lacks emotional control under stress
Energy field is sensitive and NON-REACTIVE. Wide open (sometimes naive) and is not inclined to defend itself when under attack. Will try to resolve disputes by playing the victim or getting on people's good side. Mental types can be cold and non-reactive.	Energy field is very sensitive and REACTIVE. Is inclined to boil. Goes on the offensive or defensive when under attack. Will fight for its beliefs and will try to force these on others.
The ego desires calmness and luxuries in love affairs.	The ego desires fireworks and passion in love affairs.
When it wants something others have, it is more inclined to be accepting of the way it is or willing to share	When it wants something others have, it feels intensely jealous. Will go on the offensive to take the cherished object.
More impersonal - "ours", "us", "we".	More personal - "me", "mine", "my", "I".
More lucid view of reality because of a clearer and quieter emotional field	Tendency to illusion and glamour because intense attachments and hot feelings cloud judgment.
A naturally empathetic and compassion field, mixes easily with all types of people	Attracted to those who share the same ideals and beliefs, while rejecting those who do not.
More kind and forgiving	"Revenge is sweet"
Higher Ray 2: wise, understanding and mature in love. Serene, inclusive, walks in the shoes of others, compassionate.	Higher Ray 6: warm, stable love. Emotional control, aspires for spiritual purity and growth, inspires others with fiery oratory and by example, compassionate.

Ray Three Etheric-Physical Body	Ray Seven Etheric-Physical Body
STRONG and MUSCULAR body. (Unless there is a higher ray 7) not particularly graceful - plods along.	REFINED, GRACEFUL and delicate, glides while walking
Sports: muscular body tends to endurance and strength sports, body building, physical resilience.	Sports: can be strong, but more graceful frame tends to sports such as rhythmic gymnast, ballerina.
Great activity, a busy body, restless motion, dislikes long periods of inactivity. Ease of manipulating physical environment.	Graceful, well-ordered activity. Happier with quietness and stillness.
Not especially sensitive to pain	Sensitive to pain or the thought of pain
Physically casual: relatively inattentive to physical order and detail in the environment, can live in a mess, noise or clutter.	Physically more formal: attentive to physical order and detail in the environment, dislikes clutter and mess. Loves a serene environment.
Love of freedom and activity, resists physical disciplines or restrictions.	Body is easily trained and more obedient to rules.
Hands are strong and useful instruments.	Graceful hands and fingers, the hands often "dance" when owner is talking.
Rapid brain activity, voluble, many words spun out and if there is not a controlling centre - not particularly well coordinated.	Organises thoughts before speaking, more measured in speech and life. Excellent ritualist, in magical processes.

Tick any boxes you relate to, then add up your score in each column.
Note that transformational work will bring out the positive qualities and higher rays will modify them.

3. BIBLIOGRAPHY

Bailey, Alice. A. A Treatise on Cosmic Fire. Lucis Press, London, fifteenth printing 1999.

Bailey, Alice. A. Discipleship in the New Age I. Lucis Press, London, fifth printing 1979.

Bailey, Alice. A. Discipleship in the New Age II. Lucis Press, London, fifth printing 1979.

Bailey, Alice. A. Esoteric Astrology. Lucis Press, London, eighteenth printing 2016.

Bailey, Alice. A. Destiny of the Nations. Lucis Press, London, third printing 1968

Bailey, Alice. A. The Consciousness of an Atom. Lucis Press, London, seventh printing 1972.

Bailey, Alice. A. Esoteric Astrology. Lucis Press, London, eighteenth printing 2016.

Bailey, Alice A. Esoteric Healing. Lucis Press, London, eighth printing 1977.

Bailey, Alice A. Esoteric Psychology I. Lucis Press, London, ninth printing 1979

Bailey, Alice A. A Treatise on White Magic. Lucis Press, London, 10th printing 1970.

Bailey, Alice A. Education in the New Age. Lucis Press, London, sixth printing 1971.

Bailey, Alice A. Esoteric Psychology II. Lucis Press, London, eighth printing 1981.

Bailey, Alice A. Externalisation of the Hierarchy. Lucis Press, London, seventh printing 1982.

Bailey, Alice A. From Bethlehem to Calvary. Lucis Press, London, third printing 1968.

Bailey, Alice A. From Intellect to Intuition. Lucis Press, London, sixth printing 1965.

Bailey, Alice A. Glamour: A World Problem. Lucis Press, London, third printing 1967.

Bailey, Alice A. Initiation, Human and Solar. Lucis Press, London, sixth edition 1951.

Bailey, Alice A. Letters on Occult Meditation. Lucis Press, London, eleventh printing 1973.

Bailey, Alice A. Telepathy and the Etheric Vehicle,

Bailey, Alice A. The Rays and the Initiations. Lucis Press, London, third printing 1970.

Bailey, Alice A. The Soul and its Mechanism. Lucis Press, London, fifth printing 1971.

Bailey, Alice A. The Unfinished Autobiography. Lucis Press, London, third printing 1982.

Bailey, Alice A. Telepathy. Lucis Press, London, sixth printing 1971.

Blavatsky, Helena. P. The Secret Doctrine I and II. Theosophical University Press 1977.

Barborka, Geoffrey. The Divine Plan. Theosophical Publishing House, second edition, Adyar 1964.

Barker, Trevor. The Mahatma Letters to A. P. Sinnett. 1923.

Purucker, Geoffrey de; Occult Glossary. Theosophical University Press, second edition, 1996.

INDEX

Symbols

1 Charts
    Chart 7: Rays, Psychology, Disease 100
1 Charts and Tables
    astrology
        signs and planet rulers 111
    astrology charts - people
        Astrodatabank 4221 63
        Astrodatabank 14675 79
        Branson, Richard 70
        Carpenter, Karen 53
        Dali, Salvador 56
        Ferguson, Dennis 63
        Gaddafi, Muammar 56
        Hussein, Saddam 58
        Jones, Jim 58
        Jung, Carl 172
        Manson, Charles 58
        Mengele, Josef 60
        Obama, Barack 170–171
        Paisley, Ian 59
        Princess Diana 54
        Rader, Dennis 62
        Sade, Marquis de 61
        Sizemore, Chris 77
        Travolta, Jett 80
        Whitman, Charles 57
        Winehouse, Diana 54
    chakras, consciousness, disorders 73
    consciousness - Solar System 37
    monad, soul, body 26
    principles, races, rounds 10
    psychic powers 74
    psychology problems 51
    rays
        check lists 197–204
        initiations 39
    rays Tibetan's disciples 106
    Seven
        chakras 33
        cosmic planes 5
        creative hierarchies 15
        human principles 10
        planes of the solar system 6
        rays questionnaire 197–204
    spirit, soul, body 4
    spiritual hierarchy 17
1 Drawings
    consciousness moving 26
    Djwhal Khul 191
    earth scheme 8
    egoic lotus 27
    etheric web 31
    ida, pingala, sushumna 28
    ladder of life 14
    overview: spirit, soul, body 35, 203
    seven chakras 33, 72
    seven rays 83–84
    solar scheme 7
    soul, personality 102
    spirit, soul, personality 25
    three outpourings 7

A

ACLRI technique 87
Adi-Buddhi 14
Adrenals 33, 73
Agni 20, 193
AIDS 73
Ajna Chakra 32–33, 39, 42, 73, 80
Akasa 12
Akashic Record 12
Alimentary canal 73
Angelic Kingdom 19
Angel of the Presence 43, 136, 191
Angels 11, 15–17, 19–21, 26, 28, 35, 76, 193
Animal Kingdom 9, 14, **18**, 26, 35, 134
Annan, Kofi 99
Anorexia nervosa 53
Antahkarana 7, 30, 36, 38, 40, 128, 133, 134, 135, 158, 159, 160, 177
    building 185
    defined 28, 193
Anxiety 47, 164
Aquarian Age 17, 122
Aquarius 15, 42, 53–54, 58, 62, 95, 110, 117, **122**, 126–127, 130, 138, 138–139, 140, 142–146, 148–149, 151, 153, 155–156, 163, 163–165, 169–171, 174, 182
Aquinas, St Thomas 90
Archangel Michael 21
Archangels 4, 19, 21, 84
Arhat 44, 193
Aries 15, 55–56, 58–62, 80, 109–110, **112**, 128, 130–131, 137–138, 140, 142–143, 146–148, 152, 153, 155, 165, 168, 182
Aristotle 90
Arms 73
Army of the Voice 4, 19
Artemis 115
Arteries 73
Artley, Malvin 31

Aryan 11, 32, 64, 67, 155, 167, 196
    consciousness 32, 37, 64, 67, 75
    defined 36, 155
    race 11, 196
Ascendant 111, 127, 193
    and the 1st house 133
    in signs 140
    sign 111
Ashram 18, 87, 104, 134, 136, 160, 162, 189, 193
Aspirants **36**, 37, 39, 40, 168, 179, 193
    defined 36
Assagioli, Roberto 105
Astral 29
    body 30, 31, 48, 52, 86, 88, 90, 92, 94, 96, 98, 106, 185
    desire 29
    field 30, 32, 104, 189
    maniacs 48, 62
    nature 29, 59, 132, 135, 141, 147, 154
    plane 6–7, 12, 20, 27, 32, 36, 67, 73–77, 80, 96
        plane of illusion 36
    purification 165
    ray 101, 102
    realms 174, 181
    shadows 11
Astralism 77
Astrology
    crosses 109–110
    esoteric 109
    Esoteric (Ch. 5) **107–174**
    exoteric 109
    houses 133–140, 157–165
    readings 167–174
        houses 163–164
    signs 111–123, 137–156
Athena 123
Atlantean 193
    consciousness 32, 35, 37, 54, 64, 74, 77, 105, 115, 167
    rays 105
    Race 35
Atlantis 193
Atma 8, 10, 44, 193, 195–196
Atmic Plane 5–6, 12, 15, 27, 33, 85
Atomic Subplane 193
Aura 177, 189, 193
Autism 79–80
Autoimmune diseases 73
Aversion to life 76
Awakening the Centres 71

B

Baby boomers 55
Bacon, Sir Francis 99
Bailey, Alice A. vii, 18, 88
Baptism 39
Barborka, Geoffrey 9
Base Chakra 32, 33, 43, 71, 72, 73, 129, 132, 184, 195
Beethoven, Ludwig van 92
Berners-Lee, Tim 94
Bipolar 53
Birth 39
Bismarck, Otto von 86
Bladder 73
Blair, Tony 99
Blavatsky, Helena 3, 195
Bodhisattvas 14, 193
Bohr, Niels 94
Bones 73
Borderline personality disorder 53
Borgia, Lucrezia 90
Bowel 73
Branson, Richard 70
Breasts 73
Breathing 73
Bronchial tree 73
Buddha vii, 17, 88, 193
　birthday - Wesak 182, 196
　noble truths 187
　teachings 49
Buddhi 10, 25, 26, 44
　defined 6, 193
Buddhic Plane 5–6, 12, 19, 27, 28, 30, 32, 38, 73
Buddhism 49
Buddhists vii, 50
Bulimia 53–54
Burning ground, greater 42, 153
Burns, Robert 92
Busiris 114
Byron, Lord 92

C

Cancer 15, 53–54, 57–58, 60–61, 77, 110, **115**, 127, 132, 137, 139–140, 142–143, 145–148, 150, 152, 154–155, 163, 165, 168, 173, 182
Cancer, disease 73
Capricorn 15, 54–55, 58–59, 61–62, 79, 86, 91, 99, 110, 112, **121**, 129, 131, 138–139, 141, 143–146, 146, 148–149, 151, 153–154, 156, 164–165, 169, 182
Cardinal Cross 110
Cardiovascular 73

Carlyle, Thomas 86
Carpenter, Karen 53
Carter, Jimmy 96
Causal Body 25, 26, 133, 134, 193
Celestial Hierarchy 21
Cerberus. 121
Chains Planet 8
Chakras 27, 41, 42
　and consciousness 71
　balance 184
　chart 32, 73
　defined 31
　transferences 71
Charlemagne 86
Chela
　in the Light 41
　little 40
　on the Thread 42
Chohan 193
Christ vii, 17, 88, 123, 193
　consciousness 117, 132
　force, defined 194
　in you 117
Christianity vii
Churchill, Winston 86
Circle of Necessity 25
Clairaudience 74
Clairvoyant 19, 32
Cleavage 51–53
Clinton, Bill 89
Conception, difficulty 73
Consciousness vii–viii, 3–4, 23, 25–26, 28–39, 35–38, 43, 73, 77, 84, 112–123, 126, 132, 149
　and chakras 71
　Aryan 32, 36, 75
　Atlantean 32, 115
　Christ - Neptune 132
　evolution of 23, 32, 35, 88, 109
　fixed cross level of 172
　group 74, 110, 111, 122
　ladder of 5
　Lemurian 64
　levels of **35–38**
　Piscean age 81
　signs condition 111
　thread 28, 48, 78
　through the chakras 71
　Uranus awakens 131
Constitution of Man **25–33**
Cosmic
　planes 5
　seven paths 44
Cosmos 3
Creative

　thread 28
　visualisation 188
Criticism 81
Crosses 109
Crowley, Aleister 99
Crown Chakra 33, 78
Cyber-bullies 59

D

Daiviprakriti 14
Dali, Salvador 56, 92
Darwin, Charles 94
Debussy, Claude 92
Decanates 112–123
Delirium 75–76
Delusion 48, 64, 75, 119, 123, 132
Depression 54, 92, 181
Desire 96, 113
　and sacral centre 32
　and the mind 29
　body - the astral body 30
　burning sons of 15
　controlling force 101
　defined 30, 130
　uncontrollable 48
Detachment
　abnormal 76
　integration word 95
　keynote of Pisces 123
　problem 76
　right 72, 170
Devas 19–20, 193
　kingdom 18
Devitalisation 72, 75–76
Dhyan Chohans 4, 9, 19, 21, 64, 194, 196
　defined 194
Dhyani-Bodhisattvas 14
Dhyani-Buddhas 14
Diana, Princess 54
Digestive organs 73
Disciples 33, **36–37**, 39, 41, 68, 70–71, 81, 85–86, 89–90, 94, 96, 98, 105–106, 112, 118, 135, 168, 190, 197
　2nd initiation 41
　accepted 42
　defined 36, 194
　problems of 71
Discipleship
　Cross 110
　Scorpio 119
Discrimination 74
　develop 64, 114, 117, 188
Dissociative Disorder 76

Djwhal Khul vii, 18, 67, 85–86, 105, 191
Dostoyevsky, Fyodor 92
Drake, Sir Francis 99
Dreams 68
Duncan, Isadora 92
Dweller on the Threshold 43, 136, 172
Dyslexia 69–70

E

Earth 7–8, 14, 17, 44, **129**, 141, 164, 171
   globe 11
   in houses 159
   in signs 146
   scheme 7
Eating disorders 53
Edison, Thomas 94
Egoic Lotus 6, 26, 194
Einstein, Albert vii, 90, 91
Electric Fire 4
Elementals 194
Elohim 19
Emotional - Astral
   bias, Glamour 64, 96
   body - nature 30, 187
      refine 115, 132
   detachment 94
   isolation 115, 139
   plane 6, 119
      illusion on, glamour 64
   ray 102, 204
   sixth ray 105
Endocrine System 33
Energy v–vi, 3, 7, 10, 16, 31, 32, 33, 42–43, 48–49, 51–52, 55–56, 59, 63, 71–73, 76, 77, 88, 90, 98, 106, 112–123, 127, 130, 132, 133–135, 147, 148, 157–158, 160–162, 168–169, 173, 179, 181, 183, 184–185, 189, 194, 196, 199
   fields of 49
   imbalance 51
   inter-relation of 49
Enlightenment
   and initiations 39
   defined 194
   the goal 35
Entitlement Generation 55
Esoteric 110, 194
   healing 72
   rulers 111
Esoteric Astrology **107–173**
Esotericism vii, 194
Esotericist 189

Esoteric Psychology vii, **45–81**
   defined 47
   disorders **51–81**
   goals 50
   points that distinguish it 47
   problems 51
   psychologists 49
Etheric Body / Web 10, 15, 31, 87, 89–90, 93, 95, 97, 99, 194
   connection 76, 77, 80
Evolution 7–8, 10–12, 17, 20, 27–28, 30–31, 51, 56, 60, 69–71, 76, 189, 194–196
   five planes of human 196
   of Consciousness iii, v–vi, 12, **23–44**, 71, 109
   of the monads 25
   path of 5, 8, 126, 194
Evolutionary Path 19
Exoteric planets 111
Extroverts 59
Eyes 73

F

Faludy, Alexander 70
Falwell, Jerry 96
Fanaticism 56
Ferguson, Dennis 63
Fire
   by friction 4, 90
   electric 86
   final burning ground 131
   forty nine 10
   God is a consuming 4
   Lord of, Agni 20
   solar 88
   the Mental Plane is 28
Fixed Cross 110
Fohat 4, 7–8, 14, 194
Fonda, Jane 96
Fonteyn, Margot 99
Four Noble Truths 187
Franklin, Benjamin 99
Freud, Sigmund 47, 88, 104, 172, 174

G

Gaddafi, Muammar 55
Galileo 94
Gallbladder 73
Gandhi, Mahatma 86–87
Gardner E. L. 19
Gates, Bill 91
Gayatri 186
Gemini 15, 55, 77–78, 110, **114**, 128–129, 137, 140, 142–148, 150, 152–153, 155, 164, 165, 168, 170–171, 182
Geryon 123
Glamour 194
   by rays 65
   defined 64
   dissipation formula 66
Globes 8
God
   defined vii, 3, 4, 195
   law of 12
   plan of 44
   will of - 1st ray 44
Goering, Hermann 154
Gonads 33, 73
Gorbachev, Mikhail 86
Graham, Billy 96–97
Greater Gods or Builders 19
Great Invocation 183
Griffiths, Bede 40
Group thought 81
Guidance, problem 67
Guru 194

H

Hall
   of Ignorance 39
   of Learning 39
   of Wisdom 41
Headache 73
Heart Chakra 27, 30–32, 41, 71, 73, 127, 130, 132, 135, 147, 148, 149, 152, 185
Hepburn, Audrey 99
Hercules 36, 86, 112–123
Hierarchies 5, 9, 13–15, 18, 25, 194, 196
   4th, Human 10, 13, 16, 103
   celestial 21
   defined 13, 194
   of Compassion 14
   seven creative 15
   spiritual 194
Hierarchy rulers 111
Himmler, Heinrich 154
Hippolyte 117
Hitler, Adolf 86, 154, 155
Hodson, Geoffrey 19
Holy Grail 123, 194
Hopkins, Anthony 70
Houses 133–136
Human
   kingdom 8–9, 14–19, 26, 35

and creative hierarchies 15
evolution of consciousness 23
globes and rounds 8
levels of consciousness 35
root races 11
love 74
monads 11, 16
soul 26, 129
Hussein, Saddam 58

I
Ida 28
Illumination 180
Mercury brings 128
Raja Yoga meditation 178, 180
Illusion 64, 194
Immortality 74
Individualisation
animals 18
defined 11, 196
Initiate
2nd degree 73
Initiates 33, 37, **38**, 39, 42–44, 112, 116, 168
and chakras 33
defined 194
work 38
Initiation 39
1st:- 40–41, 71, 73, 110, 134, 189
Capricorn 121
Pluto 41, 132
Vulcan 41, 128
2nd:- 41, 71
Jupiter 41, 130
Neptune 41, 132
Venus 41, 129
3rd:- 42, 73
Aquarius 122
Mars 130
Moon 127
4th:- 44, 73
Arhat 194
Mercury 44, 128
Pisces 123
Saturn 44, 131
Solar Angel leaves 196
Vulcan 44, 128
5th:-
Jupiter 131
6th:- 193
6th-9th:- 44
astrology involved 41
defined 39, 194
gate of 131
path of 12, 36, 131, 153, 194
Initiations **39–44**

Insanity 48, 72–73, 75
Integration
problem 51, 55
techniques 87
Introverts 57
Intuition
and Cancer 115
and Mercury 128
plane of buddhi 73
Intuitive awareness 37
Involution 7

J
Jackson, Jesse 96
Jefferson, Thomas 99
Jesus of Nazareth 96
Jewel in the Lotus 27
Joan of Arc 96
Jolie, Angelina 93
Jones, Jim 58
Jung, Carl 47, 88, 104, 126, 163, 172
Jupiter 7, 15, 17, 33, 41, 54, 63, 72, 89, 112, 114–120, 122, 123, 126, 129, **130**, 131–132, 142, 148–149, 160, 163–164, 166, 171–172, 172, 174
governs the 2nd initiation 41, 129, 130, 131, 132
in houses 160
in signs 115, 148

K
Kama 10, 29
manasic 35
Karma
defined 12, 195
Lord of, Saturn 131, 150
wheel of 36
Keating, Paul 86
Keynotes, signs 112–123
Khomeini, Ayotollah 96
Khrushchev, Nikita 86
Khul, Djwhal vii, 18, 191
ray allocations 105
Kidneys 73
Kingdoms of Nature
animal 18, 134
door closes 35
deva or angelic 19
dhyani chohan 9
elemental 9
evolution of 3, 8, 11
human, 4th creative 8, 15
mineral 9, 18
subhuman 18, 26
superhuman 8

vegetable 18
King, Martin Luther Jr 96–97
Kitchener, General 86
Koot Humi 17–18
Kumaras 195
Kundalini 4, 4–5, 28–29, 72–73, 181, 181–182, 181–182, 195
danger 181
defined 4, 195

L
Ladder of Life 14
Larger Picture (Ch 1) **1–21**
Larynx 73
Laws of Nature 12
Leary, Timothy 91
Lemuria 195
Lemurian
consciousness 35, 37, 64
Race 35, 196
Leo 36, 40, 55, 63, 70, 79, 110, **116**, 126–127, 137, 139–143, 145–150, 152, 154–155, 164, 165, 168, 171, 173–174, 182
Lesser builders, devas 193
Lesser Gods or Builders 19
Libra 60, 62, 79–80, 110, **117**, 129, 131, 137, 139, 141–143, 145–147, 149–150, 152, 154, 156, 163, 165, 168, 174, 182
Life Plan Reading 167
Barack Obama 170
Carl Jung 172
Life-thread 28, 48, 78
Life Wave 9, 11
Light
defined 195
forerunner of the 90
I see the greatest 89
station of light, humanity 16
Lincoln, Abraham 87
Liver 73
Logoic or God awareness 37, 85
plane 5–6, 12, 15, 27
Logos 7
1st 4, 86
2nd 4, 88
3rd 4, 90
beloved of 94
defined 3, 195
Earth 8, 44
Sanat Kumara 17
Solar 7, 20, 44, 195, 196
Lord
Agni 20

Gautama Buddha 29
Kshiti 20
Maitreya, the Christ 193
of Fire, Fohat 4
Varuna 20
Lords
of Flame 17, 26, 193
of Love 16
of Sacrifice 16
of the Rays 14, 84
of Will and Sacrifice 16
of Wisdom 26
Planet 126
Lower
nature 29
psychics 74
Lunar
Lords 19
Pitris 11
Lungs 73
Lymphatic system 73

M

Machiavelli 90
Macrocosm 195
Maitreya, Lord 17, 190, 193
Manas 10, 26, 195, 196
Manic depression 53
Manson, Charles 58
Mantrams 183, 186, 195
Manu 195
Manvantara 9, 195
Marchese, Maria 59
Marquis de Sade 61–62
Mars 7, 43, 54, 58, 60–61, 70, 79, 112, 114, 118–120, 127, **130**, 183
in houses 160
in signs 113, 118, 147
Maslow, Abraham 88
Master Morya 17–18
Masters 6, 38, 44, 92, 189, 195
and service 189–190
Djwhal Khul vii, 18, 86, 105, 191
Koot Humi 18
Morya 18
of Compassion 41
of Wisdom 111
Maya 64
Meditation 177–186
at the full moon 182
basic alignment 178
creative 184
dangers 32, 181
Raja Yoga method 178
Mediumship 74

Megalomaniacs 58
Mendel, Gregor 94
Mengele, Josef 60
Mental
health 47–48
problems 57
unit 6, 28
Mental Plane 5–7, 12, 15, 20, 26–28, 32, 37, 43, 66, 73, 85, 94, 119, 177, 181
Mercury 7, 15, 43–44, 53–54, 56–58, 63, 70, 72, 77–80, 93, 112–115, 117–120, 122–123, 126–127, **128**, 131, 140–141, 143–144, 158, 164, 166, 183
antahkarana 128
in houses 158
in signs 117, 120, 123, 143
Star of Conflict 143
Merlin the Magician 99
Michael, Archangel 21
Michelangelo 92
Mind - Manas 29
5th principle 8, 35
5th Ray - scientific 144, 203
Aquarius, 5th ray 171
cleavage 53
control of 42
defined 29
detachment 187
development of 36, 41
good mental health 47
illusion 194
its training 53
lower 10, 29, 143
Mercury 128, 143, 158
questionnaire for rays 200
Raja Yoga 178
ray 102
checklist 203
scientific, Uranus 119, 131, 162
stimulation 57
universal 3, 14, 26, 84, 141, 177, 196
Venus 129, 144, 159
Monadic
awareness 37
plane 5, 6, 12, 15, 19, 27, 35
power, electric fire 4
ray 43, 85
Monads 8, 11, 30, 44
defined 4, 25, 195
Father 16, 43
Human Hierarchy 16
Triad, body of 25, 28, 195
Monroe, Marilyn 89

Moon 11, 15, 35, 43, 53–63, 77–80, 111, 113–115, 117–120, 122–123, 126, **127**, 128, 130, 138–142, 157, 164–166, 167, 167–173, 181–183
chain 11, 35
in houses 157
in signs 111, 113, 117, 119, 126, 138–139, 170, 173
sign 111
veiling Vulcan 117, 128, 140, 142
Mother Teresa 89
Mozart, Wolfgang 92
Multiple personalities 76
Murderer, sexual 48
Mussolini, Benito 86
Mutable Cross 110
Mystic 30, 40, 42, 51, 53, 71, 74–76, 79, 119, 165, 195, 198
defined 189
mystical types 76
mystical vision 74–75, 195
problems 71

N

Nadis or nerves 31
Napoleon 86
Narcissism 55
Narcissus 53
Neptune 7, 33, 41, 54–57, 60, 62–63, 72, 77, 79–80, 97, 115–117, 123, 126–127, 129–130, **132**, 138, 140–141, 147, 153–155, 162, 163, 164, 166–167, 171–174
God of the Waters 115
governs the 2nd initiation 41, 129, 130, 132, 172
in houses 162
in signs 115, 117, 153
rules the heart of the sun 132
the Christ 132
unveiled by Sun and Moon 116, 127, 138, 166, 174
Nervous system 31–33, 73, 76, 129, 181
Neuritis 73
Neurosis 47
New Group of World Servers 195
Newton, Isaac 94
Nicholson, Jack 90
Nightingale, Florence 96
Noble Eightfold Way vii

O

Occult
defined 196

occultism vii
occultists 189
Path or Way 155
Olivier, Lawrence 92
OM 181
   defined 196
   Om mane padme hum 186
Onassis, Jackie 99
Outpourings, three 7
Overstimulation 57

P

Paedophilia 62
Paisley, Ian 59, 97
Pancreas 33, 73
Panic attacks 52
Paramatman 14
Paranoia 57, 76
Pasteur, Louis 94
Patanjali 30, 52–53, 79, 80, 188
Path
   Initiation 12, 36, 120
   of discipleship 103, 128, 131, 135, 160, 162
   of Purification 128
   of Will 189
   probationary 40, 111
   seven cosmic 44
Patton, General 86
Permanent atoms 27, 196
Personality
   astrology 109
      Leo 116
      Sun 109, 111, 118, 127, 137
   consciousness 109, 111
   defined 36
   integration 36, 111, 127
   purification at 3rd initiation 172
   ray 102–104, 173, 198, 202
   seat of power 73
   words 112–123
Perversions, sexual 62
Petals 27
   chakra 33, 73
   egoic lotus 27
Phobias 52
Physical
   body 31, 194
   plane 5–7, 15, 20, 27, 30–31, 39, 64, 72–73, 78, 81, 85, 88, 98, 115, 118–119, 122, 165, 181, 194–195
Physical-Etheric Ray 102
Picasso, Pablo 92
Pineal 28, 30, 33, 73, 78–79
Pingala 28

Piscean Age 81
Pisces 15, 53, 59–60, 63, 77, 80, 89, 97, 109, 109–110, 120, **123**, 130, 132, 138, 140, 142–144, 146, 147, 148–149, 151, 153, 155–156, 163, 166, 169, 182
Pituitary 33, 73, 80
Pituitary Body 33
Planes 5, 6
Planets 125
   in houses 157–165
   veiling 126
Plan of the Soul vii
Plant Kingdom 14, 68
Plato 88
Pluto 7, 33, 40, 41, 53, 54, 55, 56, 58, 60–63, 72, 77–80, 86, 114, 118, 120, 123, 126, 128, 130, **132**, 142, 155–156, 163–164, 165–166, 173
   alter ego of Mars 130
   Arrow of Death 62, 132, 173
   governs the 1st initiation 41, 128, 132
   in houses 163
   in signs 156
Possession 76
Practice of Right Detachment 187–188
Pralaya 196
Prana 10, 31, 133, 196
Primordial Seven 4
Principles 8
   defined 10
   fifth 8
   seven 10
   seventh 8, 30
   sixth 8
   three major 3
Prometheus 114
Psychic Powers 74
Psychism, higher and lower 74–75
Psychopaths 60, 62
Psychosis 48
Pythagoras 88

R

Rader, Dennis BTK 62
Raja Yoga vii, 30, 49, 52–53, 79, 178, 188, 196
Rapist 60
Ray Chart 101
   reading 104
Rays
   1st ray 86
   2nd ray 88
   3rd ray 90

   4th ray 92
   5th ray 94
   6th ray 96
   7th ray 98
   major, minor 84
   questionnaire 197–204
   Seven 84
   Tibetan's disciples 105
Reagan, Ronald 96
Renunciation 39
Reproduction 73
Revelation of Light and Power 80
Right detachment 187
Rockefeller, John D. 90
Roosevelt, Franklin 86
Root Races 11
   defined 196
Rounds of the Planets 8
Rules of the Road 190
Russel, Bertrand 90

S

Sacral Chakra 29, 32, 35, 40–42, 61, 71, 131, 134, 147, 184, 185
Sadat, Anwar 86
Sadism 62
Sadist 60
Sadistic 48, 57
Sagittarius 15, 54, 62–63, 80, 93, 95, 97, 110, 113, **120**, 129–130, 138, 138–139, 141–142, 144–146, 148–149, 151–154, 156, 169, 182
Samadhi 180
Sanat Kumara 17, 26, 196
Saturn 7, 15, 33, 43, 44, 50, 53–54, 56, 58–61, 63, 70, 72, 78–80, 91, 112–117, 120–122, 126, 128, **131**, 142, 150–152, 161, 164, 166
   governs the 4th initiation 44, 128
   in houses 161
   in signs 112, 115, 116, 121, 150
   lord of karma 150
Scheme, Planetary 7
Schizophrenia 48, 75–76
Schubert, Franz 92
Schweitzer, Albert 88
Scorpio 36, 41–42, 53, 55, 58–59, 61–63, 110, **119**, 130, 132, 138, 141, 144–150, 152, 154, 156, 164–165, 168, 174, 182–183
Sectarian 59
Seeger, Pete 96
Self-harm 52
Sequential Thinking 179

Serial Killer 60
Service 189
Seven
   planes of the solar system 6
   Rays iii, v–vii, 4, 14, 18, 49, 51, **83–106**, 103, 106, 167
      major rays of aspect 84
      minor rays of attribute 85
      objectives 85
      sons of light 14
Sex 74
   abnormal 48
   frustration 68
   magic 65
   organs 32
Sexes, division of 11
Sexual
   murderers 48
   perversion 62
   relationships 12
   union 11
Shakespeare, William 92–93
Shamballa 17, 196
Sherman, Dr. Gordon 69
Shoulders 73
Shylock 90
Signs, the 111
Silver Cord 28, 30
Sinuses 73
Sir Galahad. 96
Sirius 43, 44, 94
Sizemore, Chris Costner 77
Skeleton 73
Skin 73
Sociopaths 60
Solar Angel 20, 26, 28, 35–36, 44, 89, 119, 129, 196
   Venus 119
Solar Fire 88, 196
Solar Logos 6–7, 20, 44, 190, 195–196
   2nd ray of 84
Solar Pitris 19
Solar Plexus Chakra 30–32, 40–42, 72–75, 77, 97, 130, 132, 135, 148, 184–185
Soul
   consciousness 37, 109
   defined vii, 26, 196
   group soul 26
   laws 37
   ray 103–104, 169, 173, 197, 201
   words 112–123, 168
Sparks of God 13, 25
Spielberg, Steven 70
Spirit, Soul, Body 3–4

Spiritual
   awareness 37
   hierarchy 12, 182, 183, 189, 194
   light in the signs 112–123
   path 134–135, 139, 160–162, 168
   Practises (Ch.6) **175–191**
   triad 25, 30
Spleen 73
Split or Multiple Personalities 76
Stalin, Joseph 87
Stalkers 59
Stimulation 51, 57
Stomach. 73
Sudden infant death syndrome (SIDS) 78
Sun 5–6, 15, 33, 36, 40–41, 44, 53–61, 63, 70, 72, 77–80, 89, 109–110, 111–112, 114–116, 118–122, 126, **127**, 128–129, 132, 133, 137–138, 140–141, 146–147, 149, 157, 164, 166, 167–169, 171, 173–174, 182–183, 186, 195–196
   central spiritual sun 15
   heart of the sun 41, 116
   in houses 157
   in signs 111, 126
   physical sun 122
   veiling and unveiling
      Neptune 132, 174
      Neptune, Uranus 116
      Vulcan 128, 140, 142
Sushumna 28
Sutratma 28, 30, 33

T

Taurus 15, 54, 58, 60, 110, **113**, 126, 128–129, 137–140, 142, 146–148, 150, 152, 155–156, 163–164, 168, 172–173, 182
Teeth 73
Ten Commandments vii
Teresa, Mother 88
Thatcher, Margaret 86
Think an opposite thought 188
Thought form 57
Three Outpourings 7
Throat Chakra 28–29, 32, 41–42, 63, 113, 131
Thymus 33, 73
Thyroid 33, 73
Tibetan Master (DK) vii, 18, 191
   disciples 105
Trachea 73
Transfiguration 39
Travolta, Jett 80

Triad, Spiritual 25, 193, 196
Triune nature of the universe 3

U

Universal
   brotherhood 171, 174
   buddhi 14
   consciousness 111
   design 98, 104
   etheric web 31
   laws, 3 Major 12
   life 3
   light 14
   love 32
   mind 26, 135, 177
      3rd Ray 90
      defined 3, 14, 84, 196
   soul, buddhi 26, 193
   spirit 193
   system 5
Uranus 7, 33, 43, 53, 54, 56, 58–59, 60–63, 70, 72, 78–79, 99, 112–113, 116, 118–119, 122, 126–127, 130, **131**, 138, 141–142, 148, 151–153, 162, 163, 164, 166–167, 171–174
   governs initiations:
      3rd 174
      5th 130
   in houses 162
   in signs 151
   unveiled 116, 127, 138
Urinary tract 73

V

Vagus nerve 73
Van Gogh, Vincent 92
Vedanta vii
Vegetable Kingdom 9, 18
Veins 73
Venereal diseases 73
Venus 7, 15, 17, 33, 41, 53–54, 56–58, 60–62, 72, 78–80, 95, 112–115, 117–123, 126, 128, **129**, 130, 132, 140–142, 144–147, 159, 163, 164, 166, 171–172
   governs the 2nd initiation 129
   in houses 159
   in signs 112, 115, 117, 123, 140, 144
   intelligent love 114, 129
   mind 115, 117, 118, 121, 122, 129, 140, 144
   Sanat Kumara 17
   Solar Angel 119, 129
   soul 123, 129
   wisdom 121

Vinci, Leonardo da 92–93, 99
Virgo 53–54, 80, 110, **116**, 126–128, 130, 137, 139, 141–143, 145–147, 149–150, 152, 154–156, 164, 165, 168, 182
Vocations 50
   soul 50, 103, 198, 201
   via astrology 165–167
   via the rays 86, 88, 90, 92, 94, 96, 98, 104, 165, 198
Vrittis 80
Vulcan 7, 33, 41, 44, 58, 77, 86, 113, 117, 126–127, **128**, 132, 138, 140–145, 147, 158, 164–166, 173
   governs initiations:
     1st 41, 44
     4th 44
   in houses 158
   in signs 113, 140, 143, 145, 173
   unveiled by Sun and Moon 113, 127, 138, 142, 166
     pencil over Moon 128, 138

W

Wagner, Richard 92
Wesak 196
White Brotherhood 189
Whitman, Charles Joseph 57
Whitman, Walt 86
Winehouse, Amy 54
Words of power
   ray 1 87
   ray 2 89
   ray 3 91
   ray 4 93
   ray 5 95
   ray 6 97
   ray 7 99
Wright Brothers 94

Z

Zodiac 109

www.ingramcontent.com/pod-product-compliance
Lightning Source LLC
Chambersburg PA
CBHW082243300426
44110CB00036B/2380